THE

FRASERS OF PHILORTH

BY

ALEXANDER FRASER
OF PHILORTH
SEVENTEENTH LORD SALTOUN

IN THREE VOLUMES: VOLUME III.

EDINBURGH—MDCCCLXXIX.

This scarce antiquarian book is included in our special *Legacy Reprint Series.* In the interest of creating a more extensive selection of rare historical book reprints, we have chosen to reproduce this title even though it may possibly have occasional imperfections such as missing and blurred pages, missing text, poor pictures, markings, dark backgrounds and other reproduction issues beyond our control. Because this work is culturally important, we have made it available as a part of our commitment to protecting, preserving and promoting the world's literature. Thank you for your understanding.

STATUE AT FRASERBURGH OF
ALEXANDER GEORGE FRASER, 16TH LORD SALTOUN
LIEUT. GENERAL. K.T., K.C.B., G.C.H.

Contents of Volume Third.

TITLE-PAGE.

GENERAL TABLE OF CONTENTS, ... i-vi

CORRESPONDENCE OF ALEXANDER GEORGE FRASER, SIXTEENTH LORD SALTOUN.

I.—LETTERS FROM SICILY AND DURING THE PENINSULAR WAR.

To his Mother, The Dowager Lady Saltoun.

		PAGE
I. 18th March 1807,	. . . . . .	1
II. 26th October 1808,	. . . . . .	5
III. 26th August 1809,	. . . . . .	6
IV. 10th January 1813,	. . . . . .	7

To Miss Catharine Thurlow, afterwards his Wife.

1813.

V. 10th April,	. . . .	8
VI. 1st May,	. . . .	9
VII. 14th May,	. . . .	10
VIII. 15th June,	. . . .	12
IX. 13th August,	. . . .	13
X. 23d August,	. . . .	14

CONTENTS.

		PAGE
XI. 2d September,	. . . . . .	16
XII. 26th September,	. . . . . .	18
XIII. 9th October,	. . . . . .	19
XIV. 31st October,	. . . . . .	21
XV. 13th December,	. . . . . .	23

1814.

XVI. 10th January,	. . . . . .	24
XVII. 30th January,	. . . . . .	26
XVIII. 6th February,	. . . . . .	27
XIX. 17th February,	. . . . . .	28
XX. 13th March,	. . . . . .	29
XXI. 20th March,	. . . . . .	30
XXII. 16th April,	. . . . . .	32
XXIII. 22d May, .	. . . . . .	33
XXIV. August, .	. . . . . .	34

To Catharine Lady Saltoun his Wife, during the Waterloo Campaign.

1815.

XXV. 9th April, .	. . . . . .	35
XXVI. 11th April, .	. . . . . .	35
XXVII. 22d April, .	. . . . . .	36
XXVIII. 27th April, .	. . . . . .	37
XXIX. 30th April, .	. . . . . .	38
XXX. 7th May, .	. . . . . .	39
XXXI. 14th May, .	. . . . . .	41
XXXII. 18th May, .	. . . . . .	44
XXXIII. 21st May, .	. . . . . .	45
XXXIV. 23d May, .	. . . . . .	46
XXXV. 28th May, .	. . . . . .	48

		PAGE
XXXVI.	31st May,	50
XXXVII.	4th June,	51
XXXVIII.	11th June,	53
XXXIX.	14th June,	55
XL.	19th June,	57
XLI.	22d June,	57
XLII.	25th June,	59
XLIII.	29th June,	61
XLIV.	2d July,	63
XLV.	4th July,	65
XLVI.	6th July,	65
XLVII.	10th July,	67
XLVIII.	12th July,	68
XLIX.	15th July,	69
L.	22d July,	71
LI.	28th July,	72
LII.	The Dowager Lady Saltoun to Catharine Lady Saltoun her Daughter-in-law, 13th March 1815,	73
LIII.	The Same to the Same, 9th April 1815,	73

II.—MISCELLANEOUS LETTERS OF LORD SALTOUN, H.R.H. FREDERICK DUKE OF YORK, AND OTHERS, 1819-1838.

LIV.	General John Fraser to Lord Saltoun, 18th August 1819,	74
LV.	Lord Saltoun to H.R.H. Frederick Duke of York, Commander-in-Chief, 26th August 1819,	75
LVI.	H.R.H. Frederick Duke of York, Commander-in-Chief, to Lord Saltoun, 1st September 1819,	76
LVII.	Lord Saltoun to Lord Liverpool, 26th August 1819,	76
LVIII.	Lord Liverpool to Lord Saltoun, 31st August 1819,	77
LIX.	General John Fraser to Lord Saltoun, 2d September 1819,	78
LX.	Captain W. Siborn to Lord Saltoun, 4th January 1838,	78
LXI.	Lord Saltoun to Captain W. Siborn, 19th January 1838,	80

III.—LETTERS FROM LORD SALTOUN TO LIEUTENANT-COLONEL AND MRS. CHARLES ELLIS, DURING THE EXPEDITION TO CHINA AND COMMAND OF THE ARMY OF OCCUPATION.

1841.

		PAGE
LXII. To Mrs. Charles Ellis, 25th December,	. . .	83

1842.

LXIII. To Lieutenant-Colonel Charles Ellis, 1st January,	.	86
LXIV. To Mrs. Charles Ellis, 4th January,	. .	88
LXV. To Lieutenant-Colonel Charles Ellis, 17th January,	.	91
LXVI. To Mrs. Charles Ellis, 24th February,	. .	96
LXVII. To Lieutenant-Colonel Charles Ellis, 11th April,	.	102
LXVIII. To Mrs. Charles Ellis, 22d May,	. . .	105
LXIX. To Lieutenant-Colonel Charles Ellis, 4th June,	.	109
LXX. To Mrs. Charles Ellis, 9th June,	. . .	111
LXXI. To Lieutenant-Colonel Charles Ellis, 19th June,	.	116
LXXII. To Mrs. Charles Ellis, 3d July,	. . .	120
LXXIII. To Lieutenant-Colonel Charles Ellis, 26th July,	.	125
LXXIV. To the Same, 30th July,	. . .	127
LXXV. To Mrs. Charles Ellis, 6th August,	. .	128
LXXVI. To Lieutenant-Colonel Charles Ellis, 2d September,	.	132
LXXVII. To Mrs. Charles Ellis, 10th September,	. .	138
LXXVIII. To the Same, 19th September,	. . .	139
LXXIX. To Lieutenant-Colonel Charles Ellis, 31st October,	.	146
LXXX. To Mrs. Charles Ellis, 5th November,	. .	148
LXXXI. To Lieutenant-Colonel Charles Ellis, 25th November,	.	151
LXXXII. To Mrs. Charles Ellis, 8th December,	. .	155
LXXXIII. To Lieutenant-Colonel Charles Ellis, 24th December,	.	159
LXXXIV. To Mrs. Charles Ellis, 29th December,	. .	161

1843.

		PAGE
LXXXV.	To Lieutenant-Colonel Charles Ellis, 8th January,	166
LXXXVI.	To Mrs. Charles Ellis, 17th January,	168
LXXXVII.	To Lieutenant-Colonel Charles Ellis, 12th February,	176
LXXXVIII.	To Mrs. Charles Ellis, 23d February,	179
LXXXIX.	To Lieutenant-Colonel Charles Ellis, 2d March,	182
XC.	To the Same, 18th April,	183
XCI.	To Mrs. Charles Ellis, 27th April,	185
XCII.	To Lieutenant-Colonel Charles Ellis, 22d May,	189
XCIII.	To Mrs. Charles Ellis, 28th May,	191
XCIV.	To Lieutenant-Colonel Charles Ellis, 15th June,	196
XCV.	To Mrs. Charles Ellis, 26th June,	197
XCVI.	To Lieutenant-Colonel Charles Ellis, 29th June,	203
XCVII.	To Mrs. Charles Ellis, 10th July,	204
XCVIII.	To Lieutenant-Colonel Charles Ellis, 16th July,	207
XCIX.	To Mrs. Charles Ellis, 28th July,	209
C.	To the Same, 12th August,	212
CI.	To Lieutenant-Colonel Charles Ellis, 22d August,	215
CII.	To the Same, 4th September,	216
CIII.	To Mrs. Charles Ellis, 4th September,	218
CIV.	To the Same, 15th September,	219
CV.	To Lieutenant-Colonel Charles Ellis, 23d September,	222
CVI.	To the Same, 9th November,	224
CVII.	To Mrs. Charles Ellis, 14th December,	226

1844.

CVIII.	To Lieutenant-Colonel Charles Ellis, 20th January,	229
CIX.	To the Same, 19th April,	230
CX.	To Mrs. Charles Ellis, 26th April,	231
CXI.	To Mrs. George Ellis, 10th May,	232

1849-1853.

CXII.	To Mrs. Charles Ellis, 29th January 1849,	233
CXIII.	To Lieutenant-Colonel Charles Ellis, 22d June 1850,	234

CONTENTS.

		PAGE
CXIV. To Mrs. Charles Ellis, 31st August 1851,	. . .	235
CXV. To the Same, 6th August 1853,	. . . .	236
CXVI. To the Same, 11th August 1853,	. . . .	236
CXVII. Letter from Mr. Robertson of Ladykirk (the late Lord Marjoribanks) to Mr. Charles Ellis, 18th August 1853, announcing Lord Saltoun's death,	. . .	237
INDEX OF PERSONS,	. . . .	239
INDEX OF PLACES,	. . . . . .	307

ILLUSTRATIONS IN VOLUME THIRD.

STATUE AT FRASERBURGH OF ALEXANDER GEORGE FRASER, SIXTEENTH LORD SALTOUN, LIEUTENANT-GENERAL, K.T., K.C.B., G.C.H., ... *Frontispiece.*

LETTER BY LORD SALTOUN FROM THE FIELD OF WATERLOO, TO LADY SALTOUN, ... *between* 56 *and* 57

PORTRAIT OF GENERAL SIR JOHN FRASER, G.C.H., LIEUT.-GOVERNOR OF CHESTER, ... 74 *and* 75

LETTERS

OF

ALEXANDER GEORGE FRASER,

SIXTEENTH LORD SALTOUN, K.T.

I.—LETTERS FROM SICILY AND DURING THE PENINSULAR WAR.

LETTERS to MARGERY FRASER, LADY SALTOUN, his Mother.

I.

Catania, 18th March 1807.

DEAR MOTHER,—I wrote you by the last pacquet from Messina, informing you that I was fortunate enough to receive your letters at Palermo, where I was on a tour round the island. I say fortunate, as most likely I should not have received them for some time, if at all, as Palermo is three days' journey from this place by the nearest road, and the country post so badly regulated that one-half of the letters are lost, and we have no correspondence by means of dragoons with that side of the island, which is entirely under the government of the King; so if you wish me to get any letter punctually, do not send it that way, but if it does not signify how soon I receive it, they may as well go there as anywhere else, as Mr. Drummond will keep them till he has some safe conveyance for them either to this place, or indeed to this side of the island, as there is a regular military post twice a week from Malazzo to Cape Passero. I have obeyed your instructions in every particular, and sent the letters enclosed in two separate packets, as it was impossible to get them conveyed in one to Messina, where the mail for England is made up. The circular letters I have signed on the inside, but not on the back, as I do not know their separate destinies. The letters to the Dukes of York and Cumberland I have put in a cover and directed; those to the other Peers I have directed on the back, and you can put them in covers and send them. They are all open, in order that they may be sealed with my arms.[1]

Our tour to Palermo was delightful. We had the finest weather possible; the country very beautiful; but as to the accommodation on the road you can have no idea of anything so bad. We were obliged to carry our beds with us, and, as it was *starvation* time, our provisions also; and the inns were so bad that we slept more than once in lettigas,[2] rather than go into them, notwithstanding which I got my bed so full of fleas and bugs that I was obliged to boil the mattrass as the only way of getting them out of it.

Our first day's journey was to Calata Girone, 43 miles. Our way led over the plain of Catania, through Palagonia, a pretty little village. We reached Calata Girone at six at night. It is situated on an immense hill, and is the largest inland town in Sicily, and as dirty. The only thing worth seeing is the view from the top of the great church; and at the Franciscan convent, about half a mile from the town, on the road to Terra Nova, there is a most beautiful figure of a Madonna and child in marble, which is the best bit of sculpture I have yet seen in the island. They do not know who made it, but tell you some cock-and-bull story of the Virgin having made it a present to St. Francis when he was doing penance in a wood near the convent. We left Calata Girone at nine, and after seeing the Madonna, proceeded on to Terra Nova through a most beautiful country, and across the forest of Calata Girone, the second in size in Sicily. I got a shot at a partridge, the only one I had seen in the island, and killed him. He was a very fine bird of the red leg kind, but not half so good eating as our sort of partridge.

We got to Terra Nova at three, probably so called from the flat on which it stands having been gained from the sea, as it has very much that appearance. We found the way very hot, and so went into the sea, which so astonished the natives, that they turned out one and all—men, women, and children—to see us bathe, and could not conceive how we could bathe in the winter, and confessed to us that when it was very cold they did not even wash themselves.

Terra Nova has a small port, at which there is some importation of corn, but very trifling, as the exportation laws of this country are, as far as regards corn,

[1] Refers to his candidature for election as a Representative Peer.
[2] Horse-litters for journeys.

so very nefarious that the farmer cannot afford to send the corn out of the island except at the free ports, for which liberty they pay some tax to the King.

From Terra Nova we went the next day to Alicata, a well-built town and a free port. There is a castle here from which you have a fine sea view—they call it a garrison—which consists of fifty old men who can hardly stand, without arms or ammunition.

The next day we reached Girgenti; on our road there we breakfasted at Palma, a place which Swinbourne mentions as being notorious for rascals, so much so, says he, that not a jail in the country is without more than one Palmanese in it for murder or for theft. The present generation are not far behind them in that science, as they contrived to steal a couple of bottles of wine from us, and our meat-basket; however, we found them out before they could get away, and on producing our pistols they produced the meat. The approach from Palma to Girgenti is beautiful, through the most fertile country in Sicily, and close by the ruins of the ancient temples.

Girgenti, old Agrigentum, is, generally speaking, the best place worth seeing in the world for antiquarians, as the remains of the Greek antiquities are more perfect there than at any other place. However, the temple of all others that one would wish to have seen is that one of Jupiter Olympius, the columns of which were of a most gigantic size, and the fluting of them large enough to contain a man. This temple, I am sorry to say, is no longer in existence; but from what remains, the enormous size of the pillars is clearly to be perceived. Two capitals, which are the only remains of them, are broken in four pieces; and in the small part of the pillar still attached to one of them, Montgomery, who is rather a thin man, could get into the flute with all ease. What an immense block of stone it must have been to allow such cutting away from it, and afterwards to support a capital of such size, one quarter of which only, lying on the ground, hid six of us behind it, so as not to be perceived by a person on the other side. Swinbourne in his account of this temple says that the dimensions of it are not to be ascertained. True, all of them are not; but the interior breadth is very clear, as there are the remains of two old walls, which must have been the interior walls of the temple, and are at the distance of sixty paces asunder. Now by taking the scale on which the smaller temples of that time were built,—for the ancients were very regular in their buildings,—and referring to that, the length of this temple was to sixty paces, what their length was to their breadth, at least in all human probability. As to the exterior size it is not at all to be made out, but I should conceive a person well versed in these matters could easily guess at it. Of the temple of Hercules there is only one pillar perfect, of those of Castor and Esculapius there are no remains, but the temple of Juno Lucina is nearly complete, and that of Concord perfectly so, and they are extremely beautiful until you come close to them; for that goose, Ferdinand the Fourth, has crammed all the cracks which time has made in them full of white mortar, so that when you expect a fine pillar you perceive a sort of a harlequin one; and not content with this, he has put up an inscription on them in which he styles himself the illustrious preserver of the antiquities of Sicily. All the vases and other things that have been found there are shut up in a house, and you are not permitted to see them without proper credentials from his Majesty, which are difficult to be got at.

In the great church at Girgenti there is a very fine picture of the Virgin and Child by Guido Reni, and also a beautiful antique, a representation of the story of Hippolytus and Phaedra; there is also another singular circumstance, which is, that a person getting up above the altar, can hear anything said at the other end of the church even in a whisper. This is said to have been discovered in the following manner:—A carpenter was up there one day mending the figure of a dragon, and saw his wife come in to confess. He was surprised at so plainly hearing the priest speak to her, and therefore listened and heard the whole of her confession. On returning home he gave her wholesome correction for what he had overheard, and made a regular practice of mending the dragon whenever any rich person went to confess, by which means he got together a good deal of money. We left Girgenti, and the third day after reached Palermo, which will do for another letter.

The packet has arrived, but I have received neither letters nor papers. I conclude they are to come by Palermo. We are all in perfect health, and some of the men talk of going home to be married, or, in other words, to go out;—the more the better! With best love to all at home,

I am, dear mother, your dutiful son,

SALTOUN.

Catania, 2d April 1807.

II.

Corunna, 26th October 1808.

DEAR MOTHER,—We have been so bothered with orders, counter orders, and reports, that till this morning nothing certain has been known. The Rifle Corps and the Forty-third Light Infantry have disembarked this morning, and our brigade begin to-morrow.

We have a march of at least 600 miles before we can reach the enemy, and by all accounts are not likely to be very well off on the way, as the only thing the "Junta" can provide for us is black bread and sour wine, which John will not relish much; and on our arrival we may expect to be in snow during the greatest part of the [time], as our position will be on the left of the Spanish army, and on the left bank of [the] Ebro, between Bilboa and Pampeluna, which is the strongest post the French have at present, and it is whispered is to be the first affair that the British will be employed on. Should we succeed in driving out the enemy, which is not so easily done as you have settled it in the City, I daresay we shall proceed to Italy, which will be rather better than Spain.

There are at present no less than eight people packing up in the cabin, and the noise they make is such that no person can write, or indeed do anything else. I wrote Houston by the last packet, which, as the wind has been fair, he will most likely have received.

Let my letters be sent if possible in General Ward's First Guards' bag, as by that means I shall get them sooner and more securely. You must not be surprised at hearing seldom, as a subaltern has not so many opportunities of writing as a General, and our allowance of baggage is so small, that we are obliged to leave even our writing-desks behind us, which is a monstrous inconvenience, but we must put up with it. I am to carry 100 lbs., including bed, etc., which is more than half.

We have no news of any consequence, and the army is tolerably healthy. With best love to all at home,

I am, dear mother, your dutiful son,

SALTOUN.

III.

South Beveland, August 26th, 1809.

DEAR MOTHER,—Since I last wrote you we have remained in the same situation; the headquarters have been moved from Walcheren to this island, and the other day they came down to Batz, near where we are, and with them I was in hopes they would have brought our letters, and given us some opportunity of writing home; but not in the least, and we are likely to return without any opportunity of either hearing from or writing to England.

It is now the general opinion that the business is at an end, and we shall shortly retrace our steps, as the enemy have in their hurry and confusion on our first appearance inundated the country between Bergen-op-Zoom and Lillo, as well as that on the left bank of the river, which renders our further progress, if not impossible, at least attended with such difficulties and loss, as would be greater than the taking of Antwerp is worth, and it is therefore concluded that we shall either move to some other part of the enemy's coast or return home; in case of the latter a large force will most probably be sent to Spain, and I should not wonder if the brigade of Guards were amongst the number.

The army in general, officers as well as men, have been very sickly; the complaint is an intermitting fever, attended with much giddiness in the head. I never remember, even in the worst of times in Spain, so many sick as we now have in the brigade, and we are much less so than the rest of the army; the worst is that it seems to be a complaint of the country, and they are not likely to get better as long as they remain in it.

There has been a council of war sitting all day, and has not as yet broke up; it will most probably determine what is to become of us. Montagu Wynyard of the Coldstreams, who has got his promotion by the death of Ross in Spain, is just going home, and will take this with him. I think we shall soon follow.

I am, dear mother, your dutiful son,

SALTOUN.

Love to all at home.

27th August 1809.

IV.

Nel Spraida, 10th January 1813.

MY DEAR MOTHER,—I have no news, and very little to write about, but as Tuesday is our post-day for England, I just send you a few lines to say we are all going on well, and as comfortable as we can expect to be.

Lord Wellington is daily looked for from Cadiz, and when he arrives we shall probably take the field, or soon after, as our pressing the enemy here will keep up the spirit in Russia more than anything else, should Napoleon determine to try another campaign in the north. Besides there is no reason why our cavalry should not eat the green forage in Castille, instead of the enemy's, as by this means the harvest in this country will be saved to the people, which otherwise must be consumed when green by our cavalry, should we remain in our present cantonments.

I do not think I shall go to England if I can avoid it. In the first place, I cannot stay with you more than three or four days consistently with my own opinions as a military man; moreover, as I must travel with the greatest expedition, it will cost me between two and three hundred, which I have many other ways of disposing of, although none that would give me so much satisfaction.

Macdonald is here, and begs to be kindly remembered to you. He wishes you would do him a favour, which is to thank Mrs. Montgomery in his name for the music which she sent him. I do not know if you are acquainted with her, but she is the mother of the Miss Montgomerys who dance French country dances.

It is at present a hard frost, and we have turned one of our landlord's windows in the principal Sala into an excellent fireplace, to the great annoyance of the landlady; however, when we are gone she may return it into a window, and the Sala, which in our opinion is much improved by it, will not then have suffered in hers, and it is easily done, for glass is not a necessary article to a window in this country.

If any friend is coming out to join the regiment, pray send me some snuff; but it is no use sending it to Lisbon, as it is as difficult to get anything from thence to the army on a private account as it would be in England to transport Somerset House all standing to Aberdeen. Love to William and the girls.

Your dutiful son,

SALTOUN.

LETTERS to MISS CATHARINE THURLOW, afterwards his Wife.

V.

Falmouth, Friday night, [10 April 1813].

WAS ever anything in the world, my dear Miss Thurlow, half so provoking? The mail has just this moment come in with an order to detain the packet till to-morrow, so that after all I might have remained in town another night, and gone to Lady Lansdown's; not that I myself had any wonderful inclination to wait on her Ladyship or the amiable Miss Giffard—for I could have passed the evening much more to my own satisfaction in Grosvenor Street—but you wished me to stay for it, and that is quite a sufficient reason for regretting I did not. I believe the packet was detained in consequence of a dispatch, which I met between Bagshot and Egham, and which most probably brought some letters that it was necessary to answer immediately. I had a great mind to return when I found out that it was a dispatch from Falmouth; but as it might have been from America or any other place, as likely as from Spain—which I had then no means of ascertaining—I was obliged to proceed, doubting all the way, and now find that I might have returned without risk.

I have just written two long letters to her Ladyship[1] on business, and after sealing one of them, and just as I was going to send it to the Post, I by accident looked at the seal. I had put more wax on than I generally do, and in pressing my own seal some of the wax had risen from the corner, and had taken the impression of your cipher so perfectly, that I thought her Ladyship had seen that seal so often that she must have known it again; at least I should anywhere. I thought it a lucky chance that had made me look at the seal, and with a dab of hot wax blotted it out. It will, however, make me more careful in future.

This is a horrible dull place—nothing in the world to be seen except the surrounding country; but that I am well acquainted with, as I was here three weeks once. And moreover it is horribly ugly. But I am telling a bit of a story, for I see they have got the invisible girl here, and I believe the actual one that we went to see in Leicester Fields. Do you remember that? It was before

[1] His mother, Lady Saltoun.

you left St. James' Square. When I was here before, there was a play, a tolerable good set, but the waiter—who, by-the-by, is a Methodist, and a rank one,—told me that a play-house was Satan's ground, and that the people of this town would not countenance such profane works. I told him they were a parcel of d— fools, but could not convert him for all that.

By this time, I daresay, you will be tired of reading, though in this instance, on my honour, I am not tired of writing, for I *must* think, and so it is easy work to write, even although it is nothing but nonsense, and shall not therefore venture to read it over.

Pray tell me how Lady Lansdown's went off, and if my mother was there. If you write me, direct 1st Guards, 1st Division, British army, Spain. God bless you, my dear Miss Thurlow, and believe me ever yours,

SALTOUN.

Falmouth, tenth April 1813.

VI.

Lisbon, 1st May 1813.

I HAVE now, my dear Miss Thurlow, been here ten days, and am as heartily sick of the place as ever I was of anything in my life; it is certainly, take it altogether, the dirtiest town that ever a man got into.

To-morrow I leave this to proceed to Oporto, where my regiment is now stationed, which place I shall reach on the 10th, and I understand we are likely to march from thence, in order to take the field, about the 12th, when the work for the year will begin. I have been detained here waiting for some things that were left behind by my servant's negligence, and which came by the last packet. By the same conveyance I was given to understand that the A.D.C., Lord J. Hay, has had the supreme felicity of succeeding me in Mrs. B.'s good graces, and had the honour of starting Miss Di. at the second ball; but I strongly suspect, from the wording of said information, that poor I was again to have been brought forward, which would have been rather too much of a good thing, and too much, they say, is good for nothing. Had I remained, which—not on that account—I now regret I did not, I might, you know, have got tipsy and forgot it, or perhaps, indeed I may say more likely, Grosvenor Street might have seen me instead of

Portman Square. How fond the world is of manœuvring, while we poor devils have not the credit of even the slightest penetration.

Since I have been here I have gone through the regular forms of the place, dined with all the great people, been to some routs and to one ball—a most Hottentot concern. Fancy a parcel of people, whom God never meant to be active, striving to dance Scotch reels, while the fiddlers were doing their best to play them as like waltzes as the *music* will admit of. I was obliged to perform in one not to seem fine, and that I thought was quite sufficient. They are certainly the most humdrum set I ever met with; very different from Spain, equally depraved, but do not carry it off so well.

This is opera night here as well as in London. I do not know if you have been there; I, you see, have not, for by this time it must be over in both places; but I have been, if not more usefully, at least more agreeably employed. Since I have been here I have been quartered in an excellent house, and as accident would have it, it stands on the Monte de Santa Catherina, so you see my saint does not forget me even in this country.

I mean to go to Oporto by Cintra and Mafra, both which places are well worth seeing, and perhaps I may not again have such a good opportunity of going to them, and from time to time, if you do not prevent me, I shall give you an account of my peregrinations. It is now very late, though I believe I have left you later; but as I have a long way to ride to-morrow, I must go and get some sleep: so good night, my dear Miss Thurlow, and believe me ever yours

S——.

VII.

Oporto, 14 May 1813.

YOURS of the 20th April I received the morning after I wrote you. The packet came in during the night, and as I expected I should hear from you I was determined not to leave Lisbon till the letters were given out, and should have answered you sooner, but from the road that we came by not being the one of communication, I was obliged to wait till I came here, which I did yesterday; and as you assure me you will not tire of reading whenever I write, depend upon it there is nothing next to hearing from you that gives me so much pleasure as writing to you. I was obliged to leave off writing to go and fire a salute in honour of the Prince Regent of Portugal, it being his birthday; but it is of no consequence, as I find this letter cannot go before Tuesday next, which is our post-day for England, and as this is Friday I shall at all events have time enough to finish it.

The general orders for the commencement of the campaign are arrived, and the divisions will march to their separate points in a few days. Lord Wellington has, however, determined not to move *us* for the present, and they say it will be a month before we begin our march. We are certainly much better, and the men begin to look something like soldiers again, but it is shocking to think that since the month of December last we have buried eight hundred men out of two thousand, that is three hundred more than had died when I left the Brigade to go to England, but I am happy to say we have lost no men during the last three weeks, and those that are still in hospital are in a fair way of recovering; but, however, this is all Greek to you.

This is a fine large town, much cleaner and better in every respect than any place I have yet seen in Portugal, and the people have been very civil to the officers, and have given them a number of balls and other entertainments. We are to have a grand ball to-night, but I have not determined as yet whether I shall go to it or not; and if I am in the same mind after dinner that I am at present, I shall certainly not go to it, for just now I have not the slightest inclination. We have also a theatre where they act Portuguese plays, and I believe sometimes an opera, which last may be tolerable; but as to a play it must be but a very moderate performance, at least cannot have much to amuse an Englishman who does not understand ten words of the language.

And so you were disappointed in not hearing from me on the Monday after I left: I own you had hit the day off cleverly enough, and I had intended my letter to have been in town that morning; but although I knew that the mail-coach left Falmouth at three in the morning, I did not know that the post-office closed at ten at night, which was the reason you did not hear before Tuesday.

My tent and everything that had been left behind came to Lisbon a few days before I received your letter, and I have got them with me, and the only thing I now wish is that I may not be long without an opportunity of using them, for it is very provoking to be kept hanging on in this place when the army moves, as I could have passed the same time so much more to my satisfaction in England.

You say it is not fair to trouble me with cross-writing; all I can say is that, as long as the writing is not *cross*, I do not care how much cross-writing there is: I shall not, however, give you any more of it at present, but leave what is not already crossed in case anything should happen before Tuesday.

Last night I went to the ball, which was really a very good one; two sets of about thirty couple each, and some tolerably pretty women. I find everybody here can speak French, and most of them English.

I have just got my papers from England, but no letters from home. I see your name mentioned as a dancer at the Miss Pritchards' ball in Green Street; was it you or your cousin? The people appear to be quite mad about Cossacks, and the Princess of Wales,—certainly the people of England are, without any exception, the greatest fools in the world. I must own, however, I should like to see this Don Cossack myself, for if he is anything near the description of him he must be a very fine fellow. By this time you must be heartily tired of deciphering this scrawl. I long to hear from you, and believe me I remain affectionately yours, SALTOUN.

P.S.—James Macdonald, whom you know, left this yesterday for England.[1]

VIII.

Oporto, 15th June 1813.

MY DEAR MISS THURLOW,—I did not write you by the last packet, for the post leaves this place on a Tuesday, and last Tuesday was the day before our grand ball which we gave the natives, and as I had been named as one of the committee for conducting the said ball, I had so much to do that I had not time to write. It went off with great *éclat*, and, thank God, is now over, and what is not the worst part of it, *paid for*. You may guess the crush and trouble in this place —where there are no Mr. Gunters—in getting together the necessary apparatus for giving a hot supper to three hundred and fifty people, and the drill that was required previously to instruct the servants how to put the supper on the tables; but, however, we got them tolerably expert before the day, and it went off very well. This place is just beginning to be hot, but I believe they never have any heat here equal to what it is to the south of Spain; however, I hope we shall not remain here to try.

[1] Son of first Lord Macdonald. Killed at Bergen-op-Zoom, 1814.

We are now as strong as we shall be this year, and daily expect our order to march for the army, which is by this time near Valladolid; we had letters from it the day before yesterday. The 10th Hussars were engaged near Tordesillas, and defeated the 22d and 23d French Cavalry, with great loss on the part of the French. Ours was slight; one officer and seventeen men killed, and Captain Loyd wounded and taken, but left behind on his parole. This is the second time the cavalry have been engaged since the beginning of the campaign, and they have conducted themselves very gallantly on both occasions, which is a good thing, as last campaign they were rather in the background.

The principal lion here now is a man whose name, I believe, is Pearson, and he is a Pat, but he calls himself an Italian, and says his name is Personi. He certainly is a wonderful strong man. He walks about with ease to himself with seven men on him, and for his benefit, which takes place this week, he is to carry eleven; but the most singular thing that he does is, he puts a man on a cross, the pole of which is 12 feet long, and balances it on his chin. I confess I have no wish to be the man on the top of it.

I have this moment got a letter from Eleanor,[1] by which I find my mother is still at Brompton. She says you are well. I hope to date my next from some place up the country. Adieu, and believe me yours ever,   S——.

IX.

Durada, 13 August 1813.

MY DEAR MISS THURLOW,—We marched into this place yesterday, which completes our six weeks from Oporto. It is a small village, about two miles from Victoria, on the Irun road. We halt here to-day, and to-morrow we proceed to the army, which we are to join on the 18th instant.

I went yesterday to Victoria. It must have been a very fine town, but at present cuts rather a melancholy figure; not that it has been in any way destroyed, but it is a hospital for wounded, and has at present about 6000 wounded men and officers in it, many of whom are just now beginning to walk, or rather crawl about; and so many poor maimed devils do not add to the beauty of a place. Several of them are old friends of mine, but all of them, I am happy to say, doing well.

[1] His sister.

I believe you knew Cadogan[1] who was killed in this action. His death was one of the finest things possible. Being perfectly aware that he was mortally wounded, he asked the surgeon how long he could live, and was told about half an hour. He then desired the men who bore him to leave him for a short time. On their return he ordered them to take him to that part of the field where he could best see the British advance, and there died, just as the French line began to give way.

The second, fourth, and seventh divisions have had some very severe work in the Pyrenees, on the 27th, 28th, and 30th of last month, and the enemy were again completely [defeated]. You will, of course, have seen the details of these actions long before you receive this. At present we are employed in fortifying the passes. St. Sebastian has not fallen yet, and I believe it to be a very strong place. If it does not fall before the 18th, we shall probably be employed against it. Pampeluna is blockaded, and they say that the garrison are very badly off for provisions, and that they have already begun to eat horse-flesh. I wish it may be true, for if we can get possession of these two places, we may look to keeping the French out of Spain for this year at least, and next year the Spaniards *ought* to be able to do it of themselves; I say ought, not that I think they will, for they are even more indolent than ever.

By this time all the gay doings in town are pretty near over. I long much to get hold of my letters, as we have not seen a letter or paper from England since the 15th of June, and are quite in the dark as to what is going on in the north of Europe. But, however, in five days more we shall reach our Division, and then I hope to have a letter of yours to answer. Till then, adieu, my dear Miss Thurlow.—Yours ever, SALTOUN.

X.

Camp before Oyarzun, 23d August 1813.

YOURS of the 22d June I only received yesterday, but I have written several times on our march, and mentioned that I did not expect to get any letters until we reached the army. A month is certainly a most unreasonable time for a letter to take from Oporto to England, but this, I trust, will make up for it; for I

[1] Hon. Henry Cadogan, Lieut.-Colonel 71st Regiment, son of first Earl Cadogan.

understand that the pacquet is ordered to Santander, which is but a short distance to send by land, and not above three days' sail to Falmouth.

We are quite quiet here at present, and likely so to remain, encamped on the Pyrenees, about three miles from Irun, at which place the bridge over the Bidassoa is destroyed. The French are on the opposite bank, and each party mutually fortifying his position. On our left, about five miles, is the seaport of Passages, so we are well supplied with fish, which is a great luxury, and ought to be also with English articles; but the sutlers have been so often taken in by the rapid movements of the army in this Peninsular war, that they are not inclined to risk any very great speculation.

St. Sebastian is about seven miles from this place, and is besieged by the Fifth Division, under General Oswald. A breach was made some time back, and they attempted to storm, but were repulsed with great loss. Since that time we have been waiting for heavier guns and ammunition; the batteries are all ready. The guns and ammunition arrived yesterday, and on Thursday the 26th they are again to open against the place. It is of great consequence to take it, but it is very strong, and will cost a great many broken heads.

You wish to know what General we are particularly under; we are in the First Division, which is under General Howard (Lady Charlotte's husband), and the First, Third, and Fifth Divisions form the left corps of the army under General Graham. The Fifth, as I mentioned above, are against St. Sebastian, and we are covering the siege. The Third Division are on our right between this and headquarters. We shall certainly not advance unless things go wrong in the north of Europe, and I do not think the French are strong enough to try another general action, as the ground in our front is very strong, especially that part which our division would probably have to defend should they attack the positions.

By this time all the gaiety is over on your side of the water. I find her Ladyship has gone to the Lodge; I thought she meant at one time to go to Scotland this summer.

I wish you could persuade some one of our regiment to sell out. I am now first for purchase, and dread the tidings of peace more than anything; for then I should not get my promotion before it takes place, which would be a terrible bore, besides the length of time it would throw me back. However, I am not one of those who are apt to despair, and trust now to be home by Christmas as a Lieut.-Colonel.

I am going to-day to see a friend of mine who was wounded the other day in the general action before Pampeluna. I do not know if you are acquainted with him. His name is Campbell, and he is Lady Malpas' eldest brother, a Major in the 6th regiment.

Sir D. H. Blair and myself are old hunting friends. A few years back we kept house together for a season. The Victoria fête seems to have been the great lion this year. It must have had a very grand effect; for of all places in London there cannot be a better place for a public sort of thing than Vauxhall; but to be good it ought to have been very full.

How goes on loo and the Tabby set? I dined yesterday with a man whom you must have often met there, Captain R—— of our regiment. He began to talk about Mrs. H——, "a little varmin woman with black eyes." I asked him where he had met her. He said he often met her at Mrs. P.'s, and that she was very fond of play, and led her husband a devil of a life. R—— and I happen never to have met at P.'s, and he little thought I could have given him tolerable information on that subject.

You see I take you at your word, and write as often and as long as I have anything to say; and it is accidental whether I have or not, for our life is either a very active or a very dull one, no medium.

I have written this on my knees, and I fear you will have some difficulty to decipher it, for my table, which cannot be very large in camp, is laid for breakfast, and four cups rather crowd it.

We are going to have a rare wet day, but I must go and see Campbell for all that, as he is on his way to Bilboa, and I shall miss him if I do not. I hope to see you in less than six months.

Till then, my dear, my dear Miss Thurlow, believe me, yours ever,

S——.

XI.

Camp Irun, 2 September 1813.

MY DEAR MISS THURLOW,—We came here two days back in order to support the advance, as the French were making demonstrations on this point with a view of preventing our attack on St. Sebastian; they had not, however, the desired effect, for we carried the place by storm at twelve in the day on the 31st instant. Our loss was very great; they rate it, as well as it can be now got at, to be about fifteen hundred men.

The place was stormed by detachments from the different divisions of the army, and by the fifth division under the command of Sir J. Leith, who is wounded. We sent a detachment of one Lieut.-Colonel, two Captains, four subalterns, and two hundred men, fifty of whom have returned. Of the officers, Burrard was mortally wounded, and died yesterday. He is son to Sir H. Burrard, the second he has lost in action in the regiment. Ensign Bridgeman slightly wounded, and Chaplin, who belongs to the Coldstream Guards, severely; he is shot in the breast, and his thigh broke so high that they cannot amputate; he is, however, doing as well as possible, but cannot be called by any means out of danger.

On the morning of the storm Soult made a general attack on our line, with an intention to relieve the place. The ground in our front is very strong, and defended by the Spaniards of the Gallician army, under General Frere. The French attacked one hour before daylight, and carried a small height which they surprised; this enabled them to establish a bridge over the Bidassoa, and at eight in the morning they had passed over about ten thousand men, and made a regular attempt to carry the hill occupied by the Spaniards, without which they could not with safety pass any great force of artillery. The Spaniards defended it with great obstinacy, and about two, when the French had carried the hill, they made a very spirited charge, and with the bayonet drove them fairly to the bottom. Towards evening the French made another attempt, but a very feeble one, and on the Spaniards giving three cheers on being informed of the fall of Sebastian, they retired, and during the night took away the bridge, and have not since troubled us.

I have just come from the field, and from the number of dead lying there I should think the loss on both sides must be about five thousand men, of which number the Spaniards certainly lost the most. The French made an attack more on the right, and were met by the seventh division British, and repulsed with great loss. The castle of St. Sebastian still holds out, and will cost some more men; we are at present pounding away at it at a great rate.

I have now given you all the news, and must send this letter to Oyarzun to be in time for the mail if possible. I shall write should anything take place. Believe me, yours ever, S——.

XII.

Camp Irun, 26th September 1813.

THE 6th of September, my dear Miss Thurlow, I received yesterday, and am most happy to find that our letters on the march have arrived at last; for I began almost to despair about them. You have, I believe, two more still to receive at least. We halted twice between Toro and this place, and I usually wrote on those days, and did not leave you out.

Since my last, which was after the fall of Sebastian, we have been quite quiet in this part of our line—indeed I may say all along the line—and have been employed fortifying the position. You do not seem to like the marching much, and I think working would be still less agreeable to you; not that we officers work, but we are obliged to see that the others do. Since it has begun, this is the first day that it has missed me, and I have generally had the morning party from half-past five till twelve; very pleasant amusement standing on a hill for six hours seeing two hundred men dig, especially in this beautiful climate, where we never have two fine days running. I never in my life was in such a place for rain, and further on the right it is worse. I wish the *Beau*, as his Lordship the Field-Marshal is called, would cross the Bidassoa and move down into France, as then, at all events, we should not be regularly sluiced night after night in our tents, which is the case here; for no canvas, nor anything else that ever was invented, will stand the rain in these hills, and we have famous fun with the gentlemen amateurs from England with their water-proof coats and *ne plus ultra* pelisses, which they find of very little use here, and they must be content, as we are, to get wet with philosophy, and dry as soon as they can.

To-morrow I set out on a trip to the right. I mean, if I can, to get as far as Roncesvalles, where Sir R. Hill is stationed, with whom I am acquainted. I mean to see the ground of the late actions, the finest ever fought by the British yet, and on the most extended scale of military operations. I have a good many friends to call on in the way, which will make it a very pleasant trip. Colonel

Stables goes with me, and our leave is for eight days, should the army make no movement, which it probably will not till our redoubts are finished, and they cannot well be complete before ten days more, and then I hope we shall make a start.

Sir James Leith, who was wounded at the storm of Sebastian, is doing very well, and will soon be fit to join his division, which belongs to our column of the army, and, to use the military phrase, is closed up, that is, has encamped in our rear, ready to support us if necessary. They marched from Sebastian the day before yesterday, and that place is now given over to the Spaniards, who have placed a garrison in it, and are to repair the breach. It was a very fine town, but I am sorry to say our troops plundered it in the most barbarous manner, set fire to it (or, as some say, did not put out the fires which caught accidentally). Be that as it may, they have not left a single house standing in it; the Turks could only have done that.

I know Mr. Joliffe, though I am not acquainted with him. Who does not know him, at least his hat, which is tolerably conspicuous! He keeps a pack of hounds, and I have always heard is an excellent good fellow. I must finish this, for the post leaves Oyarzun at three, and now it is past two, and it is more than a league from hence to Oyarzun. Adieu; and believe me, my dear Miss Thurlow, ever yours, S——.

XIII.

Camp Urogne, 9 October 1813.

MY DEAR MISS THURLOW,—As we are now proudly fixed in France, and being on piquet within a very few yards of the enemy, and therefore not willing to sleep, I cannot employ myself better than letting you know how we have been going on since I wrote last.

I mentioned that I was going to take a trip to the right of the line with old Stables, which we put in force the next day, and were very much pleased with it. The scenery is of the grandest kind, most particularly the valley of the Alduides and that of Roncesvalles, famous in former days for the fight which we have both heard remarkably well said or sung by poor C. Anguish in these times; not less famous for one of the sharpest affairs that have lately taken place in the Pyrenees; but except at Astley's or Sadlers Wells I much fear it has a bad chance of being again remembered in poetry, unless it should graciously please Walter Scott to give us another part of Don Roderick's Vision, for which he has certainly now sufficient materials. The Pass of Roncesvalles lies over a very high mountain, the top of which is in our possession; at the bottom of it, on the French side, is the town of St. Jean Pied de Port. This pass forms the right of our line.

In the valley, on the Spanish side, stands the convent in which they show you Orlando's club and armour. It is beautifully situated amongst large woods of old beech trees, and open patches of old parkish ground, the arrangement of which would have made the fortune of any capability gentleman in England—the whole closed, in the grandest manner, by the mountains. From this pass, coming to our left, the next pass is the Alduides, which is very beautiful, but not so grand as Roncesvalles. From that, passing by the Puerto de Viscayret, you reach the Pass of Maya, and so by the Pass of Echallar and that of Vera, to Irun, to which place we returned on the 5th.

On the night of the 6th we got our orders at twelve to attack the next morning, and at three in the morning of the 7th marched to our points, so as to reach them before daylight, that the enemy might not observe our movements, and at a quarter before eight, it being then low-water, forded the Bidassoa in five columns, and advanced against their position, the enemy making but little resistance, being partly surprised; for our plan of attack was so well combined that his position was turned and attacked, hill after hill, nearly at the same moment. He ought, however, to have defended his position—which is a very strong one—with greater obstinacy. Our loss was small—between 300 and 400 men, I should guess. At twelve we had gained our present position, just above the town of Urogne, which is now the French advance, and before dark were quietly encamped upon it. During the time that this operation was going on, the Light Division debouched by the Pass of Vera and attacked the Hill of Urogne, which is a high mountain on the right of our present line, and carried it in good form.

The poor natives are terribly alarmed, and have all fled; not that they fear us (the English), as they have given us to understand, but they know well the way their troops treated the Spaniards, and they dread the retaliation which they know they deserve from the troops of the Peninsula, whom a year back they looked upon as slaves, called them brigands, and treated worse than dogs, and if they made them prisoners, for it was seldom that they gave quarter to a Spaniard, and the poor devils, from wounds or sickness, could not reach their destination, regularly shot them; and the Spanish soldiers have not forgot it. And although as yet I do not think they would stand hard squeezing, they behave well, mixed as they now are with us, and face their enemy in a better style than I ever thought they could be brought to do.

Everything looks as if we were to make a forward movement, and I trust my next will be dated from some place further in the heart of France. We can see a long way into the country from our present position, and it appears to be a beautiful and rich country. I shall go on scribbling for ever, but I am sure by this time you must be tired of army speculations, which are but dry ones at any time.

I have just heard that a mail has landed, and I hope to have a letter to-morrow when I am relieved. You most likely are just now going to bed, so good-night, and believe me yours ever, S——.

XIV.

Camp Urogne, 31st October 1813.

MY DEAR MISS THURLOW,—Yours of the 4th of this month I received a few days ago, enclosing a map most beautifully drawn on silver paper, and I have compared it with the large French map of the Pyrenees, and, considering the scale, it is tolerably correct as far as Maya, but it takes no notice of the valley of the Alduides, nor that of San Carlos, which are leading features in the frontier line between the valley of Bastan and that of Roncesvalles, and are divided from each other by the large mountain of Arola. The situation of the towns on the Spanish side is tolerably well laid down, as well as in most maps; and with respect to the French side I will tell you a little more when we have advanced further up the country, which we shall do as soon as this confounded place, Pampeluna, falls.

Our army is in exactly the same position as when I wrote you last, the left on the sea-coast above Urogne, extending to the right through Zagaramurdi and Urdax to Roncesvalles, which is our right. The right of the French rests on Fort Seres, the centre at Mondarin, and the left at Arosa and St. Jean Pied de Port. On the Nive river, on their right, they have a second line from Mondarin through St. Pé to St. Jean de Luz, on the small river Nivelles, which is not fordable from St. Pé to the sea except at low tide. They are doing everything in their power to fortify this position, and all our arrangements are complete for an attack, which will take place as soon as Pampeluna falls, which cannot hold out above a few days longer; indeed we have been in treaty for the place, but the terms that the garrison wanted were, to be sent to France not to serve against Great Britain or her allies for the space of a year and a day. These were, of course, rejected; and after a little more starvation they will surrender at discretion.

November 6th.—I was obliged to leave off to go on duty, and as to-morrow is post-day, and I have very little news, I shall tack it on here.

Pamplona surrendered a few days back; the garrison were 4200 strong, and when they gave in, they had had nothing to eat for three days. Poor devils! how very thin and genteel they must have looked when they came out after four months' low diet. I should not admire the starving much; a siege is bad enough, but a starving bout is ten times worse.

As yet we have made no movement in consequence of the weather, which has been so bad for some days back as to put a stop to all military operations, by rendering the roads impassable for artillery, and the rain has swelled all the small rivulets so much that the troops cannot ford them; besides, what is rain in our part of the line is snow at Maya and Roncesvalles, but yesterday and the day before were fine, and the weather seems again to be settled. All the arrangements for a start are complete, and we expect our orders to attack hourly. I do not expect we shall have much to do in the first instance, as the position opposite us will be turned by our right, and the enemy must either abandon it, or if he resists stoutly (which, by the by, I do not think they are in a good humour for at present), he must be made prisoner in it, and it is not their game to lose men in that way, for they have not too many to spare now.

I am on the outposts, and we have just had a parley with Johnny Crapeaux, who has been sending in money to some of their officers who were wounded and taken when we crossed the frontier. They have no later news from Nap. than ourselves. No news, they say, is always bad news for them. The officer I spoke to was at Moscow last year; he is very tired of it, and wishes to go into winter quarters. I told him we had no such word in the British service, and that we meant to be in Bayonne shortly, and perhaps Bourdeaux, on which he vociferated, "Sacre F——," and strutted off in grand style.

I am not much inclined to be civil to these rascals, for I hate them most heartily, and they swagger and *cut a big swell* on these occasions, which at present is rather our right than theirs. Some of them, however, are very gentleman-like men, and then are pleasant fellows enough.

Our posts at this part of the line are so close, that the French and our piquets at night are not more than twenty yards from each other, and no obstacle between, which makes desertion very easy, and many of our Germans who have been enlisted from the prisoners of war go off, and a good many of the French come over to us; one came in last night. He says that they are very badly off for bread, but have plenty of meat, and, generally speaking, are very dissatisfied.

You wish to know why I put a little S in the corner of the direction? it is a trick that one gets from writing reports, as it is customary to put your name on the outside, which acts as a pass for the soldier who carries it, in case any post should hesitate to pass him; and when I am afraid that my letter may not be properly directed, I always write my name on the outside, as from its being known at the post-office, they return me the letter without opening it, which is rather an advantage than otherwise.

Before you receive this you will be thinking of returning to town; I should have no objection to be there with you, in spite of what I told the French officer; and believe me, my dear Miss Thurlow, ever yours, S——.

XV.

Camp before Bidart, 13 December 1813.

You see, my dear Miss Thurlow, we are again under canvas, and have had some sharp work for these four days past; we have had two officers killed, and two wounded. I do not know if you are acquainted with any of them;—Captain Martin and Captain Thompson are killed, and Captain Streatfield and Ensign Latour wounded, the latter severely. We have lost one hundred and fifty men.

Old Soult has been manœuvring and trying to deceive Lord Wellington, by showing a large force at different points of our line. On the 9th we advanced and attacked in front of this place, and drove the enemy into his strong ground in front of Bayonne; in the meantime Sir R. Hill crossed the Nive at Ustaritz, and rested his right flank on the Adour, so as to intercept Soult's supplies, which he received from Pau and Oleron by that river. This obliged Soult to make some decided movement, and on the 10th he attacked us, but was repulsed by the Fifth Division. On the 11th he again attacked us, and got a hill in our front that covered his movements. That night we took the outpost duty, and on the 12th he appeared in force, and manœuvred under cover of a very sharp affair of tirailleurs, but finding us well prepared at all points, he during the night recrossed the Nive, and on the 13th made three desperate attacks on Sir R. Hill, and was defeated and driven into Bayonne with great loss. I do not know what our loss has been on the right, but I understand very small in comparison.

Fortunately the weather has been fine, and still continues so to be, but very cold in the tents at night; however, anything is better for soldiering than wet, and I daresay it will be some time before we again go into winter quarters, if we do so at all.

I have not had any letters from home for some time, but I understand that my mother has not as yet got her house settled, and moreover is very likely to lose it. I see your cousin the Lord is married by the papers.

The news from the north is very good, and has spread through France; for the day before yesterday three German regiments in the French service—one of Nassau, the others of Baden and Frankfort—came over to us with their officers, arms, and every other necessary; they are marched to Passages to embark for England. This shows that the *morale*, as Napoleon calls it, is not the same in the French ranks as formerly, and I very much suspect that the material is almost as low.

I have no more news to tell you, so adieu, and believe me, my dear Miss Thurlow, yours ever, S——.

XVI.

St. Jean de Luz, 10 January 1814.

MY DEAR MISS THURLOW,—Since I wrote last, which was after our brush on the 12th, I have received yours of the 30th November, by which I see you have returned from your expedition to Hampshire, which I hope you found much to your satisfaction, and at all events had better weather than we had here about that time.

Since I wrote you nothing has taken place with us in the fighting line; but for all that we have not been perfectly quiet, for it pleased Soult to cross the Adour in force on the 3d instant, above the right of our army, and accordingly on the 4th we were all put in motion, and both armies continued manœuvring until the 8th, when Soult retired across the river and resumed his old position; and to-day we have followed his example and taken up our old cantonments. At one time on the 7th he had very nearly put his foot into it, and Lord Wellington would have attacked him on the 8th, but he found it out in time and was off during the night. We have fortunately not had a great deal of rain, but it is very cold lying out at this time of the year.

I begin to think the war seems drawing to a close, but I hope we may take the field once more, and put the thing past a doubt by forcing Napoleon to make peace on French ground; for when he receives back the prisoners of war that we and the allies have taken from him, we give him an army of at least 300,000 men, and set him up at once as a formidable enemy, long before the nations wrested from him can reach their place in the scale, as he has taken care to drain them pretty handsomely during the time they were under his dominion; and even Austria will be a long time before she recovers from the great losses she has sustained in this and the last war. Little England, however, can hold up her head and say, we have beat you at last and will have at you again as soon as you please, for in peace where France gains ten we gain at least a hundred for the first years of it. I have given you a tolerable dose of my ideas of affairs in general, and shall leave off, but will not finish this till to-morrow, when the post goes, in hopes of having something more to send.

Another mail has arrived from England, but brings no particular news. . . . We are to have a grand ball here to-night—about two hundred men in fine coats, and certainly not more than ten ladies, including chaperons; [not] very gay, but it serves to pass the night. Adieu, and believe me, my dear Miss Thurlow, ever yours,   S——.

XVII.

St. Jean de Luz, 30 January 1814.

YOURS, my dear Miss Thurlow, of the 4th I received a few days ago. It had been a most enormous time on its passage, as indeed have all the packets lately; for it is the latest packet we have from England, and now we have two due, and a third will be so in a few days. I cannot conceive the reason of it, as the wind with us has been northerly for some time past, and Admiral Pickmore has arrived in a ship-of-war, and he left Plymouth on the 20th. Some people say that the road to Falmouth is snowed up, and therefore the mail cannot get down; be that as it may, it is very provoking, as I expect to get my promotion every day, and of course, you may suppose, look anxiously for the packet. I find old Hughes is a very general favourite; he is quite well, and when sober as good a servant as ever, but he has learnt to cure sore backs of horses and mules, which in this army is a very common complaint, and he, James Hughes, having gained the name of a good doctor, is consulted on every occasion, by which means he picks up so many shillings and so many friends, that he gets drunk now past all former example.

You are quite correct as to the country being swampy, but it is not by [any] means unwholesome, for the army never were known to be so healthy as at the present time; and excepting the regiments just come out from England, we have no sick in the army. It is in the summer, when these swamps are nearly dry, that this sort of country is unhealthy.

I will refer to the little map, but I much fear we are out of the district it particularly notices. Our left is at Bidart, extending to the right by Arcangues and Arauntz, crossing the Nive river in front of Ville Franche, which is in the map, so on to the Adour river by St. Pierre, also in the map, to Petite Moguere on the Adour. We then take the course of the Adour river to Urt, where Sir Stapleton Cotton is stationed with some cavalry and the Third Division of infantry, to watch the movements of General Arispe, who is at St. Jean Pied de Port with two divisions, and we shall most probably remain in this position for some time, as the immense quantity of rain that has fallen within this week has rendered the roads almost impassable.

I had a letter from my mother the other day; she likes Brighton very much, but I think her house is in very bad hands as far as expedition goes. We must soon have peace; all the French papers talk of it as a certain thing. Adieu, my dear Miss Thurlow, and believe me ever yours, SALTOUN.

P.S.—We have just heard that our army in Holland has been engaged; —*Viâ* France.

XVIII.

St. Jean de Luz, 6th February 1814.

My dear Miss Thurlow,—You, of course, before this time, know of my promotion, and perhaps are among the number that expect me home; but if so, you will be disappointed, at least for the present, for I have accepted the command of the Light Companies, in which I have always served, and mean to remain with this army till the thing is decided, which must be the case, one way or the other, in a very few months, and then I shall return without the certainty of being sent out again immediately. This is not any sudden idea of mine; for I had settled in my own mind, when I left England, if I got my promotion not to go home. I never mentioned it to my mother or you, because, although I knew it to be perfectly right in me to do so, I should have had some difficulty in persuading you of that. Now, however, that it is past altering, I think I could persuade you that it is correct for me not only to serve with a good grace when ordered, but, at the present time especially, to show that I am willing and ready to serve without being compelled to do so; and I have accordingly made an offer of my services to the Commanding Officer of the Brigade, who has been pleased to accept of the same, not but what I would give a great deal for one fortnight in London, if the fog was ever so thick. Indeed I look forward to nothing with so much pleasure, and it must soon happen, for things are now come to such a pitch, that we must have a close in a very few months. I have written this in the most horrible hurry possible, for the post is ordered out to-day an hour sooner on account of the bad roads, so must conclude with hopes of very soon seeing [you], notwithstanding my volunteering, and with loves and affections, etc., believe me, my dear Miss Thurlow, ever yours, S——.

XIX.

Heights above Anglet, February 17, 1814.

My dear Miss Thurlow,—We marched out from St. Jean de Luz on the 15th and occupied these heights, our left resting on the sea in front of Biarritz, and communicating with the Fifth Division on our right in front of Arcangues, who extend to their right as far as the Nive river, and the Sixth Division occupy the ground between the Nive and the Adour. The Light, Second, Third, and Fourth Divisions, with a strong force of cavalry, have moved upon Hasparen and the river Aran, and the French have retired from their position on the Aran, and occupy one on the Bidouse, which they will also retire from. All this is preparatory to our crossing the Adour, which we shall do in a few days, and probably without being opposed, but at what point nobody at present knows, but most probably at more than one place.[1] In the meantime everybody has his own particular favourite points, which he will back against any other; or taking the odds against the field—and they vary as they do in the Derby or any other event—my points are the junction of the Gave and the Adour, and at the mouth of the Adour, if possible; but the difficulty at the mouth will be very great, owing to the great width and the force of the tide, which is here very rapid; but should the weather continue as fine as it has been for these six days past, we may pass it anywhere, as the necessity of the high road will be done away with, for the guns will be able to move by the cross-roads, which during the rainy weather were perfectly impassable.

February 25, before Bayonne.—We crossed the river the day before yesterday in boats, and are now in position round Bayonne, and have cut them off from all communication with their rear. We passed, as I conjectured, at the mouth, and I think our bridge of boats will be completed to-morrow, when the remainder of our cavalry and artillery will pass. It is not as yet known whether we are to besiege the citadel or not, but I begin to think we shall. Lord Wellington has not as yet crossed. I have not time to write a long epistle, as I am in command of the advance posts and wanted every minute. Adieu, and believe me ever yours,

Saltoun.

---

[1] It is worth notice that two rivers in Sussex bear names nearly identical with two of these rivers of Gascony: the Adur, entering the sea at Shoreham; the Arun, debouching at Littlehampton.

26th.—All quiet here this morning, and the letters will go off in about ten minutes. We yesterday heard from Lord Wellington. He has passed the Gave D'Oleron without opposition, and is to pass the Gave de Pau to-day. Nothing as yet determined about this column, and I do not suppose it will be for a day or two.

You will probably see Reeve, who has gone home, at least if he remains any time in town, as he is a great dandy. Her Ladyship[1] is still at Brighton, and I rather think that the house will go against her whenever the Chancellor takes upon himself to determine it. She must find it a great bore, for in the present state of affairs she cannot look out for another house, for fear this suit should go in her favour. By-the-by, I see your cousin has been publishing again in verse, and not much better than the first production. I have not been in bed these four nights, nor shall I be as long as I am in command of this post, as we are rather too close for regularly going to bed. It is now just after daylight, and about my time for taking a regular good snooze; so I have tolerable good practice in late hours, and shall be a match for any one when I return. . . . Ever yours, S——.

XX.

St. Bernard's Convent, March 13th, 1814.

I WROTE you last week, my dear Miss Thurlow, from Beaucotte, a small village in the rear of this place, and the day after we advanced and drove the enemy's posts into Bayonne and the citadel, and since that time we have been perfectly quiet on our part, and have the place closely invested, waiting for orders to besiege it, which have not as yet arrived from Lord Wellington, nor is it certain whether we are to besiege or not. I have the command of this post, which forms the right of the line on this side the river, and is close in with the citadel and dockyard, our advanced posts being about six hundred yards from them; it is on the high road from Bayonne to Beaucotte and the mouth of the Adour.

My mansion has a fine name, but is not very remarkable for accommodation. It was formerly a convent, and was *abimé* during the revolution, and the ladies turned adrift. Since that period it has been made use of as a glass-house, but for want of trade they went to rack, and since we have taken possession the

[1] His mother, Lady Saltoun.

enemy have destroyed by shot and shell the small part of the house that was habitable, except the kitchen, in which I am now writing, which it will puzzle them to throw anything into; indeed for some days past they have left off firing at us, finding, I suppose, that they did us no harm.

I have no news of any sort or kind to tell you, as before you receive this you will have seen the account of Lord Wellington's victory over Soult, since which time he has been in cantonments in front of Mont Maman, and perfectly quiet. He was wounded slightly in the hip, and has been confined a few days in consequence. Soult has since the action received a reinforcement of nine thousand men from Suchet's army, which has retired from Catalonia, and we therefore expect soon to hear of another action if Soult should think himself strong enough to attack. In the meantime all the reports that we get through France are of a pacific nature; indeed they go so far as to say that the line of demarcation to be observed by the armies during the armistice is now being settled, but I rather think that this statement is premature.

The French people are heartily sick of the war, and if they could have peace, do not care whether Napoleon or a Bourbon is their King. They all seem to look towards the latter, as they say they never can have a permanent peace as long as Napoleon lives, but they are too much afraid of him to rise, as in case of failure they know he would revenge himself most properly; and as there is nothing left in the country but old men, they like to look twice before they leap. Let what will happen it cannot be long before I see you in No. 10, so for the present *adios*, my dear Miss Thurlow, and believe me ever yours,

SALTOUN.

XXI.

St. Bernard's, before Bayonne, 20 March 1814.

YOUR letter of the 1st instant I received yesterday, and as this is our post-day I do not like putting off answering it till next week, so have got up very early this morning, or rather have not lain down again, for I am obliged now to turn out every morning before daylight, in order to see as soon as day breaks if the bold Frenchman has made any alteration in his lines or not, and to report accordingly.

You seem to think that I meant to have remained in this country had I got my promotion under any circumstances, and therefore of course think it odd I did not tell you so when I was in England last year; but, my dear girl, that event depended so much upon a contingency, that, although I thought it might happen, I certainly did not think it very likely, which I will explain to you as shortly as I can. When I was in England I knew very well that some sort of arrangement was in contemplation by which the Guards would get promotion, either by taking our Generals off the strength of the regiments as Captains and giving their companies to the senior officers, letting them receive the pay and giving us the rank, or by removing them entirely from the regiment and giving them a specific pay equivalent to what they now receive. Either of these things taking place would have made a number of us Captains at the same time, and as most of them would have gone to England, there would have been a sufficient number in London to have done the duty without me; but by far the most probable thing at that time was, that I, from being first for purchase, should have got my promotion by purchase, before any arrangement of this kind could be settled, in which case I should have been the only officer promoted at the time, and must have gone home in my turn to do the duty in London, and have gone to Holland, or come out here again in the regular course of things. Now there could be no use in mentioning a thing which might never take place, and indeed which never has, at least not yet, and was not at all likely to happen in my case; but the circumstance of the augmentation taking place, which never came into anybody's head, put me exactly in the same situation as had the first happened, by promoting Reeve and Thomas at the same time as myself, and enabling me to remain, which I am glad to find you approve of, and I hope will be satisfied as to the explanation. What a lot of paper it has taken up, but I could not do it in fewer words. If I have many more military points to discuss, I shall make an officer of you by the time you thoroughly understand the different forms of speech.

Everything remains in the same state as when I wrote you last week, and as yet nobody can guess whether we are to besiege the place or not. Our casualties are very trifling. One of my men got cut in two the other day on sentry by a cannon-shot, and his comrade made the following epitaph on him:—

> On sentry I fell a sacrifice
> In cold blood to French cowardice;
> Close to my head a cannon-ball you see,
> Resembling that which was the death of me.

Not so bad for a private soldier. It is a most cowardly thing the way they fire at the sentries, as we have orders at present not to return fire on any account, and the rascals come up within pistol-shot of our sentries, at the same time that they are practising their recruits in firing at them from the works; but when our guns come up, by God we will make them look sharp enough after themselves.

Bordeaux has declared for the Bourbon, and we expect the whole of this part of the country to follow the example; so Boney must look sharp. I shall see you sooner than you seem to expect in your letter, and till then must content myself with writing. Adieu, my dear Miss Thurlow, and believe me ever yours,

SALTOUN.

XXII.

St. Bernard's, 16 April 1814.

YOURS of the 29th of March, my dear Miss Thurlow, I received yesterday, and am happy to say that my predictions about the war are not only likely to be fulfilled, but are already come to pass, sooner, I must confess, than I thought they would; for I certainly thought old Boney would have made a harder fight of it. He has made a most miserable finish, and given up all claim to the name of a great man. One can hardly conceive it possible that a man who has held the rank he has done in Europe, could hesitate an instant between death and a despicable existence, and in spite of all his talents, and all his victories, we must write him down in the same page with Whitelock. But to return to ourselves.

Since I wrote last we have had a very sharp affair, and one that has fallen very severely on the Guards. The enemy made a most desperate sortie on the morning of the 14th, about three o'clock, and were not driven in without very great loss on our side. They got through the piquet line near the Bordeaux road, and the night was so dark that it was impossible to tell friends from foes. Sir John Hope very imprudently rode to the front during the dark, met with a party of the French, whom he mistook for Germans, and in endeavouring to get away his horse was shot, and himself wounded in two places and taken prisoner. He was endeavouring to rally a piquet that had given way, which would have been a very proper place for a Lieut.-Colonel, but was a very improper one for a Commander-in-Chief. General Hay was killed, General Stopford wounded; poor Sir Henry Sulivan and Captain Crofton killed; Captain White and Shifner dead of their wounds; Colonel Collier, Captains Burroughs and Woburn very severely wounded, and in all about sixteen officers of the Guards and Colonel Townshend taken prisoners, and I believe wounded, but am not certain. What makes this loss the more provoking is, that we had heard of the abdication of Bonaparte the day before the sortie took place. We expect that a suspension of hostilities will take place to-day or to-morrow, as we have sent in the confirmation of the news to the Governor of the place, and it will not be his interest to make war against the Bourbons any longer.

I did not know till I received your letter that my mother had taken a house, but I had heard that she was looking out for one, as the Grosvenor Street house was not likely to be settled in a hurry. Adieu. I shall not be long now before I see you. Ever yours, SALTOUN.

XXIII.

Bordeaux, 22 May 1814.

I WROTE you, my dear Miss Thurlow, before I left Bayonne, but I should not be surprised if you receive this letter first, as from the packet being changed from Sebastian to this place, I much fear our letters have not been sent as they ought to have been, which is rather a melancholy thing for the friends of our poor fellows who were wounded in the sortie, as no less than nine have died of their wounds, and their friends will hear of their death before they have the least idea of their danger.

We have had a most delightful trip from Toulouse to this place, by way of Montauban and Ajen, along the course of the Garonne, through the most beautiful country. We passed through the whole of Soult's army, which was cantoned on that side of the Garonne. The behaviour of the troops, although perfectly respectful towards us as officers, clearly showed that they were not by any means well satisfied with the new order of things, and that they considered the thing as forced upon them. However, I know enough of soldiers to be perfectly convinced that, if the present Government can find means to pay them their arrears, they will be as faithful an army to Louis as ever they were to Napoleon, and the King should strain every nerve to gain that point; however, I never did, nor do I now expect much exertion from a Prince of the House of Bourbon.

This is one of the finest towns I ever saw in my life, fine wide streets, with avenues of trees, a number of public walks, etc. The Duke D'Angoulême is here;

we have just been at his levee. The natives give him a grand ball to-night, to which we are invited, so we shall have an opportunity of seeing all the beauty of the place, which, if I am to judge from the specimens I have hitherto seen, is certainly not great.

To-morrow we set out for Paris, by way of Tours, etc.; we shall arrive there in about ten days, as we mean to make several digressions to see the country. Our stay at Paris will be very short, so you may expect me soon after you receive this. I shall write from Paris, and if you write, direct—Post-office, Paris. None of the Guards are as yet ordered for America, but if they do order us, it shall not prevent me coming home and seeing you before I go. I am perfectly determined on that head, so adieu till I arrive in Grosvenor Street. Ever yours,

SALTOUN.

XXIV.

[August 1814.]

MY DEAR CATHARINE,—I shall not see you again for these three months; it is a devil of a time. I did not meet anybody this morning, being rather too late for the watchmen, but the Jubilee Jacks were returning in great numbers, and, as they call it, smoked my trousers.

I did not tell you last night where to direct to me, but in case you should ever wish to write to me *in propria persona*, my direction is—Philorth, Fraserburgh. However, as now I am reduced to my old resource, and have no greater pleasure than writing to you, I shall frequently do so, and will give you such directions about writing as you may require, although I do not see the least occasion for it, nor any reason why you and I should not correspond if we feel inclined. My head was in such whirl that for once in my life I dreamt, and could recollect most of it. It was all about you and the Park, and I was just going to kiss you, when my brute of a servant roared out ten o'clock, and I awoke not a little disappointed to find it was not reality.

By-the-by my old maid of a landlady was in the Park, knew me but not you, and has laughed at me to-day, when I wished her good-bye, about the care I took of my little woman, as she was pleased to call you. Good-bye, my dearest girl, for I could go on writing nonsense till the paper could hold no more, and believe me ever yours, S.

To CATHERINE LADY SALTOUN, his wife.

XXV.

Ramsgate, 9th April 1815.

MY DEAR CATHERINE,—We are this moment arrived and are to embark immediately, and I hope sail this evening, as this is not the most delightful place to remain in. The wind is not very fair, but we hope to get to Ostend by the morning. God bless you! Yours affectionately, S——.

XXVI.

Ostend, 11th April 1815.

MY DEAR CATHERINE,—We arrived here yesterday after a tolerable passage, and everything looks like the bustle of preparation, but except when one's thoughts wander a little across the water, I have been so used to the sort of life that it comes quite natural to me, as skinning does to the eels. To-day we proceed to Bruges, and to-morrow to Ghent. Our Brigade are at present at Enghien, a small place between Ath and Hal, where I suppose they will remain for some time, at least till every arrangement is made with respect to this army, which now will not take much longer, as the Duke of Wellington has arrived at Brussels, and is very expeditious in these matters.

This is a tolerable town, but has the appearance of much poverty, in consequence of its having suffered much during the late war by the stagnation of commerce. The garrison is at present composed of Hanoverian troops, who are clothed in red, but are distinguished from the British by their officers wearing yellow sashes. The British troops, as soon as they land, receive their ammunition, and immediately proceed by the canal to Bruges and Ghent, from which latter place they march to their different cantonments. According to our present plan we shall reach Enghien on the 14th, from which place I shall again write to you, as indeed I mean to do every opportunity that occurs.

When Hughes comes out let him bring with him a pair of saddle-bags as I have none, and also tell William[1] to get a horse at about 40 guineas, and send

[1] His brother, the Hon. William Fraser.

it out by Hughes, as they are very dear and bad in this country; the horse is not to be too tall, and by applying to Torrens he will put him into a way of getting a passage for him. He must have a saddle and bridle. We are just setting out, so God bless you, my dear girl, and believe me, ever your affectionate husband, SALTOUN.

XXVII.

Hove, 22d April 1815.

MY DEAR DEAREST CATHERINE,—I did not expect to have seen Hughes and your letter by him quite so soon, or rather, I did expect that Reeve would have arrived before; but he found, I suppose, something so agreeable in Ghent as to induce him to remain there, and I have not as yet got your letter by him; but I know that to-morrow he will be at Brussels, and of course the next day here, so that before the post can come I am certain of having another letter from my dearest Catherine, which, quiet and idle as we now are, is an event in any man's life, but in mine, considering whence and from whom it comes, a very great one, or at least one which I consider in that point, as it is one that gives me the greatest pleasure.

You wish to know where we are, what we are doing, and what we are likely to do. At present we are perfectly quiet in this village, and are likely so to remain till the army is closed up, and I do not think we shall be ready to act till about the 10th of May or thereabouts. But, however, mine is mere conjecture; yet I hope by that time—and I rather expect it—that we shall be in such form as to be able to take the field with every prospect of success.

Since I wrote you I have been to Brussels to see the place. It is a fine town, and if we were certain of holding this situation for any time, I should be the first to propose your joining me; but as we must be war soldiers now, believe me, my dear love, it is both for your comfort and mine that you should remain in England. I wish to God I was there with you, but a man must follow his line, and I have taken war for my profession. I was always ready to meet my duty—this time I have forced myself so to do; and although my heart and soul are now with you, I have no doubt they will come back the first time the French eagles want them. . . . Believe me, my dear love, I long to kiss you, and so kiss the paper you will read. SALTOUN.

XXVIII.

Hove, 27th April 1815.

I WROTE you, my dear love, on Sunday last, but, however, I am never tired of writing to you, which is the only reason I can produce for writing now, for it is half-past four in the *morning*, and I think you know me well enough to believe that I certainly should not get up at this hour to write if I could sleep without writing; but the fact is, that I had a great many letters to write by this mail, and I put yours off till this morning, knowing I should get up to write to you, and also perfectly well knowing I should *not* get up to write to any other soul alive. I might, it is true, let this mail pass by without writing to any one, but having written to others, I could not resist the pleasure of writing to you, and it is only to you, dear Kate, that I have any pleasure in writing.

Reeve has come, and brought me your letter, papers, etc., and I have written to William about the horses; for Hughes tells me that the "Larker" is likely to throw out curbs, to which all young horses are liable, and they may and must be taken off. In the meantime they will prevent him from working for a short time, I have therefore told William to get you another horse to match, so that in case of accidents you will always have two to work, and you may as well quicken him about it, as he is, like me, apt to be lazy about any and everything that he has to do. I have had a long letter from my mother, in which she mentions her wish to go with us to the drawing-room, etc. etc. I am a bad hand at etiquette, so you will find out whether you should pay your respects to her Majesty during my absence, or wait till we go together. . . .

We are perfectly quiet, and I think are likely so to remain till the 10th or 15th of the next month. The troops are closing up, and everything getting ready for war, but I hope to burn Paris, and be with you yet before August is over.

Give my best thanks to P—— for her good wishes when you see her. As to the music, take care of it, for L—— has brought out one part of the duets and left the other, so they are useless till we meet again. I have found plenty in this country. God bless you, my dear love, and believe me, ever your affectionate

SALTOUN.

XXIX.

Hove, 30th April 1815.

My dear Catharine,—I have just received your letter of the 24th, and as to-morrow is our post-day, I lose no time in thanking you for it, not that I have much or indeed any news to give you, for everything, as far as we are concerned, remains just the same as when I wrote last, and will probably continue so to do for some time yet, till the army is properly closed up.

Some gay proceedings went on last week at Brussels. The new Knights serving with this army were to be installed, and the Duke gave a ball on the occasion. He sent eight tickets to each Battalion, but by our division of four to the Captains, and four to the Subalterns, it did not come down to me; and if it had, I should not have gone, but passed it to any one who wished going eighteen miles for that purpose. I am told that it was a very good ball, and the supper magnificent.

I have a plan for going to Antwerp and Bergen-op-Zoom, which, if I can get leave, I mean to put in execution this week. The distance is about sixty miles, but the road very bad from Antwerp to Bergen. I propose setting out on Tuesday, and returning on Sunday next. Grose and Miller are of the party, and after this trip I shall have seen enough of *les Pays Bas* to be able to form a very good idea of the rest of them, for I trust when we move from this we shall go direct into France, and, if the thing is not settled before, bring the war to a speedy conclusion.

Bonaparte is trying all the means he can devise to stir up the spirit of the people by proclamations, etc., but I am inclined to think that these inflammatory publications have been so often tried upon the French people that they have lost their effect. The desertion of the troops to us continues, and the deserters say that numbers of the men are inclined to us, and will come over the first opportunity. If that is the case it is impossible that Napoleon can keep the field. The war has begun in Italy, and at first Murat had some success, but he has since been defeated; but the papers lie so in their different accounts, that it is impossible at first to know what has really taken place, and probably neither party has as yet done anything of importance.

It was rather unlucky about Hughes and the horse, but it can't be helped and was my fault for not thinking of it sooner. Should William have got one, you may send it out by Colonel Thomas, if he has not set off, or any officer of the *Regiment* that may be coming. Should he not have got one on the receipt of this, write me word by return of post, and I will provide myself here.

I did not much envy you your dinner at P———'s, particularly the Loo part of the proceeding; however, we cannot always have everything our own way, or I should not be out here at present, but much more agreeably employed communicating with word of mouth instead of pen, which last way, however, when one has no other, has much more satisfaction in it than we are at first willing to allow. . . .

I have nothing more to say to my dear Catharine at present. . . . The serjeant has just come for the letters, so I must conclude, and believe me, my dear Kate, ever yours affectionately, SALTOUN.

XXX.

Hove, 7th May 1815.

I RETURNED here, my dearest Catharine, yesterday, and found your letters of the 27th and 1st May, but the one you sent by Davis I have not as yet received. He is in the country, and we expect him to join to-night or to-morrow.

I set out, as I proposed in my last, for our trip. We reached Antwerp the first day, passing through Malines, the place we call Mechlin, a fine town, and the country very rich and well cultivated, but a great sameness in the whole of it.

Antwerp is a most beautiful city, and very well worth going to see. It has a tolerable gallery of pictures; and one picture in a private house, called the Chapeau de Paille (it is a lady in a straw hat), is very beautiful. Besides the Church of St. Jaques, which is a fine building, the Cathedral of Nôtre Dame is worthy of notice; but these people spoil all their churches by whitewashing them in the inside, which destroys all the effect which would be produced by the gloom of the grey stone of which they are built. In Nôtre Dame there is a very high tower of six hundred and twenty-two steps, from the top of which you have a most magnificent view of the surrounding country, and can see a considerable way on the seaside; but that view only had the effect of making me rather melancholy,—not that I have the least occasion to see the sea to make me think of England, for I do that, or rather think of you, without intermission. In the

Church of St. Jaques there is a model of the Mount Calvary at Jerusalem, a curious thing, and the statues as large as life.

Seeing Antwerp took up one day, and the next we went to Bergen-op-Zoom, and saw that fortress, interesting to any military man, and particularly so to us after what took place there last year. We returned the same night to Antwerp, and the next day to Brussels. It had been our intention to return through Dendermonde and Alost, but on that road they have no post-horses, and our time of leave was too short to make that detour with one set from Brussels. We rode over here yesterday.

Everything remains here the same as when I wrote last, except that the troops which are to form our army are closing, and every day more of them reach their destination. The report of the day is that the first division of the Prussians will reach the Rhine on the 15th; if so, we may look to having them in line about the 25th. They say that sixteen battalions of Hanoverians are to enter Brussels in the course of this week, previous to their being sent to the different divisions, which are to be composed of British and Hanoverians mixed, as we were in the Peninsula with the Portuguese.

I am very glad William has got me the horse, and I wrote you in my last how to send him out, and if he is not gone before you receive this, send a saddle and bridle with him, but if he is gone it is of no consequence, as I can get them here.

. . . The men Hamilton brought out were a draft to complete the battalion of the Coldstreams here, and on their arrival were distributed to all the companies here, and I must first find out what company Mr. M——[1] has got into before I can tell who are his officers; but that would be of no use, as I can do nothing for him even were he in my own regiment, for the only way he can get on is by his own good conduct, and the best thing to do is to get some of his friends to write to him to advise him to conduct himself well, and to offer to come forward as a corporal. He will be put upon the list, and in the event of his being able to write a good hand, and conducting himself well, he will be brought forward as one, and then it entirely depends upon his own steadiness whether he is made a sergeant, or broke.

8th.—I did not close this letter yesterday, in hopes of having something more to say, and we have very great news, but it will be no news to you, as you will have heard it before you get this. Ney and Mortier are arrested, and twenty

---

[1] A young gentleman who had enlisted in the Coldstream Guards.

General Officers have sent in their resignations to Bonaparte. We have for some time known that party has been running very strong, but I certainly expected Ney would have been faithful to Bonaparte. Any disagreement, however, amongst them is good news for us.

I have not had any letter from her Ladyship or any of them. I suppose she is in a fuss about houses, which, by the by, my dear love, will be your case, unless something lucky turns up; for getting a house, which one would suppose at first sight an easy thing in London, is the most difficult thing in the world. By this time, my dear Catharine, you must be tired reading, though I am not of writing to you, so I shall close proceedings till next post-day, and believe me, my dear love, ever your affectionate   SALTOUN.

XXXI.

Hove, 14th May 1815.

MY DEAR LOVE,—William's servant arrived here last Friday with the horse, which is a very nice one, just the right height, and takes very kindly to the troops. He also brought me your letter of the 4th, and yesterday I received yours of the 8th with the papers. You are so good, my dear Kate, in writing so often, that as I can't find words to express how much pleasure I have in hearing from you, I shall follow your plan, and write to you whenever I can find any opportunity.

You want to know whether I have received your letters that you sent *per* post, and the difference it makes between sending them that way or by Barnard. I can't tell if all you sent *per* post have arrived, but I should think so, for I have received eight, namely, the 11th, 14th, 24th, 27th, 28th April, 1st, 4th, 8th May. Now as to the difference of time. The letters which are sent by Barnard go in the Duke of Wellington's bag, which as soon as it lands is sent off express to headquarters, so that at present, being no great distance from headquarters, I get your letters that way a day sooner than by post; but should headquarters move any great distance from our division, and they were not at the place appointed for the post-office, then they would have to go to headquarters in the first instance, and would be then sent to me. As, for instance, when we were at Bayonne, headquarters were at Thoulouse, and the post-office was at St. Jean de Luz, the letters that came through Barnard went to Thoulouse, and then were returned to

Bayonne, and those that came by post were left with the division at Bayonne in their way through; but you had as well for the present send them through Barnard, for we are not very likely to be very distant from headquarters, as we have got H.S.H. the Prince of Orange to command our column, and I do not think the Duke will let that young gentleman far out of his sight; and if we should be sent to a distance, I can always send you word how to send them; for, thank God, my dear love, the communication here is not quite so long coming as it was in Spain. I received all the Scotch letters safe, and answered them last Sunday. I think I mentioned it in my letter to you. I went last Wednesday to Grammont to pay a visit to Lord Hill, and meant to have written you a letter from thence on Thursday last, but I found that their post had gone out on the Wednesday before I got there, as their bag goes round by Ath, and therefore sets out the day before ours, and takes our bag on the way from Ath to Brussels, so I was, much against my inclination, obliged to wait till to-day before I could write to you. . . .

I was certain that the "Larker" would, sooner or later, have thrown out curbs; however, the cure of them is perfectly simple, and not a very long job. I hope by this time you have got another horse. Indeed I now wish I had left my big horse in England, as he is an excellent match, and I find from his old master, Lord Hay, who is aide-de-camp to Maitland, that he goes very well in harness. I did not try him at Worthing, for the coachman said that he had heard in the yard that he would not go in harness. He is an excellent horse, and begins to be less afraid of soldiers, but not by any means tractable as yet, but he stands fire very fairly. We go out three times a week to practise ball at a mark which is excellent training for the nags. . . .

The 10th is past, and the 15th near at hand, but as yet we have no symptoms of a move. They say that the Prussians will be all ready in a day or two, but as yet no Russians have arrived, nor are the Austrians up, and I do not expect that anything will be done by us till after the 25th. Boney is still at Paris, and they say that he is afraid to quit it. That may be the case, but I rather imagine that he does not mean to act offensively against us, and as he knows that we are not likely to move till we are all up, he will not, most probably, join his army till he receives information of that being nearly the case. The lies that are about, some of which have found their way into the papers, are similar to all stories which circulate, no one knows how, in the rear of an army.

The story of the skirmish between the Prussians and the French is perfectly false; not a shot has as yet been fired on either side. I see also in the Courier letters about wounded soldiers passing through Brussels. Waggons with sick have passed on their way to Ghent, which is always the case when an army is preparing to take the field. These sick they choose to call wounded, and therefore there must have been some fighting. The only thing that has really taken place has not yet got into the papers. It is this:—the Saxons were not very much to be trusted, and they wished to draft them into the Prussian regiments; I mean those troops that came from that part of Saxony which was given over to Prussia. They objected to this, and did something which was very like mutiny, and they were accordingly disarmed and sent to the rear, to the amount of about 10,000 men. I am glad of it, as the rascals might have gone over to Boney in an action, in the same way as they did at Leipsic to the Allies. 10,000 men more or less is of no consequence to us, but it is of great consequence that we should all be of the same determination.

We have had most charming weather for some time, and it seems likely to continue. I mean in the course of the week to ride over to Ath, and from thence to Tournay, which is a fine town worth seeing. I meant to have gone to-morrow, but Stables is going to Antwerp, and I am therefore tied by the leg till he returns, as I am next in command at this place. I shall finish this to-morrow morning. Good night, my dear love.

I contrived to dream of you last night, but it does not always happen; I wish I had some receipt for it. I am just undressed, and recollect that to-morrow I am to see the Second Battalion Light Infantry, who are put under my orders, at five, so that I must at least get up at four, as they are a good mile from this place; and as our letters must be given in at eight to the Adjutant-General's office, I think it more prudent to close to-night.

William's man will be sent off on Tuesday. I would have sent him to-morrow, but I cannot get a route from the Quartermaster-General sooner. Hughes has been ill of a fever, but has got better. Good night again, my dearest love. You will laugh at our hours—it is just eleven—but as we get up much sooner than you and I are in the habit of doing when left to ourselves, perforce we must go to bed sooner. I shall see you yet before September if things go on well; and believe me, my dear love, your affectionate   SALTOUN.

XXXII.

Hove, 18th May 1815.

MY DEAR CATHARINE,— . . . I send you a few lines, not that I have any news or anything particular to write about, but, as you say you like receiving letters, and I certainly have great satisfaction in writing to you, I therefore have no great merit in pleasing myself.

We are going on in exactly the same way as when I last wrote. The Duke of Wellington has been for some days back riding a good deal, and we used to say in Spain that whenever the Beau, meaning the Duke, took to riding, it was time to look out. However, I believe this time he is only looking at his troops, which have been much increased lately by several battalions of Hanoverian landwehr, who are tolerably good-looking men in general, but, of course, from their having been raised by conscription since the breaking out of this business, are a good deal in want of drill and other necessary training. The spirit which the French call *morale* is very good in them, and they are pleased at acting with the British, whom they consider as countrymen. John Bull, however, does not by any means admit them to that honourable distinction, but calls them "rid Jarmins," from their being dressed in red.

At present Enghien is quite gay. Some of our officers are good cricket players, and at present a match is going on from A to G—that is, men whose names begin with any letter from A to G inclusive—against the rest of the alphabet, including the Duke of Richmond. The Duchess and ladies are also here on a visit to Maitland. I must get Lord March to introduce me to her Grace, as she and the Duchess of Bedford are the only Gordons that I am not well acquainted with. The A to G beat the others hollow yesterday, and they are to try it again to-day.

The desertion from the French army still continues, but in a very diminished ratio. Two officers came over yesterday, who report that the wish to come over is the same as it was, but that Napoleon's officers have taken so many precautions to prevent it, such as only putting men they can rely on on advanced duty, and putting all the corps they suspect into towns, that it is very difficult for the men to get away.

I have nothing further to write about, and by this time, my dear girl, you must be tired of reading this nonsense, so I shall close, and write again on Monday. Believe me, my dear love, your affectionate   SALTOUN.

XXXIII.

Hove, 21st May 1815.

YOU were quite right, my dear Catharine, in supposing that I should be in expectation of a letter from you by the last post, as I received the papers by the one before, which I believe I told you in my last. . . .

The little horse goes on very well, and I think he would make a very nice lady's horse, as he has an excellent light mouth, and very good paces, and is, besides, a very safe goer, although his feet are rather small, and have been neglected; but with the help of Mr. Hughes, who has got well again, we shall be able to get them round. I am very glad to hear that the "Larker" is going on so well. It would have been a curb if it had not been taken in time. . . .

Everything here remains exactly the same as when I last wrote, and no idea as yet got about of when we are to move. I have not as yet been able to make out my Tournay trip, and have now put it off till after Wednesday next, as on that day the Duke of Wellington reviews the whole of the heavy cavalry near Ninove, about twelve miles from this, and I mean to go and see them, as it will be a very fine sight. To-morrow he reviews the Brunswick contingent at Brussels, but we are to have a practice march, and therefore I cannot go to that show.

Old Boney has certainly not left Paris as yet, and some think that he is afraid of leaving it; but I suppose he is waiting for the grand farce of the Champ de Mai, which he will influence by his presence and that of his Guards. It is perfectly certain that party is running very high in France, and if the States-General were left to themselves they might choose to unemperor the gentleman, which would not by any means suit his purpose. It is also worthy of remark that he is now trying exactly the same means to raise the spirit of the people that he did previous to the last invasion of his empire. The attempt failed then, and we have every reason to believe that it will not be attended this time with any better success.

I am going on with the book of drawing, but with very limited improvement; however, it helps to pass away an idle hour, and besides, it always brings you to mind—not that it is necessary for anything to do that. I made a sketch of the

Parade to-day, and if I succeed in getting it up like the place, I will send you one on a smaller scale.

I am obliged to finish this, my dear love, to-night, for we are to be ready formed at Enghien to-morrow morning at six, and as it is about a mile from this, we must get up betimes. So good-night, my dearest Catharine, and believe me, ever your affectionate SALTOUN.

XXXIV.

Hove, 23d May 1815.

IN the first place, my dear love, I hope you were not disappointed in your expectation of getting a letter from me at the time you expected, and before this you have received my letter by William's servant, as I have heard from Ostend of his having sailed. In that letter you will receive £20 of Hughes (his back pay) to be sent to his wife, which, taking into due consideration his partiality for gin, is not very much against him.

I should like much to be of your party to the Caledonian benefit. It will be a fine thing to see the best actors in Europe, I may say, perform together; but I can only now hope that you may be well amused with it, and I am certain I shall derive as much pleasure from your being amused as I should from seeing it myself, you not being of the party.

My sights at present are of a different description, and I had a very fine one to-day near Ninove, where Lord Uxbridge reviewed thirteen squadrons of heavy cavalry. They were in very fine order, and worth the ride—about fifteen miles out and in. On Monday next the whole of the cavalry, light and heavy, are to be seen by the Duke and Blucher, somewhere near Grammont. I shall certainly go, unless anything turns up to prevent it, which is not likely at present, as nothing yet looks like an immediate move. However, we are all ready, and so situated that six hours would put the whole machine in motion.

In spite of your doubts about Ney, the thing is perfectly certain that he is in surveillance, and dispossessed, for the present at least, of his command; and it is also certain that he was not in the plot, and that he did his best to prevent his army from going over to Napoleon, but finding he could not prevent them from so doing, went over with them, and in consequence Boney has some doubts of his fidelity, and very properly does not employ him. As to Murat, the story of the day is that he is in Paris, and it is believed, but not by me. That he may be on his way there is very likely, for he has lost another general action of three days' fighting, at which I am not surprised, having myself seen the Neapolitan troops, six of whom are not worth one Frenchman, and therefore, by our mode of calculating, not worth half of one of England's sons.

The Bourbon cause is certainly very popular in great part of France, but they are so much under the thumb of the army that they cannot speak out. The fact is this, that they do not care a straw whom they have, so that they have peace and no conscription. They are perfectly tired of war, and they know the Bourbon will give them peace; but they are, if I may use the term, so *abimé*, that they will not turn out and fight for what they and all Europe (military men excepted) wish for. . . .

You cannot expect to hear so often now from Mrs. Cunninghame,[1] because if they go to any of the Mediterranean islands, their letters, in the present state of France, must either come across Spain to Corunna—a very long operation, according to their mode of carrying the post—or they must be sent to Gibraltar, and come home in the packet. I long to hear what sort of a turn-out you had at Lady Fraser's. Her son in the Seventh is here aide-de-camp to Lord Uxbridge. She herself is a very agreeable woman, and the old gentleman very well, if you will listen to his stories, but they are confounded long ones.[2]

To-day we have another grand cricket-match,—all those who are members of the Marylebone Club to play against the rest of the Guards. I am not much of a cricketer, and do not play, but for want of something to do have taken much lately to quoits, at which we have some famous hands. It is rather hot work, and therefore very destructive to a certain beverage called white beer.

No house, nor any chance of one! you will have plenty of bother before you get one. It is the most provoking thing in the world that, in London, where they have so many, it should be so difficult to suit one's self. I have not sent you, my dear Kate, much news in this letter; but when we are in this inactive state we can have no news. However, the sooner we get on the move the sooner I shall get home again.

I am sure you will like "Guy Mannering;" it is very well written.

I shall write again, my dear love, on Sunday, and believe me, dear Catharine, your affectionate   SALTOUN.

[1] Lady Saltoun's sister.   [2] Grandparents of the present Sir William Fraser, Bart.

XXXV.

Hove, 28th May 1815.

My dear Catharine,—I yesterday received yours of the 22d, with the papers to that date, and the whole history of the horse, and from the difference of these two professional men, F—— and D——, in their opinions, it is not very easy to decide what is best to be done. I never was over fond of making an imaginary evil a real one, and therefore see no good reason for voting a horse a lame one which is not so. The fact is just this, if you now treat the horse as if he had curbs you must lay him up for a month at least, and when he gets the curbs he will only have to be laid up for a month then. I should therefore work the horse as long as he remains sound, at the same time using this *terrifying stuff*, which I conceive to be nothing more or less than lemon's essence, which creates what is technically termed a sweat, that is, produces a slight blister on the part affected, without taking the hair off, and will keep the curbs back for a long time, and may perhaps take them off altogether. Hughes, who is the best farrier I ever saw, says, the horse in his opinion will certainly have curbs, but not for these six months at least. They may be kept back for a long time, and advises working the horse till he does get lame.

Since I wrote we have been and are to be for a day or two very gay. The Duke of Wellington gave a grand ball and supper last Friday at Brussels, to which, as I received a special invite, I thought it my duty to proceed. By far the greater part of the ladies were English, the Richmonds, Alvanley, but not Warrender, Lady Hawarden, Sidney Smith and daughters, Lady John Campbell, etc. etc. The supper was very good, and the whole thing went off remarkably well.

To-morrow we are to have the whole of the Cavalry and Horse Artillery reviewed near Grammont by the Duke and Blucher, about 5000 men; it will be a very fine sight. On Tuesday races and a *fête* given by the Hussars at the same place; and on Wednesday the Guards play the rest of the Army at cricket at Enghien. Of course a cold collation must be produced upon the occasion. I am no hand at cricket, and therefore do not play, but I attend at these places, and make very severe play at the cold beef and champagne about two o'clock.

We are all anxiously expecting Tuesday's news from Paris, as that will bring us the account of what took place last Friday at the Champ de Mai,—not that I expect anything particular will have occurred, for old Boney with his troops will be able to overawe the mob; but I should not be surprised if he went through the farce of resigning his Emperorship, of course being re-elected; but it won't do, for he is so well known that the people who are now against him—and there is certainly a very strong party against him in France—are not to be duped by any of these manœuvres. They may be kept in awe by the presence of his troops, who are certainly well-affected towards him, but as soon as he is obliged to concentrate his army, the Bourbon party will rise in all the places from which he is compelled to withdraw his troops in order to oppose our army; indeed we have reports, which are believed, that very serious disturbances have already broken out in La Vendée, and other places.

I do not see any immediate signs of a move, but I do not think anything will be settled in France till we do move, and time is getting on, and, with the old gentleman, the troops are also getting nearer the different points of the alignment, and I make no doubt, as soon as everything is ready, we shall lose no time in entering the French territory. As soon as any proclamation to the French people comes out, or any order about the strict observation of discipline makes its appearance, I shall take it for a sign that we are likely soon to start. The French have been beforehand with us, and have been forging a proclamation of the Duke of Wellington in the *Moniteur*, in hopes of raising the spirit of the people; but the fact is, that the Duke has not as yet issued anything of the kind, and will not, I should think, until the army are all ready to enter the French territory; and when he does, it will be a very different one from the proclamation given in the French papers. . . .

I hope you were much amused with the operation of laying the Southwark Bridge, although from what I know of you I am apt to suspect that you would require something very *recherché* to make up for being in the Strand at half-past ten. I should be apt to consider it much too early an hour myself were I in London. I wish, my dear love, I was there, for I begin to be deadly tired of this cantonment, although it is probably a much better one than any I shall have after we march; but they say we soldiers always like a change of quarters, and the sameness of a country village is very tiresome, especially when one knows that we must move before we can get back to where I wish to be. We have been six weeks now in this place, and I really believe if we were once on the move that ten more would see me in London. My thoughts are there pretty constantly, and when the time does come, I shall not let the grass grow under my feet in the journey. In the meantime, my dearest love, believe me, your affectionate

SALTOUN.

XXXVI.

Hove, 31st May 1815.

I HAVE just received, my dearest Kate, yours of the 25th, and, as far as post-days go, am at this moment (and that is some comfort at this distance) situated exactly as you were when you wrote yours, having just returned from a grand review by our Royal Commander, the Prince of Orange, at a place about fifteen miles from this, and as to-morrow is our post-day, and that early, I like to write before I go to bed.

Our performance was perhaps not more lively than yours; however it was very good, and those spectators who were good judges have complimented us most highly, as well as the Prince, who was pleased to say that, although he had been many years with the British army, he never before had seen so perfect a body of men. We are very good, as good as we could wish or expect. This brings me to your having heard that the Duke was not well satisfied with his infantry.

He never had so good before, for the Hanoverians are much better than the Portuguese, and John Bull has not, I should think, altered much in a year, or I may almost say half-a-year; for you know as well as myself, that I was not much above that time in England. The fact is, that the Duke was displeased at the number of staff appointments from the Horse Guards, as he thought that patronage lay with him, and this displeasure has been shifted upon us poor foot-wabblers, who have made him a Duke in three kingdoms, and are good enough to make him an Emperor; but as making him that would clash with our ideas of *limited* Monarchy and freedom of election, he stands but a bad chance of being made one. Never believe any humbugging stories of that sort until we are well beaten and afraid to meet our enemy, which, beaten or not beaten, will never be the case as long as the present race of England's sons exists. These stories are always set about either for some political purpose or by that species of animal —for man he does not deserve the name of—who, having no *esprit* himself, takes it for granted that nobody else has. You, left to your own judgment, don't respect this character; and I am sure I need not tell you what I think of him.

You want to know whether I have any good reason for expecting to be in England before September. It stands thus: our game must very soon be made up, and then it must be played off, and then we shall either dethrone him in two months, or make peace with him as ruler in France; but my idea of the matter is that the ball is at our foot, and we have only got to kick it through.

I have been running on about military subjects, and have thought you were a soldier, forgetting, my dear love, that agreeable nonsense is the only thing that a gentleman should write, but I have the unfortunate knack of not always being able to get at it. In my last I told you about reviews, races, and cricket that were to take place, but, however, His Royal Highness, as he is now called, of Orange and Nassau or Belgium, put a stop to our part of it, by ordering us to be at Le Grand Bruyere, about fifteen miles from this, which place we left, as I told you at the beginning, about twelve to-day, and are just returned,—a very hard day on the men as they were fourteen hours under arms. The review on Monday, however, I saw, and it was the finest sight I ever witnessed. There were 6400 British sabres, and the horses in such beautiful condition, that it was the finest sight possible, and I have no doubt there were plenty of spies to give a due report of them to Napoleon. The races took place, and were, I understand, very good, but the cricket was perforce put off, and the weather has been so wet, that no match could have taken place; it is therefore put off *sine die*, but they will probably play it at the end of the week.

I shall now, my dearest love, wish you good night . . . and believe me, your affectionate   SALTOUN.

XXXVII.

Hove, 4th June 1815.

MY DEAREST CATHARINE,—I yesterday received both your letters of the 27th and 29th, and I fully agree with you, my dear love, that the quick communication by letter is the greatest comfort I can have; indeed, it is even as quick as between London and Philorth; but when we begin to move it will cease to be quite so expeditious, both on account of the distance, and also the post-days of the army, perhaps, confined to once a week instead of twice; but I hope not as yet. However, we have no reason to expect an immediate move, although time is drawing on. Some preparatory arrangements are making, such as putting the men's great-coats into store, as from their weight they encumber the men in long marches; ours went in yesterday. Also the order has come out for serving out tents to the army, but the day on which they are to be delivered is not yet named.

Our news from Italy is excellent, and goes so far as to state that Murat is taken prisoner. This last comes from the Duke of Wellington, who believes it. One thing however is certain, that his army is entirely destroyed, and that is of more consequence to the Allies than anything that may happen to him personally. Boney, *on dit*, has put off the Champs de Mai, as he called it, *sine die*, and everything looks like his being in a scrape. He has been obliged to weaken his army in our front, in order to quell insurrections in the south, and we are led to believe that the north will rise as soon as our army passes the frontier. People begin to speculate about the day we are to march; some say the 10th, others the 14th, but the only thing certain is, that nobody except the Duke of Wellington knows anything about the matter, and he is a very close gentleman on these subjects, and seldom gives much notice. . . .

I wrote you a long letter the last post-day about the "Larker." The reason I did not send the other horse home is that I cannot do without two riding horses, as what with marches, etc., one has enough to do, and I want the other to ride about the country; or in case anything should happen to the little horse, I want the other, as I must perforce be mounted. The big horse is getting into very good condition, for he wanted grass, and the clover in this country is the finest I ever saw, and makes all the horses as fat as pigs. He is a very handsome horse, now that he is filled out, and a good match for the curricle horses; and it is correct, you know, that the horses behind the curricle should match those in it.

I have no more news, except that Sir Charles Stewart, who is now ambassador at this Court, gave yesterday a grand ball at Brussels, preparatory to leaving that place for the Hague, to which place the King of Holland, as he is now styled, goes in the course of the week, which also looks like our going the other way; for if we move by our left—which is the most likely line of operations, in order that we may not be hampered by the fortresses—we shall leave Brussels open on this side, and of course liable to any incursion which the garrisons of Lisle or Dunkirk may chance to make on it—and it would not do for the King to be taken by one of these parties—besides being a considerable inducement to them to make the attempt; not but what we shall have some troops on this side, but their number will be small, as we shall, I suspect, take as many men with us as we possibly can. Our force of British and Hanoverians is estimated at 61,000 men, exclusive of the Dutch and Brunswick contingent, who are also under the Duke of Wellington. . . .

I have been all day employed picking out light infantry men from the battalion companies, as some of my men are getting worn out and too old for our work, which at times requires a considerable deal more exertion than is expected from those in the battalion.[1] . . .

I was obliged to leave off, having some friends to dine, amongst whom was Hepburn, and dinner being ready; and I must, my dear love, finish this to-night, as we are to be out at six for a brigade practice; and as I have an odd fancy of never putting off anything that I ought to do, I may have some excuse in doing what I wish to do, and if I do not finish your letter to-night, perhaps we may not come back time enough for the post, and then, dear Kate, I should be in the worst rage a man can be in—one with myself. So you can't abuse me for writing at night with so good a reason as I have above given, for I should not have slept if I had not done it, and having so done, hope not only to sleep but also to dream of you, my dearest love, which, sleeping or waking, is the greatest pleasure of your affectionate SALTOUN.

XXXVIII.

Hove, 11th June 1815.

THIS morning, my dear Catharine, I received yours of the 5th, enclosing the Sunday paper; and you judged quite right with respect to Mr. Hutchinson's parcel, for I have not as yet heard of his being in the country. He is, I believe, to be aide-de-camp to Sir Lowry Cole, who is expected here to command a division. Pat. Hutchinson of our regiment, his brother, is very ill, and has been obliged to go to Brussels to take the hot-baths there.

Napoleon has at last made a start, and arrived yesterday at Maubeuge, which

[1] He had command of the light companies of the 1st Brigade of Guards.

you will see by the map is on the French frontier, opposite to Mons, and he is concentrating his force near that place. Our army at present occupies Mons on the left, extending from thence to Ath, Lessines, and Grammont, on the right, for the front line, and the second line is Braine, Soignies, Enghien, and Ninove, with troops also in Hal and Brussels. The right of the Prussians comes to Nivelles, and they are on the line of the Sambre from Charleroi to Namur. Our line, you will see by the map, is very extended, and, of course, if Boney collects any great force at Maubeuge, we must of necessity come nearer together. I have not the least idea that he can be mad enough to attack; but, of course, if we were not to take the necessary steps to prevent him, he might have an opportunity of gaining some advantage over us. I do not expect that *we* shall have to move, as we are very near our proper part of the line, but some of the other troops that are distant will, of course, be more concentrated if he, Boney, assembles any large force. They say he has about 70,000, and that the army of Metz is on its march to join him, about 30,000 strong. We are about 60,000, and the Prussians about 130,000; at the same time I do not think we shall attack him till the whole of the Allies come up, and we shall then invade with about 500,000 men.

We are going on in the same way with cricket matches, races, and so forth. The Duchess of Richmond and ladies are over on a visit to Maitland, and I have been accordingly introduced to her, and she has invited me to a ball, which she gives on Thursday next at Brussels; but I have not by any means made up my mind to go, and it will depend very much how I feel inclined for an eighteen mile ride when the day comes off.

You wish to know what the ladies at Brussels will do when we begin to act. It will depend very much upon what line we move on; and if we go by the left, most of them will, I believe, go to Spa or Antwerp, and so into Holland; but as long as we remain in our present position they are perfectly safe, as they would have time to get away even were we to retire, which is an event that I do not think likely to take place, except we go back a little for the purpose of getting a better position, but, at all events, I do not think we should give up Brussels without an action.

June 12th.—I was obliged to leave off writing in order to go to church with the battalion, which goes to Enghien for that purpose, where the rest of the troops are formed in square in the Duke D'Aremberg's park, to hear, in general, a bad sermon from a Mr. S——, who is staff-parson to our Division. I was in hopes to have picked up some news there, but yesterday, for a wonder, had not even a shave, as we call a report, and the only thing was they had a little betting about the cricket match to be played to-day between the Duke of Richmond and the ten best players, against Maitland and the twenty next best. I am included in the latter number, and we are to begin this morning at eleven o'clock.

I see by the "Morning Post," which is taken by Clements, that Mrs. B—— has been giving more grand balls, etc., and that the lovely Miss B—— danced with Lord P——, and I think that, and two or three bad puns, is the only thing in the paper. . . .

I am glad the "Larker" still remains sound. I should not be much surprised if the curb goes away altogether; however, Hughes says that he certainly will have curbs some time or another, but that is of no consequence, as they are easily cured. Both my horses here are doing very well, and getting quite fat,—indeed, everything gets fat in this country, and I do not think I have got any thinner myself; but I do not know how we shall get on when we march, for it always is the case that we have some scrambling, and the greater the number, of course the greater the scramble, and all put together we shall have certainly not less than 200,000 horses. I can fancy an English farmer seeing them grazing in his finest wheat fields and paying nothing,—what a rage he would be in. I have often thought a little war would do our farmers a great deal of good.

I have written this in bed this morning, for it is now time to get up to go to parade, from whence this must go to Enghien to the post-office. So God bless you, my dear love, and believe me ever your affectionate

SALTOUN.

XXXIX.

Hove, 14th June 1815.

I YESTERDAY, my dear love, received yours of the 8th, together with the newspapers, but, as yet, have heard nothing of Mr. Hutchinson's despatches; not that that in the least surprises me, for I am used to that sort of thing, and know that when a man first lands in a country he has to fit himself out for service before he thinks about anything else, and when he begins to think about parcels he is some time before he finds out where the owners are, and still longer before he can send them, or at least till he thinks he can send them with safety; but I make no doubt he will find his way to Brussels, and from that place he will find his way to dine with me, according to his practice in the Peninsula.

Our Royal Chief, whom you inquired about, is the very man who was to have married our Princess. The father is now King of the Netherlands, which makes his son a R.H., whereas before he was only Serene Highness.

In my last I wrote you a long account of Boney's arrival, and of our positions and so forth; but the truth is, that, as yet, Napoleon has not left Paris, and our mistake arose from the imperial salute having been fired at Maubeuge, in consequence of some person having passed through that place, invested with full powers to inspect that and the other fortresses.

Our news from France is good, in as far as party runs very high at Paris, and the risings in La Vendée and other parts of the south begin to take a more organised and respectable appearance. As yet we have no immediate idea of a move, indeed some preparatory things are necessary, such as the means of transport for the spare ammunition, and the tents, which have not as yet arrived here, and, excepting in a case of necessity, we should not certainly move before we get the necessary means for transporting these things with us.

And so, my dear Kate, you thought I was vexed at your story about our infantry: We are by far too well aware of our own strength to do anything but laugh at what the newsmongers in England choose to say of us; and if I wrote rather strongly it was only to give you the same idea of our perfection that I have. I can assure you I do not think small beer of them, and the Duke of Wellington and old Boney, you may depend upon it, are very much of the same opinion; not that the British are all together, as probably they suppose in England, but they are divided among the separate divisions in the proportion, in some divisions, of one Brigade of British to two of Hanoverians, and in other divisions two Brigades of British to one of Hanoverians, the same as we were chequered with the Portuguese in Spain. In our mode of speech we call it making very fair grog, holding ourselves, with regard to them, as brandy is to water, but by the mixture making that water a very palatable concern. Our division is as yet an exception to this rule, as we have no Hanoverians with us, and are composed of Guards only, with

Right Honbl.

Lady Saltoun

10. Lower Grosvenor Street.
Saltoun   London

June 19. Field of Battle near Waterloo

My dear dearest Katharine

I have only just time to tell you that I have lived through two of the sharpest actions ever fought by man we have defeated the French at all points & they are in full retreat our loss has been prodigious as the brunt of the Business fell upon the Guards & many of my best & worst friends are gone but these things must be — my favorite little horse was shot under me at present I have only one but I must get another here I have no time to write more at length as if I do I fear I shall be too late for the staff officer who is to take this so god bless you my dear love
& believe me ever yours
Affectionate
Saltoun

two Brigades of Artillery. You like to know all about the Army, but I suspect this is not quite so plain as the other.

Our grand cricket-match did not take place, for the day turned out to be a very rainy one, so it stands over till next Saturday, when the Duke of Richmond is to come over for the purpose. I do not feel the least inclination to go to her Grace's ball to-morrow, and shall therefore not do so.

I hope you have bought Blakemore's mare, but if you have not, pray do so. Your having a fancy for her is quite sufficient reason for me, and I hope to see you as much yourself on horseback as you used to be, some of these days; but time draws on, and we have as yet done nothing, and it will take us some time after we start before we can finish the job; however, I have not as yet given up September, but I begin to suspect that August will be far gone before we finish the business. I have no scandal or news to tell you, and must therefore, my dear, dear love, wish you good night, and believe me, my dearest Catharine, your affectionate   SALTOUN.

XL.

June 19th [1815],
Field of Battle, near Water Lude.

MY DEAR DEAREST CATHARINE,—I have only just time to tell you that I have lived through two of the sharpest actions ever fought by men. We have defeated the French at all points, and they are in full retreat. Our loss has been prodigious, as the brunt of the business fell upon the Guards, and many of my best and oldest friends are gone, but these things must tarry,—my favourite little horse was shot under me, and at present I have only one, but I must get another here. I have no time to write more at length, as, if I do, I fear I shall be too late for the Staff-officer who is to take this. So God bless you, my dear love, and believe me, ever your affectionate   SALTOUN.

XLI.

Camp, near Gourmignies, 22d June 1815.

MY DEAR CATHARINE,—I wrote you a few lines from the field of battle on the 19th, but I have just heard that letters are to go immediately to England. I take this opportunity of telling you what has taken place since I wrote last from Hove on the 15th.

A few hours after my letter was gone, we got the alarm that Boneparte had attacked the Prussians, and we were ordered to march at a moment's notice, and on the morning of the 16th, at 3, we marched from Hove, through Braine and Nivelles, to a place called Quatre-bras, which place we reached about 5 in the afternoon, and were immediately very hotly engaged in the Bois de Bossu, and at nightfall we had succeeded in taking the wood from the enemy, but not without very great loss. My old friends Grose and Miller fell in the affair, with many others, and about five hundred men of the Regiment. During this time Boney had attacked the Prussians at Fleurus, and had gained some advantages, so as to oblige them to retreat. Our position of Quatre-bras being in consequence exposed on the left, we were obliged to fall back, and accordingly, on the 17th, retired, and took post in position at Water Leud.

On the 18th Napoleon attacked us with the whole of his army. The action was extremely severe, and our loss much greater than in any of the battles in the Peninsula. . . . The infantry formed squares, and about five o'clock had completely repulsed and destroyed the French cavalry by their steadiness in square, and the excellence of their fire. About half-past six Napoleon made his last desperate attack, at the head of his Old Imperial Guards, upon our brigade. It was a thing I always wished for, and the result was what I have often said it would be; to do them justice they came on like men, but our boys went at them like Britons, and drove them off the field in less than ten minutes.

From that moment the day was our own, and the French were completely routed, and fled, leaving their artillery, stores, baggage, and an immense number of prisoners. We estimate the French army before the action at about 120,000 men, and that they lost full 50,000. The Prussians are in hot pursuit, and have taken a great many prisoners.

On the 19th we marched to Nivelles, 20th, to a village near Binche, yesterday to Bavay, and to-day we are bivouacked here. Our baggage is a long way in the rear, and I do not know when I shall get a clean shirt. I have got my toothbrush, so I am not quite a beast.

I have this moment, my dear love, got your letter of the 15th. You little thought how near we were coming to the work. I am sure you will be sorry for poor Stables; he was killed on the 18th. In short, we have lost in the First Regiment twelve officers killed and twenty-two wounded. I was in great luck again, as I had two horses killed under me, and a ball through my cap, but the head remains as good as ever. I have been very much applauded, and so forth, and been reported for good conduct, and every one says that I am sure of a medal. I am so glad that England had the first of it, I was always certain of the event, if he and the Duke ever met, and now we consider the whole thing as over. He may perhaps make another struggle at Laon, or on the Marne, but he must be defeated in the end, and I should not be surprised any day to hear of his being deposed.

You must not now, my dear love, be in the fidgets because you do not hear every post, for situated as we are, we do not know when to write; and indeed I could not have written to-day had I not been in good luck enough to borrow a sheet of paper from my sergeant; but, depend upon it, I will write by every opportunity, and as I do not expect any more fighting, you may make yourself easy on that head.

I must now, my dear Kate, send this to the Adjutant-General, for fear of being too late; and believe me, my dear love, that I fully expect to see you before August, and until I do, that I am your most affectionate   SALTOUN.

XLII.

Camp near Serain, 25th June 1815.

I WROTE you last, my dearest Catharine, from Gourmignies, giving you an account of what had taken place up to that date. We halted there the next day, and yesterday we marched to a place called Boussiers short of Cateau. To-day we marched through Cateau to this place. The weather is most horrible, and resembles more a winter than a summer campaign; for it has rained almost every day since the action, and the roads—for as yet we have been marching by the cross roads, and not the chaussées, to avoid the strong places,—are up to the men's knees in mud; but as we get nearer Paris I hope it will be better.

The news of the day is very good,—Napoleon retired from Laon to Soissons, and the Prussians occupied Laon this morning. They say also, and we have reason to believe it, that the two Chambers at Paris have deposed Napoleon, and have elected a Provisional Government, with Carnot and Fouché at the head, to manage the nation during the minority of the King of Rome. This will of course be rejected, and we shall advance and put Louis on the throne, I really think, without firing another shot. It is just a week since the action, which all hands, both French and others, agree as to having been the most severe and bloody that ever was fought, and since that day we have advanced about seventy miles, and we are now within one hundred and twenty of Paris. The old King came up to us yesterday, and to-day remains at Cateau.

I am sorry to say that poor Hughes is in a bad way. I have been obliged to leave him in the village where we halted last night, for from violent rheumatics, he was unable to sit on his horse; and the number of our wounded is so great, added to the confusion that took place in the rear, owing to the false alarm the day of the Battle, that our carts for carrying sick men have never come up, so I do not know whether I shall ever see him again, indeed I much fear I shall not; this, added to the very disagreeable task, which I have just got through, of writing to the families of all our poor officers who fell an account of their death, which as Commanding Officer I am obliged to do, the loss in the action having given me the temporary command of the Second Battalion, has made me very melancholy; so I will not write to you any more at present, for fear of making you so likewise, but finish this as soon as I can get an opportunity of sending it.

27th.—I am now, my dear love, quite out of the blue devils; for yesterday, on the march from Serain to Coulaincourt, we were halted at Vermand, and our brigade sent to the right to attack Peronne, which we stormed yesterday evening with very little loss. I have heard an old saying that everything is made for some purpose; but I do not suspect you had the least idea, when you made my little purse, that it would ever be put to the use that it was. Yesterday, during the storm of Peronne, a grape-shot hit me full in the thigh. Fortunately I had the little purse in that pocket, full of small gold pieces called ducats, which so stopped the ball, that, although it knocked me down, it lodged in the purse, and has given me a slight bruise, not half so bad as a blow from a stick. Had it not been for the purse it would have been very near a finish. So you see, my dear Kate, I owe you something. The purse is cut right open by the ball, but I shall not have it mended till it comes into your hands. What is rather odd, the little heart I had in it is the only thing not hurt, for all the gold pieces are bent and twisted about properly. I write this, first, because I promised to write exactly what happened; and next, because they are so fond of killing people in reports, especially if they have been hit in the slightest manner possible.

To-day we marched at seven o'clock, and are just come into this place. It is about two miles nearer Paris than Nesle, and about the same distance on the left of Roye. It is famous for a skirmish which took place here the day before the battle of Cressy, in Edward the Third's reign, and we are now about the same distance from Paris that Portsmouth is from London.

I have this moment received yours of the 19th, and I find you at that time knew nothing about the matter. I like your quizzing about our soldiers. We have tolerable proof now of what they are worth, and the oldest French soldiers say they never saw such a battle as the one at Water Leud. I think I told you that our Reg^t and Napoleon's Guards came in contact, and I can assure you we handled them most handsomely, and the old Life Guards completely upset Napoleon's Cuirassiers of the Guard Imperial.

The headquarters are to-day at Nesle, where a deputation has arrived from Paris to wait upon the Duke. I hope he will receive no terms till he dictates them from the Tuileries, and I rather think he will be of my way of thinking in that particular.

I must send this forthwith to headquarters to wait an opportunity of its getting to England, as we now move so rapidly that we have no notice. The baggage-horses begin to feel it, especially from want of shoeing. I have lost two—one that was stolen in the row and confusion of the false alarm, and the other died yesterday; that, added to the two that were shot, has decreased my stud much. I have, however, bought two, so I can get on, and that is all, for the large horse has just fallen lame and got a sore back, but Paris is near, and the sooner we get there the sooner I get to England. So adieu, my dear love, and believe me, your affectionate   SALTOUN.

XLIII.

Camp at Choissi, 29th June 1815.

I YESTERDAY, my dear Catharine, received yours of the 22d, and to-day the letter of the 12th, which, as it must have arrived in the country just at the time we were at work, had been delayed till now.

We are going on as well as it is possible to do. To-day we are encamped here, having marched from Couchy on the chaussée leading by the Pont St. Maxence to Paris. This is one league short of St. Martin, and about thirty-seven miles from Paris, which place we expect to reach on Sunday, if we do not halt, and we have no idea of halting at present. The Pont St. Maxence was destroyed in the last campaign, and has not as yet been repaired; but I hope our pontoons, or some other boats, will be collected, so as to ensure our passage without loss of time.

The Prussians had an affair two days ago with Soult at Compiègne, in which Soult was beat, and suffered considerably; they say to-day that Boneparte has left Paris and gone to Havre, with an intention of embarking for America, it is the best thing he can do now, for if he is taken, I do not know what the Allies will do with him, but I should think they would hang him.

We have to-day fallen into the line of a column of Prussians, who have been plundering at such a rate, that all the villages are entirely deserted, and I may almost say destroyed. To be sure they are only paying off old scores, but it is rather a bore for us, as we have great difficulty in purchasing any articles of provision, for the people are afraid of returning to their houses, as they do not know that they will be protected by us; however, it can't last long, and at Paris we shall be able to get anything that we want.

I find that some officers and men are immediately to be sent to us from England, and the sooner they arrive after we get to Paris the better, as I shall be superseded by some of them in command of the battalion, as they are all my seniors, and then as soon as things are a little settled I shall apply for leave to go home, which I could not do if I remained in command of this battalion, from the very small number of officers that are left to do duty. The weather has become very fine and hot, but the dust is terrible; however, anything is better than rain for our sort of life, and I now hope we shall have a continuance of fine weather.

I suppose people in England are half mad,—we hear of illuminations, etc. etc.; to be sure the Victory is the greatest that ever was gained, not only by us, but by any people, but it was at the same time very dearly bought, the Gazette does not contain one-fifth of the officers who have suffered in this business. I send you that of our Reg^t, as you may hear them asked for.

Killed.	Wounded.	
Lieut.-Colonel Stables.	Colonel Askew.	Ensign Batty.
„ F. D'Oyly.	„ Stuart.	„ Barton.
„ Thomas.	Lieut.-Colonel Townshend.	„ Bruce.
„ Miller.	„ Cooke.	„ Fludyer.
„ Milnes.	„ H. D'Oyly.	„ Lascelles.
Captain Grose.	„ Bradford.	„ Mure.
„ Chambers.	„ Hardinge.	„ Croft.
„ Cameron.	„ Lord F. Somerset.	
„ Brown.	Captain Adair.	
Ensign Pardoe.	„ Streatfield.	
„ Lord Hay.	„ Clements.	
„ Barrington.	„ Bridgeman.	
	„ Ellis.	
	„ Simpson.	
	„ Luttrell.	
	„ Burgess.	

We had 82 officers of the regiment in the field, of which 34 have been killed or wounded; so shot, you will perceive, did not fly very thin that morning. I should have mentioned Stables in my first letter, but I did not know what had been his fate. I saw him fall, and the next morning when I wrote, I did not know what sort of a wound he had received, and I did not like sending a false report of his death, although, from the way he fell, I was much afraid of him.

I have nothing more to say at present, and will write you again in a day or two, and believe me, my dear love, your affectionate SALTOUN.

XLIV.

Bourjet, 2d July 1815.

I WROTE you last, my dear Catharine, from Choissi on the 29th, on the 30th we marched to La Chapelle, about two miles beyond Senlis; and yesterday we came to this place, which is about two miles beyond Gonesse, on the left of St. Denis, and nearly parallel with it; and we have taken position on this ground, our right resting on the Seine, opposed to St. Denis, where the French are strong, our centre in this town, which is immediately opposite to Mont Martre, and our left resting on the canal de l'Ourcq, to the left of the road that runs through this place to Paris, which is about four miles distant; and I rather think we shall remain in this position till the Russians and Austrians come up. The Prussian army, on our arrival yesterday, made a movement to the right, crossed the Seine at the bridge of St. Germain, and are to take post on that side of Paris, at Malmaison, St. Cloud, and Versailles.

Since we came, perpetual flags of truce have been passing between the town and the Duke, but nothing has as yet been settled, and in the meantime each party is making himself as strong as possible. Nobody knows anything about Boneparte; some say he is in Paris, but no person knows for certain. Davoust commands the army on Mont Martre, and many think that Boney is there *incog*.

We were yesterday on the advanced posts with the Prussians, supporting them, until Lord Hill's corps came up, when we took our front of the line; and they told us that they took the whole of Vandame's baggage, as well as Napoleon's. One of their officers of light cavalry fell in with his jewels, and had his pocket full of diamonds. I wish I had had the same luck, I would have put them to good account, besides the *éclat* of the thing. If I fall in with him again, I will try and buy some of them, but yesterday I was not very full of cash, as the baggage had not come up; he wanted to buy a horse, but mine had such a devil of a sore back that it would not go down, even with a Prussian. They have the greatest confidence in us. They say that the French used to tell them that we were good for nothing on land, of which, however, they had doubts; but they say they had not the least idea that our troops were so good as they are. All their troops formed and cheered us as we passed them, which we answered; and as the French posts were quite within hearing, the effect upon them could not have been very animating.

I every day expect to hear from you, but our march has been so rapid that the post-office line could not have been established, but shortly I hope we shall open a nearer line. If I can get a sketch of the position, which young Nixon is making for me in the next room, done in time, I will send it in this letter; if not, by the next. I have no more news, except that we are all well and in great spirits, in hopes that the job will soon be over; and believe me, my dear love, your affectionate   SALTOUN.

XLV.

Bourjet, 4th July 1815.

My dear Catharine,—I yesterday received yours of the 26th, and also the papers.

I am at this moment on the advanced posts, and we have just heard that we are to occupy Paris to-morrow, and the French army is to retire behind the Loire, and make as good terms with the King as they can. Our army is to encamp in the Bois de Boulogne.

As to the house in Great Cumberland Street, I most perfectly agree to everything you have done. As to the distance, it is nothing, as I always go on horseback, and I hope before long to take a look at it myself. I have no time to say any more, as the A. D. C. is waiting for this to take it to head-quarters; and believe me, my dear love, your affectionate   SALTOUN.

XLVI.

Villette, 6th July 1815.

I THIS morning, my dear Catharine, received yours of the 29th, and I did not intend to have written before to-morrow, as I was in hopes that we should have marched through Paris with laurels in our caps, as we deserve to do; but the Heads think otherwise, and we are therefore to go to-morrow to the Bois de Boulogne to encamp, and as we march at five, and letters must be in at eight, I must write now or not at all. It does not suit my taste sneaking round a capital in this manner. I almost regret that they did not defend the heights of Mont Martre: to be sure we should have lost 2 or 3 thousand men in taking them, but then we should have burned the town, and that would have been some satisfaction, for I hate these rascals almost as much as I love you, and that is more than they can be hated by any other. Poor Grose and myself were brothers in that hatred, and if the brave fellow were alive, he would have gone half mad to suppose that we came victorious to the gates of Paris, and did not show the natives that we were so. So much for national indignation! Our chief has most probably good reasons; for my part I would not give a straw to march through it when the Russians come up.

As to your getting what you call a detailed account of the action of Waterloo from the Duke, you will get no other than the one you have got already. It is rather unfortunate, and the army are sorry for it, that my name was not mentioned, and but for a mistake, which I will explain when we meet, I know that it would have been; but I have been so handsomely reported by the Prince of Orange, Generals Byng and Maitland, to the Dukes of Wellington and York, that I am perfectly satisfied, and some day I shall lead a division, perhaps a victorious army; so your moralising preamble must be postponed *sine die*, as it is the only point I think you will never gain with me. To tell the truth, I do not think you remember we always agreed that a dead lion was better than a living dog.

We came here yesterday. This is, if I may use the term, part of Paris, as much so as Connaught Place is of London, for it is the same distance from the Barriere as that is from Tyburn. Lord Castlereagh has arrived: I saw him as he passed by here, but I understand he has not gone into the town, but has gone to the Duke's head-quarters. Party is running very high in the town, but I think we shall have no more fighting.

I have no doubt myself that Napoleon is with the army, *incog.*, but his chance gets more and more desperate as the Allies come up, and he probably will start for America, for the army will never give him up to us; at least if they do, they will lose with me that little respect I still have for them.

Your story of ears and noses is quite morning post. They had something else to do about that time, but the Prussians treat them much the same as if their noses and ears had been cut off, and I suspect that the Russians are not far off, for the people have come in to-day from the country, saying that the pillage is still going on: they are perfectly thunderstruck at our men not doing the same, as their own troops plunder them, and how we prevent our men from doing it perfectly astonishes them.

As soon as things are quiet, and I am superseded in the command—which I shall be when the people from England arrive—I shall ask leave to go to England. I have as yet heard nothing of Hughes, but as soon as we are quiet I shall send after him; and I shall now, my dear love, wish you good-night, and believe me, your affectionate   SALTOUN.

XLVII.

Paris, 10th July 1815.

HERE we are, my dear Catharine, well established, and the old King as regularly crammed down their throats as anything could possibly be. He made his *entrée* yesterday at the head of the National Guards, and all the Eagles are upset, and the Fleur-de-Lys everywhere; not but what there is a very strong party against him, but I do not think they lean towards Boney, they are rather for a Republic.

I was at the opera last-night, and the people had Vive Henri Quatre played over and over again, and a great deal of holloaing and so forth; but I am told they did just the same when Napoleon came: if so, it all goes for nothing. They say that the army have sent deputies to make submission: if so, the game is over, for this time at least, and I shall apply for leave as soon as I possibly can.

At present we are encamped in the Bois de Boulogne, and I suppose we shall remain there. I am in a house half-way between the Bois and the Barriere de Roule. The distance is not above two miles, so it is nothing on horseback; not that there is much to see here since I saw it last, but one rides in to dinner, as the *traiteurs* here are rather superior to our soldier cooks. I only yesterday got her Ladyship's letter, but as she had put no date to it I could not tell if it was written on the same day as your last, which I received three days back, and answered from La Villette, in a great rage at not marching through Paris.

The people here, I mean the gentlemen, are inclined to be particularly civil to us; indeed they are much struck with the strict discipline we preserve, so totally different from Continental armies now-a-days, and which gives us such a decided advantage over them; and lucky for them it is so, for if our army were permitted to plunder and destroy as the Prussians and others are, they would first of all get drunk, and then they would burn down the town, or commit some horrible massacre or other.

I am going this morning to see the Louvre, and I shall afterwards ride out to Boulogne to see Lord Hill, and dine there, if he is at home. I never was a good hand at playing at soldiers, *surtout* when I wanted to get away; if not, I can do that well enough. But I now want much to cross the herring pond, and shall be with you as soon as I possibly can.

I have as yet heard nothing of poor Hughes. I mean to send a man back to the village to enquire about him, for it is rather out of the direct road. He was perfectly well in health when he was left, and therefore I am not afraid of him—at least the surgeon is not,—yet I think he ought to have turned up before now.

I have not a particle of news, and in hopes to see you before I write many more letters, believe me, my dearest love, your affectionate   SALTOUN.

XLVIII.

Paris, 12th July 1815.

MY DEAR CATHARINE,—I have not got a word of news or anything else to say, but the day being very hot, and therefore not worth slaving about seeing sights, I cannot employ it better than in writing to you.

I forget if I told you in my last that the Kings and Emperors were arrived. They are however come, and, what is worse, we have to mount guard over them, which, in our present reduced state of L^t.-Colonels, comes rather sharp; and what I am most afraid of is, that when our draft comes, they may, in consequence, take it into their gracious heads to refuse me leave, which will be rather a bore, as it will fix me here till the end of the chapter. Now, if that event takes place, and they refuse me leave, you shall, if you like, come here; for, as Mahomet observed (and he is very good authority), if the mountain would not come to him, he must go to the mountain. My only reason, next to seeing you, for wanting to go home, is that I wish to go to Scotland : now, if I can't go there, I see no reason why you should not see France. Should this be the case, I can manage to meet you at Calais, and William can escort you that far. I shall make the application as soon as our people come up, and write you the result, and if you approve of this plan, instructions how to proceed, and when to set out so as to meet me. I think all the fighting over, but if anything else should blow up before these grand continental matters are settled, you can only return. I do not think these things will be settled under three or four months, and if you were here I don't care if they take as many years to debate it, for the country is a very good one to live in.

A mail has come in up to the 4th instant, but as I have had no letters or papers I suppose that you were too late, or, what is now very likely, the bag was so full, Lord Castlereagh being here now, as well as the Duke, that they did not send them, should you have sent them to the office, as they have not arrived. You had better send your letters per post; but if you did not send them to Barnard, you need not, as yet, make any alteration.

They talk of some Generals having come from the French army with proposals of submission; but I do not know if anything has been done. However, I suppose they must shortly come to [terms.]

No one knows anything certain about Napoleon, and nobody seems to care anything about him. Paris is just the same as when I was here last, and the rascals are calling Vive le Roi now as lustily as they last week cried Vive L'Empereur. God bless you, my dear love, and believe me, your affectionate   SALTOUN.

P.S.—Your last letter that I have is dated the 29th June. Hughes came up yesterday, his rheumatism has left him, but he is very thin, as he got very little to eat on the road.

XLIX.

Paris, 15th July 1815.

MY DEAR CATHARINE,—You may see by the paper that I am not at home. The fact is that I am on guard over H.M. the Emperor of all the Russias, and as he gives nothing but long paper, I am obliged to manœuvre it as well as I possibly can.

We have just done dinner, six o'clock, about an hour before you are thinking of dressing for yours; it is very well this hour for His Majesty's household, who can go out and walk in the cool of the evening, but for us, who have to remain here, rather too early. However, I will do him the justice to say that the dinner was a very good one, and by a fortunate accident we had a clean table-cloth, for the waiter, a regular ruffian of a fellow, had put such a beastly thing on the table that it was even too much for us, who of late days have not been much used to luxury. However, I had the satisfaction to make the most unfortunate mistake in the world, just as he put some wine down, by breaking a bottle of it, which so sluiced the table-cloth, that we were perforce obliged to have another, which was clean. Some of the Emperor's household dined with us, and they were tolerably genteel fellows, and spoke very good French, and some little English, indeed most of the Russians are good linguists.

I received yesterday, my dearest girl, both your letters, one of the 6th, and the other of the 10th, but I still suspect that you wrote a letter either on the 3d or 4th, which has not as yet turned up; it will however, I make no doubt, come to hand some day or another. . . .

About Gazettes, etc., as if 500 others were not exactly in the same situation as I am, and as if I do not know that it has been the only outcry against the Duke of W. ever since he commanded an army, that he seldom or never mentioned people, excepting Generals and others high up in the army; and as to being returned wounded at Peronne, it's all fiddlesticks. I do not intend that my military reputation, if ever I get any, shall have so hollow a foundation. I see a parcel of fellows figuring about who have returned themselves severely wounded when they only had scratches and bruises, who are the perfect laughing-stock of their companions, and therefore not very far from being so of other people.

We expect our people up in a day or two; they were last night at Roye; to-day they will therefore be at St. Martin's, to-morrow at Senlis, then Bourjet, and from that here, which will bring them up on Tuesday or Wednesday at the farthest. I shall then immediately make my application, and if I find any difficulty in obtaining leave, shall apply for leave merely to bring you over, which I rather think will certainly not be refused. I shall sound the ground first, and then apply. I rather suspect you will have to come here, for General Vivian has gone to England for the same purpose, to bring his wife, and if any person could have got leave, I think he might. Besides, if they only give me a month, it will not be worth while, so you may, if you feel inclined, make your mind up to soldier a little. You may continue to send letters and papers after you receive this, as my leave will take some time going through, and should they come here after I am gone they will be very well taken care of, and sent to any place I may direct, or kept till I return, as the case may be.

No news of any kind, and nothing as yet known of what the remains of Boney's army mean to do. They have not as yet made submission, nor will they, I suspect, as long as they can get anything to plunder where they are. I hope the King will cut off a good many heads, but I am told he will not, and the consequence will be that he will be deposed in less than two years, and France a Republic.

My paper begins to run short, so I shall wish you, my dearest love, goodbye for the present. I shall write you again in a day or two, and also as soon as I know how my leave goes; and I am, my dear Catharine, your affectionate

SALTOUN.

L.

Paris, 22d July 1815.

THIS morning, my dear Catharine, I received yours of the 17th, and also the papers up to that date. I have put off writing from day to day in hopes of being able to say when I should set out for England. Our draft from Town joined three days back, and I immediately sent in my application for leave, but as yet I have not had any answer. I am told that General Barnes meant to have made the application yesterday, but that the Duke was in such a devil of an ill-humour about something or another, that he could not speak to him on any subject with any chance of success; I expect, however, an answer in a day or two, and shall then write you further. This place is horridly stupid, and I shall be most happy to leave it.

To-day we had a review of the Prussian Guards, 13,000 strong; the finest body of men I ever saw in my life, the only horrid thing is that the French have licked them like sacks. On Monday next, at ten o'clock, the Duke of Wellington's army is to be reviewed. We shall be about 65,000, and it will take up nearly the whole day marching past. We shall not be able to show such fine men as these Emperors and Kings have, but yesterday, as the Prussians, etc. were marching by, Lord Wellington said to Lady Kinnaird, 'On Monday I will show you some men that can lick those fellows.'

The remains of the French army, under Davoust, have not as yet made submission, they say they will acknowledge the King if he will retain them as an army; but the King says they shall be disbanded, and they are at issue on that point. I think probably the end of it will be that we shall send some troops against them and give them a good licking: that army will never have the King. It is a curious fact, that during his short reign before Boney came back, the soldiers, in telling off from the right, never mentioned the number eighteen, but said, 'dixsept, groscochon, dixneuf,' and so on; and whatever man it fell to to be 18, he was the butt for the day; that shows how little they cared for him, and he now ought to hang every twentieth man by lot, and then, such slaves are these rascals, that he would be very much respected, and thought a very good King.

This is the most rascally pen that ever was, and I have got no penknife by me, so I much fear you will not be able to read this letter; however, as I hope soon to follow it myself, it will be of less consequence. My next will probably tell you about my leave: till then adieu, and believe me, my dearest Catharine, your affectionate   SALTOUN.

LI.

Paris, 28th July 1815.

I HAVE this moment, my dear Catharine, received yours of the 25th instant, and two days back I got yours of the 20th, and as to your letter of the 4th, it was the one that came by Mr. Prince, but I did not receive it till after two other mails had arrived. I shall take this letter to the post, and forward the other, which is very likely one of mine which my servant has taken there by mistake, instead of the military post.

I have put off writing from day to day, in hopes of being able to say something about leave. Yesterday I was ordered to send in my reasons in writing, so I went this morning to Barnes, the Adjutant-General, and told him my reason was not one that could well be sent upon paper, but I would be much obliged to him to tell the Duke that I had been married a fortnight, and I wished to go home to bring you out here. I am to have my final answer to-morrow, and I shall then either write you how to proceed, or shall forthwith proceed to England, as the case may be.

We expect that the army will shortly move into Normandy, as we begin to be short of forage for the cavalry, but they say the First Division is to remain in Paris, or near it; however, if I get my leave, that will make no difference to us. Hughes, I told you in one of my letters, has turned up, and he is now quite well again, and the horses consequently begin to show the improvement. I have not a word of news, and as I am always anxious as long as anything that I particularly wish for remains undecided, I shall finish this; and in hopes of following it very shortly, believe me, my dear love, your affectionate   SALTOUN.

P.S.—I have not as yet got the papers, so the post is at present the most expeditious.

Two Letters from the Dowager-Lady Saltoun to Catharine Lady Saltoun, her Daughter-in-law.

LII.

March 13th, 1815.

My dear Lady Saltoun,—We all wish you and our dear Saltoun all happiness. I shall rejoice to embrace you both, and I hope you and he may enjoy many years of felicity, at least if the best that mortals can enjoy may be termed felicity. I do not like to allow a post to pass without writing to your Ladyship, and having not above two minutes and a half to write in, must be my excuse for this hurried scrawl. The girls join in love with your affectionate mother,
M. Saltoun.

LIII.

Philorth, 9th April [1815].

My dear Lady Saltoun,—I have just received Saltoun's most distressing letter. Alas! it seems my evil destiny never to be for any time free from some very heavy pressure,—some cause either of deep regret, or some object of constant anxiety. I have enjoyed more ease of mind for the last ten months than I had known for years, but the term is over; I have now only to join my prayers with yours that the Almighty may be gracious and protect him. For you do I feel most truly; it is a severe trial for you, and not the less so as—except in the loss of your kind father—you have not as yet felt the iron hand of affliction. God grant you never may, and that this trial may be happy in its issue and short in its duration: all will depend on the promptitude with which the combined powers set their immense force in active operations.

I am very much vexed that I have so long delayed being in town, but my letters from some who ought to know, and one from Saltoun two days since, satisfied me entirely as to any immediate orders for service. I am unhappy at not having seen him; do, my dear Catherine, tell me if he is quite well, and how you are yourself. You have no friends more anxious for you than the girls and I, and it will be a great comfort to us if by our society we can add to yours, particularly during Saltoun's absence.

If you should not feel disposed to write directly, make William write. I need not, I am sure, recommend him to your sisterly protection; you will, I know, be a real sister to him without any solicitation. I hope soon to see you; a very few days will make me fix my day for setting out; I wait some letters.

I began to write on half a sheet, which pray excuse; and with the united love of Margaret and Eleanor, believe me, your affectionate mother,

M. SALTOUN.

P.S.—It strikes [me] as just possible you may be going with Saltoun, if so, I double my entreaties that you will write to us very often.

LETTER from GENERAL JOHN FRASER to LORD SALTOUN.

LIV.

Kensington, 18th August 1819.

MY DEAR LORD SALTOUN,—Upon going to town yesterday I was informed that your brother officers were of opinion you ought to be appointed King's Aide-de-Camp in consequence of the late promotion, and that they regretted you were not in the way to make your own application; and having consulted with Colonel Christie, who is much about the public offices, he advised me to endeavour to see Lord Liverpool without delay. I therefore went to Fife House directly. Fortunately Lord Liverpool was at home, and saw me immediately, when, introducing myself as your only military relation in town, and referring to the delay which must attend waiting for a letter from Scotland, I stated to him, in the strongest terms I could, how much you had distinguished yourself upon many occasions, but more particularly in the battle of Waterloo; and that as M'Donnell, and others of your standing, had all been promoted to the rank of Colonel, how gratifying it would be to your feelings to see yourself now appointed Aide-de-Camp to his Majesty, in consideration of your share in the honour which the Grenadier Guards had acquired.

I referred also to your conduct in Parliament, as the ground on which I was more particularly authorised to address his Lordship; and I endeavoured to impress strongly that, as the rank of Colonel was your object, you would be

GENERAL SIR JOHN FRASER, G.C.H.
LIEUT. GOVERNOR OF CHESTER,
DIED 1843.

equally satisfied with the appointment of extra Aide-de-Camp as if you were put upon the establishment.

He listened to me with great attention—expressed himself very desirous to attend to your wishes—promised without delay to do what he could, but reminded me that it did not come exactly within his department; that is to say, was not in his gift.

At all events, I trust you will not disapprove of my going to Lord Liverpool under the existing circumstances. Possibly, upon receiving this letter, you may write both to Lord Liverpool and to the Duke of York; and if you should not be included in this promotion, surely your claims are so great that you ought certainly to have the first vacancy that may occur. You are now a Lieutenant-Colonel of six years' standing, and although there may be a considerable number above you, yet Barnard, Willingham, and others, are sufficient precedents for the promotion, when supported by such strong claims as yours.

Uncertain where you may be at present, I shall direct this letter to be forwarded, in case it does not find you at Philorth; and with best remembrance to Lady Saltoun, in which Mrs. Fraser begs to join, believe me, my dear Lord, most sincerely yours, JOHN FRASER.

LETTER from LORD SALTOUN to H.R.H. FREDERICK DUKE OF YORK, Commander-in-Chief. [Copy.]

LV.

Philorth, 26th August 1819.

SIRE,—The gracious condescension with which your Royal Highness has been pleased on many occasions to honour me, and the distance that I am at present from town, will, I trust, be considered by your Royal Highness as a sufficient excuse for trespassing on this occasion on your Royal Highness' goodness.

I shall not trouble your Royal Highness with any statement of my services, they being known to your Royal Highness as Colonel of the regiment; but having nothing to depend upon for my advancement in the service but my own exertions and your Royal Highness' goodness, I am induced to call your Royal Highness's attention to the great advantage I should derive from being appointed extra Aide-de-camp to His Royal Highness the Prince Regent, and I trust your Royal

Highness will graciously condescend to take my claims into consideration, and that I shall be honoured by your Royal Highness' recommendation on this or some future occasion.

I have again to trust to your Royal Highness' goodness for my excuse in thus trespassing upon your Royal Highness' gracious condescension.—I have the honour to be, Sire, with the greatest respect, your Royal Highness's most devoted and dutiful servant, SALTOUN.

Answer from H.R.H. Frederick Duke of York, Commander-in-Chief, to Lord Saltoun.

LVI.

Horse Guards, 1st September 1819.

My Lord,—I have to acknowledge the receipt of your Lordship's letter of the 26th ultimo, and to assure you that I entertain the most favourable opinion of your claims and services; but as the Prince Regent has already many supernumerary Aides-de-camp upon his establishment, it is not at present His Royal Highness's intention to add to them. Your Lordship's claims, however, with those of other officers, will be considered on future occasions, with every disposition to show them attention.—I am, my Lord, yours, FREDERICK,
Commander-in-Chief.

Letter from Lord Saltoun to Lord Liverpool. [Copy.]

LVII.

Philorth, 26th August 1819.

My dear Lord,—My absence in the Highlands prevented me till my return here yesterday, from knowing that the promotion which His Royal Highness the Prince Regent has been graciously pleased to extend to the service had taken place on the 12th instant. By this promotion some vacancies have occurred in the situation of Aide-de-camp or extra Aide-de-camp to His Royal Highness the Prince Regent, and I have taken the liberty of addressing your Lordship on this subject, to solicit the favour of your Lordship's interest in procuring my appointment to one of the vacancies so occasioned. I shall not trespass on your

Lordship's time by entering into any detail of my services, military or political; but I must beg leave to call your Lordship's attention to the length of time which elapsed before I could obtain the rank of Lieutenant-Colonel, the greater part of which was passed in active service as a Lieutenant of the Guards, and also the advantage I should derive in looking forward to the higher ranks of my profession should I succeed in this application.

I am aware that this situation is not immediately in your Lordship's gift, but should I succeed in inducing your Lordship to exert your interests in my favour, there are circumstances which have occurred which would prevent the appointment being in any way unprecedented, and I shall always consider your Lordship's exertions on my behalf as a personal and most particular favour.

I have to apologise for troubling your Lordship at this length, and have the honour to remain your Lordship's most sincere and faithful servant,

SALTOUN.

ANSWER from LORD LIVERPOOL to LORD SALTOUN.

LVIII.

Fife House, August 31st, 1819.

MY DEAR LORD,—I have received the favour of your letter.

You will perhaps have been apprised of General Fraser having spoken to me on the subject of it at the time that the Brevet was announced.

I did not fail to communicate with Sir Henry Torrens, in the absence of the Duke of York, but I found it impossible to press the matter, as he assured me that the Prince Regent had determined to adhere on this occasion, and in future, to the rule which had been followed by the King respecting his Aides-de-camp. You may recollect that the King never gave this rank to any Lieutenant-Colonel who was not at the head of the list.

I stated to Sir Henry Torrens that if this rule was adhered to, I felt I had no right to interfere, but that I wished he would say to the Commander-in-Chief, that if it was in any instance departed from, I could not but press upon His Royal Highness's consideration the just claims I thought you had to such a mark of favour. I have the honour to be, my dear Lord, your very faithful humble servant,

LIVERPOOL.

LETTER from GENERAL JOHN FRASER to LORD SALTOUN.

LIX.

Kensington, 2d September 1819.

MY DEAR LORD SALTOUN,—I should imagine that you were perfectly right in addressing your letter to the Duke of York himself, both as a Peer and as an Officer in his own regiment, more especially as you wished it to reach him without loss of time, and I shall be happy to hear that his answer is favourable.

Should further application be necessary, what think you of applying to the Duke of Wellington? He was abroad when the Brevet came out, but is now returned.

You speak modestly of your own claims when you term W———'s to be equal. The Spanish General Alava had good opportunity of judging of what passed at Waterloo, and what did he say of you in his Official Report of the engagement?

I have heard even strangers say that the stand you made at Hougomont decided the fate of the battle. We ought not perhaps to say this to the Duke of Wellington, but I trust he appreciates your conduct as he should. . . ..

Pray remember me to William when you see him, and with our best compliments to Lady Saltoun, believe me, my dear Lord, very sincerely yours,

JOHN FRASER.

LETTER from CAPTAIN W. SIBORN to LORD SALTOUN.

LX.

Dublin, January 4th, 1838.

DEAR LORD SALTOUN,—As rumour assigns to you the command of a Brigade of Guards for service in Canada, I am anxious to avail myself of the only opportunity which time may allow, to beg you will, with your usual kindness, favour me with your recollections of Quatre Bras, as also with a few particulars concerning the French attacks upon Hougomont during the *earlier* part of the day. I enclose a rough sketch of that portion of the former field upon which the Guards were principally engaged, as also a plan of Hougomont and its immediate vicinity.

It appears that during the interval between the commencement of the battle of Waterloo—half-past eleven—and the attack upon Picton's division about two o'clock, the action was, with the exception of a general cannonading along both lines, confined to Hougomont; but in drawing up my history of the battle, I find considerable difficulty in giving a clear and satisfactory view of the *progressive* course of the contest at the latter post during the above interval, and I should feel truly grateful for any hints with which your Lordship may be kind enough to favour me on that point, including the remainder of the period during which you remained at Hougomont. I am also anxious to learn whether any artillery were brought to bear against the orchard or the garden from the rising ground on our left of the long outward eastern hedge, which I have marked *a, b,* and of which the highest point was at *c.* I think I heard you mention your having at one time attempted to get possession of a French gun, which was worked *à la prolonge.*

I am rather doubtful as to an attack by the 1st Brigade of Guards upon French *Infantry previously* to that of the Imperial Guard. I am aware that a strong column of French infantry, flanked by Cuirassiers, advanced against a part of our line more to your right, sweeping by the outward north-east angle of the orchard of Hougomont, and that they were driven back,—perhaps another column made a simultaneous attack against the 1st Brigade of Guards; of the time and circumstances of the latter attack I know literally nothing.

Should I be warranted in stating that when your Lordship discovered the mistake caused by the passing of the word "form square" immediately after the defeat of the *first* column of the Imperial Guard, you gave the order, as well as your voice at such a moment would admit, for every man to retire to the original position, that the Brigade accordingly retired, though in considerable confusion, re-formed in line four deep, and brought up its left shoulder to meet the attack by the *second* column ? Such a circumstance as their accidentally retiring in confusion, and then re-forming for another attack, redounds so highly to the credit of our Guards, that I should wish particularly to notice it, if such actually occurred; for certainly none but British troops would have halted to re-form, aware as they must have been that a second immense column was rapidly moving against them; foreign troops would not have stopped until they had fairly crossed the main ridge of the position.

The model, I am happy to say, proceeds very satisfactorily though slowly, and

I am now fagging with all my might to bring it out in London on the 18th of June, as also my history of the whole campaign at the same time.—I remain, my dear Lord Saltoun, yours very faithfully, W. SIBORN.

P.S.—I have just this moment heard that you are to command the Light Division in Canada, upon which I take the liberty of congratulating both your Lordship and the service.

May I ask if it be true that the Duke of Wellington made use of the expression, so often attributed to him, of, " Up, Guards, and at them," at the attack of the first column of Imperial Guards ? An officer belonging to the Battery on the immediate right of the Guards informs me that he heard the Duke say, " Look out, Guards,—ready ;" perhaps these were the precise words—a point, however, of very little consequence. W. S.

LETTER from LORD SALTOUN to CAPTAIN W. SIBORN.

LXI.

London, 19th January 1838.

MY DEAR SIR,—Your letter of the 4th reached me on my way to town, but I have not had time to answer it sooner, and by this time you know that one of your Generals from Ireland goes instead of me with the Brigade of Guards to Canada.

I can give you little or no information regarding Quatre Bras. On that day I commanded the Light Companies of the First Brigade of Guards, and the post we occupied was in and about the wood on the right of the field of battle; but from the circumstance of your plan of the ground not being shaded, I am unable at this distance of time to trace our operations upon it. When we debouched from the wood (which we had cleared of the French light troops), we had on our right a deep ravine, or perhaps I should rather call it a hollow, and about 150 yards to our left, and about half that distance to the rear, was a low scrubby hedge, behind which the 33d Regiment was posted. This point I cannot make out on your sketch of the ground, but as far as information goes it is not of much importance. That was the extreme point we advanced to, as did also the Brigade; and although we were driven back from it, we recovered it again, and held it till the firing ceased at dark. I perceive you have a small brook or marshy bottom running through the wood. But as far as my recollection serves me, we met with an obstruction of that description much nearer the Nivelle road, from which we commenced our advance, than it appears to be in your plan, but I most likely am wrong in this; for hurried into action as we were into a large, and in some parts thick wood, without any instructions, and nothing to guide me in my advance but the fire of the enemy, it is not likely at this distance of time that I should retain a very clear recollection of distances.

Next with respect to Hougomont. From the first attack to the period mentioned in your letter (till about two o'clock), during the whole of which time I was at that post,[1] the whole was a succession of attacks against the front of that post, attended with more or less partial success for the moment, but in the end always repulsed. And it was in one of these attacks, when I had been driven from the front hedge of the orchard to the hollow way in the rear of it, that they, occupying the outward side of the front hedge with infantry, brought a gun along the line marked by you *a, b,* to a point I have marked *d* on that line. This gun I endeavoured to take, but failed. I however regained the front hedge of the orchard, from which I never was again driven. Whether the enemy had artillery at the point marked *c*, I am unable to state. We suffered very little from artillery on the post, but it is quite clear that the house and farm-yard of Hougomont was set on fire by that arm.

Your next point is the attack (as you call it) of the First Brigade of Guards against a body of infantry previous to the attack of the Imperial Guard, etc. You seem to have mistaken the advance not of that Brigade, but of one battalion of them, viz., the Third Battalion Grenadier Guards, and have concluded that this was an attack against a regular body of infantry, but that was not the case. The circumstances were as follows :—

During the cavalry attacks on the centre, a great number of the enemy's sharpshooters had crept up the slope of the hill, and galled the Third Battalion, who were in square, very severely. At that time the Second Battalion Grenadier Guards (the other Battalion of the Brigade) was likewise formed in square, about 100 yards in rear of the Third Battalion. The Third Battalion, who suffered severely from this fire, wheeled up into line, and drove them down the hill, and advanced to a point I have marked *E*, and there re-formed square. A small

[1] He omits to mention that he had to retake the orchard first of all.

body of Rifles were at a point I have marked with a ✕, and the 52d Regiment in line at *F G G*. In this position we received the last attack of cavalry I saw that day, who, refusing us, passed between us and the *inward rear angle of the orchard*, [and] receiving our fire, did not pass between us and the left of the 52d, where the Rifles were, but rode along the front of the 52d, with a view of turning their right flank, and were completely destroyed by the fire of that Regiment. After this, we, the Third Battalion, retired to our original position in square, as I conclude the 52d did also, as the next I saw of them was their attack, with the rest of General Adam's Brigade, on the second column of the Imperial Guards. As to any attack made about that time by the outward angle of the orchard of Hougomont, I could not from my position see or know anything about it.

Your next point is with respect to what took place towards the close of the action, and during the momentary confusion that took place in the First Brigade from the cry of " form square."

It will not do, in an account such as yours, to put down any order that was not given, however scientific it might be, still less to make me give an order to retire, when that was the last thought that came into my head at that moment. The word of command passed was,—" Halt! Front, form up ;" and it was the only thing that could be done—any other formation was impossible ; and as soon as this order was understood by the men it was obeyed, and everything was right again. To prove this, I must take you a little into the drill-book. The original formation of this Brigade at the commencement of the action was in contiguous column of Battalions, at quarter-distance, right in front. From that they formed squares on their respective leading companies. When they were ordered towards the end of the day to form line of four deep, instead of being deployed into line to either flank, they were wheeled up into line from square (in order that they might get the quicker back into square should that formation be required again). It followed from this that when in line the Grenadier Company and No. 1 formed the centre of each Battalion, and the right sections of each Company formed the right wing, and the left sections formed the left, thus completely separating the Companies, and rendering any formation upon our principles of drill utterly impracticable, except the one before mentioned of wheeling back into square. From this you will at once, I should think, see that any such account as you suggest would, to any soldier acquainted with the circumstances of the formation of that Brigade, prove its own inaccuracy, and do your account more harm than good. For such person would at once know that no fresh formation was practicable with those Battalions, until one of two things had been done.

Either they must have been re-formed into square, from that to column, and then deployed in the regular way; or they must have been ordered to fall out, and formed again as at the beginning of a parade to their respective covering serjeants, when all the process of a fresh telling off would become necessary. You had better therefore, I think, have it as I have given it to you, viz., that as soon as the men were made to understand they were not to form square, but to *Halt, front, and form up,* they did it; the left shoulders were then brought forward, and we advanced against the second column of the Imperial Guards, but which body was defeated by General Adam's Brigade before we reached it, although we got near enough to fire if we had been ordered so to do; and, as far as I can recollect at this distance of time, we did fire into that column.

Your last point is, whether the Duke made use of the words, " Up, Guards, and at them!" I did not hear him, nor do I know any person, or ever heard of any person, that did. It is a matter of no sort of importance, has become current with the world as the cheering speech of a great man to his troops, and is certainly not worth a controversy; if you have got it I should let it stand. I have endeavoured to answer your queries to the best of my ability, and I hope I have made them intelligible to you, and as I am not going with this army, I hope to see your model on the 18th of June next, and that the result will be of use to you. I remain, my dear Sir, yours very truly, SALTOUN.

LETTERS from MAJOR-GENERAL LORD SALTOUN to LIEUTENANT-COLONEL and MRS. CHARLES ELLIS, during the Expedition to China and Command of the Army of Occupation. 1841 to 1844.

LXII.

Belleisle, at Sea, 25th December 1841.

MY DEAR JULIA,—In the first place, to prevent all mistakes in future, I now write to say that I shall number my letters, whether written to you or to Charles, in one list, for I have so long been in the habit of writing to you both as one and the same, that it is not worth while numbering your letters separately, and this being Christmas-day, I begin now by wishing you both many happy returns of merry Christmas; and although I cannot expect to pass the next one with you, still I have passed so many that I hope to do the same with the one after.

As yet we have had fair wind, though not much of it, but to-day it blows a strong breeze, and we are about opposite to Vigo, that is, looking at the chart that Charles got at Plymouth, if you fancy a line from Ushant to Madeira, and then a line from Vigo across the chart to America, where the line from Vigo crosses the other is about the spot of ocean that I write this from. We get on very well; the Captain[1] is a good rough fellow, at the same time a gentleman; he gives us a good soup and a bit of roast meat, which we have cold the next morning for breakfast, and his cook makes a good curry and a fair hash. We breakfast at half-past eight, then walk the deck, read, etc., and at eleven the band of the regiment practise in the officers' room, and play pretty well. At three o'clock we dine, and after that walk the deck; and if it is very fine the men dance hornpipes, and play at a game they call the goose, or the hare. One of the 98th has been at Astley's, and he can tumble and sing comic songs, and so they pass their time till eight o'clock, when they pipe down; and about six of them sing very well in parts, and they keep it going till nine or so. At eight we have tea, and then Grant[2] and I play duets for a couple of hours, and then the grog comes in, and the Captain says, "All nights at sea are Saturdays, so let us drink sweethearts and wives," to which I agree, and we then turn in about half-past eleven; and as at sea, except as to weather, one day is the same as another, you may take this as a specimen of our usual life. I expect that I shall send this from Teneriffe, where we now hope to be before New Year's day, or on it, so I shall write no more now, but I shall add to it between this and the time it is to go; so for the present, dear Mr. Dick,[3] good-bye.

29th.—We made Madeira yesterday at about two o'clock, and passed the north end of the island about fifteen miles distant; and although we got becalmed under the land for most of the night, the breeze got up again at daylight, and we have been going at about nine knots all day, and they expect to see Teneriffe before dark, and to get in there to-morrow forenoon. I am told by some one on board, that a mail goes from this twice a month to Cadiz, where it meets our

---

[1] Captain Kingcombe, R.N.   [2] The late General Sir Hope Grant, then his Brigade-major.
[3] Mrs. Charles Ellis's nickname.

packet, so this will go that way if it is so; if not, we are to make a bag on board to go by the first chance to England. Either way you will hear by this sooner I should hope than you could have expected to do.

I have, for the first time, been playing with Grant this day, in the morning, things we found too difficult to play at night, and we have plenty of them. Somehow it made me a little melancholy, even at this distance, so I am come to *write it out* if I can. He plays his instrument better than I can play mine, and is a good timist; so I have no scolding, as I have had before now at that time in the morning, and mean to have again when I come home, unless you are very much improved indeed.

Our weather, which has been fine all along, has become very mild, but nothing like heat as yet, nor will it be till we have left Teneriffe for a day or two; and as yet we have not a sick man on board, which, as far as it goes, is very satisfactory. I shall add more to this when we see Teneriffe, and if this is not required to go at once I will add a description of that place, and what we find there. I have some letters to write, and we must stay two days, and very likely three, but that will depend upon whether they will let the native boats bring us water, or whether we must do it with our own boats. So no more, my dear Mr. Dick, just now.

30th.—We made Teneriffe at daylight; a fine bold barren rock on the side we saw it from, and we sailed along until we came to an anchor here at about one o'clock to-day. The Consul came on board, a Mr. Bartlay, and then I put on my undress toggery and went with the Captain to see the Governor, a gentleman-like Spanish General; but I found myself rather out in speaking Spanish to him, but for a visit of ceremony got on pretty well. From that we went to see the place where Lord Nelson failed here, and no wonder, for the parties landed in different places, and never getting together were beat in detail; for both gained their object as far as landing and getting into the town was concerned. From that we went to see their colours, which are preserved in the church here, and they have a right to them as a fair trophy of war well disputed; for our men, who, under Troubridge, were driven into a convent we also went to see, made so good a defence, and took such an imposing position, that they were permitted to retire to their ships, leaving their colours. I did not know till I asked our Captain that Jack takes those flags on shore with him; but it seems they do, and

I love them the more for it; so after all, under these feelings, I did not feel that disgust at seeing our flag here that I should do, if they have one to show at New Orleans. After seeing this we went to the Consul's house and saw his wife, a Gaditana, and a finish-looking woman. Arthur[1] and Grant are gone there to a party to-night, but I had to write this and other things besides. He has got a daughter also, by a former wife, but I have not seen her; however, my boys are to bring back word at what hour the ladies would like to hear the band play, and it will go on shore to-morrow for that purpose, and I shall go to see what sort of beauty the town of St. Cruz can turn out, for they will all be there. I was obliged to go through this official work, which put off time, for the first thing I heard was that the boat that takes letters from this to Cadiz sails to-morrow morning, and therefore that this letter must be with the Consul early in the morning; so if you cannot read the last written of this easily, you must put it to writing by a bad light.

We have made arrangements that the water we require is to be sent on board by the natives, and therefore we most likely will sail from this on Saturday evening—that is what our Captain says, and I have accordingly (as many of my young ones want to see as much of the Peak as they can, and others to shoot) ordered all hands to be on board by three o'clock on Saturday, which will be New Year's Day; but I will not take any notice of that here, but reserve that day to put another letter on the stocks for Charles, and now, as it is late, and this letter must be closed, I shall conclude with my love to Charles, and wishing you, my dear Julia, every good, believe me, yours affectionately, S——.

LXIII.

Teneriffe, 1st January 1842.

MY DEAR CHARLES,—Many happy New Years to you and Mr. Dick.

My letter to her, begun on Christmas Day, went from this yesterday by the Spanish post; but as we are going to send a bag with the sailors' and soldiers' letters by a ship that will sail in a day or two for England direct, I write this to give you an account of how we have got on here during our short stay. I have had again to interfere about that row in the "Sapphire," not to any extent; but the fact is, I do not think the officers in that ship have the least idea of the

[1] General Sir Arthur Cunynghame, G.C.B., then his Aide-de-camp.

position in which they stand with respect to Mr. C——, who commands the ship; for I find that Assistant-Doctors and other Subalterns seem to think themselves his superior officers, whereas he, being a Master in the Navy, ranks with the junior Captain, and, of course, is superior to any Subaltern in our service; and I have been obliged to send Grant on board to-day, to show these young men the exact position in which they are placed, and how much real power he, the Master, holds if they force him to exercise it.

The Middies all went on shore yesterday, and as usual rode the horses' tails off, galloping up and down the stony streets as if they were mad, to the great astonishment of the natives, who exclaimed, " Como questos chicotos son locos!" The band went on shore and played pretty well, but very few ladies turned out, and those nothing remarkable. In the evening they had a play: I did not go on shore, but Cunynghame and Grant did; and it was very bad.

The "Wanderer," that sailed two days before us, came in yesterday, having been to Madeira, and the Captain asked Mr. Boyd, I think his name is, and his friend Captain Bushby, R.N., who sails with him and takes care of the craft, to dine; and from them we heard that the "Harlequin" only left Madeira the day before yesterday, and that the "North Star" is not to sail till to-morrow, so we shall most probably be at Rio as soon as they. The "Wanderer" goes from this to the Cape de Verd Islands, and then from that to Rio, where we most likely shall meet again.

We have had the us[ual] allowance of drunken men, etc.; but the best thing that happened was to Major R——, who sent his servant and his servant's wife on shore to wash his things: they took their child with them. As they proceeded to drink before the washing they got drunk, lost or pawned the clothes, wandered out into the country, where they lost the kid and themselves; but the whole have luckily been found this morning. And now, as far as this ship is concerned, we have by good luck and exertions on the part of the officers got all our men on board again, where we mean to keep them; for Blue Peter will be hoisted at twelve o'clock, and as we have completed our water, we shall sail at three this afternoon, and if in luck, will be at Rio by the 1st of February.

The climate here is most delightful at this time of the year, but must be very hot indeed in the summer; for even now, when you get into the influence of the sun and the Rock, it is warmer than England is in general in the summer, and to-day is warmer than any day we had after the month of June last year. The only resident here for pleasure is a Doctor M——, with his wife and two children. He is a medical man, and attended William and his children when they lived at Battersea. He went to Madeira a year ago for his own health, and came to pass this winter here by way of a change; but it must be a horrid place to live in,—no society, no books, very little, if any sporting: in short, I take it to be what an old cook of mine used to call as "one-eyed" a place as I ever saw. This Mr. M——, who is well now, intends to go home *viâ* Cadiz and the S.E. of Spain to France. The houses here are just like the Cadiz houses, built in a square with a court in the middle, in which there is a well; and when you pay a visit, as I did yesterday, you walk straight up and stamp about till somebody comes; the rooms the same as in Spain, but all the floors I have seen are of wood, and not of brick, as many of them were at Cadiz.

As yet we have not got a sight of the Peak, as the mountain has been covered with clouds ever since we came here; but to-day is fine, and perhaps we may see it towards night, when we get a little out to sea. The breeze has just come from the land, and we shall get under weigh at three o'clock, which was the time I gave the officers to be on board by; and we have every chance of getting into the trades at once, and carrying on to the line; but of that you will hear by my next, which will most probably be sent from Rio, as, from the course we take, we are not very likely to meet any homeward bound ships. I must now finish this, for the captain is to send our bag on shore to the consul at one o'clock; so, with best love to Julia, believe me, my dear Charles, yours very truly,

SALTOUN.

P.S.—You are the only person I have written to by this bag.

LXIV.

Belleisle, at Sea, 4th January 1842.

MY DEAR JULIA,—I wrote to Charles letter No. 2, from Teneriffe, on New-Year's Day, and left it to go by a private ship that was to sail in a day or two.

St. Cruz, in Teneriffe, is a new, clean town, with water brought into it in a covered aqueduct from a distance of about three leagues. The island, as most likely I before wrote, is entirely volcanic, and very barren looking, but at the same time very picturesque. We sailed about four o'clock on the afternoon of the 1st, got a momentary look at the Peak as we went out of the Bay, but the next morning was clear, and we had a magnificent view of it at day-light about forty miles distant.

This is the fifteenth day since we sailed from Plymouth, and as yet we have never tacked ship or had a moment's foul wind; and I write to-day because this morning we have got within the tropics. I slept last night with a blanket and counterpane, and I am dressed to-day in the usual clothes I should wear in England, and as yet nothing like heat, and we are going along at nine knots an hour, in a climate as near what the month of May is in England as anything I can liken it to. As yet we have seen no dolphins, nor indeed any sort of fish except porpoises, and we had a large shoal of them alongside yesterday.

I have finished Timousky on China, a book of great information for Russia, but gives little or no information about the part we are going to, except as to the climate at Pekin. I began Alison yesterday, and like him much. To-day the Lieutenants of the ship have invited us to dine with them; so you see we have our gaieties here as well as on shore. I shall leave off this now, my dear Mr. Dick, till I have something more worth writing about.

7th January.—We made the Cape de Verd islands yesterday at 12 o'clock. The one we first saw was a low island called Sal, from quantities of salt being found there. Next we came right on the island of Bonavista, about half-past one. By our calculation we should have been about fifteen miles to the east of it; and our calculation was right; for it seems that in the chart the island is laid down fifteen miles more to the west than it actually is, so we came right on it. This mistake in the chart is mentioned in a book they all sail by, but it is very odd they do not either alter the chart, or at least mark the mistake on it. We sailed along it all day, and lost sight of it before dark, and we do not expect to see land again till we make Rio, if we go there; but that is not as yet certain. To-day, for the first time, we have seen flying-fish, but as yet no dolphins or sharks. The thermometer in my cabin was 76° this morning, and with the port open, is at 74°. We all dined yesterday with the 98th. No more news, dear Mr. Dick, just now.

10th.—We have had a fine run since I last wrote, at the rate of 200 miles a day, and we are now in the latitude of 5° north, but last night it became quite calm, with an immense quantity of thunder and lightning, and to-day it rains, but not so hard as it sometimes does in these latitudes, and it is very hot; the thermometer in my cabin, where I am writing with the port open, is at 82°; but we must expect to have it much hotter before we are done with it. Captain Little, who is on board—he belongs to the Madras Artillery—tells me it will be as high as 105° when we get to the other side of the Line. The Captain said at dinner yesterday, "I shall write a line to-morrow, as we may meet a ship on the Line going home" (for as yet we have not seen a sail since Teneriffe); so I am adding to this in case we fall in with a ship homeward bound.

To-day, for the first time, a shark has come alongside, and the Jacks are fishing for him. Some dolphins have also been seen to-day, but I do not expect that the fishermen will get anything as long as we lie like a log on the water, as we are doing just now. The flying-fish, of which the sea seems to be full, are the prettiest thing possible. They spring out of the water in coveys of ten or twelve, fly about fifteen to twenty-five yards, and then drop in again; and some of the single ones fly quite far enough for a double shot at them, and often just touch the water, as the swallow sometimes does, and then fly on again for twenty more yards. They are about six inches long, and altogether put one much in mind of swallows. For these last three days we have been coming through them, but I have not seen any of them to-day.

As yet it is not by any means certain whether we go to Rio or not; it will depend upon how long we are kept here about the Line by calm weather, for if we get into the south-east trade-wind before our water gets too low, we shall go to the Cape direct. No more now. I shall add good-bye to this if we meet a ship.

12th January, 3° North Latitude.—A ship has just come in sight, homeward bound, and we are likely to speak her; at least we are trying to do so, for as yet we cannot make out what she is, or whether this can go by her.

It was quite calm yesterday, but no rain after the morning. The Captain had the commanders of the other ships to dine, and the commanding officers of the troops; in short, a state dinner, and a very pleasant party it was, as they were all agreeable men enough, particularly Captain Frederick, who commands the "Apollo." They went away about dark, and this morning we have a nice breeze, and if it lasts we shall probably cross the Line by to-morrow night or the next morning.

The thunder and lightning here are the nearest I have ever seen, and we had a most tremendous crack yesterday morning, but no harm. It was the loudest clap of thunder I ever heard, but the sailors say we have had less of it than usual.

The Jacks caught a shark yesterday while we were at dinner, but I did not see him, as he was cut up before we heard of it; he was not a very large one—about six feet long. The band played after dinner, and pretty well; and after that the boys had a game at what they call swinging the monkey. They hoist a fellow up by his shoulders; the rope passes under his arms, and as he swings away they all hit at him with handkerchiefs made into what we used to call Westminster knots; and he has one also, and any fellow he hits gets into his place and becomes the monkey. After that, as the drums and fifes played a very good valse at tattoo, they all set to work to valse; so you see, as we used to say in the Peninsula, there is always some fun going, up at the army.

If you look for 3° N. latitude, and 20° W. longitude, where we expect to cross the Line, you will see on the chart where about we are. The stars at night are beautiful, but we are fast losing an old friend, the North Star. I could just see him last night, and took leave of him till we come to the north of the Line again, but we shall not see him till about Sincapore. I have written to Willy Macdowall[1] by this opportunity, so he will tell my mother that he has heard from me.

After all, dear Mr. Dick, the ship is not going home; she was becalmed, and when they saw her they thought from the way her head pointed she was homeward bound, but she turns out to be a Swede, going the same way as we are, so this must wait for some other opportunity.

14th January.—A ship has just come out of the haze, and our boat is lowered to speak to her. We are in 2° north, and shall most likely cross the Line tomorrow; so with love to Charles, believe me, dear Julia, yours affectionately,

S——.

LXV.

17th January 1842, Belleisle, at Sea on the Line.

MY DEAR CHARLES,—On Friday last a ship called the "Acteon" from Callao (she had come originally from Sydney), spoke us, and as she was bound for Liverpool we sent letters by her, and I sent No. 3 to Mr. Dick by that ship.

Whether we are ten miles over the Line, or ten miles short of it, we shall not

[1] His brother-in-law.

know till twelve o'clock; but whichever it is, we have made an excellent run for this is our twenty-eighth day from Plymouth, and we have never yet had occasion to reef a top-sail, and the wind has been nearly fair the whole way, that is, at the worst times we always have made some southing.

The men are quite well. We have not a single man with fever on board; and the only thing that is not so well is, that with men who get hurt on the shins, etc., by falls, which some half-dozen of them have, these sores, since we came into this heat, have taken an ugly appearance like gangrene, so we made a requisition for lime-juice, which the doctor hopes will have a good effect on them. We are entitled to said lime juice after being fourteen days at sea without an issue of fresh meat, which we had not then been; however, the Captain gave it on requisition.

Neptune came on board of us last Friday night; they manage that very well at eight o'clock, when it is always dark in these parts. They make a great light at the bows with phosphorus, and he hails from under the bows, with a speaking-trumpet, "Ship a-hoy!" and the first Lieutenant answers, and then he asks leave to come on board to speak to the Captain, and a conversation takes place, in which he ascertains that some are on board who have never paid him his tribute, and he takes leave saying he will return the next day at nine o'clock in the morning to claim it, and as soon as he is supposed to have got over the side, they cut away a lighted tar barrel, which drifts away for some miles. The next day at nine o'clock he came in procession in a fine car, attended by all his myrmidons, painted and tarred in the most various fashion, and some of them feathered all over, with a coachman and sea-lions to draw his car; and after a speech to the Captain, in which his Majesty of the Deep observed that as I had been a good boy, and had come to visit him after having seen so much service elsewhere, he would make me free of his dominions without undergoing the ceremony, the fun began, and they shaved and ducked every man in the ship, and it lasted till twelve o'clock, by which time they had got through them. They began with Grant, then Cunynghame, next the little boy Fred, and then Campbell,[1] and the Captain introduced all these and went through the sail with them; after that they took all the officers as they might come, and then the men. The process is thus: in the lee-gangway they

[1] The late Lord Clyde, then commanding 98th Regiment.

have a sail full of water, about three or four feet deep, kept full by the fire-engine. The victim is seized, then they blind his eyes, on which all who have passed before sluice him with buckets of water, and he is taken behind the sail, where, if they do not like him, they give him a drink of salt water; then he is taken on to kiss Amphitrite, and then they shave him with tar and an iron hoop, more or less severely, as the case may be, and that being done (which it is in the boat on the booms, in the centre of the ship), they pitch him, if he is shy of jumping, into the sail, when the Tritons take and duck him well, and as he tries to get out they play the hose in his face and shy water on him in any way they can, and as soon as he is out he begins at the next; but as we were so many they could not all get at the victim, so our boys shied water at each other till the fun was over, or they were tired of it. It all went off well, no row of any kind; some got hurts with falls, but nothing to signify. I cannot find out from any one the origin of this absurd ceremony, but I conclude it is of Buccaneering origin.

19th.—Yesterday a man of the 98th jumped overboard and was drowned. The Captain brought the ship to, and the boat was down in less than four minutes, but he could not swim well; perhaps a shark took him, for a very large one has been seen about for some days. He was one of the recruits, a bad-conditioned man and a thief. His company were going to cob him for stealing other men's messes, so he jumped overboard,—no great loss to the regiment. The doctor reports all the men with ulcers to be much better since they got the lime-juice.

24th January.—Five weeks to-day from Plymouth. We are to-day in lat. 14° South, long. 31° W., and still going on with the same steady breeze and smooth sea, at between four and six knots an hour; in short, since Teneriffe, except just when we were in sight of the Cape de Verd Islands, it has been like sitting in a drawing-room as far as motion is concerned. In the evening of the 20th a man fell from the main-top-gallant-mast rigging and was killed. From what we can make out he had been drinking; he was a sailor of the name of Dunbar. As yet it is uncertain whether we go to Rio or not; when we get to lat. 20° South the Captain must decide.

25th.—The Captain decided at dinner yesterday to go to Rio, and ordered the ship to be steered accordingly. I think what made him decide was that our master told him that he would not be responsible for the lower range of tanks being full of water, for he had not seen them filled himself, as it was done before he was appointed; that they were given over to him as full, but he could not prove it; and from the hurried way that many other things had been done in the fitting out of the ship he would not be responsible for them, and it was impossible to sound and prove what they had in, as the upper row of tanks was not empty. Rio was distant about 1200 miles, and as we are going along at from nine to ten knots, so we shall be there on Saturday or Sunday. Provided we are not too late for the fun in China, I am rather glad of it than otherwise, as by this means we shall see all the four quarters of the globe in one trip.

This morning we saw a three-masted craft, schooner-rigged, going the same way as we were, but as soon as she saw us she hauled her wind and stood right away to windward. Mr. Bradly, our master (referred to above, and a very nice fellow), told me he had no doubt she was a slaver, and he ought to be a good judge, for he was for nine years on the coast in that service, and was at the taking of more than 5000 of them; he thinks that nothing will stop it but making it piracy. Hope Grant has been very unwell for these two days. He got a fall playing at leap-frog, and got some concussion of the head or brain. For twenty-four hours he did not know where he was or anything; he is much better this morning, and before this letter goes I hope to be able to report him quite well.

Wednesday, 2d February.—Since I wrote last on the 25th we have had nothing but very light winds, and made very little way, but yesterday at daylight we made Cape Frio, and sailed along the land all day in the direction of Rio Janeiro, and at about nine o'clock last night, after a smart squall, it became calm and we moved but very slowly, and we are now close to an island called Raza, which is about twelve miles from the harbour of Rio, or rather from the town of St. Sebastian, as the capital of the Brazils is called. We expect the sea breeze about twelve, and in that case we shall be at anchor in a couple of hours, and I shall go on shore.

I am happy to say that Hope Grant has got quite well again, and we have been fiddling for these four or five last days, which he could not do at all at first after his accident. The fact is he got a very severe shake, and the hot weather made it worse. Our doctor is a very clever fellow, and as soon as he rallied he told me he would get quite well and no ultimate harm would come of it.

The entrance to Rio is one of the grandest and most beautiful views I ever saw, but upon too large and grand a scale either to be drawn or described; fine high rocky hills in all directions,—some bare and others covered to the top with fine wood, and we have from sixty to one hundred sail in sight, all making for the port. These ships are coasters, and bring the different products of the country from the different ports to this place, where the greater part of the trade with Europe centres. If I have time I will send what we see here in this letter, but if not it must go in the next, which will be from the Cape, where I hope to be yet by the end of the month.

Rio Janeiro, 3d February.—We anchored about two o'clock, and after dinner came on shore in the Captain's gig, and have established ourselves here in a fair enough place called the English hotel,—good airy rooms, and they have just given us an excellent breakfast of fish, beef-steaks, with eggs, fruit, etc., and all good of its kind. The harbour is the finest I ever saw, quite land-locked, and large enough to hold all the navies in the world, if the nations had twice as many ships as they have. It is quite impossible to describe it; but it is altogether the most beautiful and grand-looking thing I ever saw.

I expect the Captain and Campbell on shore in half-an-hour, and then we shall go and call on Mr. Hamilton, our minister here, dine with him if he asks us; if not, all hands dine here with me, and we will then go out in open carriages, with tops to them to keep off the sun, to see all the lions. It is very hot, but no fleas or bugs in the house; and last night we had no mosquitoes, to my great astonishment; they have them, however, for the beds have the proper curtains. As we stay here to-morrow, I shall finish this now, and if I have time, write Mr. Dick what we see here; if not, it must go from the Cape. Give my best love to her, and believe me, my dear Charles, yours very truly, SALTOUN.

P.S.—February 4.—I found Mr. Hamilton in bed, and very unwell, so we did not see him; but we saw Mrs. Hamilton, whom I found I was acquainted with, having met her at Kinfauns, when they were in Scotland before they came out here.

As these letters will not go from this for fourteen days, I shall not write any more from this place, for our letters from the Cape may be so soon after this in England that it will be nearly the same thing. We cannot get our water on board till to-morrow, so we shall not go on board till after dinner to-morrow, and sail with the land wind on Sunday morning, and then on our way to the Cape I will put down all we have done and seen here for the benefit of Mr. Dick and yourself.

They gave us an excellent dinner yesterday, and as we have ice here for the wine and porter, it goes down quite another thing. I have no thermometer with me, but it cannot be less here than 86° or 87°, but still, when the sun gets behind the hill, it becomes very pleasant and tolerably cool, and driving out very pleasant. Love to Mr. Dick and Aunt Anne.[1] Yours very truly, S——.

LXVI.

Belleisle, at Sea, 24th February 1842.

MY DEAR JULIA,—I did not intend to begin this letter so soon; I meant to have waited until we were in the meridian of Greenwich before I wrote; but since we left Rio we have been going on so slowly that we were still yesterday twenty degrees to the westward of that meridian, so I have got tired of doing nothing, and therefore write a bit this morning.

I left letter No. 4 to Charles with Mr. Hamilton, to go by the packet. I called the last day to take leave of Mrs. Hamilton, and he was so far better that he came into the drawing-room while I was there, and I found he was an old friend, and a man I had known at Paris years ago.

After all, we were much more at our ease by his being unable to entertain us, because we had all our time to ourselves without being bothered with any ceremony. Accordingly I gave a dinner to eight every day, and we drove out in the evening; and except, as I think I wrote Charles, that I was disappointed in the size of the tropical growth here, it is certainly most beautiful. The natives say that the *ensemble* is as fine as Constantinople, but I have never found any person who has seen *both* say so; I shall therefore put it next to it. The landing-place is in a fine square, built after Black Horse Square at Lisbon, from which the streets branch off inland on a small square bit of ground between the harbour and the mountain; and this is the city. A road or rather street branches off each side between the sea and the mountain, for about one mile and a half each way, of good well-built houses, and the number of inhabitants is, I am told, about 15,000, the much greater proportion being black. They have three theatres, the

[1] Mrs. George Ellis.

Opera, Portuguese Play, and French Play; the two last only were open while we were there. They say the Opera is good, and I should think it was, from the very respectable manner that the orchestra at the Portuguese Play (which is the one at the Opera) performed several things. Most of the performers were men of colour, and the fault was they wanted bass.

Everything here is progressing, and shows a thriving place. Instead of, as at Lisbon, houses falling down in all directions, nothing here is going to ruin; on the contrary, all decayed houses are rebuilding, and new ones putting up in all directions, and exports and imports and general trade in a regular progressive state of improvement. At the same time, I was told that the Government was in a very unsettled state, and that at any time it might be upset. Indeed while we were there a deputation from the country came in to present, and they did present, a petition to the Emperor, which his ministers had refused to lay before him, as they said, on account of the way in which it was worded; but, however, if they go on prosperously and getting rich they will not rebel as yet.

We sailed from Rio on Tuesday the 8th, and lay becalmed all that night and the next day, just outside of the Island of Raza. All Wednesday evening it lightened in the most beautiful and at the same time fearful manner; and at about twelve at night it came on one of the most tremendous squalls of wind, rain, and thunder that even our old Captain had ever seen. Our top-gallant sails and our fore-top sail went to rags in a second. However, we got before it, burnt our blue-light, which was answered by the "Sapphire," but not the "Apollo," and at day-light the "Apollo" was missing, and we have not seen her since, but we expect to find her at the Cape, as, if she had been struck by lightning and seriously damaged, she would have thrown up rockets and made signals to us; so we suppose she is all right.

I had gone to bed about eleven as usual, and I was woke (my port being open) with such a splash of water in my face that I thought the sea had come in. I bundled out of bed to shut the port, but it was pitch-dark, and I could only see the ropes to pull it up by the flashes of lightning; so before I could get it shut I was wet, and the bed wet, and everything at the same time so infernally hot, it was difficult to say whether it was cold water or warm. I got my shirt off, and not thinking the bed was so wet, I rolled myself up in the blanket and fell asleep again. However, I caught cold, which after a day or two turned into a fit of the gout, of which I got well the day before yesterday. It was a good smart fit, but then I have not had one for more than two years, and if this one will keep me well for two years more I shall have made a good job of it. I have to-day got my regular shoe on, and walk quite sound; so, my dear Mr. Dick, I shall inflict no more upon you just now, but unless something very particular occurs, add to this when we reach the meridian of Greenwich.

March 5th.—At last, my dear Mr. Dick, we have reached this meridian of Greenwich. We crossed it about ten o'clock last night, in lat. 35° south, and we are accordingly, being in a straight line, nearer England than we shall be again for some time to come, our distance now being about 5000 miles as the crow flies.

On the 27th of last month, being then about 70 miles to the north of the little island called Tristan D'Acunha, we saw a large ship to leeward, but it was so foggy we could not for some time make her out. She turned out to be our missing ship, the "Apollo." We had lost her in a squall on the 9th, and found her in a fog on the 27th. It being calm the next day, her Captain came on board and brought his chart with him, and on comparing it with ours, we had constantly been within fifteen miles of each other without knowing it, for the weather had been for the most part very thick and hazy; indeed, we could hardly have seen less sun if we had been in England than we have done since we left Rio, and our thermometer has gone gradually down till it is now at 65°, and as this is just the end of summer here, it shows how much colder it is to the south than to the north of the Line.

I have been looking over your book of astronomy, but I find, what is very natural, the author rather confines himself to the northern hemisphere, with which for the present, at least, we are done; and I took leave of the North Star the day before we crossed the Line, but we shall see him again when we get to Java Head, where we cross the Line again, and during the rest of our proceedings he will shine upon us as well as on you. In the meantime we have a very fine constellation here, and as conspicuous in this hemisphere as the Great Bear is in the north; it is called the Southern Cross, composed of six bright stars in the form of the Roman cross; and as the bear shows the way to the north, so does this show the south.

After all, one gets very much used to this sort of life. I get up every morning at half-past six; we breakfast at eight; the band of the regiment practise in the officers' cabin from nine till half-past eleven, during which time the deck is crowded with drills, parade, etc., but from that till one o'clock it is clear, as the men are all at dinner, and during that time I walk, really for exercise; at one the drill begins again, and then Grant and I fiddle till half-past two; then I take my bath and dress for dinner,—dine at three; at five the sailors muster at quarters and drill at great-gun exercise till half-past six; the deck is then clear again and we walk till eight, when we have tea; after tea, play whist till ten or a little after, when the grog comes, and at about eleven I go to bed,—what one must call, my dear Mr. Dick, a very regular life.

We hope to be at the Cape before the end of next week, and there we expect to hear a good deal of China news, and I will finish this from that place. So good-bye for the present.

Saturday, 12th March.—Yesterday at twelve o'clock we were in lat. 37° 26′ south, long. 11° east, giving us still 400 miles to the Cape, so I write a little bit more, because I see I have forgot to put in the right place that when Captain Frederick of the "Apollo" came on board, he told us he had had the misfortune to lose an officer. He was a Mr. Craven, the son of Mr. Fuller Craven, going out in the "Apollo" as a passenger to join the ship he belonged to, which is in China in the navy. Under these circumstances they sometimes do duty in the ship they are in, and he was on watch: how it was they do not know, but he fell overboard from the poop and was lost. They had some anchors and spars stowed over the side, and they think he must have struck against them and got stunned, as he never rose after he fell into the sea. He was a fine handsome-looking young man, but I only knew him by sight. I shall finish this from the Cape, which we must get to at last; but the passage has been a very long one from Rio.

16th.—We anchored in Simon's Bay at five o'clock on the 14th, and yesterday we came over here. The distance is about twenty-four miles of a not very good road, a great part of it sand; and Cunynghame and I did it in a buggy in four hours. I called on the Governor to-day, an old friend, and we are going out to dine with him at his country house;. it is about five miles out of the town. We dine at rather a different hour from what we have been used to, viz., half-past seven.

This is a nice town, but the mosquitoes got hold of me last night and have bunged my eyes up funnily. Everything here English—language, money, and goods, and they have many very nice things from England; and I am looking out for a horse, as our Captain can take one on for me, as also one for Campbell and each of the staff—in all four.

Our news from China is good, but no use sending it to you, as you will hear it overland long before you can receive this, as ours gives no further than to October last, at which time they had taken Ningpoo; but we have also just heard the bad news from India, which you know also. I am glad poor Elphinstone died a natural death, and was not insulted and murdered by these fellows. The worst part of it is that it compels us to fit out a force sufficient to really crush these people. How absurd my writing all this to you! but somehow I always write to you what comes into my head at the moment; so I will not write any more now, but give you an account, when we come back, of our dinner with Sir George and Lady Napier, as I shall learn from them when the post goes from this to England.

18th.—We had a very nice dinner with the Governor and his wife, a very pretty woman for a grandmother. They have a nice little house out there, which they hire during the hot months, as she cannot exist in Government House for the mosquitoes during the hot weather. We met at dinner Colonel Chambers, who commands the 25th Regiment here. You and Charles may remember him in the 1st Regiment, to which he belonged before the reduction in the year '19, when our two companies were reduced. He has asked us to dine with him and his regiment on the 21st, Monday; but I am in hopes that we shall be obliged to return to our ships before that or on that day, although yesterday we heard that it blew so hard there they could not get any water on board, which was curious, for here it was quite still and very hot. The Governor is to drive me out this afternoon to his country house, and I am to sleep there, and he is to show me all the lions the next day.

I have just got a horse at £25, which is not too much; but they have been asking £70 and £80 for them. I daresay we shall get three, and when we land I shall take my choice of the quietest one.

I walked all over the town yesterday. The old part of it is very Dutch. The streets have a run for water in the middle, but as the water is very scarce, it is more like a muddy ditch than a canal, with a row of trees on each side of this ditch; the consequence is that the mosquitoes are bred in thousands. They do not touch Cunynghame nor his servant, as they have just come from the Mediterranean, but they attack Grant, Thomas,[1] and me most furiously; this shows how long a time climate will to a certain degree affect a constitution.

I am, as you may suppose, my dear Julia, most anxious to hear from England; and we may, and I hope will be at Sincapore in seven or eight weeks from this, and then I shall, I trust, hear that all of you I have left there are well. I expect certainly to get your February letters, and perhaps we may get the March ones before we leave that place, not that our stay there will be long, but this is the tenth or twelfth letter I have written to one or another, and I am tired of writing without something to answer; however, you shall always hear, if it is only a line by any opportunity I have of sending, and I shall put a letter on the stocks for Charles as soon as we leave this, to send by any chance conveyance we may meet with. I find a ship sails for England on Wednesday next, at least they say so at the post-office, for they have no regular mail here, but send by any ship that may be going to England. So now, with love to Charles, good-bye, but I will keep this open till the last, to add love to you and Aunt Anne.

21.—We are to return to Simon's Bay to-day, and dine with the Admiral, go on board, and I hope sail to-morrow morning, for I am quite tired of this place; however, we have done our business and got three horses at a fair and a reasonable price, and now we have only to get them safe to China, and we shall then be complete.

We had a very pleasant time of it with the Governor. . . . The first day we drove out and called upon Sir B. D'Urban, whom I had known in the Peninsula, and who is settled here, having been Governor, but he and Lord Glenelg could not hit it off, so he resigned; and the next day, Saturday, we went to Constantia and tasted all the wines, and after that all the grapes they are made from. The wines are all of them very sweet. . . . I thought the grapes were much better eating ones than I have seen out of England before, and much better as grapes than the wine made from them is as wine.

I have now, I think, my dear Julia, given you all my adventures, and I do not expect to be able to write again till we get to Sincapore; indeed, a letter will probably be faster that way than any other, and you will get this about the middle or perhaps 20th of May, by which time I trust we shall have left said Sincapore for our work at China. Give my love to Charles. I hope

[1] His valet Thomas Phillips.

he finds Bath a nice place, and I long to hear how you get on there. I have not written to Aunt Anne, but when you do, send her my love and say that I will write next time; perhaps you may be with her when you get this. And now, with best love, believe me, my dear Julia, yours affectionately, S——.

LXVII.

11th April 1842, Belleisle, at Sea,
Lat. 38° 40′ S., Long. 80° E.

MY DEAR CHARLES,—We have made a capital run from the Cape as yet, and everything looks like a continuance of it, so I put a letter on the stocks to-day, as this day last year was Easter-day, and I dined with you at the Hill, when I was staying with you, before I went to Eglinton races.

The day before yesterday about five in the evening, we made the Island of St. Paul, distant about forty miles, and as it is marked in your chart, it will show you whereabout we are; and I am glad to have seen it, because it is the land furthest removed from any continent in the world. The Island of Desolation, discovered by Cook, is not quite so far removed. You will also see what a roundabout we make to get to the Sunda Straits; but we do that to get the wind, and we have had it fair ever since we left the Cape, and they expect to carry it on till we get to 105° east long. in this same latitude, and then we shall get the south-east trade, which will take us to Sunda.

On the 24th, the day after we left the Cape, we had a very strong gale and heavy sea. One of our ships, the "Sapphire," got hit with a sea that carried away all her bulwarks amidship, her boom-boats, and all her spars, as also all their sea-stock which was stowed in the boats, and, unfortunately, a sergeant and one of the sailors were washed overboard and lost. We had several of our ports driven in on the main-deck, and some of the officers well washed in their beds, and the sea was so high that it came once or twice into my cabin. On the 27th the weather had moderated, but it was dark and hazy, and we lost sight of both the other ships, and have not seen them since, which was unlucky for the "Sapphire," as we meant to have sent some of our stock on board her, we having plenty to spare. The horses, of which we bought three at the Cape, stood it beautifully, and they are now so reconciled to the ship that they lie down just as if they were in a stable. These horses have been a great delight to old Shean,[1] as he has something now to look after; and he lives in the boat with them all day long.

What is curious, this passage, in which we have been further from land than any other, we have been constantly attended by birds,—the albatross, noddy, booby, and two sorts of sea-swallows exactly like our land ones, except that they never flew up in the air, but only skimmed along the sea as ours do on water. We have also had at times a great many of the snow-bird with us, but he is rather larger than the one we have in the north, so we must have been near icebergs, though we have not seen one.

I am now in the 8th volume of Alison. It is beautifully written, and being, as he is, a clergyman, or the son of one, one has no right to object to the religious view he takes of these convulsions; but he goes very much into detail as to the military movements of all the armies, and finding him not very correct in our own details, has staggered me a little as to the movements of other armies. For instance, he makes the troops from Cadiz go to Lisbon by sea, and so join Lord Hill, whereas we know we marched up, and only just in time. Again, in the retreat, he excepts the Guards and Light Division from the misconduct of the army at large, but then he words it, "The Guards that landed at Corunna," leading you to suppose there were no other Guards with the army,—the fact being that of the four battalions with the army, the one that landed at Corunna was by no means the best on that particular occasion, being, as we know, all raw young soldiers, who never did, nor ever will do, so well in distress as the older soldiers do. Then, again, he is very fond of generalising events, and in a note, in which he records the different charges of cavalry that gained victories for Napoleon, he goes on to state, "and a charge of light cavalry at Waterloo hurled him to St. Helena," as if that charge of Vivian with a few horse, after we had taken the position, had anything to do with gaining the battle. Then again, he more than once, describing the great advantage that Napoleon got from his flank and turning march at Ulm, and again of Ney's corps at Bautzen, hauls in as a parallel case what he calls Blucher's flank march from Wavre on the 18th, it being notorious that no man came from Wavre, that the corps that came up to us was General Bulow's from the rear, and, moreover, that they never turned the French flank at all, for we had beat the French before they had got

[1] His groom.

over the Dyle. These inaccuracies in a historian of our own country lays his book open to be doubted as to the detailed movements of other armies.

10th May.—The island of Bintang in sight. This island forms the beginning of the Straits of Sincapore, and is about fifty miles distant from that place.

We had a capital run from the Cape to Java Head, the entrance of Sunda Straits, having sailed from the Cape on the 22d of March and made Java Head the 28th of April; but since that we have had calms and currents and all sorts of delays, so we were obliged to stop at an island in the Straits of Banca, called Nanka, where we took in water, which kept us a day and part of the next. This island, although not inhabited, is frequented by the natives for fish. . . . Cunynghame and others went on shore. He shot a very fine pigeon, they say a scarce bird even in India; it was excellent eating. The island is a complete jungle, into which they could not get fifty yards; but they saw wild hogs and parrots on it, and brought off some of the most beautiful flowers I ever saw. They got some fish from a native boat, but they were bad before they got on board, the heat was so great. Since that we have been moving along, until we have reached where this is dated from.

We nearly got on shore twice in the Straits of Banca, but the Captain let his anchor go in time, and by sounding round with the boats we got clear of the danger. We can hardly get to Sincapore to-day, but I hope when we do, to hear from some of you, although I very much fear my letters, being directed to the army in China, may have been sent forward. I shall add no more to this till we get in.

13th May.—We anchored here yesterday evening, and the Captain went on shore, and I sent Arthur with him. The Governor, an excellent fellow, insisted upon our taking up our quarters with him, not in his own house as to sleeping, for he has some officer with him who is sick, so we are put up in a very nice house about 100 yards from them for sleeping, and we dine, etc., with his Excellency. He is a Mr. Bonham, well known in the East for his hospitality and kindness to all people coming here.

The heat from the time we entered Sunda Straits has been very great, and I have suffered a little from it, but our doctor has given me some quinine for these last two or three days, and I am beginning to get better, and a day or two more will quite set me right again. I have not weighed yet since I landed, and I only did that three hours back, under a salute (the custom here, so they gave me eleven guns when I left the ship, and the same number from the battery when I landed), but still when I do weigh I am certain that the perspiration which has run off me ever since we reached Java, will have taken off all the extra beef I had laid on before. Here it is quite cool and comfortable, and rather pleasant to us in a large cool room after such a voyage as we have had, for we have been 152 days getting here, and yet the "Thalia," which did not go to Rio, and the "North Star," that sailed before us from England, and ten days before us from the Cape, only got here two days before we did.

We had only one heavy squall near Rio, and the gale I mentioned in this letter, and all the rest has been beautifully fine weather. Neither of our missing ships has as yet turned up. I suspect after we parted they did not go so far to the east as we did before we steered north. We went as far as 105° east in 39° south latitude before we turned north, and we consequently got the trade wind strong and went on merrily to Java Head. Now if they went to the north in longitude 90° or so, they probably had no trade at all, or at least very light wind, and that has kept them back; however, they will probably be here in a day.

Many thanks for your letters, of which I have found here Nos. 2 and 3 from you and Mr. Dick, but both your Nos. 1 have failed. I suspect they are gone on, and I shall find them at Hong-Kong, where we go to from this. I am glad you like Bath, and you seem to be comfortably put up. I shall send this on Sunday by a ship going to Calcutta, and shall leave a letter here for Mr. Dick, to go by the first opportunity that occurs. All well, not a sick man on board, and Grant, Arthur, and Campbell send their best regards; and believe me, my dear Charles, with best love to Mr. Dick, yours very truly, SALTOUN.

LXVIII.

Belleisle, at Sea, 22d May 1842.

MY DEAR JULIA,—It is not your turn for a letter, but still, as I wrote the last along shore one to Charles, I send this one to you, as probably what I may have to send from Hong-Kong may be more in his line, as there at least, I think, we must hear something, so I proceed to detail to you what happens from time to time as we go on, having in my last sent you the account of how kindly and civilly the Governor at Sincapore, Mr. Bonham, behaved to us all, which, as you now know, would have been added to his, Charles', letter, but for the alarm that came of the post going, which obliged me to cut his letter short.[1]

We sailed from Sincapore on the 17th, and just as we began to weigh our anchor our two missing ships, the "Apollo" and "Sapphire," came in sight. Our Captain went on board the "Apollo," and they are all well in both ships; and after we parted they steered north too soon, and lost all the fine wind we had, which made them so much behind us. They are to follow us as soon as they get their water and provisions. In the meantime we have picked up another consort, as they call it at sea, a Peterhead ship, the "Flower of Ugie." She has got on board the followers, as they are called, for the 98th, and is going with us to Hong-Kong. The Captain came on board yesterday, and seems a decent sort of man. He has 317 of these people on board for the 98th and artillery, consisting of cooks, hospital men, barbers, bearers, etc., which are always attached to all European regiments in India, so you see we shall be ready for the field as soon as we arrive, and I am happy to say our horses go on beautifully, and after a day or two took to the new forage we laid in for them at Sincapore, called gram, just as if they had been used to it all their lives. We had very light winds for the first three days, but on the 20th, that being just five months since we left Plymouth, a breeze came from the S.-W., and to-day, being just off the Gulf of Siam, it blows strong; and they think we have now got the regular monsoon, and therefore that we shall make a good passage.

The guitar has met with an accident. On Thursday last as I was fiddling with Grant the glue of the bridge gave, and it came away at once. We have got some glue calculated to hold in this climate, so we have glued it on again, and it is now hanging up to dry, and we will try how it holds to-morrow. It will then have had three days, and I will write again, my dear Mr. Dick, after trying it.

Saturday, 28th.—I am sorry to say, my dear Mr. Dick, that on stringing the guitar, as soon as I tuned it to a very low D, away the bridge came again, and on examining it we found the glue was not half dry, so we had nothing for it but to do it all over again, and I shall give it ten days or a fortnight this time before I try it. The fact is, that although this climate is very hot, and we have plenty of

---

[1] From this it appears that one or two letters written at Sincapore have been lost.

wind, yet it is so damp that hardly anything is really dry. Knives, razors, and all articles in steel or iron, including keys, unless in daily use, rust immediately, and even the leather in the inside of dressing-cases and writing-boxes, unless constantly wiped, is covered with a sort of mildew, and this sort of climate will of course prevent the glue drying so soon as it does at home.

We have been going on well since I wrote, having had fair winds with occasional calms, and to-day we are in the channel which runs between the Paracels and the Macclesfield Banks (it is laid down in your chart), and we are therefore about 400 miles from Hong-Kong, our present destination, though I do not expect that we are likely to be kept there, at least for more than a day or two, and that will depend upon whether we land the women there or not. We have had one child die since we sailed, but then we have had three born, so we have not diminished in numbers in that respect.

I heard at Sincapore that our great man, Sir Henry Pottinger, was at Hong-Kong. If so, I hope we may stop for a day that I may make acquaintance with him; but if he is gone on, the sooner we follow the better. We must lay in some stores there, for, strange to say, I hear we can get no tea more to the north, and I have not laid in any of that as yet.

We have now entered upon our sixth month, and if we get fairly landed, and *au pied de guerre* before it is out, we may think ourselves in luck; and after all we have not made so bad a passage, for the day before yesterday we overtook the "North Star" frigate that sailed some days before us from Plymouth, did not go to Rio as we did, and had sailed from the Cape before we got there. I should not wonder if we beat her in after all. We sailed up to the "Thalia" also, and several ships that left Sincapore before we did; but we have lost them all again to-day, as they all stood more out, I conclude to go round these banks that we are going through, and therefore so much more out of their way. No more now, my dear Mr. Dick, so good-bye for the present.

2d June.—After passing between the Paracels and Macclesfield, we found the wind from the north-east; in short, that that monsoon had not ceased in these parts. Under these circumstances nothing but steam can go on from Hong-Kong, so we are not so much behind-hand as we might have been. This wind being dead against us, we have been beating ever since; and on the 31st at daylight we made what we took to be the Great Ladrone, but when we got nearer to it, finding none of the bearings agree when we had taken our observation at twelve o'clock, we found we had been set by the current far to the westward, and that the land was part of China to the west of Macao. The next morning, that is yesterday, at daylight we made the Great Ladrone, and about ten o'clock a pilot came on board,—a good-looking Chinese, at least an intelligent-looking man, who has since proved that he knows his business well. Under his directions we have been beating to windward ever since; tacking ship whenever he told us. About dark we got inside the Ladrone island, and at eight o'clock this morning we were about fifteen miles from Hong-Kong; but what between the wind and current, which are both against us, we do not make in our line above five miles in four hours, so it will be dark before we can anchor in Hong-Kong to-night, but they say when once there it is easy to go into the bay.

Ever since we have come in sight of land the sea has been covered with Chinese fishing-boats, which, with their mat sails, look very picturesque. They are in every direction, and they work in pairs, having a net between each two boats, but as yet we have not had any communication with them; indeed, it blows rather fresh and a sort of sea on. In the meantime they (the boats) and the various-shaped rocky islands we are sailing through look very pretty, but they would not look the worse if we had a good dish of fish for dinner. Our friend the pilot's boat is known to them, and he says if an opportunity offers he will board one of them.

We have been now for two days in sight of land, but as yet no one has detected a single tree of any kind. Such a contrast with the last land we saw, where you could see no open spot whatever,—all trees and jungle, and trees of a very large size growing as it were out of the sea, and from that to the tops of the highest hills. Captain Little, of the Madras Artillery, who is on board, and has been here before, tells me that fuel is the article they are worst off for, as the only sort they have is a sort of stunted fir they grow for that purpose. I have not as yet strung the guitar, and now I think I will let it stay till we sail from Hong-Kong, which ought to give the glue a fair chance. So good-bye, my dear Mr. Dick, for the present.

2d June, at Night.—We anchored here this evening a little before dark, and find that a mail is to start early to-morrow morning for Bombay, so I have no time for any more. At this moment they brought me my letters, and I have received Charles' and yours, No. 1, which you will hear from Sincapore I had not received there, so now all is right as far as it goes. The only news is that they have a report here that a small party of our people up in the north have been beat, and Lieutenant Tomlinson killed; but after all it may not be true. This is the only letter I have time to write by this mail, and you may get it before those from Sincapore; so as it is the latest, send word to my mother that you have heard. If the mail is kept I will write to her. So, with love to Aunt Anne and Charles, believe me, my dear Julia, yours affectionately, S——.

LXIX.

Hong-Kong, 4th June 1842.

MY DEAR CHARLES,—I had begun a letter to Mr. Dick on our passage from Sincapore, and on our anchoring here on the night of the 2d, we heard that a mail was to sail that night, and so I finished it and sent it at once. However, it seems another mail is to sail on Monday, so it is just possible that you may get this letter as soon as the other. On getting here, as I expected, I found your letter No. 1, as well as Mr. Dick's, . . . and now, pray, as I had not read these letters before I sent my last off, thank Mr. Dick 10,000 times for me for all the trouble she took about my music, and I have no doubt it is all packed and put away in the most careful manner.

On landing yesterday I went of course to call on Sir H. Pottinger. He seems a quiet, sensible, strong-minded man, quite used to the business he has to transact. He went very much into detail with me as to the actual state of things here; and it is impossible to say what effect this great display of force we are making may have when it comes to be known by the great Emperor, but as yet nothing whatever has been done in coming to a settlement, and in point of fact things are exactly in the same state they were in when he (Sir H. Pottinger) came here.

When we get up, which I suppose we shall do in ten days from this, Sir H. Gough will have an efficient force of from 8000 to 10,000 men, at least they say so here. Now whether he has the head to seize such a position, and maintain himself in it, as will really be felt by the said great man, remains to be proved. As yet anything that has been done has been a sort of marauding warfare, taking a town one day and giving it up the next, and so forth; but that is not the way to conquer a great and obstinate people. We must take and hold such a position as, by cutting their resources off, will be felt by those at the head of the Government. Such a position is to be found (I think) in the Yan-tse-Kan river, and we are certainly going there in the first instance. A steamer has come in from the north, and it seems they have sustained some severe loss. I do not know the particulars, but I am going now to dine with Sir Thomas Herbert, who is the senior naval man here, and I shall hear them there, and will add them to this to-morrow.

5th June.—It seems they attacked a town called Chapoo, and took it without loss. A quarter of this town was inhabited by Manchu Tartars, and this quarter they had not properly secured; and when the men had dispersed, these fellows attacked, and before they were beat we lost twenty men killed and seventy wounded; Lieut.-Col. Tomlinson, who commanded the troops, killed, as also Col. Mountain, the quartermaster-general, and a Captain, whose name I do not know, badly wounded. When these Tartars were beat they proceeded to kill themselves, their women and children, and our people had great difficulty in preventing the women from smothering their children in a little drain that ran through the town, about four inches deep. This must arise either from an idea that we murder everything that comes in our way, or from an edict of the Emperor condemning all these people to death if defeated by us. We have treated their wounded the same as our own, and we have sent back all prisoners in order to do away with the first notion; but I believe the Emperor has published some such edict.

This is a most singular place, for they tell me that last September it had not four houses, and now they have a street of nearly a mile and a half long: most of the houses finished and inhabited, good shops of every kind, a bazaar, and an excellent covered market-place, divided into a meat-market and excellent fish-market on one side of the main street through it, and a vegetable and fruit market on the other side, all kept clean and well. If this place becomes a British colony it will put an end to Macao, at least as long as they keep it a free port, or levy very low duties; but I understand Government do not seem inclined to make a colony of it, and therefore all grants of land, etc., are for the present suspended.

The garrison to be left here is one regiment [of] natives, about 400 of the 26th come out in the "Apollo," some Madras artillery, and some sappers. A wing of a native regiment is to be sent to reinforce Amoy, or rather an island off it, and these garrisons are sufficient to secure these places, and will show the Emperor that while we are very much increasing our field army, it is not done at the expense of weakening our depots; on the contrary, that they are increased in an equal ratio; and as it is well known that not a man or ship comes that is not reported to him, we having one of his spies in our employment here, it must make his Court think rather seriously about what we may be able to do with a large force, having done so much, and upset so much of his trade, with a very small one.

We expect to sail on Tuesday, and I shall be right glad of it, for the plan here seems to be to throw everything off their own shoulders on mine; I have a pretty broad pair as you know, and I have therefore authorised all I thought was for the good of the service, but as yet I can know little or nothing. I will write again from the north, so, with best love to Mr. Dick, believe me, my dear Charles, yours very truly, SALTOUN.

LXX.

Belleisle, at Sea, 9 June 1842.

MY DEAR JULIA,—It is your turn for a letter, and I now write you what I call another along shore letter, which will probably be the last of that description, as I conclude, before I finish this one, we shall have arrived at our destination and be in communication with the army, when our voyage may be considered as terminated; not but what I suspect we shall have a good deal of ship-work for some time yet, but most probably our present ship will draw too much water, so we most likely will be shifted out of her. Our two ships, the "Apollo" and "Sapphire," which reached Hong-Kong two days after us, would be complete in water and provision, and were to sail in this direction the day after us, but if we keep this fair wind they will not catch us before we get in.

Just after I had sent my letter to Charles to the senior officer's ship, we had a Chinese row in the boats near us, the funniest thing one ever saw. I will try to describe it. We had been surrounded all the morning with a crowd of boats with fruit and other things to sell, in such numbers that the Captain only allowed a certain number to come alongside; and how it happened I do not know, but from something unfair, I conclude, one boat had drawn upon itself the anger of three others, and the abuse went on in a furious war of words, and from not understanding one word of it I have no doubt we lost some excellent Billingsgate. I was sitting in the cabin with Cunynghame when the tones got so loud and angry that I said "this must come to a fight soon;" so we ran to the stern window to look out just as it began. First of all they began with what they had to sell, and the three attacking boats threw plums, pears, all sort of fruits, salt-fish, bread, and everything they had to sell, at the culprits' boat, who returned it at the three in the same manner. Next they threw all the wooden bowls, baskets, and what they held the fruit in, then china plates and basins and all their crockery, making the most infernal jabbering all the time that ever was heard. This ammunition being now expended on both sides, they took to the stones they carry for ballast. The attacked boat seemed to think this sort of missile rather serious, and five of them, men, took to the water and swam away, leaving on board two women, two children, and another man, who up to this time had been in the sort of shed cabin they have, giving out the things for the others to throw. The women and children made their appearance, and a volley of stones went at them. One woman and the two children took to the water at once, but the other stood a round or two; but seeing them prepared to board with their boat-hooks, which have a spike of three or four inches long at the end, she took to the sea also, just as they boarded, and just as the last man was coming out of the cabin, but they poked him back again with these hooks, and kept poking at him for some time, and I believe ran these spikes into him and wounded him severely. They then abandoned their conquest, took to their own boats, weighed their anchors, and went off. The crew of the defeated boat, who had been in the water all this time, got on board again, and so finished the battle of Hong-Kong. What is curious—there were at least fifty boats looking on all the time, who took no part in the row, except that they picked up one fellow who jumped into the sea and could not swim well. I never saw a more comical scene than the rage and gestures of these people when throwing away the whole of their property at each other.

The guitar is again a failure. I put the strings on yesterday, but the bridge went again, so we held a council of war on it, composed of Grant, Colby, an officer of the 98th, who is a great mechanic, and the ship carpenter. The glue was quite wet, and our opinion is that glue once melted will never dry in this climate, but is kept in a constant state of fusion, so we determined not to try any more till we come to a colder climate. Even the pieces of glue, which ought to be as hard as a stone, are all like India-rubber. I am certain, whenever the glue will hold, we shall make a good job of it, for, for the half minute it held, the tone from the strings was as good as ever.

I do not know if you have a chart of this sea we are in, but we are steering for the island of Formosa, and are about 200 miles from Hong-Kong. No more news to put in to-day, so good-bye, dear Mr. Dick, for the present.

13th.—We have not as yet reached Thusan, for the wind, which looked quite like the monsoon on Saturday, fell calm yesterday, and last night we had a great deal of thunder and lightning, and it is calm and thick fog to-day. Still we can see a little distance, and we are about five miles from the island on the chart called [Hainan ?], about eighty miles short of Thusan.

I got hold of another guitar in the ship. The Doctor of the 98th had one which he could not play on (I believe he does a little), but he lent it to me, and as soon as I had strung it and tuned it up, the bridge of that went also; so that was a second floorer. By the bye, my dear Mr. Dick, this guitar puts me in mind that I have never written to you about three little pieces of music, called *Les Murmures de Rhone*, by Frederick Bergmuller, one sheet each. They are published for guitar and violin, or guitar and violoncello. We have got the violin set, but Grant plays it all the same, and they are beautiful, and you would be able to play the guitar part in an hour. They are the prettiest things I have heard for a long time, and put one in mind of running water. I was told by the Doctor that lent me his guitar, that at Hong-Kong he saw guitars in a china shop constructed like ours. If so, these people have glue that will stand, and I shall get mine put right if we get to any quiet town, but I do not expect that for a time yet.

We are all most anxious to reach Thusan, as we shall probably get some orders there, but I only expect to be sent on to some rendezvous further up the coast, and near the river called Yan-tze-Kan, where we shall find the advance of the army. I have no more to say now, dear Mr. Dick, but will add to this as we go on.

15th.—Last night we entered into the channel of the group of the Thusan Islands—in many maps spelt Chusan, but I believe the T is the right way. We anchored at dark, and had a night of rain, thunder, and lightning. This morning we got under weigh again, and are progressing but very slowly.

The islands on each side—for the channel is very narrow—are very beautiful; a great want of wood, however, but still they are cultivated in all directions up to the very tops of the hills, and the whole line of shore covered with houses, or rather the huts, of the people. At the same time the sea is covered with fishers' boats, but none have come to us to sell anything. It would almost seem as if the men fished, from the number of boats they have, and the women cultivated the ground,—not that I know this to be the case.

We have still a long way to go before we get to the island of Thusan itself, as we are just now passing Gough's Island, named by us after Sir Hugh, and from that we steer to Roundabout Island; so that even if we got a fine breeze we shall not get in to-night, for it is now two o'clock, and we have still some thirty or forty miles to go. The day is fine, not by any means very hot, and the whole scene very pretty. The "Rattlesnake," which has been here all the war, is ahead of us and shows us the way, and the "Apollo" has just caught us up with a nice breeze. She sailed a day after us from Hong-Kong, but then we have anchored two nights, being, as we were, so near the coast, which she from her distance did not do, and that makes us even as to time.

Whether I shall have an opportunity of sending this from Thusan I do not as yet know, but if I have I will do so, adding what news we get there. My belief is that we shall go on immediately to the Yan-tze-Kan river, but we shall know more about that when we get to the island, which now I should say will be to-morrow morning.

I am quite well, which I was not in the great heats, but this cooler climate has set me quite right again. In the hot climate I drank no wine, but plenty of bitter ale by the doctor's advice, and it agreed very well with me; but I have now come to my sherry as usual, and one comfort is that our Selzer water has kept perfectly, and is as good now as when we started.

17th, Harbour of Thusan.—We anchored here about half an hour ago, and are lying in the outward harbour near the little island of Just-in-the-way. We are to remain here till to-morrow at noon, when the tide will serve, and we are to have the "Venus" steamer to go with us.

Captain Grey commands here at present. He came on board and gave me a letter from Sir Hugh Gough. Grey is a hunting friend of mine, as I have met him out in Berwickshire, and he is a very nice fellow, a son of Earl Grey's.

Gough's letter is a very nice one, telling me what he is going to do, and wishing me to come to him as soon as I can; so, as we could not go any sooner than to-morrow, I lose no time here. The whole sail from the time we entered these straits has been very pretty, and the quantity of cultivation extraordinary.

The Chinese are beginning to be more civil; they have constantly when they could kidnapped our people; but when we took Chapoo we made several prisoners that we used well, and sent them back, and I understand they, the other day, sent in sixteen of these kidnapped people, whom they have treated very well, and they do say that the mandarins have written to kidnap no more. However, I for one shall not trust them, for I intend going on shore after dinner, but I take my arms with me, and will add what sort of a place the town looks like.

We have here a French frigate, sent of course by their Government to see how we are getting on in these parts. They are of necessity very polite and civil, but then we have ships enough here to blow them out of the water, and Johnny Crapeau is always very civil under these circumstances.

We should not have got in here so soon, but the "Cumberland" steamboat was sent to us last night, and she took us in tow at daylight this morning, and saved us three or four hours in getting up. No more till to-morrow.

17th June.—We anchored about one o'clock, and after dinner went on shore. It is well worth seeing. The town is a large one, the streets about wide enough for three people to walk abreast; the houses of one story, and low for that; the streets, if you may so call them, not straight, but turning round, as Charles may remember at Seville; the Joss-house worth seeing, and in a good state of preservation: on entering, facing you is a jolly-looking god in bronze, or painted so; on the left hand two very gigantic figures, one of a man and the other a woman, having nothing emblematic; on the right is a god with a drawn sword, and next to him one playing a guitar. These figures are made of delf or terra cotta, and painted. Behind the jolly god is what we should call the altar, with several figures on it, but all either brass or painted to look like it. This they told me was a Bhuddist temple, but the curious thing is, that all this should be so well kept in a country that has no religion of its own, or rather none ordered by the State. We walked about for two hours, and saw all worth seeing. The commanding officer was a relative of Mrs. Oliphant, wife of the brother of the man that Charles knows at the Madrigals, his name Lieut.-Col. Craigie, and he showed us where the town was taken, and all the rest of it; in short, I walked myself tired, and slept like a top.

I shall leave this letter here to go to England by the first opportunity, and will put one on the stocks for Charles. I have a very nice and civil letter from Sir H. Gough wishing me to join him as soon as I can, and we are to sail in an hour or so, having the "Venus" steamer to go with us to tow us over any narrow or bad ground we may meet with; in four days or thereabout we shall be in the Yan-tze-Kan river. So now, with love to Charles, believe me, my dear Julia, yours affectionately, S——.

LXXI.

Belleisle, off the Amherst Rock, outside the Bar of the Yan-Tze-Kan, 19th June 1842.

MY DEAR CHARLES,—I left letter No. 10 to Mr. Dick with the naval commanding officer at Chusan, or Thusan, for they spell it both ways, and we sailed from that place on the afternoon of the 17th. I do not know if you have the charts of these seas, but they are published, and you will probably find them at some of the reading-rooms; they are the surveys by Captain Bethune. We went out of Thusan by what is called the Blackwall passage, from a small island of that name, and anchored at dark. Yesterday we passed the rock called Gunstatt, again anchored at dark, and came this morning to this place, called by us Amherst Rock; but in the chart only mentioned as "rocks, a few feet above water."

Here we found a brig of war at anchor; she had no orders for us, but as the "Childers" went up yesterday, we shall probably get our orders this afternoon. They heard here heavy firing on the 16th in the direction of Woosung, and they suppose the place was carried that day, so we may now be said to be up with the army, as they can get us in a tide if they want us for any purpose, and most likely we shall join them to-morrow, being exactly six months since we sailed from Plymouth, and the same day of the week also. Yesterday, the 18th, the 98th gave a dinner in honour of the day, and we drank the Queen, and the Duke, and your humble servant, in due form, and I told them in reply that I was happy to find we were in time for this business, and although I did not wish them quite so much fighting, I had no doubt we should be equally successful in gaining our ultimate object for our country.

The fog is so thick now that, even if we had our orders, we could not stir till it clears. Indeed, ever since we have been in these seas we have had a great deal of thick weather, which, as it hides the sun, makes the climate very pleasant, and I sleep under a sheet and counterpane at night. Indeed, it is even betting that yesterday was hotter in London than with us. Our thermometer for the last week has ranged from 72° to 75°; to-day it is at 74°; and I remember last year when I was at Stockbridge for the "May Fly" it was never less than 75°, and sometimes higher, but we must expect it to be much hotter at times as the summer gets on.

21st June.—Going over the bar of the Yan-tze-Kan river, having been six months and one day since we sailed from Plymouth. We remained at anchor, the weather being thick fog, and yesterday Captain Collinson of the "Plover," who is here surveying, came to take us in—a clever sharp fellow, and they say an excellent officer. He is the son of a clergyman somewhere near Newcastle.

The affair at Woosung was entirely a naval one. The water was deep enough to allow the ships to get within 400 yards of the batteries, and as the landing for troops was very bad, they were not to land except in case of necessity. The ships took their stations on the 16th, and after a sharp cannonade of about two hours, drove the enemy from their works, and landed from their own boats on the batteries at once. The fire was a sharp one, the Admiral's ship, the "Cornwallis," firing 900 rounds to her own share. The Chinese stood pretty firm for a time, and returned a better fire than they had done on former occasions. Our loss was twenty-five killed and wounded. The only officer I have heard of is a lieutenant of marines killed.

This Woosung is a very poor place—of no importance but for its military position, completely commanding the channel of the river, so we were obliged to take it. The Admiral and the General the next day went up the river Woosung to a large town, Chang-Hai, or some name like that, which is a place of importance as a city, but which we hear they have abandoned.

If I get in early this afternoon, and the authorities are still there, I shall go up in the "Venus" steamer that is with us, to report myself to Sir Hugh Gough. Captain Collinson, who is now piloting us, as soon as we get in will go up the river Yan-tze-Kan to buoy the channel, after which we shall proceed up. If he meets with batteries that must be taken, he will return, and we go on; and so we intend to proceed till we get to the position we are to occupy; but of that I will write further as we proceed.

Our receiving letters here is, I understand, very uncertain; they get well enough from England to Sincapore, but then it depends upon when they get an opportunity to be sent on to Hong-Kong, and also from that place for another to come on here. The consequence is, that we sometimes get two or three mails together. So you must not be surprised if your letters are not acknowledged as regularly as they would be in a civilised country. The last mail we have from England is the March one, and the April mail had not reached Hong-Kong when Sir Henry Pottinger, who passed us yesterday in a steamer, left that place, which he did on Sunday the 12th.

23d June.—Yesterday a steamer went up the river to the town of Shanghai, where the General and Admiral had gone. This steamer was sent for Sir H. Pottinger, and I went up in it with our Captain; they took our boat up, and we returned in it in the afternoon. The Admiral had gone some miles higher up the river, but was to return at night, and when we came back the whole force had orders to return here, as to-day, unless something new occurred. I reported myself to Sir H. Gough, who is looking uncommonly well, but I believe as yet nothing is settled as to our proceedings.

After taking this place, Woosung, the ships went up the river to Shanghai with half the troops; the other half, with four guns, marched, and a very severe march it was. They had a battery of fifty guns about four miles below the town, which they fired as the ships passed, and immediately ran away. The marching column found no resistance; but when our force was about four miles from the town it was abandoned by the authorities and better classes, and forthwith pillaged by the lower orders, and pretty regularly sacked before the troops reached it. This seems to be the regular practice, and these wags always begin by plundering the pawnbrokers' shops, on the principle, I suppose, of getting their own things back first of all. I walked over great part of the town, and I saw no plundering amongst the men, but the followers as usual were actively engaged in it.

The town is a large one, has a wall round it, and large suburbs extending on each side along the river bank, and is a place of very considerable trade and riches, most of which they say was embarked in junks and sent out of reach up the river and canals. The back streets were much the same as those at Tinghay, but the principal streets were not much narrower than the generality of the streets at Cadiz.

This sort of passive resistance is the most extraordinary way of making war that ever was, and no one can guess when it will end. Since Sir H. Pottinger came out last year we have taken Amoy, Chusan, Chinghai at the mouth of the Ningpo river, the town of Ningpo, where they wintered, and were abundantly supplied with everything. This summer we have taken Chapoo, and where we are now, and yet no sort of communication has taken place between him and any Chinese person in authority. The only thing is that, after we have taken any of these places, an order comes out in the *Pekin Gazette*, ordering the General and his army to drive the red-haired barbarians into the sea, which they obey by giving up the next place attacked without hardly firing a shot for it.

I am going on shore this forenoon to look at the batteries the ships carried the other day. We have still about 2500 men to come up, and I conclude we shall stay here till they join us. In the meantime the surveyors are examining the river Yan-tze-Kan, which, in my opinion, we must go up, and establish ourselves in some position which will bring the matter to a climax, or at all events give us entire military possession of all the south and richest part of China, and having by so doing cut off their means of sending their effects to the north, we can levy contributions at our leisure.

I have just come back from seeing the batteries. The fire of our ships knocked them about a good deal; but they had a square tower, which they had faced with piles and split bamboo, in a sort of stockade, about four feet from the wall; this they had filled up with loose bricks and stones, and rubbish of all sorts, and the guns had made no sort of impression upon it. No shot that I examined had penetrated above two or two and a half feet.

A party of our boys went out shooting, but did not find much. One of them shot a hen pheasant, and we had it for dinner, and a very good bird it was.

24th.—This morning I went on board the Admiral. He seems a fine sailor-like fellow, and very civil.

I believe it is now settled that we are to go straight up the river to the place where the Grand Canal crosses it. They say it is the strongest place in this country, and the garrison Tartars; so we shall see what sort of a hand they make of it. The last Tartars they met with, when they found they were cut off and could not get away, cut their own throats. If these fellows take to the same plan, they may save us some trouble; for from what I see by the maps we ought to be able to invest the place on all sides.

I calculate it will take ten days to go up the river, so my next letter will probably be from that place. As yet we get nothing from the shore, for as soon as we land the natives run away up the country; but they tell me after three or four days they get bolder, and then bring things for sale—pigs, butter, etc., and all very good and reasonable.

I believe we could with the greatest ease revolutionise the country, for it seems the day before we went up to the town here, the people rose on the Mandarins and soldiers, and drove them out of the place with some loss; but this is not the plan our Government is going upon. They want peace, and expenses paid, and I do not think they will get either in a hurry. We could go to Pekin with great ease, but we should be no better off there than here; for the Emperor would go into Tartary, where he is said to be gone already, and we should have nearly four hundred miles of communication to keep up, which we could not do. The Pei-Ho river is rendered impassable, and therefore we cannot presume to stay at that distance from our base and supplies. We may, however, do something that way after we are well established on this river, but it can hardly be done this year; for the ships cannot stay in the Yellow Sea after a certain time. Best love to Mr. Dick, and believe me, my dear Charles, yours very truly,

SALTOUN.

LXXII.

Belleisle, Woosung Harbour, 3d July 1842.

MY DEAR JULIA,—On the 26th of last month I sent from this place a letter, No. 11, to Charles, and I brought up all that had occurred to us to that time, and since that we have remained quietly in this harbour, while Captain Collinson and some small ships and steamers are gone up the river in order to find and mark out the channel for our larger ships, and therefore, my dear Mr. Dick, I have very little to write about. I have been on shore two or three times for a walk, and we have established a sort of intercourse with the natives by means of a Chinaman that Major Malcolm has sent me as a sort of servant and interpreter. His name is Atang—at least it sounds like that; and he is a very handy and expert fellow, and he has a friend with him—for they will not come alone—but his friend has no English, though he speaks a little Portuguese. When we landed, the natives all ran away up the country by twenties and fifties, but at last one stopped to speak to Atang, and so we got a parley with them; but our man did not speak the language of this part of the country. However, we went into a house and got pen and paper, and as the written language is the same all over China, and every one of them can read and write, we soon came to an understanding, and they got us fowls and ducks, but they said the cattle were driven far up the country. We paid for these things, but I am sorry to say that is not the general custom, for the boats from the transports and other ships land and plunder them in a manner that ought to be prevented, and if it was, we should have had a good market long before this.

This army was divided the other day into three brigades, and I have the right brigade, consisting of the 26th and 98th British, the Bengalee regiment, and the flank companies of the 41st Madras regiment—in all, about 2200 men, with very few sick; and I was not a day in command before I had, as usual, a bother. There is here a Lieutenant-Colonel Montgomery, of the Madras artillery, and Sir H. Gough has made him a Brigadier. Now he is seven years junior to Campbell, who has accordingly complained, and I have been obliged to forward his grievance to the General. As yet I have had no answer.

Our post here is very badly managed, at least for us who only write to England. We have no post-office here, and our letters go by some ship or another till they get to Sincapore. From that, if a ship goes to Bombay, they go all safe to England, but if they are sent from Sincapore to Calcutta, we are by no means certain that they will be sent across to Bombay, as they are not paid; and the hard case is, that we have no place that we can pay for them here; and I mention this in case you should miss any of them, for this letter will go by a friend of our Captain's who is going to Sincapore and will pay for it there, so I hope it will get safe.

I dined the other day with the Admiral. We had the Plenipotentiary, the General, a French captain of a man-of-war that is here seeing what we do, and several captains of the navy—a pleasant party, and the Admiral an agreeable man about sixty, and he gave us a very fair dinner.

We expect the April mail from England every day, and I hope it will come before the ship sails that will take this. So, dear Mr. Dick, good-bye for the present.

7th July.—After all, the ship I intended this to go by was kept to embark the brass guns we took here on board of her, and as yesterday morning the signal was made to sail, I have taken this up the river with us. We are told off into five divisions, and sail as thus :—1st, the Admiral, with the Army headquarters, including Engineers and Sappers ; 2d, in order of sailing, my brigade, under the charge of the "Belleisle," eleven sail; 3d. General Schoedde's brigade, in charge of the "Blonde"; 4th. General Bartley's brigade, under the "Endymion"; and 5th, Lieutenant-Colonel Montgomery, the Artillery, with the powder ships, etc., under charge of the "Dido." We made yesterday about twenty-six miles, and then, the tide running out, got on shore, but we got off during the night, and are just getting under weigh again now. The Admiral also got aground yesterday, but got off as we did.

The answer about Campbell has come. Montgomery gets no rank or command by his being made Brigadier of Artillery, only as head of a department it gives him more pay, so all parties are satisfied.

I was right about the post, for an order came out stating that letters going across India must be paid to go overland; so I have written to a Mr. Johnston, from whom I got about £100 worth of things at Sincapore, making him my agent, with directions to pay and forward my letters overland, so in future they will go under cover to him at Sincapore, but we get your letters direct, as you pay for them in England as far as Calcutta, and we get them free from that, so send yours as heretofore.

The river is too wide here to make anything out on shore, except with a glass, and we have about 100 miles to go before we get to where the Great Canal crosses, which we now think will be our place to begin at. *Nous verrons*, no more now.

10th July.—Here we are at anchor, and I suppose we shall stay here to-day. We have got as far up as he had gone in the "Conway," if you should happen to see a chart of Captain Bethune's survey, without meeting much difficulty; that is, we are about sixty miles higher up than Woosung, and our steamers and surveyors are gone higher up to see if they can find a passage for us, and I conclude they will send some report down to-night. Curious enough that we now are sailing up this river in China to take their ancient capital, with as little knowledge of what the river is before us as our ancestors, or partly so at least, the old Norsemen, had of the river Seine when they sailed up it to attack Paris. The current of the river is very strong, which looks as if we should find plenty of water; for we have now got as high as the tides go, or nearly so, and the current to-day, when we tried it, was four knots and a half an hour; but then, at this time of the year, we have a right to expect strong winds and fair ones.

As yet we have not been able to do anything with the guitar, for the weather is still hot, about 80°, and next month they say it will be hotter still. We examined the glue the other day, and it is still quite soft. Much of this effect is, I think, produced by the damp that comes with this heat, which is very great, and penetrates everywhere; even into the writing-box you gave me, which looks very close, and besides has a cover to it, but in two days the whole of the leather inside is covered with a sort of white mildew; still the men remain very healthy as yet, and as we have been in this hot damp climate for now two months it cannot be unhealthy. I am afraid we shall find that the hot weather in August and September will be worse, after that again it begins to get very cold in these parts, and last winter was as severe as in England; they had the ground covered with snow for six weeks.

The Artillery were moved just before we sailed from Woosung into another ship, and I have now on board only the 98th. This gives them more room, and I am now getting them in proper order to land whenever the time comes for that purpose; and if the enemy make a stand at the mouth of the Great Canal, we shall be at work in a few days; but the interpreters and people who know, or are supposed to know these people, differ much in opinion upon this point. We got some bullocks yesterday, which is a great thing for our men, who have only had fresh meat about twenty days since we left England, now six months and a half. I have no more news now, my dear Mr. Dick, so this must stand still for the present.

18th July.—We reached this place three days ago. It has no name, but it is about an hundred miles up the river, and about fifteen miles below where the

Great Canal crosses it. They had a small battery here, but they only fired a shot or two from it, and then ran away. The Admiral's people landed, and burned it and the barrack. The weather for these last three days quite calm, with a very hot sun, and the thermometer never less than 92°, day or night.

We are anchored near some curiously-shaped rocky hills, of considerable extent, standing out into this flat country in a very odd manner, so as almost to give you the idea that they have been here from the beginning, and the low country has been formed by alluvial deposits. I went on shore yesterday in the evening, and walked up to the top of one of them, and saw the view all up the river. These heights keep along it on the right bank, but the other is the same low flat country that the rest of these parts are, and, as far as the eye can reach intersected with canals of all sizes and large lakes of water. Indeed, I believe the whole of the country between this and the Whang-Ho river to be of this description.

We have no communication with the shore, and get nothing from it, and are beginning to be rather badly off. We still have some sheep, for I laid in ten at the Cape, but our potatoes are done, and we have no sort of vegetable—only some pickles.

Our steamers are up at the canal, and they report that the town there, Chinkiang-foo, where we expected resistance, has been abandoned by the troops and all. If so, we shall push on for Nankin as soon as possible, and perhaps find the same there. What the end of this passive resistance may be is very difficult to say, for we must, and shortly too, devise some means of supplying ourselves, for 12,000 men and upwards cannot live upon air; but we shall find little difficulty in that. No more now, dear Julia. I will add to this when we move.

19th July.—We sailed this morning to get up the river, and had a steamer to tow us—the Admiral, in the "Cornwallis," having gone up this morning; but the wind is so scant round one point that the sailing ships cannot make it out. We have done capitally, and now, at near dark, we are anchored near the Admiral, and close to the Golden Island, which is very pretty, and has on it an old palace of the former Emperor of China, who lived here when Nankin was the capital. The Admiral has landed a party of marines to see that no harm is done to anything, and we have hoisted Old England's flag on the top pagoda of the old palace.

20th.—The Admiral sent me word this morning that he was going in a steamer up the river, and would take me with him, and we were to return to dine with him; so I went up, and a very nice trip we had. We went up about sixteen miles, and are just come back. About three o'clock the wind came fair, and all our fleet that were left below are come up and anchored here. The town is full of troops, and they have a camp of them about six miles up the country. The orders are to land to-morrow at day-light, so I shall write that history to Charles. So, with love to him, believe me, my dear Julia, yours affectionately,

S——.

LXXIII.

Kian-Kong, near where the Tartar camp was, and about
two miles from the city of Chin-kiang-foo,
26th July 1842.

MY DEAR CHARLES,—The order came out on the 20th to land the next morning at day-light. Two brigades, mine and General Bartley's, above the town, and General Schoedde's below it. My orders were to attack and carry the Tartar camp, and to make certain, Sir H. Gough intended me to have a battalion more added to my brigade, instead of which I had one and a half less. I landed at day-light, and found, of my brigade, the 98th, the two companies of Madras 41st Regiment, and two companies Bengal volunteers (two others joined me afterwards); and three three-pounders under Major Anstruther, and as there was no chance of getting any more, I set to work at once. I had to march from five to six miles over a low hilly country, with very difficult and bad bottoms to get over, from marshy ground, but as I and my staff were mounted, by riding forward we found a passage, although frequently so narrow as to be obliged to cross rank entire. The artillery found a more practicable road to the right.

After marching about three hours I got to about 900 yards from them, and halted there to close up the column. They immediately opened upon us with their gingals, which carry well that distance, but they did us no harm. They fired them in salvos, and shouted and roared after each discharge. They were well posted—about 1600 men—on a rising ground, the front covered by one of these marshy bottoms, a high hill on their left, which circled round so as to take us in flank and nearly in the rear. This was occupied by rather a strong body of men, and on their right flank they occupied some houses in front. After resting the men, for it was very hot, I moved to within 300 yards of them—about the range of my three-pounders. Here I saw the two companies of the Bengal coming up in the rear, and I sent them at once against the right flank. The other two companies of the Bengal I sent against their left flank on the hill; the Light Company of the 98th against the front, backed by that regiment and the two companies of the 41st Madras—the guns covering the attack. They stood a few shots from the flank parties, but before the guns had fired six rounds (and they were admirably managed by Major Anstruther), and long before we got within reach of them, they broke and dispersed in the greatest confusion, and scampered away over the hills in their rear, and we saw no more of them, I having only three men of the Bengal wounded; but the sun was the worst enemy, for thirteen men of the 98th died on the ground from the heat. I went into a village in the bottom in rear of the camp, where I cantoned my men, and am there now, very comfortable. My Light Companies killed about fifty Tartars.

The town was a worse business. They got in easy enough, but the Tartars fought in the houses, and before we got it we had five or six officers killed and wounded, and about 140 men. Here also two officers died of the heat—Lieutenant-Colonel Trevor of the 6th Madras, and Major Uniack of the marines. The blue-jackets got peppered here. The boats of the "Blonde" went up the canal that runs round the town, and got so severely handled that they were obliged to abandon their boats with the guns in them, and run for it, having lost from 20 to 25 men, but we got the boats again.

So ended the taking of Chin-kiang-foo, said to be the strongest city in China, and what between soldiers, sailors, transport men, and the lower order of Chinese, it has been burned and plundered in a way that those even who saw Badajos and Sebastian can hardly form an idea of. All the rich and principal people had left the town, and the Tartars, when they found they were beat, set fire to their own houses, cut the throats of the women and children, and then killed themselves. Sir H. Gough suffered from the heat, and is gone on board his ship. I conclude we shall stay here a day or two. General Schoedde, with his brigade, the 3d, is to be left here in charge, and I believe we are to quit the Belleisle and go up to Nankin in the ships that had his brigade. This puts me to much inconvenience in shifting baggage and stock, etc. etc.; but these are war chances, and must be made the best of.

You will hardly believe in England that the only three mounted officers with this army are myself, my Aide-de-Camp, and Brigade-Major, and the consequence is that no orders can be given, and all the evils arising from disjointed operations are severely felt. I am certain if orders could have been transmitted we should not have lost half the men we did here.

We are well provisioned from the ships, and we have plenty of vegetables. I am in a Joss-house, a square building, with a court in the middle. I have the Temple end open to the front, my servants the verandah, the 41st Madras the centre court, and their officers a place over the entrance opposite me. I have just succeeded in getting Colonel Trevor's servants, and they tell me they are very good ones, so for the future I shall be better off—a butler, cook, and three helpers. I am quite well, and have not suffered from the sun in the least; but if I had not been mounted I could not have done it. Poor Thomas was very bad the first day with the sun, but he is better now. As to old Shean, he stood it like a brick. Best love to Mr. Dick, and believe me, with love to Aunt Anne, my dear Charles, yours very truly, SALTOUN.

P.S.—We have no mail in as yet, and our last letters from England are the three we got at Sincapore of the 4th March, but they say the mail is in the river.

LXXIV.

Belleisle, off Chin-kiang-foo, 30th July 1842.

MY DEAR CHARLES,—You will by this mail get another letter with the account of our proceedings, and I certainly should not have written this, but the April mail from England came in last night, and our mail that was to have sailed to-day is detained on that account, so I take the opportunity of writing to thank you and Julia for your very kind letters of 2d April, and hers with several dates prior to that one.

Since I wrote you the account of our campaign I am sorry to say that a great deal of sickness has broken out amongst the men of the 98th. The length of time they had been on board on salt provisions, and the heat of the weather, 110° and 120° being common in the sun, made them lay into the raw vegetables, in spite of all that could be done. Several have died of cholera, and we have from 80 to 100 sick on board. Nor is it confined to them, for we have 60 sick out of the ship's crew, which is only 220 men. They have just sent to me about moving my sick, but the doctor says they are unfit to move at present, and moreover they are as likely to get well here as anywhere else, so I have declined moving them. The English doctors call it cholera, but I believe it is English cholera aggravated by the heat of the weather, and not that epidemic they call cholera in India, and the doctors of the India regiments bear me out in this opinion; but for all that men die very suddenly of it, and turn blue; however, I hope a day or two will set us to rights. I have had a little gout for these last three days, and a little diarrhœa also; but I think the one has counteracted the other, for to-day the gout is nearly gone, and the other quite.

I have many people waiting to see me, owing to some appointments made in consequence of our loss here, and as they affect my brigade I must go and see them, and finish this. With best love to Mr. Dick, believe me, my dear Charles, yours very truly, SALTOUN.

If you see my mother tell her I have received her letter by Captain Clarke Kennedy, whose father was in Dublin with me, and I know him well.

LXXV.

Belleisle, at anchor off Nankin, 6th August 1842.

MY DEAR JULIA,—As I wrote to Charles, I got all your letters safe by the April mail, for which many thanks, and long before you receive this you will have been in London and back again at Bath, and seen Antonetta and all the rest of it; and as Bath seems to agree pretty well with you, I conclude I shall find you there when I return.

As to ourselves, we came on board again on the 29th, and after dinner each day, for as long as we remained, I went and saw something in the cool of the evening. First I went to see Kian-Shan, or the Golden Island. It is the ancient residence of the Chinese Emperors, but it is now deserted and in ruins, except a part of it inhabited by some Buddhist priests, who have a large Joss and temple here. The view from the top of the pagoda is very fine, and it is 238 steps, and high ones too, to the top of it. They have here in the court a very large bronze vase on a marble-pedestal, finely engraved, and curious, not so much as a work of art, but that these people should at any time have been able to execute anything so substantial and lasting. They have also here a very fine library, which the Admiral very properly sealed up, so I did not see it; but they say it contains a curious work—"The History of the Conquest of this Country by these Manchu Tartars." This work has prints or drawings of all the battles, which it seems were done at Paris about 200 years ago, through the Jesuits, who had a great deal to say at that time in this country; and if you look about carefully, you see a good deal to prove that at some time Catholicism formed one of the religions of these people; to say nothing of the Buddhist priests using beads, though not put together in the same shape as the Catholic rosary.

We, as I have before told you, left a brigade at Chin-kiang-foo, and my two next evenings were employed in looking over the positions they occupy to hold that place. The next and last night, I went down to the island at the entrance of this reach of the river. I do not know its right name, but we call it "the Silver Island," in opposition to the other. It is much the most picturesque of the two, and has also its Joss and temple and priests. It is in much better preservation, better cultivated, and they have many flowers, and also several of the dwarf trees and plants this country is so famed for. It is a high rocky island, covered with trees, in which millions of white herons have made their habitation, and roost there at night, which gives a pretty effect to it. The next day, the 3d, we sailed on, and got here last night. We had a steamer to assist and tow us, so we have beat the fleet a good deal, and I do not expect them to get here before this evening, and most likely not till to-morrow.

When our two little surveyors, the "Plover" and "Starling," came up, the enemy "hung their banners on the outward wall," and made a very warlike show; but when the Admiral and our ship came in sight they abated their valour, and a flag of truce is now flying, and some sort of negotiation is going on between them and the Plenipotentiary, which at all events I hope may save the town from the inevitable fate which must follow if they defend it.

As to the poor 98th, they are done up for this campaign, and if I can get 200 of them into line it is as much as I expect. They left a company and also 100 sick at Chin-kiang-foo, and of those I brought on here we have buried two serjeants and 70 men; 44 are in hospital, and of the men who are not, many are in such a state that it would be madness to land them for work in this climate, for we are still between 87° and 92° thermometer in the shade, and in the sun it runs up 20° to 30° higher, and often much more. It is a sad thing for poor Campbell, for I never saw a man take such pains about his men as he did all the way out; so much so that to me, a Guardsman (and we take pretty good care of our men), it appeared almost preposterous; but my experience has proved to me that the more men are exposed the more you get to the front, the more they are petted the severer the blow when it hits them.

We are at anchor near the outward wall, which they say is thirty miles round. The city is about five miles further inland; so I can say no more now, my dear Mr. Dick, but will add to this as events turn up.

Camp near Nankin, 16th August.—We landed, my dear Mr. Dick, on the 11th—that is, my brigade did—at a place called Can-Si-Ming, and the artillery with me, and I marched on to this place, a large village, where we are cantoned, about one mile and a half from the wall. I have with me the 26th Regiment, 450; Bengal, 700; flank companies of the 2d Madras, 6th Madras, 41st Madras, 550; rifle company, Madras, 140; flank companies 55th British, 140, and sappers, 100—about 2100 men, with four three-pounders, four six-pounders Horse Artillery, four nine-pounders British, four twelve-pounders, and six howitzers 3½ inch, and rockets; and if this matter goes on, we are to attack the wall at a place about two miles from this, to which we have a good road, and we must carry it, I should think, with very little loss. In the meantime we are at a stand-still, as negotiations are going on, and the reports say favourably. The 98th are left at the place where we landed, to secure our communication with the ships. They have landed 350 men, as the shore will do them good, and in case we attack, I shall bring up their flank companies, made up to 200 men.

The inhabitants have all fled the country, and no wonder, from the way these Native troops plunder, particularly the Bengal, although I flog pretty freely with the Provost; but still the mischief is done, and provisions getting very scarce; and although we have two chief commissaries on board at £3000 a year each, neither of them has ever landed, nor has any step been taken to establish a market, or secure provisions for the troops, though nothing could be easier done; so we are obliged to get our rations from the ships, at a long and very fatiguing distance for the men of both services, for the boats have to bring them five or six miles to the landing-place, and we have to carry them about the same distance afterwards; but if we take this place we shall then be near the ships again.

We have no news here, but our remaining inactive proves something to be going on, and reports say the Commissioners here have agreed to our terms; but how that will be at Pekin remains to be proved. The reports go so far as to say that of the twenty-one millions of dollars required by us, they have twelve millions ready to pay down as soon as matters are in train. If this be true we shall most likely stay here a month longer while things are settling, and if everything was settled to-morrow, we could not go sooner; for although we can get out of this river, we cannot get out of these seas till the monsoon changes, and that never changes till the end of September.

I have not been well since I came on shore this time. I got a touch of the cholera the last time we were on shore, but I got rid of it before I landed this time; however it had set the stomach wrong, and I had a little fever the day after we came on shore, but I got hold of the Bengal doctor, a Dr. Grey, and I am a great deal better to-day, but I am not quite the right thing yet; however, I am to take no more medicine to-day, and see what comes of it to-morrow. The sickness has been very general, but except where it took an aggravated form, as it did with the 98th, it has not been very fatal.

I am going in the cool of the evening to have another look at the wall, that there may be no mistake if we are ordered to act; and as I have no more news now I must put this by, my dear Mr. Dick, till something turns up. So good-bye for the present.

19th.—Late last night I got an order from the General, with the extract of a letter from Sir H. Pottinger, in which he says that negotiations for peace have gone to that extent that he recommends, for the present, a total suspension of hostilities, and accordingly an order is given to that effect, that no plundering or foraging is to go on, and the people are to be treated as a friendly nation. This order has just come in time to be sure of being obeyed, for the people have all fled for six miles round, what plunder there was has all been taken, and nothing is to be got by foraging within any distance we can send out; but I conclude in a day or two we are likely to have a regular market.

I am getting better by degrees. I live very quietly, eat plain food, and drink about one-third of a bottle of port wine, sleep well, and, in short, could do anything in the shape of service, but still I am not quite the bold thunder. I suppose a mail will go soon, when I will finish this.

21st.—Just eight months and a day since we sailed from Plymouth, and not on that account, but as we heard last night that a mail was to sail on Tuesday, I sit down to finish this; not that I have much more to say than what has been already written in this, as things remain in the same state, and as yet nothing has been done in the way of market.

All the great Chinese authorities had tiffin yesterday on board the Admiral; and the only thing I heard was, that one Mandarin got opposite a bottle of cherry brandy, about which he said nothing, but drank the whole of it, and got as drunk as Chloe,—all the rest went well. To-morrow a return is to be given to our people on shore. I should like to see it, but I fear I shall not be able.

In the meantime all seem to agree in thinking that the Emperor will confirm the treaty; if not, he will have to come to harder terms, for we shall take this place to a certainty, and drive our steamers up to the Poyang lake, which will give us some thousand more miles of his country.

I sent Thomas on board yesterday for some snuff, and he came back at night and was taken ill. To-day it turns out to be ague, which is much going about; but the doctor says he has it very slightly.

Give my best love to Aunt Anne. I do not bother her with letters, as she will always hear of me through you and Charles, and the payment would be greater than any nonsense of mine is worth. I think it likely that you will not get this letter so soon as the next, as it goes by Calcutta. However, I send it to take its chance. So, with love to Charles, believe me, my dear Julia, yours affectionately, S——.

LXXVI.

Camp, near Nankin, 2d September 1842.

MY DEAR CHARLES,—The May and June mails have arrived from England, but as yet we have seen nothing of their contents, as far at least as the army is concerned.

On the 24th of last month, the peace having to a certain degree been settled, the Chinese authorities gave us an entertainment, at eleven o'clock A.M., at a Joss-house on shore, outside the wall; of these there were present Elipoo, the Chief Commissioner, Neukeen, a relation of the Emperor's, in the said Commission, Tzing, the Governor of the Provinces. These three wore plain dresses of fine China crape, and no arms; they had each of them a pale red coral button in their caps, and Elipoo and Neukeen wore peacocks' feathers. The Tartar General was not present, being unwell. On our side, as great men, we had the Plenipotentiary, the Admiral, and the General, and next came your humble servant. The officers who chose came regimentally dressed. They received us with a good deal of ceremony, and we marched through ranks of unarmed soldiers, with their bands making queer noises, to the Joss-house, where a table was laid with seats round the room, and they served tea, all sorts of cakes and sweetmeats, and a sort of wine, not bad in itself. They are three fine-looking old men, and conducted the whole thing with a good deal of dignity. I sat next to Elipoo, with an interpreter near, and through his means kept up a sort of conversation. After about an hour we took leave and returned to our ships. I dined in the "Blonde" and rode back to the camp.

It had been settled at this meeting that they were to sign the Treaty of Peace on board the "Cornwallis" on the following Saturday, but the next day they sent word that they wished to see Sir H. Pottinger in the city; he was accordingly provided with an escort of twenty picked men from the Horse Artillery, mounted on very fine Arab horses, and he went to the Viceroy's palace in the city for this purpose. He there saw a letter from the Emperor entirely approving of the treaty, of which they gave him a copy, and fixed to sign it on Monday, the 29th, on board the Admiral's ship, where we met at 12 o'clock on that day. In addition to the three who were at the former meeting, we had the Tartar General, a fine-looking old man, with white beard and moustache, dressed also in crape, and without arms; he wore a clear crystal button, having been degraded from his button for that Chin-kiang-foo job I had with him, but they had left him his peacock feather. There was also another great man who had commanded at Chusan, and had been degraded from his button, and wore a dull white one, but in consequence of his having been active in sending down fire-rafts against our ships in the Ningpo river, they had given him a peacock's feather. A very clever sharp-looking man was there also, dressed in yellow crape (the others all wore blue); he was the treasurer for the province, and he seemed to have a good deal to say to them. Four copies of the treaty were then sealed and signed by Pottinger on our part, and Neukeen, Elipoo, and Tzing on the part of the Emperor. This being done, the China flag was hoisted and saluted with twenty-one guns, and we drank the Emperor's and the Queen's health, and so forth. One copy of the treaty was sent to Pekin to be confirmed by the Emperor, and one to England; so you will know all about it before you get this, as this will go by the steamer to Bombay as soon as the confirmed treaty comes back from Pekin, which we expect on the 9th, and then we are to retire and leave the river, the first instalment being paid, which they say is ready. This being done, Sir H. Gough goes to Madras with half the force, leaving the other half under me as an army of occupation, having a brigade with artillery at Chusan, a garrison in Ching-Hai, another in Colansoo (which is Amoy), and head-quarters at Hong-Kong, where I am to have Greenwood's Artillery, the 18th Regiment and 98th Regiment—all British.

It is conjectured, by people who know these Chinese, that the Emperor, to get us out of Chusan, which commands the whole of his empire, will pay the money at once; if so, good! but, if not, I shall write to be relieved, as it never formed part of my bargain to stay here five years, which they give him to pay in, doing nothing: and as Hong-Kong is a very nice place, I should think they would have no difficulty in finding me a successor to the five thousand a year in a reasonable time.

I went yesterday with a largish party to see the famous Porcelain Tower; it is between eleven and twelve miles from this,—riding, as we had to do, outside the wall. We started about a quarter before five, with our followers carrying provisions, etc., and got there at twenty minutes before nine, and soon got an excellent breakfast; after that, we went up the tower. It is a building of eight stories high, and 200 very high steps, and the view from it in every direction very fine and extensive: you see the city of Nankin quite under you, and can make out where the Tartar city is divided from the other by a wall, which is always the case in these towns. A very large Joss-house is attached to the tower, and the whole built of brick, and in a very good state of preservation, and covered, the walls as well as the roofs, with a porcelain tile, like our Dutch tiles, but of various colours, which in the sun look very pretty and gay; in short, it is well worth seeing, and the ride to it from this is over a very pretty wild country in some parts, and cultivated in others. We passed close to the south gate of the city to get there, through a very large suburb, and the crowds of people to see us were something enormous, but not one single woman did I see amongst them. They brought us fowls, fish, vegetables, and fruits to purchase; so our cooks gave us an excellent dinner at three o'clock, and we rode home in the evening; in short, we made a very pleasant day of it, and I drank the Queen's health, as did all the rest of us, in a tumbler of champagne at 12 o'clock on the top of the tower.

This in the winter must be a very good sporting country; we have very fair snipe-shooting now; a fair gun can get from five to ten couple; but 57 years of age, and the thermometer in the shade at 86°, do not suit, so I have not tried it. A good many pheasants are found, and now and then a hare and some deer of the antelope kind have been seen, and as great part of the wild uncultivated ground is covered with a sort of brushwood, the shooting must be good when the cocks come in. The snipe, I think, is rather larger than ours, and does not fly quite so fast, but they are excellent eating. The best day I have heard of was, two officers of the artillery killed twenty-five couple of snipes and three pheasants.

In going over to the Porcelain Tower we crossed a clear burn of running water, the first thing of the kind I have seen in this country. It came out of the hills close by, and lost itself almost immediately in a marsh on our right hand, and if it had had a longer course I am certain it would have had trout in it, and I have no doubt in the more mountainous parts of the country they have plenty of them. The fish we have had here are a sort of tench, and also carp, a large fish like the grey mullet, a fish that eats very like pike, but I have not seen either pike or perch, eels also but not very large, and roach and dace. They also get a fish in the river that runs from eight to twelve pounds, and I hear it is a good fish, but I have not seen it as yet.

I see several flowers like those we have in England; the blue bell is exactly the same, but I think the colour rather darker. I also saw the other day, in two places, the Campanula magna; it certainly was darker in colour, but not near so fine a specimen as you had at the Hill. The groundsel and chickweed are the same as ours, but I have never seen a common daisy. The convolvulus is common; I have not seen the dandelion, but I saw the foxglove the other day.

I have seen no heather, nor cranberry, nor blaeberry; I am told they have the strawberry wild, but I have not as yet seen it growing, although I saw a dish of them at Hong-Kong.

The General came on shore the day before yesterday, and went to see the Porcelain Tower, where he met Sir H. Pottinger, who came there by the canal from the ships, and they returned on board with Sir Henry, the General having been taken ill, and his Adjutant-General and Quartermaster-General also. It certainly is a most unhealthy hole, but the sickness is not formidable, for, with the exception of the 98th, the men have not died of it; but every officer in the force on shore, except Captain Eady of the 98th, and Hope Grant, my Brigade-Major, has been more or less ill. The prevailing disorder is fever and ague, but it is odd that Campbell, and his Adjutant, who are martyrs to the ague, and I, who am somewhat that way inclined, have had none of it. I suppose the diarrhœa, which we all three had severely, kept all fever away.

Our horses that we got at the Cape are a great comfort, and I ride out most mornings, and every evening as soon as it gets cool, for an hour or two, but the days are getting very short now—quite dark at seven o'clock; and the worst is, the sun does not get cooler any earlier than it did when the twilight lasted till eight o'clock.

5th Sept.—I went this morning to see the burial-place of the ancient Emperors of China of the Ming dynasty, and it is the most curious thing I have as yet seen. It lies a little out of the road to the Porcelain Tower, and about half-way there. You approach it through an avenue of stone figures of colossal size, on each side of a grass road; first some lions, then camels, then elephants, then rhinoceros, then tigers, then horses, two pair of each of these, one couchant the other standing; then comes a high pillar of stone, then two pair of warriors, then judges or other civil functionaries, lastly priests; then three arches through a straight wall; then three bridges over a brook; opposite them three doors which enter the outward wall of the building; opposite the centre door one door having two stair cases on each side; and in the centre of this building (something of a pagoda shape), an enormous tortoise in stone supporting a stone pillar, which supports the roof (some think this is the tomb). Passing through this, at a distance of about sixty yards you enter a magnificent hall (seventy-five of my paces long by thirty-five wide), the roof very lofty, and supported by four rows of pillars at equal distances, eight pillars in each row. In the centre of this hall is a sanctum of some kind, which I am inclined to think is the tomb; beyond this again is a very wide paved road through what once had been a very fine garden, but now wild;—the whole of these buildings, from where you cross the three bridges to the end of the garden, being inclosed in a high brick wall, the length of the whole being about the third of a mile, and the breadth about an eighth. These Mings I believe reigned some two thousand, or so, years back, and it is certainly a very curious remnant of antiquity, second only to those found in Egypt.

I think now, my dear Charles, I have given you a very fair account of all here, if you have patience to decipher it. I shall close this letter now, and send it on board Sir H. Pottinger's ship, as from a report I heard to-day, although we do not expect to move till the 9th, we may move so suddenly that I might miss the opportunity of sending it; so, with best love to Mr Dick, believe me, my dear Charles, yours very truly,   SALTOUN.

This morning in riding out I saw the wild buckwheat, the same as in England.

P.S., 6th Sept.—I conclude our Rulers are satisfied with the state of things, as our retreat has begun. The 98th embarked yesterday morning. The six companies that came up from Chin-kiang-foo marched to embark this morning, and I sent my horses and heavy baggage I had on shore on board. To-morrow and Thursday the guns move to the coast and embark. The Bengal regiment embarks on Thursday, and on Friday the 41st Madras flank companies, and the Rifle company bring up the rear, and everything will be on board. I go on board to-morrow, and the "Belleisle" will then sail at once for the salt water, in hopes of that doing good to the 98th, as well as their own crew, who are very sickly.

As I must see our Plenipotentiary about certain matters he only can settle, I shall leave this with him to-morrow to go by the mail, as probably I shall have no means of writing or rather sending again till we get to Hong-Kong. As my means of giving dinners have gone on board I live on the public. I dined yesterday with the Bengals, and they gave an excellent dinner. To-day I dine with the 41st Madras, who I know live well. I have got quite well again, given up medicine and the doctor. Once more, with love to Mr. Dick and Aunt Anne, believe me, dear Charles, yours sincerely,   S——.

LXXVII.

Belleisle, off Nankin, 10th Sept. 1842.

MY DEAR JULIA,—I have written by this same mail a long letter to Charles, to which I must refer you for all our news in this quarter, and I expected that that letter would have sailed yesterday; but it seems that a letter had been received from Pekin stating that the ratified treaty cannot be down here till to-morrow morning, and accordingly the steamer is detained till it shall arrive, and they expect to sail to-morrow evening; so this just gives me time to thank you and Charles for your very kind letters by the May and June mails, both of which reached us here this morning, and our letters were given out about two hours ago, and I am happy to find, my dear Julia, that you and Charles get on so well at Bath, and that Charles got my letter from Rio; but by the book I find I did not write to *you* from that place, but I wrote to you from the Cape of Good Hope, which letter I trust you have long before this received, as I put it into the post-office at that place on the 21st of March, and paid for it, a thing required there. I have also by this mail heard from my mother, from Willy and Eleanor,[1] William, and many other friends, and I am quite delighted to find that May,[2] whom I had some doubts about, is thought so well of by Dr. Clarke.

Our sickness still continues on board this ship, and generally through the navy. The poor 98th have only eighty-six men fit for work, and in the men-of-war they have more than 600 men on the sick-list. I was sent on board in a great hurry, as they said that the ship was to sail as soon as I could embark, but I have now been on board three days, and I see no chance of sailing; indeed, to-day we are taking in provisions. I have got quite well, Grant has not been ill an hour, and Cunynghame has now got quite right again; but poor Campbell is still very ill with fever and ague, and Sir H. Gough the same, so much so as not to be able to see people, and Campbell has been in bed ever since I came on board; but the weather has got much cooler, and I expect all will rally now and get well.

All my people and guns I had on shore are re-embarked, and we are now quite ready to quit this as soon as the treaty comes down, and the first instalment of the money is paid, and most of it I hear has been received. My destination is

---

[1] His brother-in-law and sister, Mr. and Mrs. Grant Macdowall of Arndilly.

[2] His niece, Mr. and Mrs. Grant Macdowall's elder daughter.

Hong-Kong, to remain in command of the army left here, but I have written home to be relieved in case this thing is likely to last; so you are not to consider this as a regular letter to you, but only a chance one to acknowledge the receipt of yours, and I shall put a regular one on the stocks for you as soon as we begin to move down the river, as then things will be finally settled as far as peace is concerned. I have a letter from Aunt Anne which I will answer if possible by this opportunity, but we may weigh our anchor at any moment, and I have many letters to acknowledge: so no more from me just now, but, with love to Charles, believe me, my dear Julia, yours affectionately,   S——.

P.S.—I have just remembered to add that you may tell Gunthorpe[1] I have made many attempts to get acquainted with his nephew and I may succeed yet. When we were on shore last at Chin-kiang-foo I asked him several times to come and dine with us, but he was in General Schoedde's brigade, which was at some distance, and he could not make it out; he was left at that place, and did not come on here, but perhaps I may catch him on our way down.—Yours affectionately,   S——.

LXXVIII.

Belleisle, going down the Yan-tze-Kan River,
19th September 1842.

My dear Julia,—In my last hurried line, sent with the steamer that took the ratified treaty, I told you I would write you a letter on our way down the river; so here I shall give you an account of this very slow operation, as far as we have got in it.

We started on the 15th, the "Vixen" steamer being ordered to come with us, but she could not get her anchor up, so we went off by ourselves, leaving her to follow. All went on very well till about five o'clock, when we went aground just as the "Vixen" was coming up to us. She would not answer her helm, so she came against us, doing herself some harm but not much, in trying to go round us. The same thing took place again, and this time she did herself some damage, carrying away her jib-boom, but nothing to signify. At last she got anchored in a good position, but nothing could be done that night. The next day, with very hard work, we got a hawser to the steamer, and a cable on her cable, and began

[1] An old brother officer in the Grenadier Guards.

to try to haul off; the ship very soon got off; we slipped the cable, and trusted that the hawser would hold us on to the steamer, but it snapped at once, and the consequence was that we drifted bang into the "Belle Alliance" transport, and did her a great deal of damage. However, we got clear, and drifted away, leaving the steamer to assist the transport, and then come after us; and that night, the 16th, we anchored about two miles from Chin-kiang-foo.

On the 17th we started again, and just close [to] Kian-Shan or the Golden Island we got what they call here chow-chowed; that is, we got into one of the eddies of the stream, and were turned round and round, and the wind being light, no sail could get her clear; at last we went nicely into a nook of the island, our bow being aground in the mud, and the rest of the ship in from ten to twenty fathoms. Here we lay very snug, and as nothing could be done till the steamer came up, we took in the men of the 98th that had been left here as we went up. Just before dark, the steamer and all being ready to haul off the ship, she was floated off of her own accord by some rise of water which destroyed the chow-chow; we luckily went clear of the steamer and got into the main stream, and came to an anchor for the night. We got the steamer alongside yesterday morning, and came a long way down the river and anchored for the night; but this morning we are in a difficulty; we are not aground, but the channel is here so narrow, the wind being against us, that we cannot get the ship's head round, we are now getting an anchor out from her stern to the bank, to which we are quite close, to try and cant her head round that way. We have just got her head round, and going away down the river; so no more now, my dear Mr. Dick; I shall add to this as we go on.

25th September.—Here we are at Woosung, from which place I sent letter No. 11 to Charles, on our way up. We made, as you see, a very long business of it in coming down the river, for, as nothing had been prepared, we had to send our own boats before us to make out the channel, which in many places is very difficult. However, we only got aground once more, and that was on the 22d, but as it was near low-water the rising tide soon got us off again, and we came to anchor here yesterday afternoon.

It was very hard work for the men in their reduced state of numbers, but I hope that things will get better, for it is as bad now as can be. Our ship's crew is 240 men, and of those we have only 80 fit for work; and the 98th have lost about 160 dead. They have 100 sick men on board the "Belle Alliance"; and of the men they have here they have not above 60 fit for anything, and they expect to lose several more of the bad cases; Campbell is better, but can only crawl about; our captain is in his berth, as is also the captain of the "Vixen" steamer that brought us down; the ship doctor has only just got well, and the regimental surgeon is still in his bed; but the people in the ships here are all healthy, so I think our people will begin to recover also.

To-day Cunynghame and Grant, with Captain Seymour of the "Wanderer," are gone up to Shanghai, to see if they can get anything worth having. I did not go; it is a long way in a boat, and I was there when we were here last; and to-morrow I am to go on shore and dine with Sir Everard Home, the senior officer here, who has pitched a tent where he is to give us a dinner; and on Tuesday, if the wind remains fair, we expect to sail for Chusan, having the steamer with us over the bar as far as some rocks they call the Ariadne, from that steamer having found them out by getting on them, and being nearly lost there. We then go on to Chusan (but the steamer goes back to help others), where I conclude the whole of the fleet will rendezvous as fast as they can get down the river; but that will be a long business.

We know that the July mail has come out, for, as we were anchored off Round-tree Point, it passed us up the river in the "Memnon" steamer. The ship got her letters out, as they make up the naval letters by ships; but the army ones are all directed to the Adjutant-General, who is our postmaster. However, we shall get them at Chusan when the headquarter ship comes down there; in the meantime we have nothing for it but patience, a virtue much required in a service like this.

I see by the paper of the 2d June that Charles was presented by the Bull.[1]

We have also heard by a ship that has come from Sincapore that they had heard there that the Queen was again shot at on the 2d of July last, but that the pistol only flashed in the pan.

I am happy to say that as soon as the weather got dry I had the guitar glued again, and when we came on board this time I put on the strings, and it holds as well as ever, and the tone quite as good; so Grant and I pass an hour and a

[1] Nickname, among his brother officers, of Colonel Townshend, Grenadier Guards.

half every day now in that way; but my fingers were so sore at first that I could hardly keep them on the strings, for I had been more than three months without touching it; but they are getting quite hard again now.

I have no more to say now, my dear Julia, so I must put this away for the present.

2d October, Chusan.—On the 27th we sailed for this place, but just before dark got aground again on the bar. This was the worst scrape we had been in yet, for, if it had taken to blow, we might have been badly off; but it was fine all night. In the morning it blew a strong breeze, and having sounded and found water ahead of us, we set on a press of sail, and as the water rose a little and a sort of swell got up, after some bumps for about an hour, we forced over the shoal and got away, and anchored that night near the Rugged Islands; and the next day, the 29th, we came in here, and are now comfortable enough: the market good; plenty of fish and meat, fresh bread, and vegetables; so I trust our sick will mend rapidly. We have sent fifty of the 98th, and ten seamen, on board the "Minden," which is here fitted as a hospital ship, and this gives us a little more room.

I went on shore and walked all over the town, and all the shops are open, but very little, indeed nothing that I saw, worth having in the shape of curiosity. The senior officer here is Captain Hope of the "Thalia," and I am to dine with him to-morrow. We have also subscribed and are to get up a regatta for the boats, by way of some gaiety; for we shall most likely stay here till the fleet comes down, and about six of them have come in this forenoon.

The weather has got cool and pleasant enough, and we are all looking out anxiously for the "Marian" transport, our headquarter ship, as, when she comes, we most likely shall get our letters. I have no more news now, dear Mr. Dick, so good-bye for the present.

13th October.—Captain Justice of the "Pelican" offered to take me to see a curious place here—the island of Pootoo, or the Worshipping Island; in short, the Mecca of the Buddhist religion; and Captain Hope, the senior officer here, gave him leave to do so. But first we were to go over to Chin-Hai, which is at the mouth of the Ning-po river, with orders for the garrison to evacuate the place.

We accordingly sailed on Thursday last, got to Chin-Hai in about four hours, saw the place—a strong rock—where the garrison was, and then saw the town, dined on board and slept there that night, and, on getting under weigh the next morning, got aground, which was a fortunate circumstance for some Chinese, for their boat was upset, and all their countrymen left them to their fate, but followed the boat till it got on some rocks, and plundered it. Our boat was getting an anchor out, and saved the people; we gave them some rum and some tea, and sent them on shore. By this time we floated and sailed back to Chusan, but did not go in, having signalled and got leave to go on, and we proceeded and passed out by what is called the Surat-Galley passage, and at dark anchored for the night. The next morning we got under weigh, and about one o'clock came to an anchor near this famous island of Pootoo, and a most beautiful sail we had of it. We went on shore that afternoon, and saw the things worth seeing that were near, and at dark returned on board to dinner. The next day, Sunday, the Captain had prayers at ten, and after that we started for the day and went over a great part of the island. It is a very beautiful place, about twelve miles round. The inhabitants, with the exception of a few working-people, are all priests, and the island covered with Joss-houses, as we call them, or temples of different sizes and, I conclude, sanctity, and all dedicated to Buddha. It is, moreover, the only place in China that I have seen any wood in, and here it grows in many places as large as our fine trees in England, and what with the fine wood, the high points of rock, water in some places, and the pagoda tops of the Joss-houses, mixed with some cultivation, it contains some of the most beautiful views that ever were seen. We walked about the island all day, and wrote our names down at two of the very large Joss-houses, where they have books for the purpose, which have been kept for many years. We could not make much of the Chinese names, but there were English and other European names sixty or eighty years back, most likely of missionaries. At night we returned on board, sailed in the morning, and got back here to Chusan about four o'clock.

Nothing as yet come in from the river except the "Modeste" frigate, by which we hear the Admiral is at Woosung, and, I suppose, will wait till the next spring-tides to come over the bar; so as yet we have got none of our letters.

We have been very gay here with our regatta, the principal feature of which has been that a boat rowed by the 18th Regiment beat all the sailor boats, to the great delight of the said regiment, and the only news is that Mr. Shadwell of the

98th and Captain Wellesley of the navy had a very narrow escape of being kidnapped. They missed Wellesley, but got Shadwell down, tied his arms and legs, and began dragging him away; it was close to the town, and Wellesley alarmed the guard; just at this time Shadwell got one of his hands disengaged, drew a pistol and shot one of them, but not so as to drop him; this produced a sort of check, and the villagers ran out calling "mandarin," which so alarmed the kidnappers that they left Shadwell and ran away. These rascals are not supposed to belong to this place, but all these islands are more or less frequented by a set of ruffians, who live in their boats, and land and plunder whenever opportunity offers, and they no doubt expected a good ransom if they had got Shadwell away. It would have made a bit of a stir in London if the Duke of Wellington's nephew and the Vice-Chancellor's son had been carried off. I have no more to say for the present, so, my dear Mr. Dick, I must put this away till something turns up.

16th.—Yesterday evening the "Blonde" frigate came in from the Yan-tze-Kan river, and brought a box of letters for the 98th Regiment, and with them came Charles's letter of the 2d July, No. 7, and also your supplement to No. 7, by which I find you have received mine from the Cape, which ought to have come as soon as the others, for I went to the post-office myself on purpose to put them in, and paid for them all at the same time, so I conclude some sort of accident has delayed your letter No. 7, about which you took the same trouble; for I have not yet received it, nor any letter from any of my relations, although most of the papers (we never get them all) are come, and Cunynghame told me he had received your letter.

The "Blonde" also brought me my orders, which are to proceed to Hong-Kong and take command of the troops there; but as no orders are as yet come from the Admiral, we shall not sail till they do. I am to have at Hong-Kong about 1700 men, and I conclude about the same number will be left here under Major-General Schoedde, and after Sir H. Gough takes his departure, both forces will be under me, besides the garrison at Colansoo, which is the name of the post we hold near Amoy.

After church I am going on board the "Blonde," and I will then decide whether I will send this letter home by her, or take it on to Hong-Kong; she has got three million of the dollars on board, and will therefore probably sail for England direct in a very few days.

Our men, I am happy to say, begin to look better, and we have only had one death this last week. I hope Hong-Kong may agree with them; it is far from being a healthy place, particularly in the summer, but the sickness there is of a different nature from that which we have been visited with in the river we are just come from.

I agree with you about the "Bull" and myself in the Waterloo dinner picture; but the best of the two is the one by Knight, of the company in the drawing-room before dinner.

I was glad to see by Charles's letter that the Duke was so well on the 18th, but I heard by the mail before this from Lord Fitzroy, who said he had not known him so well for some years, and Dr. Hume gave a good account of him also in a letter of introduction he sent me by a private hand.

I have at last got hold of Captain Gunthorpe; he came and dined here the day before yesterday; he is quite well, and a very fine-looking young man.

No more now till after I have been on board the "Blonde." I shall send this letter by Sir Thomas Herbert, who goes to-morrow in the "Modeste," and will send it from Sincapore with his own letters, as he is ordered home with his ship, the "Blenheim," which is at Hong-Kong; this will be quicker than sending it either by the "Blonde" or the "Modeste" which go home with the money, and may be four or five months on the passage.

We are to sail to-morrow, if we can, for Hong-Kong, so my next letter will be from that place; and one advantage of being there is, that, at all events, we shall have our communication with home more direct.

I hear to-day that Sir H. Gough means to go with the rest of this army, in the first instance, to Sincapore, there to wait for instructions from India, and he will be very handy there if the Burmese are inclined to give trouble; but my opinion is, that whenever they hear that we have forced these Chinese to make peace, they will draw in their horns also.

I have just got a pony from Captain Hall of the artillery here, which, they say, is a very nice one, but I have not as yet seen him; he will be very useful in the scrambling sort of riding we shall have at Hong-Kong, much more so than a fine horse, and I hope to get him on board to-morrow morning before we sail.

A great lot of ships are just come in sight from the river, but neither the Admiral nor General is with them; they are under convoy of the "Childers" brig, and the "Columbine," another of the ships going home with money, is with them also.

Give my best love to Aunt Anne, and say how glad I was to hear by your letter she was so well. I wrote her a letter from Nankin, which I hope got safe to hand; it went by the "Auckland" steamer, which had Major Malcolm and the Treaty on board. I have written by this opportunity to Eleanor, and my brother, and also to Tudor, so if you see or hear of them you can tell them I have done so, if their letters should be lost, not that many are; and I have very little doubt but I shall get your letter, of which I have got the supplement, at last. So now good-bye, and with best love to Charles, believe me, my dear Julia, yours affectionately, SALTOUN.

LXXIX.

Hong-Kong, 31st October 1842.

MY DEAR CHARLES,—I wrote my last letter to Julia with an account of our proceedings down the river, and sent it from Chusan before we left that place. In that letter I mentioned that I had received yours from Bath of 2d July, as well as Mr. Dick's supplement to her letter; and on getting here I found her letter No. 7, to which the supplement referred. Pray thank her for me for it, and all the news it contained. I have also a letter from Aunt Anne, which I will answer the first opportunity.

On the 22d we sailed from Chusan, and, after a very fine-weather voyage, anchored here on the 29th, and I only heard this morning that the Admiral here, Sir Thomas Cochrane, was to send a steamer to-day to Calcutta, so I write these few lines as you may get them faster than by the regular mail.

I have not been on shore as yet, but I have secured a house, and Cunynghame went on shore yesterday and saw it, and thinks it a very good one; I am to pay 1000 dollars for furniture and fixtures, and 40 dollars a month rent. The plan here is, you engage a man, they call him a compradore, a major-domo in fact; he finds cook and helper, wine-cooler, table-decker, etc. etc., and these worthies cost about 60 dollars a month; so house and servants come to about 100 dollars a month. My pay may be put at 2000 dollars a month, and as I have received six months' pay, and have not as yet spent one, Cunynghame ought not to get me much into debt. Things here are what they call dear, but 1000 dollars a month ought to pay everything, house and all.

When Sir H. Gough and the rest of the army go away, which they will do in another month, Grant, who is now a Field Officer, and therefore cannot hold the Brigade Majorship, is to be made my Deputy, or rather my Assistant, Adjutant-General, which gives him much more pay; and I am going to make Mr. Haythorne of the 98th, by this time Captain Haythorne, my Brigade Major.[1] In England, as you know, the Horse Guards appoint the Brigade Majors, but in this country the officer commanding the Brigade does it—that is, he recommends, and the authorities confirm.

I have just seen the letters about Elphinstone in the *U. S. Journal*, and from my own personal knowledge they might have written even stronger. The fact is, poor fellow, his health was so bad it deprived him of all energy; and the political agents threw him regularly over, not intentionally, for they fell themselves by it, but from too much confidence in their power over the natives. I have seen his journal, written and signed by himself, to a few days before his death, and sent by him to the Secret Committee of army matters in India, and it quite puts the saddle on the right horse.

I am going to dine to-day with the Admiral quietly, and to-morrow I am to dine there to meet a party. Young Grant, whom you saw at Plymouth, is here in the Admiral's ship, and dined here yesterday, quite well, as you may tell his father if you chance to see him. There is also on board that ship a nephew of poor old Miller's[2] that I must be civil to if I get an opportunity.

We have heard of the August mail being at Sincapore, and I have seen a paper from that place, with date of the 4th of August, by which we have heard of the death of the Duke of Orleans. But this will make no difference to your French brother-in-law, as, if I remember right, he is now in the Royal household.

I must finish this for fear of being too late for this steamer, which sails about mid-day; so, with best love to Mr. Dick, believe me, my dear Charles, yours very truly, SALTOUN.

[1] Now Lieut.-Gen. Sir Edmund Haythorne, K.C.B.

[2] Lieut.-Col. Miller, 1st Guards, killed at Quatre-Bras, 1815.

LXXX.

Hong-Kong, 5th November 1842.

MY DEAR JULIA,—My letter of the 31st of last month, to Charles, left this yesterday by the "Bombay Castle," going first to Macao, and then to Bombay direct, and by it I sent all our news, as far as coming down here from Chusan went, and my having taken a house here, into which house we got the day before yesterday, and this is my first letter written from it; and as most ladies (I do not mean you in particular) are as curious about houses and dresses as about those who inhabit the one or wear the other, I must begin with giving you a regular description of our habitation.

The house stands on the top of a hill, of which it occupies the whole, looking over the sea and harbour, with a fine view of the opposite coast of China, distant about three miles in the narrowest part, and very mountainous and rocky; in short, a very fine view. The width of the house is about 30 yards, and its depth 25. The entrance is at the back, where the stables and kitchen and offices are in a sort of yard. One passes up some steps into a small entrance passage, from that into the dining-room, and through that to the drawing-room, which has a bay-window looking over the before-mentioned sea view; these rooms occupy the centre of the house. On each side of the drawing-room there is a good large bed-room, and smaller rooms on each side of the dining-room, and a small bath-room on each side of the entrance passage; I occupy the right-side rooms looking to the front, and Cunynghame and Grant the left, which rather crowds us at present. Grant has got a house about a hundred yards off, a little lower down the hill, but he does not get into it till the 1st December, and then we shall have more room, as at present we are very badly provided with places to put things away. Round the whole the roof projects about five yards, supported by pillars, with a walk under it made of a sort of stone preparation; so some part of it has always shade, and the sun is off the front face by half-past seven in the morning, and it makes a very cool walk all the day. The stable is within the offices, but I want that to make a room for our English servants to dine in, so I am going to put up a stable, and also a house for my guard, which at present is in a tent; and after this is done we shall be very comfortable, as far as room goes.

Our major-domo, a Bengal man called Haro, seems a very decent sort of man, his cook a very good one, and his wine-cooler perfectly understands his business —a great point in this hot place. We breakfast at eight, lunch at one, and dine at half-past six, and, not much liking to lead a hermit's life, we generally sit down eight or ten to dinner, and when we have drilled these black waiters a little more into our ways at table, the whole will be very respectable. Grant and I tried the room yesterday, and it is very good for music, so that will go on, I trust, prosperously, as the guitar stands quite well, and the tone as good as ever it was.

10th November.—I went yesterday over to the other side of the island to a place called Chuck-Choo, where I have barracks for about 250 men, a nice ride of about ten miles on a very scrambling road made over the hills, and it took us three hours to get there, and the same to come back.

This morning the August mail came in, and I have, my dear Mr. Dick, got your letter, beginning on the 6th July, also the music, which I will try the first opportunity. I have also got Charles's letter, one from Aunt Anne, also letters from my mother, Eleanor, Willy Macdowall, and my brother; but these letters have been a long time coming, as the north-east monsoon is quite against them all the way from Sincapore; and between this and Chusan it makes so great a difference, that whereas a ship comes from there in six days, it takes six weeks to go there, and this wind will now blow most likely till next June; but then our letters go home the faster, that is, if they happen to catch the steamer at Bombay; therefore, if this letter is in luck you may get it in February, but most likely not before March.

By that time you will know in England what they have settled to do with me, and I shall hear the same here, for I calculate that my orders will come out by the January mail from England; and you will be guided by that as to writing, for Lord Fitzroy will tell Charles what these orders are as far as my staying here is concerned. If I am ordered to stay here, of course you will write on; but if I am put off the staff, or ordered to be relieved, I shall proceed at once to Bombay, where I should hope to be by May. In that case you will write to me, " P. O. Bombay," by your March and April mails, and I should find your letters there in May, as they take just about a month to that place, and I am rather in hopes that the report of our Plenipotentiary will be so favourable as to matters in general, that they will not at home consider so large a force necessary here as I am at present left with, and very likely put me off the staff.

I daresay you were much amused by the China exhibition, but nothing whatever of China is known in England except Canton; and therefore, an exhibition of the same sort taken from Glasgow would give as good an idea of England as one from Canton does of China, for even the Canton language is not understood in the country we have been serving in; although from one end of China to the other they all write the same, and as all writing in China is done by symbols, and not by letters, they all understand what the symbol means, although the name of it is pronounced differently in the various dialects of the country.

This morning I had Kingcome's son, little Frederick, and the other Mids of the ship, to breakfast, and I have sent them up the hill, to come back to luncheon, after which I am going in a boat of the Admiral's to call on a Yankee commodore, Captain Kearney, who has come in here in his frigate, and called on me yesterday; and from that I am going to the upper end of the bay, to call on a Mr. Morgan, who manages here for the great opium house of Jardine and Co., and acts as my landlord. He lives at the upper end of the anchorage in a sort of palace he has there, and is a married man, although I have not as yet seen Mrs. Morgan.

This house of Jardine, they say, has made an immense fortune since the war began, by smuggling this poison into China in all directions, for the Chinese will have it; and as they do not trade in anything else, and receive payment in money only, they run very little risk, and are supposed to have realised an immense fortune. They have their vessels, beautiful sailing ones, called clippers, in all directions, and they are in concert with Chinese boats of an equally beautiful construction, who purchase the opium from them, and then smuggle it into the smaller waters; and, if all accounts are true, these Chinese smuggling boats, when not so employed, are little better than pirates, and plunder in all directions. But now that peace is made, and the Chinese war-junks may put to sea again with safety, they may perhaps be able to put some check upon these illegal proceedings. The best thing the Emperor could do would be to put a duty on this opium, for as they cannot prevent its getting into the country, they may as well get a good revenue from it as not; and as far as our people are concerned, they would far rather trade in it fairly than smuggle, and would make equal profit;

and it is an article of such profit to India that they cannot afford to give it up, —the land on which it is cultivated paying a very high rent to the Company.

11th.—I saw the American Captain, went over his ship, and had a glass of wine with him, and on coming away he fired a salute—all very grand; and the singular thing was, that he prided himself on having a farm in his own country, which had been in his family before the Revolution broke out, and he was collecting Chinese things to fit up a room there.

Mr. Morgan was not at home, but I saw Mrs. Morgan; she is a Bombay lady —a fat little woman, with pretty eyes, and in a way likely soon to increase the race of Morgans. From that we walked home, about two miles, as here, after four o'clock, the sun gets behind the high hill, and one can walk in shade all the way, which makes it very pleasant.

I have not been able yet to try the music, for Grant has had a good deal to do in writing and returns; but I have had a letter from Miss H——, sent out by Mr. Miller of the "Agincourt," a nephew of our poor Miller that was killed.

This mail is going to close almost immediately, so I must finish, and with love to Charles and Aunt Anne, believe me, my dear Julia, yours affectionately,

SALTOUN.

LXXXI.

Hong-Kong, 25th November 1842.

MY DEAR CHARLES,—On the 31st of last month I wrote to you, and on the 12th of the present one I sent a letter to Mr. Dick by the "Bombay Castle," and since that we have been going on very quietly here, and the ships that have the troops on board have been coming down from Chusan in small divisions at a time, and are now all here, except the ships having the horse artillery; they had landed their horses at Chusan, where they got good forage on shore, and it was no use bringing them down here; so they stop there till the orders come to return to India, when they will embark, and only touch here to take in water and provision. In the meantime the Vice-Admiral remains at Chusan, and, they say, will be there for another month.

Sir Henry Pottinger is visiting the ports where the consuls are to be [stationed], on his way down, and we have heard that Sir H. Gough went into Amoy last

Sunday, so we may expect him here every day, and the sooner he comes the better; for, besides plenty of ordinary business to do here, he has several cases for boards and general courts-martial, that no one here has authority to dispose of but himself.

I am just getting well of a touch of the gout, rather a sharp one, in the hand and wrist,—not that it has lasted longer than usual, but it was severe while I had it. On Monday last I tried to get to a height about two miles from this to the east, to see what sort of a place it was to put a barrack on, for the authorities here have disposed of every bit of ground fit for that purpose to private individuals. There is no road to the place, so I went scrambling on, sometimes getting round a point by riding through the sea, at others scrambling over the rocks. I tried to get round one point, but the water began to get deep; I did not care much about that, but the bottom, instead of being sand, got deep and muddy, so I gave that up, and, by way of being very prudent, led my horse up the rock, but in going down the other side my feet slipped from under me, and I came down a very heavy fall on my side, and hurt my left arm and wrist, but nothing to speak of. However, that coward the gout laid hold of it that very evening while sitting at dinner, and I am now, Friday, just getting well of it. I conclude the impurities of that rascally river are coming away in this fashion with me, for I escaped all fever and ague, which very few did, and of which a very great number have died. The 98th are still very bad: they have not more than 104 men fit for duty, including officers' servants and tailors; they must have buried now 300, and they have many yet in hospital not likely to recover: and when this sickness has passed away, as it will in this very fine climate that we have here at this time of the year, if they can muster 350 men I shall think them very lucky.

We have been employed these last ten days in landing the native troops to cook and wash, etc., while their ships were cleaning out, and I think by Tuesday that will be done, and those who formed the garrison of this place, and are now to go on to India, will be embarked, and as many of the garrison that is to remain, as I have cover for, landed, and the rest will remain on board the "Belleisle" and "Jupiter," which ships are to act as barracks till we can get these things built on shore.

We have no opportunity of sending letters just now, so I shall not finish this till I hear of one. In the meantime tell Mr. Dick, with my best love, that I have tried the music she sent, with Grant, and it goes remarkably well on the two instruments.

30th November.—The wind, which has been in the east for these three weeks, changed the day before yesterday to the north of north-east, and here I am writing to you in this latitude, sitting before a good fire of English coal; for no sooner did the wind change than it began to rain, and the thermometer fell to 51° or 52°. I have not as yet had a fire in my bedroom, though I have not for years in England got up in such cold weather without one; but it is a great point this cold weather, and sets all us English on our legs again.

If it did not rain so hard there would be some tolerable shooting on the other side of the bay, or rather strait, on the mainland of China, for they say this, which falls rain here, is snow in the upper country, and drives all the snipes down before it, and many of them come this length, but the woodcocks never come so far to the south, though they are so numerous about Ningpo and Chusan, where the army wintered last year, that many officers killed two at a shot, and one officer three.

Sir H. Gough came in here the day before yesterday, and has ordered a Court of Inquiry on the nature and causes of the sickness in the 98th Regiment, and after that, one on the sickness of the part of the 26th Regiment, who were very sickly, and lost a number of men at this place in the last hot season. I am President of the Court, and we met yesterday, and I never remember sitting for five hours in a colder place than the room we met in. I hope we shall finish the 98th to-day, but the 26th will take a day or two longer, as some reflections have been made about the want of discipline, or rather of proper restraint, that existed in this detachment of the regiment, which we are ordered to inquire into. The fact is, these recruits, who had never even been drilled, came out with me, 450 of them, and their officers were three subalterns who had never joined a regiment; they were left here in this state, when we went up to the north in June last, with one assistant surgeon: a great many of them died, and when we came down we found what were left of them all sick, under the care of this man who had done his best, but was himself very ill with fever and ague; however, they are now much recovered: under these circumstances I have no doubt every sort of irregularity was permitted, and probably very much increased the sickness.

But this is not the real cause of this inquiry. The fact is, a party here, with the Plenipotentiary at their head, all interested in this infant colony, wish to make Hong-Kong out to be the most healthy place in the world. On the other hand, those who have suffered call it the most unhealthy hole that ever was. I do not believe it to be either the one or the other; but this controversy has been the real cause of this inquiry. All places in the tropics are more or less unhealthy, but I should say, from the great change of climate between winter and summer, that this place is less unhealthy for Europeans than most other tropical places; we are in the same latitude as Calcutta, but the cold we have here now is perfectly unknown there, or in any part of India, unless you go up the country.

The September mail from England has not come yet, but we look for it every day, nor have I as yet heard of any opportunity of sending letters home, so this must wait for a time.

December 4th.—I have just heard that a clipper belonging to the house of Matheson and Morgan, the great opium people here, is going to Bombay direct, and that if I send letters to-day they will take them; so I send this as it will probably be in time for the February mail from Bombay, and you will get it the beginning of March, and I will write to Mr. Dick by the next opportunity.

The transports are still here, waiting till the General makes up his mind what to do with them; and Sir Henry Pottinger came in yesterday, and sent word he would land under a salute. The Artillery Officer did not know what number of guns he was entitled to, so sent to me; I knew nothing about it, so I wrote back that, provided he did not fire twenty-one, he might fire any number he liked. So he gave him nineteen, two more, I believe, than he ought, I understand to the horror of the Admiral, for in the Navy they have books to show these things, but they are not mentioned in our Regulations.

They have built a theatre here, which is to open on Wednesday, but who are to be the actors I have no idea,—I believe some amateurs from the Navy. Love to Aunt Anne and Mr. Dick, and believe me, my dear Charles, yours very truly,

SALTOUN.

LXXXII.

Hong-Kong, 8th December 1842.

MY DEAR JULIA,—I wrote to Charles by the last opportunity, and the letter went from this on the 4th by a clipper of Mr. Matheson's, the great opium merchant here, direct to Bombay, and ought to be in time to go home by the February mail from that place. No mail come in from England yet, though we look for it—the September mail—every day; but at this time of the year the north-east monsoon is very much against its coming, and it is impossible to reason with any regularity about the mails. I hope it will come in before the "Vixen" sails, which steamer will take this letter to Bombay, and is expected to sail in a few days now, in charge of part of the fleet returning to India, which she will convoy as far as Sincapore, and which will probably sail soon after Sir H. Gough's return from Macao, where he has gone for a few days to see his friends in that place, and go up to Canton; and also, I hear, to have his picture taken by a Chinese artist, who is said to be very clever at likenesses. We have here a very clever fellow in that line, a Captain Platt of the Bengal volunteers, who has been taking the whole of us; he intends to paint a picture representing the signing of the treaty of peace on board the "Cornwallis" at Nankin. He has made an excellent likeness of me sitting, with Cunynghame standing on the right and Grant on the left, and Campbell looking over my shoulder—all remarkably good likenesses, as indeed are all the rest of the people he has taken—the three Chinese Commissioners, the Plenipotentiary, the Admiral, Sir H. Gough, etc. This picture it is his intention to have printed in England, and we have all taken some copies. I have taken two proofs before letter, two after letter, as they are called, and two prints. One of the first I intend for Charles and you, and the other for my mother; one of the second for William, and the other for Willy Macdowall, and the two prints for any one. These are to be delivered at Cox and Co.'s; and when I write to them next month, sending the paper for my quarter's Guard allowance, I will say that if they are delivered before I return home (a thing not very likely), he is to send them to Charles, for, being your agents as well as mine, they will always know where to find you at all events. It will be a curious work, as representing the first treaty ever entered into by any nation on a system of equality with these celestial people.

Our weather just now is very pleasant—a little hot in the sun; but as the thermometer is never, during the day, higher than 62° (at this moment it is 59°), fires are very pleasant in the house, and riding or walking exercise can be taken at any time of the day. However, I find my Emily Pringle[1] leg, as I call the one that broke down dancing, rather troublesome, and it gets very painful after walking a couple of hours or so, I have therefore taken to the bandage again; I am inclined to think the relaxing nature of the hot weather in this country has produced this, and I am half inclined to try a sort of douche for it.

We have plenty to do here, and no time ought to be lost about it, for we have thousands and thousands of pounds' worth of stores lying about in the most insecure places possible. But nothing will be done till Sir H. Gough and his part of the army are gone, for while he is here people do not consider me as commanding, neither do I command, and I see clearly that nothing will be done till I am left to myself, when I shall at once submit to Sir H. Pottinger, the head of the Government here, the necessity of hiring from the merchants secure places for these stores, till buildings can be erected, and I do not anticipate any objections in that quarter; and everything I have had occasion to require from the Admiral here, Sir T. Cochrane, has been done at once, so I am in hopes that things will go on pretty smoothly. No more news now, so good-bye for the present, my dear Mr. Dick.

11th December.—No mail as yet come in, and they tell me last year it was the 15th before it arrived; and I fear when it does it will not bring any answer to my letters sent from Sincapore in May last, for I fear they did not get in by the mail received in England in August, and therefore all your letters will be written before you get them (which I trust you will) by the September mail, as I think you are obliged to close your letters before the letters arriving from India are delivered.

The music which you were so kind as to send is very well put together, and goes remarkably well with the violoncello; I thanked you for it in my letter to Charles, but I do it again here, as, though not likely, it is possible that a letter may miscarry.

They have had a row at Canton. It seems, in the highly civilised countries of France and China, that the students in both are an influential body, and at

[1] His dancing partner when the accident occurred.

Canton these students are adverse to the Peace, and have expressed themselves strongly against it in a proclamation which they issued in the Canton paper. They, moreover, got up a row, and at first got the better of the authorities, killed some people, and burnt one of the factories,—I hear the American one; but to-day, they say, the regular authorities have put them down, and very little mischief has been done. Sir Hugh Gough, who is over at Macao, sent me an order to have everything in immediate readiness to move in the event of the Plenipotentiary requiring it. They were all ready enough, as he well knew, for they were all on board ready to sail for India; and as to the Plenipotentiary, he could not in any way interfere, unless requested to do so by the Emperor from Pekin.

The Plenipotentiary and Admiral dined here two days back, and I am to dine with His Excellency to-morrow. They tell me he has a Chinese establishment, and I shall like to see what sort of a hand they make of a dinner; I shall be a better judge of that on Tuesday, and as, even if the mail comes in to-night or to-morrow, nothing will sail till after that, I will send you, my dear Mr. Dick, the result of how his dinner comes off. So no more now, as the horses are come, and I am going to take a ride for an hour or so before dinner.

13th December.—We had a very nice party yesterday at Sir Henry Pottinger's, and he gave us an excellent dinner, and the soup and fish, the only dressed things I eat, were very nice and clean, and spoke well for his China cook; we had besides a roast turkey. They have no turkeys in this country, but they have them at Manilla, and very fine ones after they have been fattened here; and Mrs. Morgan, a Bombay lady, the wife of Mr. Morgan who lives in this island, and either is a partner of, or employed to a very large extent by, the house of Jardine and Matheson, has these turkeys brought over regularly, and fattens them, and sent this one as a present to Sir Henry, who is an old acquaintance of her's, he having been employed in the Bombay Presidency during his service in India, before he was sent on this service. He, Sir Henry, has been a great deal employed in India in the diplomatic line, is a gentlemanlike pleasant man, and I have every reason to believe very well calculated for the situation he now fills here.

Amongst other things here we have what is called a Sheep Club; that is, a certain number of us subscribe, and sheep are brought from Bengal, and also from Sydney in Australia. We graze them here on the hill, and feed them with gram, which makes them very fat and good. The plan is this:—they kill a sheep for each four members, and at one killing you get a hind-quarter, and at the next a fore-quarter, so that all get their share regularly. It happened to be our turn for a hind-quarter, and as we dine to-day with the Admiral, and it would not have kept till to-morrow when I have a grand dinner, we sent it to Sir Henry; so you see the main-stays of his dinner were easily come at. He gave us an excellent dessert, and his wine is of the very best; and after dinner he brought out some of the curiosities he got when up in the north, and a very fine collection of them he has. To be sure in his situation he had more opportunities, and they brought him a number of things they never brought to us; besides, he has visited all the great towns since the peace in his way down, and so got a number of things that are only to be got in the north, and are never sent down here by any accident, and in point of fact are very much more curious than anything you can get either at Macao or Canton, where the principal curiosities consist of china and silk, and various things curiously cut out in ivory; and from long dealing with the English they have a very good notion how to charge for these articles. Our General, Sir Hugh, is still over there; he was to have been back here last Saturday, and every ship was quite ready to sail; but if he stays much longer they will have to fill up provisions and water again before they can start.

What stuff all this must be for you to read three months after it is written, but I have nothing else here to write about; however, my dear Mr. Dick, I will not inflict any more of it on you just now.

18th.—No mail yet in from England, but a ship came in yesterday from Sincapore, bringing good news from Cabul; but you will have heard all that months before you get this letter. The Admiral dined with me yesterday, and just as we were sitting down Sir H. Gough came in, having returned from Macao. Sir H. Pottinger goes over to Macao to-day, but is expected back by Christmas.

When we were up in the north the "Dido" frigate intercepted and took a post-office junk with a great quantity of letters in her; those that the interpreters made out to be directed to great people were opened to get intelligence, and I got three or four of them (the common ones), as curiosities, and I send you one of them for your museum; and certainly the nice way in which they are folded up, directed, and secured from being opened, show what care these people take in this sort of thing.

A ship came in yesterday from Chusan, and they have had a fall of snow there; but this has made no difference here, and our weather remains as fine, and the temperature just the same as it was before. To-day it is even a little warmer, being 64° in the shade, with little or no wind.

19th.—I am obliged to finish this in a hurry, for the "Vixen" is to sail to-night or to-morrow, and letters must go on board to-day. Everything quiet again at Canton, and I hear Pottinger has received a very satisfactory letter from the Viceroy. Sir H. Gough is to sail at daylight to-morrow, and has been here for an hour, and left me papers enough to read to last me all the evening, as he has not time to get them copied; so I must finish this. With love to Charles and Aunt Anne, believe me, my dear Julia, yours affectionately, SALTOUN.

LXXXIII.

Hong-Kong, 24th December 1842.

MY DEAR CHARLES,—Our mail, which we had been long looking for, came in at last this morning, and I have received yours of the 1st September from Bath, with a note from Julia in the same letter, of the 2d, as well as her other letter, which I will answer by this conveyance, as I shall have time to do so, I expect, before we get an opportunity for England.

By your letter I find you had not heard of the bad fall my mother got, and how much she was hurt. But I have had an account of it from herself, and also a letter from Margaret,[1] and one from William, by the same packet, in which, I am delighted to say, they report her quite well again, which is so far fortunate, as it prevents me from being over-anxious about the next mail, which I certainly should have been had I not heard she was so. But from her own account it was a bad cut on the head, to say nothing of the shake of a fall of that sort at her time of life.

This last mail has been three months and twenty days coming, but I hope we shall get the next in more reasonable time. I believe I have received all your letters, though you have not put numbers on them; at least I have received a letter from you by every mail. I am afraid you will not get mine so regularly, and several of them will come tumbling in at the same time, for we have more

[1] His unmarried sister residing with his mother.

opportunities of writing than you have, as we write by every ship that goes from this to any part of India; but then that is no security for them going to Bombay, and it is only when they reach that place that they are fairly started for England.

In my last to Mr. Dick I mentioned the Canton row, and everything has been quiet since, and the Emperor's proclamations are all very peaceable, and order the parties charged to settle the terms of trade to do so on a basis that may last long into the future; and the fact is, they suffered so much from the stoppage of all sort of trade and communication, that neither he nor his people, certainly not those in the north, would willingly get into another row with us. But the case is different at Canton. They have been in the habit of insulting us in every way for more than a century, and this last row was got up at the instigation of a man nearly 100 years old: moreover, Canton is likely to suffer in trade by the opening of the other ports; and as all this is our work, they are angry with us: besides, they have not had the good dressing that the towns in the north got.

The Admiral, Sir W. Parker, is still in the north, but we expect the "Memnon" steamer every day from there, and she will take the next letters to Bombay, to which place she goes direct. And we are also expecting the "Apollo," who is to take the supernumerary marines to England, and Captain Greenwood of the Artillery goes home in her for the recovery of his health, he came out with us in the "Belleisle," and has been very ill indeed, but is much better now. Our Admiral here is over at Macao, but is expected back in a day or two. Campbell is made my Commandant here, which gives him 150 rupees a month extra; and I have appointed Haythorne of the 98th, whom I wanted to make Brigade-Major, what they call here Resident Staff Officer, that gives him sixty rupees a month, and I have made him extra A.D.C., which saves him thirty rupees a month by his ceasing to be a permanent member of his mess: it is not so good a thing as Brigade-Major, but it is about £100 a year, which is always something.

I have now given you all our news, and although it is not yet Christmas, tomorrow will be so, I wish you a merry one, and many happy returns, and will, if I can, dine with you on the next. So, with best love to Mr. Dick, believe me, my dear Charles, yours very truly, SALTOUN.

LXXXIV.

Hong-Kong, 29th December 1842.

My dear Julia,—First of all I must wish you a merry Christmas, and many, many returns of them; and although months must pass before you receive this wish, you must think it as fresh as if I had come down to breakfast at the Hill, and made it.

Our long-expected mail, the September one from England, came in yesterday morning, and brought me your kind letter; as also the one with the music on the blue paper, which I have not had time to try over yet. I have also letters from my mother, and Margaret, William, and Eleanor. Neither Eleanor nor you seem to have heard of the bad fall my mother had; but as both Margaret and William report her perfectly recovered, I am now quite easy about it; although, at her time of life, to fall from a chest of drawers, and cut her head open with a wound two inches long, is no joke; but I think it runs in our blood not to suffer much from these sort of things, and soon to get over them. I know, my dear Mr. Dick, that you could not receive my letter from Sincapore in time to answer by the September mail, but I trust that you will have got it in that month; but of that I am by no means certain. It was, however, paid for at the post-office at Sincapore, and ought to have gone; but I am sorry to say, that letters sent from this army, where we had no office at which to pay them, have been stopped at Calcutta, notwithstanding the Government had notified they were to go free, which, to say the least of it, was a very shabby thing on the part of the Indian authorities; and as I hear other letters have been stopped, I fear some of mine may have been also.

I like your crying out about the heat. This is our cold season, but it has got warmer within this day or two; last night when I went to bed the thermometer outside of my window and looking north was at 70°, and when I got up this morning at 69°; we, however, have been much cooler than that, and shall be again, they tell me, next month. This being our winter, the sun, on the south of the line, is now 40° from us; but when the summer solstice comes in, he comes to our side of the line, and about the middle of the summer into the same parallel, and then we are all in the same scrape that the German student was in who sold himself to the devil,—that is, we have lost our shadows,—and it is very curious to us, who have always been used to see objects in nature throw shadows from them, to see that they have none when the sun is thus vertical; and things look to our eyes more odd than you can easily imagine.

The news I like least, that has come by this packet, is the change at the Horse Guards, because it was clearly understood between me and Lord Hill that I was not to be kept in this place; that is, that I was to be relieved or allowed to go home, things being quiet in this quarter; but this may not be acknowledged by the powers that come in, and I may be thrown over. However, I can know nothing till I hear in March next, so it's no use thinking; but I had made my mind up that I was to dine with you and Charles at Christmas 1843; so I shall only now still hope for the best, and that it may turn out so.

I mentioned in my letter to Charles that all was again quiet at Canton; and I hear that the Plenipotentiary has sent a letter to the merchants (the English ones), in which he gives them a rare dose of Goose—tells them distinctly that they or their people were the aggressors, as far as he has heard yet of the matter, and that, unless it is clearly proved to him that the Chinese began the row, he will not make any demand for compensation. I have not seen the letter, but I have heard this, and we shall have it in our paper next week, and you will probably see it in the London papers before you get this letter, for it may probably go by the "Vixen" steamer, which was still at Macao at that time, and which has got my last letter to you, begun on the 8th instant.

Talking of Goose, I have given my mamma a bit of advice, for I have written to her that, although it is generally admitted that ladies of a certain age may do as they like, still it is not either wise or prudent to go scrambling on the top of a chest of drawers, when you have a bell in the room that you can ring, and tell your maid to get what you want. The said bells are a dead letter in this country, for when you want anything you call out "Quy Hy," which in Hindostanee means Who is there? or, Who waits?—and then one of the black fellows comes, and you tell them to send such a servant, or to bring what you want, for our fellows understand the English for most things you are likely to call for. They are very willing, quiet, nice servants, but they have such a want of memory, or want of mind, that you can never get them to do exactly the same thing two days together, and you have no chance of having the dishes put in their proper places on the table. At first they put all the dinner on the table at once, soup, fish, meat, and all; by dint of worry we have got them to bring the soup first, then the fish, and then the meat course, but they have never yet, twice running, brought the fish right; they always bring the two fishes, but one day they forget the sauce, and the next day the potatoes. It is the custom here to take your black servant to wait on you at table when you go to dine; and the other day, at Pottinger's, I sent my fellow (who, by-the-by, is a very nice servant, called Achar) for some turkey, and when he brought it sent him for some ham; now he had seen me eat fowl and ham twenty times on the same plate, but turkeys are very scarce here, indeed the only ones they have come from Manilla; so he took away the turkey and brought me a slice of ham; when I explained to him it came all right: but some days after, dining with Major Cain, who is magistrate here, and a ham being on table, he remembered something about the ham, so brought me a slice of it with the roast beef. One advantage is, that, being Hindoos, they drink nothing but water, so drunkenness is unknown with us, and so far better than the Madras men we had up in the north, who being in India a lower race of people—and, as they expressed themselves, all the same caste as Massa—were fonder of drink than Massa himself.

You in your letter talk of writing stuff, but what stuff this is to send such a distance! However, one can only write what comes into one's head, and as it is impossible to put all that comes into one's head in the space of a letter, one writes what comes first; so, stuff as it is, it must go.

I am happy to say the 98th are getting better; they still bury some men, and have more yet who, the doctor fears, will not recover. But those who have got over the disease are recovering fast; and, as soon as the new barrack on the other side of the island, at a place called Chuck-Choo, is finished, there will be room there for 300 men, and I shall march them over there, as it is proved to be the most healthy part of the island.

Charles will tell you about Campbell, who is very well, and dines here to-day; for, having dined last Christmas-Day with them, I have a party of them to dine with me to-day.

I am glad to hear of the marriage of Wynyard's[1] daughter, but I have not heard of it from him; I got a letter from him which I see I answered from this place on the 4th of June last, in our way up to the north; but when he wrote

[1] General Wynyard, an old brother officer in the Grenadier Guards.

that letter he could not have known about it, and I have not heard from him since. It is so far fortunate that she is going to the same place that her brother has gone to; but it by no means follows they will meet much, for these Presidencies are very wide districts; for instance, the Bengal Army that went to Cabul marched in the whole 2170 miles. I have gone over about 30,000 miles to get here, and if this letter could go as the crow flies it would even then have somewhere about 8000 miles to go to you, I being one hundred and ten degrees to the east, and some thirty odd to the south, of any part of England that you can be in just now.

Our Admiral here returned from Macao yesterday, and I am to dine with him to-morrow. He sent the steamer "Proserpine" back for Sir Henry Pottinger, whom we expect back here to-day. Some letters that you will see in the papers passed between the merchants, Sir H. Gough, and Sir Henry Pottinger on the occasion of the late riot at Canton, which the papers here have taken up. Our paper, the Hong-Kong one, is in favour of Pottinger, and the *Canton Register*, as it is called, but published at Macao, on the side of the merchants; so they have got a very pretty matter to argue upon, which is a great thing for them in this place, where news is a very scarce article.

Yesterday, Grant, Cunynghame, and I dined with Mr. and Mrs. Morgan. The only other person was a Dr. Young from Macao, who is the first doctor there, and I presume is over here living in the house till Mrs. Morgan is confined, which, to all appearance, must soon take place. He was quite in favour of the merchants' side of the question, which did not please the lady, with whom Sir Henry Pottinger is an old acquaintance and a great favourite.

Aunt Anne will, after all, I think, pass some of the winter with you; for, if she is going to clean up her house, she must go somewhere during the time; and if she cannot pass all of it away in visits, she must pay for a lodging somewhere, and she may as well do that at Bath as anywhere else; so you will see her down there. I have not written to her as yet for this packet, as I wrote her on the 18th of last month, and that letter will most likely go by the same mail that this one will; so you can tell her that I send my love to her, and, as they say, all the compliments of the season.

I saw Miss A. Kemble in "Norma" just before I left England, and I liked her singing very well; and also Miss Rainforth, who had then made very great improvement. I daresay Miss Kemble will sing well in English, but when I saw her she took the Italian words for all the difficult parts.

The "Orestes" transport that we have been expecting for some time has just come in; she sailed from Gravesend on the 17th June, so she has been six months and some days getting here. She brings out recruits for the 18th and the 55th, which Regiments are here, at least they are in my command; and she has some men also for the 26th Regiment, who will have to be sent to Calcutta as that regiment has returned there. A Captain Butt, who belongs to the 57th Regiment, at present at Madras, has come out in command of them, and he has brought me a letter from Lord Brougham; so I must be as civil as I can to him while he remains here, as it may be some time before we can find him a passage to Madras, and this I should have been whether he had brought a letter or not.

31st.—I had just wafered my letter to Charles when a report was brought me that the "Memnon" was to be detained, but I am not certain of it. The Plenipotentiary wishes to keep her till after the next mail comes from England, and has written to our Admiral here to that effect. But then she has come down from the north with despatches from the Vice-Admiral who commands, with orders to proceed direct to Bombay; moreover, a ship came in yesterday with orders to the same effect. Now, as communication with the Vice-Admiral is quite impossible, and as the Rear-Admiral cannot know what store he may put on his despatches, I think he will hardly venture to supersede the Vice-Admiral's orders; but we shall know in the course of the day, and as the Captain of the "Memnon" steamer, as well as the Admiral, dine with me to-day, if it is settled that he is to sail to-morrow, this letter will be in time; if he is detained, it will only be the longer and more bother to read when you receive it.

As I expected I have just received word that the steamer is to sail to-morrow morning at nine o'clock, and the bag to be made up to-night at our post-office here. And as we are now so near the New Year, that this letter will start on it, I must wish you, my dear Mr. Dick, and also Charles, many happy returns of it, hoping not to have to do so another time till I have seen you, and perhaps wish you the next one in person. I was afraid at one time that we should not be able to get an almanac here, but I find they make a short one up at Macao, which I have sent for and got; but still I shall miss my pocket one much. Perhaps if you can find a light one you will take the trouble of sending it out to me. Perhaps, my dear Mr. Dick, you may have done so, for I know you like to have an almanac yourself, and are very thoughtful in these things.

Cunynghame, who is quite well, is going over to Macao in this steamer to see the place, and if he can find anything that we want, to bring it back with him. I am glad he is going, as he will see the nature of the place, and know exactly where I am to go, and what I am to do, when I make my trip over there, which I shall do shortly now, if I can, when Sir H. Pottinger is up at Canton, as more lions will be to be seen then in the Chinese line. And now having got through my paper, nearly my time, and said all I have got to say, give my love, and all good wishes to Aunt Anne, and with love also to Charles, believe me, my dear Julia, yours affectionately, SALTOUN.

LXXXV.

Hong-Kong, 8th January 1843.

MY DEAR CHARLES,—Our mail from England, the October one, has not as yet come in, but we have received all the general news by a mail that came yesterday from Calcutta, bringing with it papers from Bombay, coming across India with news from England of the 4th October; by which we know that Lord Wellesley is dead, and all general news of that sort. We also calculate that our English letters cannot be very far off, but most likely the ship they came in from Bombay had a long passage to Sincapore; however, they will come in a few days, and I care much more about them than any general news. That from India is very satisfactory about our prisoners in Affghanistan having got away; as also the falling back of our army into the Punjab, where they will be in a plentiful country for the winter; but all this you will hear long before you get this letter.

We have also heard by this mail that the steamer with the news of our peace here was at Aden on the 25th of October, and the one with the ratified treaty was at the same place on the 29th, so about the middle of November you heard of all these successes in the East; and as things have been settled in America, the ministers will be in clover, for all this will set the manufactories going again.

We are going on here in the same quiet jog-trot way; the health of the troops is very fair, and I am getting temporary barracks made to hold some of the men that are required for the duty of the place. I have got the Artillery and

Sappers in a barrack called Cantonment Hill; the wing of the 55th are at West Point and Chuck-Choo; this last place is on the other side of the island, about ten miles off, and they have 100 recruits just arrived on board ship; the 41st Madras Native Infantry will all be on shore in about a week in temporary barracks; the sick of the 98th are on shore, and about fifty of their duty men, in a small barrack we have here; the rest of them are still on board the "Belleisle," where also there are 100 recruits of the 18th Regiment just come out, waiting for a passage to Amoy or Chusan, where the regiment is; but in this monsoon we have very little communication from here to those places. What I am most in want of is a drill-ground. Drilled troops might be moved on some parts of this very steep and rugged island, but not without subjecting the men to great fatigue, and even then only as light infantry; but we have not on this side of the island a single spot where a battalion, or even wing, could drill. There is a small parade at West Point, which will hold from eighty to a hundred men in line, that will do for recruits' drill, but that is the only spot we have even for that purpose, for the sea-shore is all rock. In the plan I have sent in for a new barrack (a permanent one), I have required ground for a parade large enough for a battalion to drill on, but the authorities want ground so much for houses, that I doubt if they will give it me. I am going to-morrow to Chuck-Choo to inspect the 55th there, and I shall see if I can find a place there for this purpose, for it is absolutely necessary we should have some place, as the recruits come out here for the most part quite raw, not knowing how to shoulder arms.

10th.—I went over to Chuck-Choo and saw the troops; they are healthy, and in as good order as men who have been nearly three years in a ship can be expected to be; and at that place I found a bit of ground that will do for my purpose, with a little levelling. The new barrack there is getting on, as are also the huts made of bamboo and matting for the officers; I think in about a month they will be ready for the troops, and I shall then send over the 98th, who will be about 300, and relieve the 55th, who are there at present.

Yesterday morning, just at day-light, the 41st Madras Native Infantry set fire to one of these temporary barracks, large enough to hold about 100 men; and being made of bamboo and matting, floored and lined with deal boards, you may suppose how it burned. It had only been finished four or five days. I believe it was set on fire by the men smoking; but these native troops are so careless about fire that it might have been done in any way. They were pretty quick getting out of it, for I hear they only lost six muskets and one knapsack. Fortunately the wind, which had blown hard during the night, had lulled, and no more harm was done, for it stood within fifty yards of about £300,000 worth of commissariat stores, all put up in these mat buildings, where they have been for more than a year in the most dangerous position possible. I am taking steps to move them into hired places of a safer description, until a proper building of brick or stone can be made to hold them, but in a new place like this it is not very easy to find places to hire; and besides this, we have several ship-loads more coming on shore, in order that the ships may be paid off. This all speaks well for the care the Government took that this expedition should not suffer from want of supply; but as my garrison here of about 900 men makes very little way in eating through supplies calculated for 15,000 men for a year, the putting them into any place reasonably safe is very difficult, and what are not now required can only be disposed of gradually and in small quantities, as merchant ships here may be in want of provisions; besides which, the first of the market will be got hold of by the merchants, many of them having speculated largely in this sort of cargoes, with which, during the time the war lasted, they did well.

13th.—Our mail has not as yet come in, nor is it likely to do so to-day, for it is quite calm, so I must finish this letter or lose the opportunity, as our bag is made up here to-day to go over to Macao by the "Proserpine" steamer, to be put on board the "Anonima" (she is one of Jardine's clippers), which sails direct for Bombay on the 15th; so, giving her the usual passage of forty days,—and as she is one of the fastest ships they have she may do it much sooner,—I trust you will get this letter by the 4th of April. I have no more news, so give my best love to Mr. Dick, and believe me, my dear Charles, yours very truly,

SALTOUN.

LXXXVI.

Hong-Kong, 17th January 1843.

MY DEAR JULIA,— . . . Our mail from England, the October one, has not as yet come in, and last year it did not reach this till the 23d of the month. I am anxious for this mail (as I am for all of them), but this one will bring answers to our letters from Sincapore, written and left at that place on the 16th of May last, just eight months this very day. What a time to wait for an answer! But this is an extra case, as, upon an average, we here can get an answer in about five months, and the mail that left London on the 4th of June last year was received here on the 5th of August; but at that time of the year the wind all the way from Bombay is south-west, and at this time it is north-east, which makes all the difference.

We have fine cold weather just now; the thermometer has not been higher than 52° for this last week, and it is very pleasant either riding or walking; and yesterday I had a long ride for this place, about ten miles out and the same back. I went to a place called Seywaan, not above six miles from this, but it is nearly impracticable to get there direct, even on foot; the way I went was to a place called Titam on the road to Chuck-Choo, to which we have a made road, and from Titam I found a track over the hill to Seywaan by which, with a little scrambling, I got my pony over very well.

My reason for going over was to see if I could find a place in which to post a small body of men, to keep the pirates, by whom these islands are infested, in some sort of check; not that we can prevent their plundering boats at sea, but we can prevent them from landing and plundering the inhabitants, and I have found a very good place for this purpose; the only way to put them down at sea would be for the Navy to take it on hand, but the Admiral does not seem inclined to move in it. These pirates plunder a good deal in and about the mouth of the Canton river, and we heard yesterday that as Mr. Sharpe, who had one of these large lorchas, as they here call the trading boats, was going over from this to Macao, they boarded him at night, it is supposed by the connivance of some of his crew, killed him and six or seven of his Malay men, and left his ship-steward, a woman, and a Mr. Wilson, a passenger, as they thought, dead in the cabin; they plundered the boat and set fire to her. Fortunately the little boat astern was left, and Wilson, recovering a little, got the steward and the woman into this boat, cut away from the burning vessel, and drifted with the tide to one of the small islands, where the fishermen were kind to them, but the steward died of his wounds; however, the fishermen for a reward landed Mr. Wilson and the woman at Macao, where we hear they are likely to recover from their wounds. This lorcha of Mr. Sharpe's was an opium-trader, and the Chinese authorities have several fellows in custody on suspicion, they having been taken selling opium at a very unusually low price; but whether they can bring the piracy home to these people is not known. However, in this country they act very differently in these cases from what we do in England. We let ten guilty men escape if the proof is not direct, rather than run the risk of hanging an innocent one; but in China they reverse that plan, and they hang a dozen men on suspicion, rather than the guilty should escape, more particularly if they have not the means to bribe the Mandarin.

Grant has hunted up a fiddler at last; his name is Rawstoun; he is first Lieutenant in the "Agincourt;" he has a nice tone enough, has been well taught, and at some time or another has been in the habit of playing in concert with other instruments; but he is out of practice, and does not read quite so well as we have been used to. However, he makes a tolerable trio to pass the time with; moreover, it does Grant good, as in most of these trios he has to play the tenor on his violoncello, so it is excellent practice for him, and the music went very fair after dinner yesterday. No more now, my dear Mr. Dick, as I have some business.

20th.—Nothing as yet heard of the mail. Our weather still continues cold, thermometer from 50° to 55° or 58°, as a little more or less sun shines; but for the last week the weather has been cloudy, though no rain; indeed, since we have been here, we have not had two rainy days together, and not above five days rain in, now, nearly three months.

We have in these waters, besides our own ships of war, the American frigate "Constellation," commanded by Commodore Kearney, and the French frigate "Erigone," Captain Cuille—the same that I wrote you we met up in the north last summer. Captain Cuille was at Macao the other day, and was walking out with some of his officers; they met a party of Portuguese, who cautioned them not to go further on, as some Chinese were there who had insulted them; the French party, however, continued their walk, and when they came to these Chinese they were insulted and pelted, and in a sort of fight—for they were not armed—they got the worst of it, and Captain Cuille got more or less hurt and lost his spectacles; however, they all got away and got on board, and began to talk very big about what they would do in consequence. Now, at Macao they speak a sort of jargon composed of English and Portuguese, which all the Chinese and other residents there converse in; they call it English, but we English call it "talky-talky." Cuille, when he landed again, was telling one of the principal Chinese who live there, what he would do, who answered, "Why you make so great bobbery bout dis, you catchee one sheep, Englishman he catchee hundred sheep, he very great bobbery can, you, one sheep, no can, you no sabe dat." So this Chinaman thought his countrymen would have no great respect for the Frenchman and his one ship. Cunynghame has been over to Macao, and reports it as a nice place, and I intend going over there shortly, so I shall defer anything about it till another letter after I have been there myself.

Elipoo, who is the chief commissioner on the part of China to settle the tariff with Sir Henry Pottinger, came down to Canton some days ago, and wrote to Sir Henry to say that he wished he would give him a personal interview, as he had a communication to make to him from the Emperor that he could not trust to writing; this we suppose to be some complimentary message from the Emperor, which this people think as much of as we should in England of making him a duke. Pottinger sent over to beg he would fix the place of meeting, which Elipoo did at a place a little above Whampoa, in what they call the inner water, for which place Sir Henry started yesterday in the "Ackbar" steamer, taking with him a guard of honour of an officer and twenty-five men, with a drum and fife, to present arms and make a noise when Elipoo comes on board. I do not suppose they will do any business at this meeting, but most likely they will fix the time and place for meeting for the tariff business after the Chinese New Year, which takes place this year on the 29th of this month, and is kept as a great holiday in this country for a fortnight or three weeks; so we expect Sir Henry back again here before he goes up to Canton for business. I also wish our Vice-Admiral, Sir W. Parker, would come down, as I want to send men and provisions to Amoy and Chusan, and our Admiral here will not order a ship to go, or make any alteration, till the Vice-Admiral comes; and it is no use writing, as in all probability he must be here before a letter could reach him, as it takes upon an average five or six weeks before a ship can get to Chusan against this monsoon.

I have now been over a great part of this island, but there are two places I have not been to: one called Ty-Py-Waan, and the other Little Hong-Kong. They lie in two valleys just over the hill, or rather mountain, just behind this house; I have been to the top of it, but to do the whole on foot is rather much for my game leg; but I have taken a pony over a worse hill in the Highlands, and as these Chinese ponies are very good scramblers, I have no doubt I can get mine up the hill, which, by riding or walking, as the road suits, will make it easy work. One can get easily to these places in a boat; but being a soldier and not a sailor, I like better to make out the land communication.

25th.—I went yesterday to see these places on the other side of the island; our party were Major Moore, Mr. Haythorne, Cunynghame, and myself; Campbell was to have been of the party, but the day before he had been kicked by one of these ponies, who are all of them as vicious as devils, and he had so much pain in his side where he was kicked, that the doctor bled him, so he could not go, and I have not heard as yet how he is this morning. We had a very nice day, and a rather hard day's work,—riding, walking, and scrambling over these rugged hills. We went right round the west end of the island, and got, after five miles of very hard work, to a very pretty village of three or four houses, called Put-Foo-Lun, and from that in about two miles more to a place called Chuk-Py-Wan, a considerable fishing village; from that about two miles more of tolerably easy road to Little Hong-Kong, at which place we have built by subscription a small Bungalo, as these Indians call it, which is a wooden house with mat roof, and a clean comfortable place enough, like a Highland shooting bothy. Here we had our luncheon, and rested ourselves and ponies for about an hour. From that three miles right over the hill back to this place,—in all, twelve miles; and you may suppose it was pretty rough work, when it took us from nine in the morning to five in the afternoon. My Miss Pringle leg, as I call it, stood it very well, much better than I thought it would, and is none the worse this morning; I conclude that the cool weather we have had, and the colder water that I have been using in consequence, have brought the muscles back to their proper tone. The bungalo at Little Hong-Kong is very prettily placed, having in its front a plain covered with bush and rough stuff, mixed with cultivation, about a mile square, and behind it, on the face of the hill, a very thick wood of about half a mile square, and very rough and rugged, and I project a party over there some day of from six to ten guns, and with a body of about fifty Chinese as beaters, to drive the whole covert, and see what may be in it; we have partridge, pheasant, and deer on the island, but not many. However, I think some of them must be in this place, at all events it will be a pastime, and some of these Indian officers are very pleasant fellows, and understand this sort of shooting very well; if, when we go, we have any sport I will send Charles an account of it.

I suppose the "Bull" sent you your roots for the glasses as usual; we have something of the kind here, but we grow them in little China trays, holding about three roots each, and we fill up the intervals with stones, over which we occasionally pour water; they look very pretty, and mine are growing very well, and just going to blow, but they are not Hyacinths—nor have I seen any here—but a sort of Jonquille; when they come into flower I shall know what they are, but they look like that at present.

1st February.—No mail come as yet, my dear Mr. Dick, which is very provoking; but this north-east monsoon has blown very strong this year. A ship of war, the "Wolf," came in the day before yesterday, having been six months from England, and when she left Sincapore our mail from Bombay had not reached that place.

This is New Year with the Chinese, and the poorest of them will do no work for three or four days, and the better sort shut their shops and do nothing for ten days, except playing at cards, and walking about letting off crackers and other fireworks. This practice is not a little dangerous in a place like this, where one-third of the houses as yet are made of bamboo and matting, and accordingly they yesterday set fire to one of these bamboo houses on the property of a merchant, a Mr. Fletcher; this set fire to a large stack of timber, from that to certain mat houses, the property of another merchant, a Mr. Harour; he was next to the Ordnance store, and so rapid was the fire, that in ten minutes from its breaking out, and before it was possible to get any number of men, a mat building in the Ordnance store had caught fire, as well as a very large pile of wood, composed of what they call sleepers, and platforms for batteries. Things now began to look very serious, for next to the Ordnance store, and only separated from it by a wall not yet finished, was the Commissariat, where we have about half a million worth of stores, the greater part of them under mat buildings; and in the Ordnance store next to the pile of wood and burning mat house, was a building used as a store for arms, in which, from the want of any other place, and until the magazine could be finished, we had some loaded shells, a good many rockets, and a large quantity of musket ammunition. By this time the men were all assembled, and the sailors had landed from the ships, and all hands worked like horses, and behaved beautifully. Notwithstanding that the building had partially taken fire, we removed the whole of the powder, shells, and rockets, and then the spare arms; we then got an engine into the building, which, by playing on the window frames, prevented them taking fire, and the walls were built of a composition of lime, sand, and clay, which will not take fire, and here, by great exertions, the fire was stopped from making any further progress. The fire broke out at twelve, and it was now two o'clock, and the only remaining danger was from the sparks that might be carried by the wind to the Commissariat mat buildings, not above eighty yards distant; engines were stationed to play against them, and keep them wet, and the burning masses of timber, which it was impossible to extinguish, were left to burn themselves out, which they did by twelve o'clock at night. Fortunately no one was hurt, although three or four shells, and half a dozen rockets, exploded in the middle of the burning mass; how they got there no one can tell, but it is supposed they were left there by accident when landed from the ships, and this stack of gun-carriages and other timber piled over them; we had taken every precaution against fire that man could do, and so far it was satisfactory that it did not originate with us. As yet I do not know what the loss is, but I hear not so great as at first one would take it to be, as most of the things burned were put aside there to be inspected by a Board as unserviceable.

Next month, and perhaps in this one, we shall hear what they have decided at home to do with this place. But the more I think of it, the less chance I see of my being relieved at this time. When things are settled they will not keep so large a force here as to require a General Officer, and therefore I very much fear they will not relieve me at present, but direct me to remain here till the Treaty is completed, and then put me off the Staff, sending the troops not wanted back to India. However, another month will put this out of doubt.

8th February.—I had begun to think that we should never get another mail at all, when yesterday afternoon an American schooner came in from Bombay and brought our mail, the November one, and I have just read your kind letter, No. 11, latest date October 27th; so our October mail is still absent and a month behind time, but that is nothing odd in these monsoons. I have besides your letter, one from Charles, from my mother, Eleanor, and William, and am happy to find all well.

You tell me always to mention my health in all letters. I am afraid I said too much about that in my letters from the north, where, although amongst the best of them, I was but so so, but ever since we left the river I have been as well as ever I could have been in England, and at this time of the year this must be a healthy climate. I am writing this with a fire in the room, and dressed in the same clothes I should have on were I with you at Bath, except that I have got on an old shooting jacket, instead of a morning coat. So far so good for Hong-Kong, but it certainly is the most stupid place any mortal ever was confined to. I get here about £4000 per annum, and cannot spend above two; but both the Admiral and I agreed yesterday, when I dined with him, that if they would offer us the government of it, with £10,000 a year, we would not accept it, and he is so disgusted that he has gone to sea to-day by way of a change for two days, and comes back to dine with me on Saturday.

I am glad Charles has been out shooting, and he gives a good account of his sport in his letter to me; and if we had anything here to shoot at, from a rabbit to a tiger, I would shoot here, but we have nothing. However, if I can organise it, I mean to beat some day a large wood we have on the other side of the island, where perhaps we may see an antelope and a pheasant or so.

During the time that the war was going on the country was filled with proclamations and papers of encouragement to induce the people to continue the war and keep up their spirits, and I send you one of them, which the interpreter tells me is very well translated, so you can judge for yourself of these very extraordinary people.

Every thing is, I hear, going on satisfactorily as far as the treaty is concerned, and our authorities seem to have no doubt that they will keep faith with us. Indeed, they got such a lesson that they are not likely to forget in a hurry; and the more the loss they sustained all along the coast, which was the seat of war, becomes known, the less likely are they to run the risk of incurring another. These people call the tribute paid by the south of China a present to the Emperor, and it forms more than half his yearly revenue; and I see by the *Pekin Gazette* that the present for the year 1842 is remitted by the Emperor in consequence of loss sustained by the people from the stoppage of the trade and other losses inflicted by the Barbarians. To be sure, if the present Emperor were to die, his successor might change the state of things, but still, in the most absolute government, the state of the people must be taken into consideration, and he would most likely remain quiet for fear of a regular revolution; for, since we have shown the Chinese that the Tartars are not invincible, they have on various occasions shown their teeth against these their hard task-masters.

I am very sorry for poor Sir W. Geary, although I know him but very slightly; it was a most unfortunate accident, but Lady Geary deserves great credit for her presence of mind at the time. . . .

I have just heard that a ship is to go in half an hour from this to Macao, to catch a ship that sails from there to-morrow to Bombay. Love to Charles, and believe me, my dear Julia, yours affectionately,   SALTOUN.

LXXXVII.

Hong-Kong, 12th February 1843.

MY DEAR CHARLES,—On the 8th of last month I wrote you a letter, which went on the 13th to Bombay by the "Anonima" clipper; and two days back I sent a letter to Mr. Dick by the ship "William Grenville," which I hope may get to Bombay in time to go by the April mail from that place. But when this letter will be sent, I have at present no idea; we have two ships here, transports paid off, that I hear intend to go to Bombay, but as yet no time fixed for sailing.

Many thanks for your letter of the 2d November, which I got on Tuesday last, the 7th inst., by the November mail from England; but we have not as yet received our October mail. It is coming from Bombay in a ship called the "Elizabeth Anne," which is known to be a very bad sailer, and it may be some time yet before she comes in; and I shall not be much surprised if the December mail from England beats her. We are all here very anxious about the said December mail, as we know that the news of our proceedings here reached you in the month of November, and we are anxious to know what they think of the Peace in England; but I do not expect to receive any directions about this place till Major Malcolm, who went with the ratified Treaty, comes back, and he is expected early next month.

I am glad you have had some shooting, and by your letter you seem to have had some very fair sport. I have not heard how William found the game at Philorth, but the partridges ought to be getting well up again now. We have nothing on this island worth going after, but I wrote in my last letter to Mr. Dick that I meant to organise a party to beat a large wood that is on the other side of the island, and the fun is to come off on Tuesday next. I get the beaters at five for a dollar, so twenty dollars will pay all the expense; I am to have sixty men, with a leader to every ten, and a man to direct the whole line. Six of us guns go over on Monday afternoon, and dine and sleep at a small bungalow that we have built near the place, and six more guns will join us in the morning. We know that a few deer, pheasants, partridges, and quails are on the island; and as this wood is very thick and rough, and so large that no ordinary shooting party can make anything of it, we may perhaps see something to shoot at; I will send you the result after I come back.

We have no sort of news here. The Plenipotentiary is over at Macao, and I believe things are going on for settling the Tariff; and Grant, who has not been very well, has gone over there and on to Canton for a change, as taking charge of his office had been rather much work for him; for, as Adjutant-General to the Force in China, he had to make himself acquainted with many points that are quite different in India from what they are in Europe; and the consequent confinement and want of exercise, added to a great deal of detail correspondence, had disagreed with him; I expect him back in a week or ten days, or as soon as he has spent all the money he took with him.

17th.—We went over on Monday last, the day after I began this letter, and the party all got over to dinner, on a rainy evening, but in hopes it would clear for the next day. However, it rained all night and all the next morning, so we could not try the wood, but I shall give it another turn, as we ascertained some deer to be always in it. I suspect the rain we had was a fall of snow in the north of this country, for the weather has been colder and quite fine since then: thermometer at 55°, and this morning at 51°.

The October mail not yet come, but we got one in yesterday from Calcutta, which had been ever since September getting here. The usual direction of this monsoon is from the north-east; ships therefore get away to the east till a north-west course will fetch this place; but when they are in that situation, if the wind shifts from north-east to north or north and by west, it becomes dead against them, and this year it has been more shifty than usual, which accounts for so many very long passages.

The Emperor has issued a proclamation about the manner in which the people who were wrecked on Formosa were treated, and ordered an inquiry into the conduct of his authorities there. In this document his Celestial Majesty uses the old tone of superiority over all other nations. In consequence of this, Pottinger sends a proclamation in which, with reference to this paragraph—"The Celestial Dynasty has for its principle in *governing* all foreigners without its pale"— Pottinger remarks, "That his royal mistress, the Queen of England, acknowledges no *superior or governor but God*," and requests that his proclamation may be sent to the Grand Council; and in a private letter to Elipoo tells him, if he has any objection to forward it he will send it himself. Pottinger is quite right, for the egregious vanity of these people is very apt to come out in their papers, and if not checked at once, the next paper is certain to have a double dose of it, and if this was permitted to go to too great an extent, it might embroil matters again; for with absolute monarchs, as with men, it is more difficult to make a man eat his words in a great insult than in a small discourtesy.

From what I heard yesterday, the letters I sent off in a great hurry on the 10th—one of them for Mr. Dick—were too late to catch the "Thomas Grenville" ship at Macao; if so, they will go by the same mail as this does, but I send what I have ready by any opportunity that offers, for it is all a matter of chance when they get to Bombay. I have no more news to send, but I will not seal this letter till the last moment, as, if the October mail from England, which is still absent, comes in, I will mention it in this; so, with best love to Mr. Dick, believe me, my dear Charles, yours very truly, SALTOUN.

P.S.—19th February.—No mail come in as yet, and this letter must go into the post-office to-night, as the boat sails for Macao in the morning, and the Admiral and a lot of them breakfast with me at eight o'clock, and then we are to walk over the hill to a place called Chuk-Py-Wann, where there is a very pretty island in a little sandy bay, with a Joss-house on it, and some nice trees and good water. The Admiral sends a boat round with his tent and fishing-nets, and everything right for dinner. We are to drag the bay for our fish, dine in the tent, and after dinner either walk back or come home in the boat, as we like best. I am told the island is very pretty, with some curious things in it; but I have not as yet seen it.—Yours truly, S——.

LXXXVIII.

Hong-Kong, 23d February 1843.

MY DEAR JULIA,—My last letter to Charles begun on the 12th inst., was sent from this on the 20th, and I should not have begun this one so soon to you had not the ship "Mor" come in yesterday from Bombay, and brought me the *United Service Magazine* for May last, with a letter from Jane Onslow introducing her brother, to whom, as you know, I shall be most happy to shew any civility in my power, if we chance to meet; but I conclude he is in India, and not at all likely to come here; but I am much obliged to him for his kindness in sending me the *Magazine* and letter, and also a book he brought out for me from my mother when we were up the river last year. I heard of these things coming out in a letter of June last from my mother; and also, either from you or Charles, about the *U. S. Magazine* and *Reminiscences of Bayonne*, which I have read, and they are a very nice article for a work of that description.

Our party, on Monday, to Chuk-Py-Wann with the Admiral went off very well. The party breakfasted with me at half-past eight, and we then walked over the hill, and got to the place about eleven; the men dined at twelve, having come round in the boats, and we proceeded to draw the sein, but the bays were rocky, and we got no fish that way; however, we got plenty from the Chinese fishing-boats; and at four o'clock the Admiral gave us a good dinner in his tent, and we left in the boat about six, and got home about nine. We had a very fine day, which made the party go off very pleasantly. Our Vice-Admiral, Sir William Parker, has just come in sight; and by a boat from Macao, I have received a letter from Sir H. Pottinger, which I must answer, so I cannot write any more now, my dear Mr. Dick.

25th.—After I had finished my letter to Sir Henry, it was time to start upon an expedition I had formed to a place, Sy-Wann, where I have a post of fifty men, to protect that side of the island from the pirates; this party had taken some of these gentlemen at a place called Chuk-Wann, on the east side of the island, and I wanted to see that place and the east side altogether. It is difficult to describe this island so as to be understood. It is about forty miles round, composed of ranges of high hills, diverging like an irregular star from a common centre; and the average height of these hills is such that it takes from an hour and ten minutes to an hour and a half to walk over any one of them. This place, Hong-Kong, is on the north side of the island, and from this we have made a riding road to Chuck-Choo, which is at the end of the south promontory, and distant about ten miles. At about seven miles on this road you come to a place called Titam, at the head of the bay of that name, which bay divides the south from the east promontory of the island, and the place called Chuk-Wann is near the end of the east promontory. The distance from this, Hong-Kong, to Sy-Wann, going east, is about the same that it is to Titam; but as the Sy-Wann bay runs into the land, the distance from Titam to Sy-Wann is not above five miles, forming the base of the east promontory of the island. The distance from Sy-Wann to Chuk-Wann is four miles, and from that round the promontory to Titam about six, and the track by which you can go is very steep and rugged, but not more so than other tracks. My excursion was this:—We sent our tents and beds by water to Sy-Wann in the morning; in the afternoon we rode to Titam, and walked from that over the hill to Sy-Wann, where we dined with the party, and an excellent fish dinner they gave us, I sending over with the tent half a sheep, a scarce article here. The next morning, after breakfast, walked over to Chuk-Wann, saw the place where they had taken the pirates, parted with them there, and walked round the promontory to Titam, where the horses met us, and we rode home to dinner. The day was very hot, and I found the walk quite far enough for my game leg; they told me a pony could not go the road, so I did not take mine; but I found he could have gone all the way quite easy, and I could have ridden him two-thirds of the way. I have now been over every bit of the island, except a track from Chuck-Choo to Chuk-Py-Wann, which I mean to have a turn at shortly. This word Wann that comes so often is the Chinese for bay, and at the head of every little bay they have a fishing village and a little cultivation; so going round this east promontory we went from Sy-Wann to Chuk-Wann, then to Tuti-Wann; from that to Ali-Wann, and then to Titam, which they have not put a Wann to;—I suppose because the bay of Titam is very large, being four or five miles long, and six or seven wide; and some of these little villages are at the head of little bays that run out of it.

I find I was wrong about Mr. Onslow; for, by the *Canton Register*, a newspaper published at Macao, I find the "General Kidd" ship is there, last come from Madras; so I hope to have the pleasure of seeing him here.

No October mail yet: we cannot think what has become of it. A ship called the "Eliza Stuart" came in yesterday, being 104 days from Bombay; she brought some of the October mail letters, but only such as had been directed to the care of agents at Bombay; but the post-office bags by which my letters come, are on board some other ship, and it is supposed she is at Ceylon getting in some more cargo; if so, she may be another month. I do not know how they manage this at the post-office, but I have been told they are obliged to put the mail on board the first ship that sails; but then it ought to be some ship going direct to the place, and not one going to some other port to look for cargo.

Grant came back yesterday from Macao and Canton, and liked his trip very much; I think he is better in health from it.

We are now beginning to look out for our December mail, but I think I shall have an opportunity for sending this letter before it will come in, as it must be in a sailing ship; for if they had sent it from Bombay by steam, it most likely would have been here before this, and it is very likely that Major Malcolm, who we calculate left England in January, will get here first, as he will certainly come by steam from Bombay, and will probably be here in ten days from this time; and as he will most likely bring with him the decision of Government about this place, he is anxiously looked for.

Our Naval Commander, Sir William Parker, came in here on the 23d, just as I was setting out on my excursion; he is to dine with me to-day, and I conclude will stay here now till he hears from England; he is very anxious to remain out here, and I believe thinks himself ill used by being sent home before his time is out. They certainly will not keep two Admirals in these seas; they never before have had more than one, and as Cochrane is on our side of the question, and Parker a Whig, why I think it most likely they will keep their own friend; so, as things often go exactly the way one does not wish, they will probably send Admiral Parker home, who wants to stay here, and keep me here, who have no sort of wish to stay here a day longer than I can help.

We have a report to-day, which comes in the *Canton Press* newspaper, that the mob at Canton are inclined to kick up another row, and that it is their intention to attack the factories as they did in December last; and this is rather confirmed by a private letter. Our two interpreters are living in one of these factories; they are Messrs. Morrison and Thom, and Morrison writes that the authorities are quite ready and willing to protect them; so the only question is, whether they are strong enough to beat the mob, who, since our proceedings in this country, have lost a great deal of their dread of the Tartar soldiers, having seen that we so easily defeated these troops, who had for years been looked upon as invincible. However, notwithstanding these rumours, I believe that all the business of the Treaty is going on smoothly and satisfactorily to both parties; but it must be rather a long business, being obliged to be carried on in a language very difficult to translate with correctness.

I must finish this letter now, my dear Mr. Dick, for they have just sent up word from the post-office that the ship "Mor" sails for Bombay early in the morning, and the letters must be in to-night; they are in hopes, as she sails well, that she will catch the April steamer; if so, you will get this in May, but I fear it will not reach you before June, as the chance of the "Mor" finding the steamer from Calcutta to Suez at Ceylon is, I think, very small; however, she ought at all events to reach Bombay before the May steamer starts for that place. No October mail come yet, and no more news to send from this; so, with love to Charles, believe me, my dear Julia, yours affectionately, SALTOUN.

LXXXIX.

Hong-Kong, 2d March 1843.

MY DEAR CHARLES,—I wrote the other day to Mr. Dick, and the letter went into the post-office on the 28th, as the ship was to leave early on the 1st; but the mail, so long missing, came in during the night, and I see the ship is still in the harbour, and as I cannot get my letter back to add to it, I send this one to you to say that we have at last got this October mail: and, after all, I am not sorry it was delayed, for by these letters I find that Eleanor had been very unwell with cholera, and also that Mr. Dick had had a touch of the same complaint, and after the awful examples I have seen of it in this country, it is an alarming disorder to hear of. However, as by the delay, we had received our November mail nearly a month before the October one came in, I had heard that both of them had recovered before I heard that either of them had been unwell.

By this October mail I have received your letter of 2d October, and also one from Mr. Dick. I have letters besides from all my relations, and also one from

Salomons, in which he mentions having written me in April last, that is April 1842, which letter I never received, and I believe it is the only letter that has failed. However, I wrote him in December last, and as I did not mention the receipt of his letter, he will guess that it had failed; for, if idle and lazy about writing of my own accord, I have at all events acquired that military habit of answering every letter I receive,—and a great bore it is when you cannot do what the writer wants.

I have no sort of news, having written so lately to Mr. Dick, and this place does not furnish much. However, I have just heard that Campbell, who is very well, returned yesterday from Macao (he is stationed at Chuck-Choo), and on landing sent his things over by some of his black fellows, and the story is that they were robbed at a place called Titam of everything, the curiosities he had bought, and his clothes, etc.; but I believe his black servant Jeshair to be a bit of a rogue.

Our December mail is what they call due now, so we are looking for it every day, and it will bring us some news; I fear nothing good for me, and I shall have to stay here till the Treaty is carried into effect; but all this you will know at home long before I can hear.

As soon as I hear anything certain from home I shall take a trip over to Macao and Canton to see the lions, and will write you an account of them.

So, with best love to Mr. Dick, believe me, my dear Charles, yours very truly,
SALTOUN.

XC.

Hong-Kong, 18th April 1843.

MY DEAR CHARLES,—I was writing this day-week to Julia, when they came in a great hurry to tell me that the post was to go that day: so I finished the letter[1] as fast as I could, as well as one to my sister Margaret, and the next day they found out the mistake, and the mail is not to go till to-morrow; so this, at all events, enables me to send you a week's later news as to how I am going on,

[1] This letter has been lost; it probably contained an account of the severe accident which had befallen him on the 29th of the previous month, as related at page 300 of vol. i. in his memoir; but the letter of the 7th April, there quoted, was not written to Colonel or Mrs. Ellis, and is not now available for publication.

and a week, particularly the third week, makes a great difference in broken bones, and I am happy to say I am going on remarkably well.

I had been for some days very restless, could get no sleep at night; I had no fever, still I was in pain, sometimes in the chest, then stomach, then where the hurt was; in short, I was all no how. However, on Sunday last, soon after dinner, the gout got hold of my left foot; I went to bed, and, on lying down, no pain in the back, no pain in the chest, or anywhere, and I fell asleep before ten, and did not wake till half-past six in the morning.

I had the gout bad that day and the next night, but it is now all gone, and in ten more days the bones will be hard, and I shall be fit for horseback again.

You did quite right to send me the substance of what the papers had been at about me, for it so happened that I have not received any of my November papers, and I should have been quite in the dark but for your letter. I saw, however, in a monthly paper, a letter to the editor of the *Morning Post*, for which, I suspect, I am indebted to you, for I think no one else is so well acquainted with the circumstances. Be that as it may, we will have a bumper to the writer's health, whoever he may be, when we meet. I read the letter in a paper called the *Monthly Times*, but extracted from the *Post*, with a statement that they had published it, because if any person doubted it, they were at liberty to verify the writer.

Everything concerned with the Treaty is, I believe, going on as well as it can, and they have heard from Pekin that the Emperor has appointed Keying to be the Chief Commissioner to succeed Elipoo, and that he is likely to be at Canton by the 7th of next month, when I conclude the exchange of the Ratifications will take place, and if that is done here, I must be present; and as our gracious Queen's birthday is on the 24th, I suspect I shall not get to Macao and Canton till June. It will be hot work there, but it is equally hot here; and even now we are beginning to have it, for the glass to-day is at 80°, which is much higher than it has been any day these last six months.

Pottinger has issued a very strong Proclamation in to-day's paper on the subject of certain smuggling that has come to his knowledge, as carried on in the Canton river; it is too long to copy in the present state of my bones, so I cut it out and send it you. It will at all events show the China authorities that it is our wish to trade fairly with them, but what I fear is, that the system of corruption has existed so long in China in all departments of the State, that the Emperor will find it impossible to get honest men to do his work.

We are looking out now for our next mail from home, the February one; it is on board the "Anonima," a very fine fast clipper, and is expected in every day; but as this letter must go by the steamer at eight o'clock to-morrow to Macao to catch the mail, it will be too late to answer by this opportunity; so, with best love to Mr. Dick, believe me, my dear Charles, yours very truly,   SALTOUN.

XCI.

Hong-Kong, 27th April 1843.

MY DEAR JULIA,—I wrote you last on the 11th inst., and that letter was sent, by a mistake of the postmaster, a week too soon; and since that I have written to Charles, which left this for Bombay on the 20th, and I now find myself beginning another letter to you; not that I have anything very particular to say about myself, for sufficient time has not elapsed yet to be certain about the bones, but the doctor tells me that the collar-bone is safe, and only wants time now to harden; as to the ribs, we cannot tell about them yet. Since I sent my last letter to Charles I have had a terrible week of gout, perhaps a little owing to my own obstinacy, but then I have been borne out in that by my doctor, our Surgeon-General here, a man of the name of Thompson. You know that in England I never did anything for gout, but grin and bear it till it got well; but when I had it coming out on board the Belleisle, the doctor gave me colchicum for it, and it certainly drove it away very rapidly, but still it returned at much shorter intervals. At home I had it about once in eighteen months, whereas under the colchicum treatment I had it four times in the year 1842—slightly, certainly, and it gave way at once to the remedy, but still it was gout. When it broke out this time in the left foot I asked Thompson what he meant to do with it. He said, "I would rather keep it where it is, as if I was to drive it away I cannot be certain that it will not go somewhere where it will be worse: but what have you been in the habit of doing for it?" I told him, and he said, "Let it alone; you will probably have a very severe fit for having been playing with the colchicum; it will probably now pay you off old scores: but depend upon one thing, the oftener you use the colchicum the oftener will the gout return upon you; whereas if you have the resolution to let it wear itself out, it will probably not return again till your constitution requires to throw it out." As this advice agreed with my theory I did nothing for it, and consequently I have had fourteen days of as severe pain as a body could wish, and it is not gone yet; but the foot, which at one time was as big as my head, has got back to its natural size : and I think it is all on the go; and if after it is gone I keep well for say ten months or more, I will take no more colchicum.

I have just been reading *Percival Keene* and James's new book *Morley Ernstein*, brought out by Colonel Malcolm. The worst of *Percival Keene* is, that the principal scene, the one with the black pirate, is borrowed from a similar one in *Tom Cringle's Log ;* and I suppose because *Tom Bowline* finishes by losing his frigate, they have made *Percival Keene* do the same thing, which, however, takes away a good deal from the originality of the work. As to James, as long as he stuck to the wars of the Fronde, or the League, troubles in Flanders, or Burgundy, or Piedmont, etc. etc., such was our faith in the powers of our forefathers, added to our general ignorance of these events, that it did not signify what he put down, nor how improbable it might be; it all went down as fact, and no one thought it either *outré* or dreamt of disputing it in a work of fiction. But when he chooses to take for his time the year 1822, or somewhere thereabout, and above all, the high life of England, for his actors, you constantly say, "how could a man imagine such things could ever happen to these people!" It is, however, a very entertaining book, and you have read it long ago.

We are looking out every day for our mail, the February one, from England. Not that I expect you will have received much from me by the mail that you got in January, for we were in a state of movement after Malcolm left the river. I see by my book that I wrote to you, to Tudor, Eleanor, and William, which letters left Chusan on the 18th of October, and might have been in time to leave Bombay by the mail that would reach England in January; but it was not likely they would get there soon enough : I sent them from Chusan by Sir Thomas Herbert, and he had sailed for Sincapore before we got down here, at the end of October, and he was to send them on from Sincapore the quickest way he could; still I fear they will be too late for that mail. Sir Thomas is a nice old gentleman-like sea captain, and I am certain you will like him if ever you should chance to meet him.

5th May.—Still no mail, and the ship it is on board of is so fine a sailer that nothing is at all likely to beat her; so we are not likely to hear of her, which we constantly do of our mail, till she comes in.

I meant to have added to this letter yesterday, but I had a long and difficult letter to write (only so far difficult as it may, and probably will, be quoted hereafter as my opinion) on the subject of barracks in general, and those of officers in particular; and as we are about to lay out some hundred thousand pounds in these matters, it was necessary, I thought, in my letter to our great man here, to well-weigh the case in all its bearings, as to how things would best act, now being, as we are here, on an Eastern footing; and how they might be so regulated as to merge in the easiest manner into the European system, should the Government at home, at any time hereafter, choose to have them so regulated; and as this required a good deal of consideration, both as to the facts and the best manner of wording them, I was tired when I had done it, and put off writing to you till to-day.

And now about myself, the gout is all gone, and I have got my regular shoe on again, but I have been passing an odd life, for me, for these last eighteen days or so. Old Thompson, who is a good doctor, and tells you what he wants you to do, about that time back told me that the time was come for curing the ribs. "I can do nothing for them," he said, "but bandage you round to keep you steady, and you must do the rest for yourself by sitting quite quiet all day in a chair, and lying as still as you can at night. But if you do this, and eat and drink, you will, from want of exercise, get fever, and that will not do. So, at eight o'clock you may have tea and toast for breakfast: at two o'clock you may have some chicken broth with the chicken in it, and a rice pudding; and no more to eat for the day. No wine, or beer, or brandy, but as much lemonade as you like." And accordingly for these last eighteen days I have led this life, getting up at five o'clock, daylight, and sitting in my chair till seven, dark, when I went to bed, and for the most part slept tolerably well till getting up time at five. Yesterday they had an examination, and the ribs are all right: they were broke off, close to the back-bone, but it is all joined now, and only wants a few days to get hard, for the bone there takes as long to harden as a leg, from forty to forty-eight days, and it is now only thirty-seven days since they were broken. In the meantime I have got rid of the flannel bandage, and I now wear my hunting-belt, which I had brought by accident; to be sure, hunting, I wore it rather lower down, but I am so large round the chest that it is quite small for me, and by putting a pair of braces to it, I get it just under the armpit like a pair of stays, and I can by the buckles and straps draw it to any tightness required. I can now walk about in the verandah, but I am still for some six days more to be kept on the broth plan, though he lets me have a glass of wine, ONE, if I like, and accordingly I had one yesterday. Next Thursday will be six weeks, when I suppose I shall be let loose again. This, as I think I wrote you before, has prevented my going to Macao and Canton, where I meant to have been this month of April, but I must now put it off till June, as, in this month of May, I have to make my half-yearly inspection of the troops here, and on the 24th, Her Majesty's birthday, we must fire away, and do all that sort of thing.

We yesterday got a despatch from Pekin, by which Keying is appointed High Commissioner in place of the late Elipoo, and ordered to Canton; he is expected there before the end of the month, so the business will go on again. His appointment looks well, for he is a great man in the State, of the Imperial blood, and one of those who has from the first counselled peace, and argued the utter impossibility, constituted as their forces are at present, of standing against us in war.

I have not seen Campbell for some days, and I hear he has been laid up at Chuck-Choo with fever. Poor fellow, he suffers much from that. Old Shean has also not been quite well, but I suspect his disorder was too much meat and too little work, for two of old Thompson's bolusses (and from experience I know they are no joke) has set him all right again.

May 6th.—Our mail, my dear Mr. Dick, came in yesterday evening, and brought me your kind letter, for which many thanks, though I have hardly any time to write, for the Admiral has ordered a steamer to sail for Calcutta this evening, which will take these letters.

The hot damp weather has set in, and the guitar bridge given in consequence, but I have sent for a Chinaman who tells me his glue will stand this weather, as it is very first chop; so you will hear in my next whether it will or not.

I must now leave off, as I have all my returns and papers to sign, which must go by this post to Calcutta; so, with love to Charles, believe me, my dear Julia, yours affectionately,   SALTOUN.

XCII.

Hong-Kong, 22d May 1843.

MY DEAR CHARLES,—I wrote on the 6th to Mr. Dick, which letter left this on the 13th to go to Bombay by the "Anonima," which brought our last mail, the February one, from England.

We have coming out here a Major Aldridge, a Brevet-Major of our Engineers —a young second Captain, but they tell me a good man in his line, and he is to have entire control over all barracks and buildings, fortifications, etc.; indeed, the letter announcing his coming out directed all works to be suspended till he came. However, as suspending works is neither more nor less than vitiating contracts, and thereby paying a great deal of money for nothing, I have suspended no works; for, in the first place, he may approve of them, and if he does not, it costs no more than throwing up the contracts would have done; and many of them, commissariat and ordnance store-houses, are nearly completed. We have heard of his having reached Bombay, and the sooner he comes here the better; but none of the clippers that carry out mails will bring him, as they are prohibited by the houses they belong to from carrying passengers, as they could not with them on board play the tricks they all do, in order to give their owners some days' earlier intelligence about prices and the state of trade than the rest of the community.

I intend to get through my half-yearly inspection this week, if the weather will let me, and I meant to have begun this morning, for six o'clock is our time here, to get things over before the heat of the sun comes, but it rained cats and dogs, so it was no go. I have got a wing of the 55th and one of the 41st Madras here, and the 98th at Chuck-Choo, but I shall go over and dine with them the day before, as it is rather far to ride over in the morning for that early hour, and after I have got this done I shall be all ready for my trip to Macao and Canton; not that my bones are all right yet—at least at times they feel very queer—but the doctor tells me they are all joined, but that I must be careful not to get any sudden wrench, as that might do harm; it will be nine weeks to-morrow since it was done, so they ought to be pretty firm.

29th.—Still no mail come, which is very provoking.

I have got quite well now, and sit a horse as comfortably as ever; at first it hurt me, but it was only the muscles brought into play after being quiet so long.

I have gone through the inspections, and the 55th are in tolerable order, all things considered. They have been more than two years on board ship, and half of them that are here are still so, and the other half recruits joined since we have been here, and they have only a very small parade where they can do recruit-drill; indeed we have not a spot anywhere here, as yet, that four companies could change front upon, except a high road that runs across the bit of ground that the 41st have for a parade, and having got into this line, you must re-form your column; for it can only be done by deployment. However, I found the said 41st Madras Native Infantry in excellent order, stood well under arms after their fashion, marched well, were very silent and steady, and I put them through a regular quadrille, and you know I can do it, the cautions and all words of command given in English, and neither the men nor Captain Hall, who commanded them, ever made a mistake at all; their hospital is in good order, as also their barracks, and the books, although in some respects different from ours, just as well and as regularly kept. Having seen these regiments I rode over the next day to Chuck-Choo, and dined with the 98th, and slept there; and saw them the next morning, or rather what was left of them, for they are now only 370 men. They are however healthy, having only 56 sick, but they furnish several detachments, so on parade they had only three companies, 135 men, but their drill was perfect, stood under arms, and marched as well as I ever saw the Guards do; they must have been a most admirable corps before they left home. They were commanded by their Major, Roberts; for Campbell being my Commandant here, is obliged to give up the command; he was there, however, and indeed lives mostly over with them, but he is very bad, poor fellow, with ague, and has it nearly every other day, and it lasts five or six hours, and then he complains that the immense perspiration by which the hot fit is followed reduces him very much. However he is in excellent spirits, and is not near so much pulled down as you would suppose, and the officers tell me that he does not suffer so much from it here as he did in England.

7th June.—Our mail has just come in and brought me your letter of the 1st March. I have also a letter from Lord Fitzroy, who can give me nothing certain about being relieved; his words are, "I am commissioned by the Duke of Wellington to say that he has not lost sight of your wishes, but he has not yet been able to make an arrangement for the appointment of an officer to succeed you in the command of H.M.'s troops remaining in China." I did not expect to hear anything till the next mail, if so soon; so you may continue to write on, for when you hear of an officer being appointed, he cannot get here under three or four months, and most likely six, if he comes by sea, and it will take me three months at least to get home; so that March next is the earliest I can expect to get back by; however, the sooner it comes the better. Love to Mr. Dick, and believe me, my dear Charles, yours very truly, SALTOUN.

XCIII.

Hong-Kong, 28th May 1843.

MY DEAR JULIA,—As yet no word of our mail, although those who profess to know these things have been expecting it every day for this last week.

We have been very gay here since that time, having had two G.C.B. to invest, the Vice-Admiral and the Plenipotentiary; and I was well enough to be able to go and support the Admiral, who came first, and was invested, under a special order from the Queen, by Sir Henry Pottinger, and after that, he, the Admiral, by a similar order, invested Sir Henry, to whom I went also as supporter. The ceremony was this:—We were directed to assemble on board the Admiral's ship at half-past two, at which hour Sir Henry embarked in the barge and was saluted from the shore. On coming on board, where we were all assembled, he was saluted by the ships; soon after that the Royal Standard was hoisted at the main, and all the ships of war and the shore fired a Royal salute. The quarter-deck was covered with an awning, and a throne erected at the end near the mainmast, and very neatly decorated with flags and so forth, with a print of the Queen over the Chair of State, a small chair being placed on the right for Sir Henry, and the Marines formed on each side of the deck. Some of the party were told off as Sir Henry's procession, and they moved out of the larboard cabin-door and took post, some close to the Throne, and the rest on the larboard side of the deck. This being done, we, the Admiral's procession, went out by the starboard door, and lined that side of the deck; I and Captain Richards advancing with the Admiral up to the Throne. Colonel Malcolm then read the Commission from the Queen, ordering the investment, also a letter to the same effect from the Duke of Sussex as acting Grand Master of the Order; the Chaplain then read a prayer for the occasion, and Sir Henry made a speech to the Admiral, and invested him with the Ribbon and Star, after which the Admiral made a reply, which finished the ceremony, and another salute was fired from all the ships and the shore as the Royal Standard was lowered: we then had luncheon on board, and all dined with Sir Henry. This was on Thursday the 18th, and on the 20th the same thing was done over again on shore, the Admiral acting the part that Sir Henry had done in the former ceremony, and investing him, and we all dined with the Admiral on board.

As this was my first time of showing since my accident, and as the distance from my house to Sir Henry's is considerable, they would not let me get on a horse, but Sir Henry sent his sedan chair for me, which is the way the mandarins and all great people move in this country. However, I have been on horseback since then, and rode over the day before yesterday to Chuck-Choo, dined with them there, inspected them yesterday morning, and they dined at three o'clock, and I rode home after dinner; and as far as the bones are concerned am all the better for it.

At Sir Henry Pottinger's investment we had a grand turn-out of all our ladies here: first came Mrs. Wilson, a nice-looking old lady of between fifty and sixty, the wife of our Paymaster-General; then the Admiral handed out Mrs. Bamfield; she is a nice lady-like woman, with a little girl with her about ten years old, and has since gone on to Chusan where her husband is; then I had to hand out Mrs. Morgan, who is a regular residenter here; then we had Mrs. Gilespie, a pretty American woman, and her sister, also residenters here; then a very pretty woman, a Mrs. Lockhart, wife of a doctor and English Missionary, and her sister, gone or going immediately to the north where his mission is to be; they say she speaks Chinese better than any one of the interpreters; we had besides a very pretty woman, a Mrs. Mathieson, a native, I heard, of New South Wales, she is the wife of a clerk, or, as they call them here, writer, in Dent's house, and was over with her husband from Macao to see the place, and probably to look after a residence here, as all these merchants' houses will have to come here sooner or later from Macao, and it is by no means an easy thing to find a place to put one's head into here at present, but all the heads of houses are building, and by the end of the year will most likely be settled here with their families.

I have now given you a very fair dose of Hong-Kong gossip, and have no news except that the Chinese glue will not stand in this climate any more than the English. The Chinaman said it would, or, as he expressed it, "can secure," and accordingly it stood for a week, but on looking at it this morning I find the bridge is gone again, so I fear I must put it by till the dry season comes, about two months from this, and it is of no great consequence, for I could get no chanterelle that would stand for more than an hour even at A flat, and I got some thin fiddle-strings too to try, but they were just as bad; besides, all the instrument seems to lose its tone; it did the same last year, and as soon as the dry weather set in got all right again; so I have no fear of it, and I think it very likely if the Chinese glue had held the bridge that the manche might have come off, and that is a more difficult thing to put back exactly in its right place than the bridge is, for on the way in which the manche is set depends the distance that the strings are from the finger board, which after all is the greatest difficulty in guitar-making; if too near, they give no sound, and if too far, even so strong a hand as mine can hardly execute upon them, and I like tone so much that I have them the least thing further off than they are usually made, but it is a nice point.

June 2d.—This day last year we sailed into this place, and I that evening sent off that letter that you received so much sooner than the other letters that were sent from this some days afterwards. I also found here at that time yours and Charles's letters of January and March, having received your February letters at Sincapore; but this year the March mail has not as yet arrived, and we have had the wind fair for it now for five or six days, and consequently the weather has got a good deal hotter, and fever and ague are beginning to show themselves again, particularly with those who had it badly last year. Up the river poor Campbell suffered very much from it. It is a curious disorder, as it comes and goes without any warning, lasts from six to eight hours, and during that time knocks a man completely down, and as soon as the perspiration breaks out he is quite well again. Six or seven officers of the 98th have it as well as the Colonel.

After all, the guitar has gone back to the Chinaman; he had heard that it had given way, and came here in such distress, and seemed so confident he had certain glue that would stand, that I let him have it back again yesterday for another trial, not that I think he will succeed.

We hear that the New Commissioner, Keying, is to reach Canton on the 10th or 12th of this month; after that, business, which, ever since Elipoo's death, has been at a stand-still, will begin again. The first thing will be to exchange the ratified treaties, and I hear he is to come over here for that purpose, and then I hope they will begin in earnest; and those concerned now say they hope to have the Commercial Treaty settled about the month of August.

I have parted with one of my black servants, or rather he with me: he got leave to go over to Macao for three or four days, and when he came back he brought another man to Cunynghame, and said a ship was to sail for Calcutta that day, and as his heart was at Calcutta he could do no more good here; Cunynghame being of the same opinion paid him his wages, and he went off to Calcutta; but the reason came out in a day or two. It seems when he went to Macao, a countryman of his employed in the Commissariat gave him a hundred dollars to buy him a wife, and a hundred rupees to pay the expense of bringing her over; he, however, bought a wife for fifty rupees, and fearing his friend would find it out, bolted for Calcutta with the hundred dollars.

I believe, from what I can find out, that all the women in China are sold as wives from the highest to the lowest, and a man may buy as many of them as he can afford to do, and they become his domestic servants; for he can only have, by law, one wife, who, I suspect, has certain privileges; but then the man has no choice in this wife, for this is the one that his father fixes upon. The father of the young man agrees with the lady's father what shall be given for her, and this one becomes the wife properly so called. My interpreter is very angry at this: he wants to buy a wife and make her his real wife, but his father has fixed upon another, and he complains that his father "no sabe chuse wife like him;" not that I know whether he has seen the one his father has fixed upon, for they very seldom do that,—the old people settling the whole matter in the shape I believe of a regular bargain. For instance, a man in power gets a large price for his daughter, and in return puts the husband's father in the way of making some money. The women are not actually shut up in this country, but are kept a good deal out of sight; though in towns they go to the play and other representations; but they form no part of society, and are not supposed to sit down in the presence of their husbands; and whereas they teach all the young men to read and write, they teach the women needlework and embroidery.

We had a complaint sent some months back through the Mandarins about what Mr. Gutzlaff, who is our magistrate at Chusan, was doing, and it turned out that he had established a school, where boys and girls were taught to read and write, and this being explained to the Chief Commissioner he was quite satisfied; but his answer was, it was quite right to teach the boys to read and write, as they had to make their way in the world, but as to the girls it was useless, as they were only supposed to learn embroidery.

7th June.—I am very glad you like "Les Murmures,"—the more you play them the more you will like them, which is always the case with really beautiful music, and I agree with you about that passage in the first one where it goes into the major of the key. As to the low F you mention as difficult for you to finger, playing with the violoncello it must be used, but I should think you might substitute the octave above with a violin or concertina, and that the effect would be as good, as it is quite impossible to play that passage too piano; it should just be heard, and afterwards it gets a little more forte.

9th.—You are now in London, and I conclude Charles is to dine on the 18th with the Duke, you are probably sitting in Aunt Anne's little drawing-room, where I wish I was with you, but I see no chance of that for some time, for I had a letter from Lord Fitzroy by this mail, who writes :—" I am commissioned by the Duke to say he has not lost sight of your wishes, but he has not as yet been able to fix upon an officer to command the troops left in China." I did not expect to hear anything by this mail, nor for a mail or two to come, for they cannot before that time know at home how quietly everything is settling itself here, and until they do, I cannot expect them to attend to private matters, and I am quite certain that although nothing would induce the Duke to inconvenience the service, yet as soon as it can be done without inconvenience, he will send out some one to relieve me, so you need not be expecting to have to direct to Bombay so soon as you seem to think. If the officer who is to relieve me comes overland, you must give him four months to get here, and if by sea, six, so if he started now by sea, you might write with perfect safety till August, as he would not be here till November, and if he got here in November, the odds are that I should not reach Bombay till some time in January; but you may continue to write, and I hope you will, as, if even I should be gone when the letter gets here, it would be sent after me to England, just as I have been sending Sir Hugh Gough's letters to India after him; but as soon as I hear of any one coming out, I shall be able to calculate, and write you when to direct to Bombay and when to Malta. As far as this place is concerned, I was wrong in what I wrote you about Marseilles, for now that our post here is perfectly settled, *viâ* Falmouth is just as good and quite as fast.

The Admiral has given me the "Proserpine" steamer for my trip to Macao and Canton; I start on Monday next, and shall be away till the 24th or 25th, when I hope to be back here, as we expect the next mail in about that time, so in my next I shall have to give you an account of my adventures there; I go to Mr. Drummond's house, he is a son of Lord Strathallan, and head partner here in Dent's house.

Give my love to Aunt Anne, who I am delighted to hear is so well as your letter states her to be; I must write her in a mail or so: so now, with love to Charles, whose letter goes with this, believe me, my dear Julia, yours affectionately,

SALTOUN.

XCIV.

Macao, 15th June 1843.

MY DEAR CHARLES,—I wrote you last on the 22d May, which letter went by the "Ann Eliza" that left Hong-Kong on the 9th of the month for Bombay, but I find here that a ship called the "Water Witch" is to sail in a day or two to Calcutta, and they calculate that letters by her will get over India to Bombay faster than they will get there direct by the "Ann Eliza," so this letter may perhaps be in time for the August mail and the other may not, and as this letter will go with those of the house where I am staying here, Messrs. Dent & Co., it will stand a good chance of going right; therefore I send a line to you and one to my mother by this conveyance, as I have ten letters to various people in the "Ann Eliza."

The Admiral has given me the "Proserpine" steamer, and I left Hong-Kong on Tuesday at ten o'clock, and got here at half-past five, and I stay here till Sunday, when I take the steamer up to Canton, stay there Monday, Tuesday, and Wednesday, return here Thursday, and back to Hong-Kong on Sunday, which will be the 26th, where I hope to find your letters by the April mail, which ought to be in before that time.

It is very hot here, more so than at Hong-Kong, but the houses are fine large houses like those at Lisbon; it is very odd, and shows what very little intercourse these people had formerly with the Chinese, that although the Portuguese have been here two hundred years, and the English one, they have never managed to get ice, although it is in abundance during the winter within ten days' sail of them: we got a lot down to Hong-Kong last winter, but from the ice-house being improperly built, it all melted with the first heavy rains.

I called yesterday on the Governor, and found him an old Peninsular soldier, his name Silviara de Pinto, he was in the Corps de Guides under Sir George Scovell, and inquired particularly after him, and all the headquarter people. He is a gentleman-like man, and speaks fair French; he has been here seven years, and expects to be relieved shortly.

17th.—We live very well here, dine out at the other merchants' houses, and a Mr. Kerr has lent me a very nice Arab horse to ride in the cool of the evening, and since the war ended, they are no longer kept within the barrier, as they used to be, but can ride six or seven miles in any direction quite safely.

The merchants here do not like shifting over to Hong-Kong, and I do not much wonder at it, for they have all fine large houses, well-built and comfortable in every respect, and at Hong-Kong they have all that to do, and are not likely for a long time to be half so comfortable; but as all the trade will shift over to Hong-Kong, they must go there also, or run the risk of losing a good deal of it.

We are creeping through the summer, hardly knowing how the time passes, for to-morrow will be the 18th, and I am going up to Canton, and you I conclude to dine with the Duke.

I must finish this now and give it to Mr. Dent, who will take care of it; so, with best love to Julia, believe me, my dear Charles, yours very truly,

SALTOUN.

XCV.

Hong-Kong, 26th June 1843.

MY DEAR JULIA,—I returned yesterday from my trip to Macao and Canton, and found your letter, which had reached this place on the 20th. Many thanks for it and all the news, and I am happy to find that my long missing letter to Charles has turned up at last; and although you do not mention it, I conclude you have received mine, dated 19th September, because by a letter I have received from my sister Eleanor, she has received one that went at the same time from Chusan.

I have heard nothing positive about my recall, but by a letter I have from Lord Fitzroy he writes that he hopes by the next mail to be able to send me the name of the officer that is to relieve me, and also the probable time at which he will be here.

We had a very pleasant trip to Macao and Canton. I left this on the 13th in the "Proserpine" steamer, which the Admiral had placed at my orders. Cunynghame and Haythorne went with me, and we got over to Macao in seven hours, and I took up my quarters at the house of Dent and Co., having a letter to them; I stayed there four days, and on the 18th went up to Canton to their house at that place; returned to Macao on the 22d, and got back here yesterday, the 25th, having promised the Admiral to be back by that day.

Macao is a very pretty, nice, clean town, with excellent large houses built on the Portuguese plan, and must at one time have been strong and well fortified, but now, like all other things belonging to Portugal, the fortifications are in bad order, and the garrison only 300 men, but good-looking troops enough. The English residents do not mix at all with the Portuguese, but they are very hospitable, and give a great many dinners. Some of them are married; and I saw there Mrs. Kerr, Mrs. Burns, and an unmarried sister; Mrs. Burns is a pretty woman, as is Mrs. Kerr; I also saw a Mrs. Stuart, who had been a very pretty woman, but is now a great invalid; however, she beats you in chattering all to sticks; I called on her when I went over, and also to take leave, and I did not get a word in edgeways either time. The sort of life they lead is this: get up when you like, and breakfast is ready at nine; lunch, here called tiffin, at one; at four or half after, go out to ride in the country—and Kerr lent me a very nice horse; return about seven, and dine about a quarter to eight, and go to bed about twelve.

At Canton the merchants live in what are called the Hongs; they are a row of large fine houses, built close on the bank of the river, and each merchant-house has one of these, where all the trade business is done. These houses are surrounded by the suburbs of the city, which are fully as large as the city itself, and full of excellent shops, and Europeans can go all over this, but as yet none are permitted within the city : I do not believe they are prevented going in, as the gates stand open, but they never do go in, as they are certain to be insulted if they do; so they confine their operations to the suburbs and the river. In the three days I was there I saw all the lions, so it must be a desperate dull place to live in for years, as some of them do. They keep the same hours as at Macao, and they go from one place to the other at any time they like, or rather as their business will permit; but no one goes to Canton that can help it, the whole life is so much more comfortable at Macao. The first thing you go to see at Canton are the shops where the curiosities are sold, and they are very well worth looking at, particularly the things done in jade-stone and in bronze; I contrived to get through about 1000 dollars, and when you see them in England I hope you will think them pretty.

The next place I went to see was the Joss-house in the island of Honan. To us who had been in the north it was nothing particular, but it has much land belonging to it, and is said to be the richest Joss-house in China. The next day we went to pay a visit, by invitation, to a very rich Chinese at his town house, and he showed us over the whole of it, from the entrance, to his wife's bedroom; and a remarkably good and finely-furnished house it is. This Chinaman's name is Linqua, and he is said to be one of the richest people in Canton (Howqua is the richest man, but he is a merchant, which our friend is not), and, like some of our Englishmen, seems to be getting rid of the money his father made—who was a merchant—as fast as he can. He received us in a sort of anteroom looking out upon a pond, where there were fish and ducks and curious aquatic birds of all sorts, with artificial rocks and grottos, and trees and little bridges most perfectly Chinese. Here we had tea and cakes handed to us, and his two sons and his daughter were introduced to us; his eldest boy was fourteen, the second eleven, and the girl ten years old, and likely to be very pretty, but with the small feet, which showed her to be Chinese and not Tartar. A funny thing was, that in going over the house, whenever we sat down, which we constantly did, he always sat with his back to the place from whence the women could see us— and a good lot of them he seemed to have—and every now and then he looked round, and seeing them, gave a whisk with his fan, when they all ran and hid themselves as fast as they could. After going over a great many rooms, including a sort of printing-office, where he is printing a new and very extensive dictionary of the Chinese language, which he has nearly completed, we came to the great room of the house, well furnished, and the walls covered with looking-glasses, pictures, and so forth; and from this, while we were having more cakes, tea, and champagne, I saw a very pretty woman, with several attendants, looking at us out of a window across a very small court; she, I suppose, was his wife—not the mother of his children, who, they told us, was dead. After sitting a short time he took us across the court, and we entered a very nice anteroom and sitting-room, beautifully furnished, with embroidery frames and all sorts of ladies' work things, and then the bedroom, the women hiding themselves behind screens and anything they could get behind. When we had seen all the place, we took our leave, and he asked us to lunch with him the next day at his country house. In the cool of the evening we went on the river, and saw the way the troops came up for the attack, and where they landed, and so forth.

The next day we proceeded by the river to our friend Mr. Linqua's country house, and a more singular thing I never saw in my life, and it must have cost loads of money, but it is next to impossible to describe it. Fancy a shallow pond of water, about a foot or two deep, and about a mile in circumference, entirely covered with water-lilies (the lotus), in full blow; in the centre, built upon piles, a magnificent saloon of an oblong shape and open, with Venetian blinds on all sides for air. At the end of this, but separated from it by about five yards, another building where they can have what they call a sing-sing, or theatre, the company sitting in the saloon, the actors being in the other building. The above-mentioned pond is studded in all directions with little islands of earth that must have been brought from a distance, some long, some round, others triangular, all planted with various sorts of trees, several having small pavilions on them, and others with aviaries for all sorts of birds, gold and silver pheasants, etc., and some with rocks and grottos all artificial, others with pens where they have deer and hares and rabbits; all these islands and buildings communicating by bridges, some high arches, others low, all fantastically made and painted of the most gaudy colours; in short, the nearest thing I ever saw to it is one of the old china plates, but infinitely more extensive than that gives any idea of. One gets to this curious place by a small canal that comes out of the river, and at the landing-place there is a very nice dwelling-house, where the people who take care of it live, and this has two or three rooms *en suite* for company; and when we had tired ourselves with walking about, we went there to lunch. Linqua lets his friends go there to amuse themselves, and the effect was much increased to us by several parties being there that day, as it enlivened the scene with the people and dresses which belonged to it.

We did not return by the river, but followed the canal, which, after passing through an immense town built in the water on piles, brought us through the enormous boat population which has been so often described, and is the most extraordinary thing that ever was seen. They calculate that five hundred thousand are born, live, and die in these boats. Many of the boats (and they are of all sorts and sizes) are stationary, and fitted up as coffee-houses, eating-houses, theatres, etc., others are movable, and the rich Chinese hire them for a day, or a week, or a month, and go with their party or family to live on the river for the sake of coolness. It was just dark as we passed through them, and they were all lit up with their curious lanterns, more or less brilliant, according, I conclude, to the funds of the parties occupying them; altogether it is a thing very well worth seeing.

The next day, the 22d, we returned to Macao. At this place the only things worth seeing are the front of the church of St. Jose (the interior was burned down long ago, but the front saved, and it is a fine piece of architecture), and a place they call the Caza Gardens belonging to a Portuguese; they are extensive and well laid out, with some pretty views from certain points, and they have a grotto where they have put up a monument to the poet Camoens.

On getting here on Sunday we found the Chinese Commissioners had arrived, and the next day, Monday the 26th, was fixed for exchanging the ratified treaties, and the time fixed for five o'clock P.M., at the Government House. The troops were drawn up in front of it, and the Commissioners came in their State sedan chairs, and had arms presented to them, and so forth. The Treaties were then carefully examined and exchanged, when a Royal salute and feu-de-joie was fired by the troops, and they marched past the High Commissioner in slow and quick time. The Queen's Proclamation was then read, appointing Sir H. Pottinger Governor of the Island, and he was accordingly sworn in, after which a salute of nineteen guns was fired in honour of him.

We then got rid of our full-dress toggery as soon as we could, for it was infernally hot, and at seven o'clock sat down to dinner, a party of fifty. The High Commissioner sat next to Sir Henry, on one side of him, and I on the other, having the Tartar General Heyling next to me, and Whang, the other Commissioner, sat opposite, each of these having an interpreter next to him. They did very well with the soup and the fish, but when it came to the meat, they could not use the knife, so we cut it up into small pieces for them, I feeding the Tartar as if he had been a tame sparrow, and they ate and drank enormously of every thing.

Soon after dinner they began to play amongst themselves a game with the fingers, exactly as the Italians do, throwing out one hand each, and whoever guessed the right number of fingers displayed won; the loser drank a bumper of wine. The only thing I observed, for the play was quite fair, was that, whenever the Chief Commissioner lost, the other stood up as a mark of respect when he, Keying, had to drink the wine, he being of the blood-royal. By this means each got at least a bottle of wine more than any of us, and after a bit Keying, who is a natural musician, and who had been singing the tunes that the band were playing, said he would sing us a Chinese song, which he did, and had his health drunk according to English custom. He called upon Sir H. Pottinger for a song, which he sang very well, then Whang gave us another Chinese song, and then it came to my turn, and after me the Tartar General, the other two had sung Chinese songs, and they were rather pretty, but the Tartar General gave us a Mongol Tartar song, and it reminded me of some of the wild chants I had heard the gipsies in Spain sing; several others sang songs, and Keying was greatly delighted with several of them; and about eleven o'clock the Mandarins went away in their sedan chairs as jollily drunk as any three fellows I ever saw in my life.

This morning they paid me a visit before going round the island, which they are doing to-day in the steamer, and they complained that they had drunk too much wine the night before; I gave them lots of tea, but they would not have anything stronger. They are to lunch at Chuck-Choo with Campbell, but I made an excuse, saying I had letters to write, and to-morrow they return to Canton; and Hong-Kong has now become a colony of Great Britain.

When I was up at Canton the Chinese Commissioners sent me their cards of State; they will do for your book, so I send them: of course I had mine made out by the interpreters in the same form, and sent to them; and what with my rank in the army, my rank as a peer, and my four orders of knighthood, and the countries they belong to, my line of Chinese letters was as long as any of theirs.

If you happen to see Tudor you can tell him, that before I had received his letter introducing Mr. Bloomfield, I had granted what he wanted, which was leave to go to Calcutta for the purpose of resigning his Commission, being obliged to go home on account of some family business.

The weather is now very hot, but Charles knows of old that hot weather and I are very good friends, the only difference is I drink about as much again as I do in the cold. Love to Charles, and believe me, my dear Julia, yours affectionately, SALTOUN.

XCVI.

Hong-Kong, 29th June 1843.

MY DEAR CHARLES,—On the 17th of this month I wrote you a letter from Macao, to which place I had gone on a visit, and from that I went on to Canton.

I was very much pleased with my trip, and saw many things well worth the trouble of seeing; but as I have given a long account of it in my letter to Mr. Dick, which goes by this same mail, I shall refer you to that for the history.

The merchants at Macao were a good deal taken aback by Lord Aberdeen's letter, which Peel read in his speech on opium, and which has been here these three months, but kept secret, a proof that Pottinger does not altogether approve of it. It had been the intention of all these merchants to come over here to reside, instead of at Macao, which would very much increase the trade and prosperity of this colony; but the principal reason for so doing was the opium, which they meant to store here, and overlook with their own eyes; but if it is not to be permitted to come, as Lord Aberdeen's letter says it is not to be imported here for the purpose of exportation to China, they have no object in coming, and most likely will remain where they are at Macao, and carry on the opium trade by storing it in ships in the harbour of the island of Lintin, as they did before we got Hong-Kong, and this place, instead of being a thriving colony, will sink to nothing, and be a great expense to the country to maintain.

I believe that Pottinger is not without hopes of being able to get the Chinese Government to legalise the importing of it, which would remove all difficulty, give the Emperor a great increase of revenue, and do away with the smuggling; but, at the same time, the great profits made by smuggling it would be done away with also, and the merchants would only make the fair profit they do on any other article of trade. The great difficulty is, that the Emperor has issued such edicts against opium that he does not like to eat his words; but these edicts were not against opium for itself, about which he does not care a straw, but in hopes of preventing the silver going out of the country to pay for it, which would be done if it were made an article of trade, as merchants would then take produce in exchange for it. The people of this country will have it; and if we do not bring it others will, and British capital will be employed for the benefit of other nations, instead of our own, if we prohibit the trade in it.

I have given you all the news, so, with love to Aunt Anne and Mr. Dick, believe me, my dear Charles, yours very truly, SALTOUN.

XCVII.

Hong-Kong, 10th July 1843.

MY DEAR JULIA,—On the 26th of last month I wrote to you, and on the 29th I wrote to Charles, and both these letters left this on the 1st July to go to Bombay in a ship called the "Mor," and they ought to reach you in October.

The Chinaman was right about the guitar, and he so glued the bridge that it has stood quite well, but then came another difficulty, the strings would not stand, and my chanterelle broke when the instrument was tuned as low as G, instead of A. I saw in our paper that some one here had some fiddle-strings to sell, and as the usual firsts are much smaller than mine, I sent to buy some, but it turned out that the man would not sell the strings unless you also bought a fiddle; so as Thomas had not brought his fiddle with him, I made him a present of one, and so got some strings, but these broke just the same as the others; they would tune up to A flat, but would not stand at that, still I heard the fiddle going in the servants' room, so I asked him about the strings, and he told me they all broke, but he had found a Chinese fiddle-string that would stand, so I got some of them. They are very thin, but have a fair tone, so I began to tune my instrument as thus :—I had one of these Chinese firsts; I took one of my thick chanterelles for a second; I had some very thin G's for Turin guitars, and I made one of them the third; one of my thick G's for a fourth; a D silver string for fifth; and an A for sixth. The proportions are very good, and although the general tone is not so strong, it does very well, and Grant and I play away again, but it hurts the fingers more, and at first was more difficult to finger. The strings I brought out with me in the guitar-case have lasted till now, so I have not opened the stock I brought out hermetically sealed, but whenever the damp weather is over, and the regular strings can be used again, I must do so; but by that time I hope to be able to give a guess when I shall be playing with you again.

A ship came in this morning from Madras, bringing back some of the officers belonging to the Native Regiments here, and one of them has sent me a fine turtle; we have turtle here, but they are very small, and it takes two or three of them to make a soup; but at Sincapore, from whence this one comes, they are the same as in the West Indies; I have sent to see if the cook can dress it to-day, as I have the Plenipotentiary and all the big-wigs to dine with me.

I got also by the same ship a letter from Sir H. Gough, sending me the vote of thanks of the House of Lords; and a letter from Lord Tweeddale, from which I am happy to find that both he and Lady Tweeddale are quite well and like Madras, but they complain of the great heat of that place. I understand things are going on well with respect to the Commercial Treaty, and that they hope to have it all ready by the 1st of August, in which case this letter may very likely go with it, as Colonel Malcolm will take it in a steamer, which will be the best opportunity we shall have for writing for months.

21st July.—Our mail came in on the 11th, and brought me yours and Charles's letters, as also one from Lord Fitzroy, who had nothing certain about me, but wrote that, by orders of the Duke, he had that day written to an officer to propose to him the command here in my succession, and that he hoped by the next mail to send me a more complete communication.

We have received accounts from Bombay that a Mr. Commissary-General Coffin has reached that place with a host of other commissaries who are to come on here and take charge of all money, stores, etc. etc., and relieve our Indian establishment, and as soon as that is done, the account with the India Company is to close, and the officers of that establishment will of course return to India.

This will make no sort of difference to the troops here, who will be paid the same as heretofore, but it will simplify the matter; for, as this Commissary Coffin is to receive all the money paid by China, he will pay us out of that, sending the account direct home, whereas now we are paid from Calcutta, and they charge it against the Home Government; moreover, all the stores, etc., will come into one account, and be furnished direct from home, instead of coming from India, thereby incurring nearly double the expense of carriage.

This is the anniversary of the taking of Chin-kiang-foo, the action that decided the fate of China, and accordingly the 98th Regiment gives a grand dinner at Chuck-Choo where they are quartered, and I am going over there to dine with them; I shall start about five o'clock, it will be rather hot for the first hour, but after that the hills are so steep that it will be shady all the way; I shall get in plenty of time to dress, as they do not dine till a quarter before eight. I have a bed at the Colonel's (who by the by has been uncommonly well for a long time); the next day they are to dine early, and I shall ride back in the cool of the evening.

We are all making up our letters to go by the steamer on the 1st of August, but they sent me word yesterday that a mail would be made up for Bombay by a sailing ship, and although I think the steamer will beat that vessel, yet as these things are uncertain, I shall send this letter, and one to my mother, by this sailing ship on the 24th, as I shall have plenty of time to write to you, and to her, other letters to go by the steamer on the 1st of August; this steamer is to go direct to Suez, and I hear that a steamer is waiting for Colonel Malcolm at Alexandria, so in all probability that will be the fastest communication that ever will be received from China, still if the ship that takes this letter reaches Bombay in thirty-seven days, which is not impossible, you will receive this letter first, so I send it for the chance.

24th.—We had a capital party at Chuck-Choo, and I came back the next day after dinner, and as I am certainly none the worse for it, I conclude it did me good, got me a little out of the very regular life I pass here.

I must close this letter now, my dear Mr. Dick, and send all other news by the steamer that starts on the 1st of August, which letter you will get before you get this one I think; so, with love to Aunt Anne and Charles, believe me, my dear Julia, yours affectionately, S——.

XCVIII.

Hong-Kong, 16th July 1843.

MY DEAR CHARLES,—Our mail came in on the 11th instant, and brought me your letter of the 4th May, as also one from Mr. Dick, which I shall answer by the first opportunity.

I find that others, than you, of my friends at home thought the appointment of Sir Henry Pottinger would relieve me, but he is Civil Governor here;—all Governors, Civil as well as Military, are Commanders-in-Chief in their respective Governments, and in most they are also Vice-Admirals,—and this gives him no direct control over the troops, for all orders he may wish to give to particular guards or officers he cannot give direct, but must give them through the officer commanding, even in his own colony; and he has no more control over the Army of Occupation here than he had before as Plenipotentiary, which is pretty full, for both the Admiral and myself have received orders to carry into effect any instructions he may give us. One difference exists, that whereas, before he was Governor, I could carry into execution a sentence of death, I cannot do so now in this colony without his concurrence in the same, expressed in writing, but this does not extend to Chusan or Colansoo, but only in this particular colony, just as we never execute a man in a town without notifying it to the resident Governor for the time being.

You congratulate me on having found a drill-ground, but it is of no use to me, for it is thirteen miles at the least from where most of the troops are, and the only road to it is a good deal worse than the short road to Coignafearn,[1] for you can ride that road, but on this one you must lead your pony in many places for near half a mile on end, and even if the road was good, the distance is far too great to go in this climate merely for drill.

It is very hot here now, the thermometer at night not lower than 83°, nor higher in the day as yet than 91°, the mean heat last week was 88°, and I suppose it will be about the same for two months more, when we shall begin to get cooler at night, and it is clear now that I shall have to see the hot weather out, for nothing was settled about relieving me when the last mail came away.

I hear the commercial treaty, and tariff, are settled, and it is to come into operation at Canton on the 27th of this month, and at the ports in the north on

[1] His grouse-moor in the Monadhliadh, Inverness-shire.

the 7th September; Colonel Malcolm will leave this on or about the 1st August, and take it home with him in the "Ackbar" steamer, and most likely this letter will go by the same opportunity, the last we shall have for some time, so I shall not close it for some days yet.

We are at a regular stand still here just at present; the engineer, Major Aldridge, has given in a plan for fortifying this port, which, by the purchase of certain houses, would at once have given us cover for our troops here, and those we expect out, but it would have cost a good deal of money. The Governor objects to the outlay, and says we want no fortifications at all, and the Admiral does not like the Naval Station selected. Under these circumstances nothing can be done in the shape of barracks till they settle where the forts are to be, and the consequence is that when the depôt of the 98th comes out, I shall have seven or eight hundred men without any cover for them; the only thing I have for it is to put them under canvas; but the evil of this is that I can only encamp them in places so distant that they are not available for duty, which is very hard here just now : in any formed place one could billet them, but the houses of the Europeans are all building, nothing finished, and therefore not as yet registered, and in the Chinese houses it is impossible, for a Chinese house consists of two small rooms, the lower one the shop, the upper one where they all pig together, men, women, and children, as thick as herrings in a barrel.

I have just heard of a Sir —— Coffin, a Commissary-General, having got to Bombay in his way out here, with a host of Commissaries who are to take charge of all the departments from the Indian authorities, and close the account with the India Company; it will make no difference to the troops, who, being on the Indian Establishment, will receive pay and rations the same as heretofore; so the only thing I hope is that they may turn out as gentleman-like and pleasant a set of men as the officers they relieve are.

July 30th.—Since writing the above, the port of Canton has been opened for trade upon the new system, and Mr. Tradescant Say is Consul there, pro tempore, and the "Dido" is at Whampoa to support his authority, where she will remain till the "Childers" brig comes, which is the regular ship-of-war for this station. The mail closes to-morrow, and this will go with Malcolm. No more news, and, with love to Aunt Anne and Mr. Dick, believe me, my dear Charles, yours very truly,
SALTOUN.

XCIX.

Hong-Kong, 28th July 1843.

MY DEAR JULIA,—On the 10th of this month I began a letter to you, which was sent to the post last Monday to go to Bombay by a sailing ship, but I very much suspect it will only get as far as Macao, and go home by the same conveyance that this does, in which case you will get them both together; but this will be the quickest communication you will have received from China, or probably ever will, for this letter is to go direct to Suez by the "Ackbar" steamer, which starts from this on the 1st of August, and takes Lieutenant-Colonel Malcolm and the commercial treaty, and tariff, and I hear he has a steamer waiting for him at Alexandria, and we therefore calculate that he will get home in between sixty and seventy days. The said treaty, and tariff, came into operation yesterday at the port of Canton, and it is expected to be in force at the northern ports of Amoy, Souchu, Ningpo, and Shanghai, on or about the 1st of September.

I heard yesterday from Colansoo, the island we hold near Amoy, and the cholera, it was hoped, had passed away, as they had not had any fresh cases for some days; they lost twenty-three men of the 18th Royal Irish, but the Native troops did not take it; and on the whole they are by no means sickly, having 82 sick in 960 men. We are much worse here, and I have removed the wing of the 55th Regiment from West Point, on board ship, where I shall let them stay till the hot weather is over; and in the meantime I have set parties to work to drain the barracks at West Point, and to destroy some pieces of stagnant water there, to which the doctors attribute the sickness. I think the hot weather has something to do with it, and it is very hot here now; however, as yet it agrees quite well with me. To be sure I do not trouble myself with much clothing, and I should be starved to death in England with what I wear. I have a pair of silk socks, nankeen trousers, a blue calico shirt, and a very thin white cotton waistcoat and jacket, and at night I sleep on a Chinese mat, and, for the honour of the thing, have a sheet that I can pull over me, though I generally sleep without it, and this in a room with three windows in it all open; but in another month or so, the nights will begin to get cool again, which is a great comfort,—not but what I sleep very well in general; sometimes I do not get to sleep directly, but not often; I generally go to bed between eleven and twelve, and never wake till about half-past six, and that is longer than I ever sleep in England. Under these circumstances I ought to get very fat, but the perspiration is so enormous that I do not think I am a bit heavier now than when I left home; I got very fat on board ship, and I shall most likely do the same going home, whenever that time comes.

We heard yesterday of our Commissary, who is coming from England; the ship he is on board of got some damage in the Bengal sea, in a gale of wind, and is in Sincapore refitting, so we may expect him here any day. He is a great man, Mr. Commissary Coffin, for he is to have charge not only of the money required for this place, but of all that China is to pay.

30th.—I dined the other day on board the "Cornwallis" with the Admiral, and he told Grant he should like much to hear us play. Grant mentioned this to me, so I wrote him word if he would come and dine quietly at half-past six we should probably give him enough of it before he was obliged to return on board; so he came yesterday, and is a remarkably good listener, for we played from half-past eight to ten, and he never went to sleep. We first played "Les Murmures de la Rhone," and after that "Dolores," and the things from the "Somnambula," "Guillaume Tell," and "Lucia di Lammermoor," and finished with some things we have by Ball, taken from different operas, Italian and German; they are called "Pot Pourris," and were published at Bonn and Cologne.

We have got a change of weather to-day; it blows hard in squalls, with showers of heavy rain, and has greatly cooled the air; the glass this morning was at 84°, and it is now, at three o'clock, only 85°, and we have not had it so low these two months; in general, at three o'clock, p.m., it has been 89° to 90°.

Cunnynghame went yesterday to Sy-Wann. A party of the 98th are there, under Captain Ranier, who is very fond of singing; and as some of the young ones of the Regiment sing pretty well, they have a sort of a Saturday night club there, and they go there from the different stations of the Regiment, and Cunnynghame, who sings the "Vale of Avoca," and things of that sort, is a pretty constant attendant. He will get a rare ducking coming home to-day, which will cool him and do him good; not that I ever heard of any hard drinking, but I know from experience that young men's singing parties are not the driest things in the world; at least they used not to be in my time, and I do not suppose they have changed very much; it makes people thirsty.

You may have seen in the papers, and most likely I wrote you about it at the time, of a Mr. Wilson who made a narrow escape when the lorcha (the name they have here for a passage-boat) he was in was attacked by pirates. We have had another case of the same kind, in which a Doctor M'Kinlay of the 18th Royal Irish has been murdered; at least he has never been heard of, and it is now a month since he left this for Macao; he had come down here in bad health, and a Board had been held on him which had ordered him home, and he was going to Macao to settle for his passage; but in this instance it is supposed that the Chinese part of the crew attacked the Europeans, probably when they were asleep, murdered the whole of them, and ran away with the boat. After a lapse of ten days, two of this crew were seen in a village near Macao; one of them escaped, but the other was taken, and he told a story of their being attacked by two other boats, who murdered the Europeans, and they, the Chinese, jumped overboard and saved themselves by swimming; but this was not believed, as, if they had been honest, they would have come and told the owners what had happened, instead of keeping out of the way for so long a time. He was given over to the Chinese authorities, who, I hear, have extracted the truth, and as the crew are all known they will soon get hold of them, but we shall never see anything more of the poor doctor; he had no money of his own with him, but the boat had 20,000 dollars of other parties' on board, which was the temptation.

The Chinese have a way of their own in these cases; if they cannot find the man, they seize his family and relations; and as these generally know where he is, they give him up to save their own heads, which they cut off without any warning if they cannot find the culprit. Under any circumstances they take all the property, which the Mandarin pockets, and this is what they call squeezing, of which process there are endless varieties, by which the Mandarin extracts more or less according to the crime committed; and when the parties are rich they generally buy the Mandarin off; for when a rich man is convicted the higher fellows step in, and take the lion's share. I have no more news, my dear Mr. Dick, nor do I expect any, but I will not close this till to-morrow.

31st.—The rain lasted all night, and it is much cooler to-day, and as this must go to the post, I must finish it now, as I have at least three hours' good work with the returns, and various letters to the authorities. I have written to Aunt Anne by this opportunity; give her my love, and with love to Charles, believe me, my dear Julia, yours affectionately, S———.

C.

Victoria, Hong-Kong, 12th August 1843.

MY DEAR JULIA,—My last letter to you, dated 28th July, left this by the "Ackbar" steamer on the 1st of this month, and I trust by this time is passed Sincapore, and well on its way to Penang, where the steamer is to take in coal, and means to go from that to Aden. We are looking for our mail, the June one, every day, at least I am, because I expect by this mail to hear something certain about my being relieved; we have a ship in here that left Bombay on the 5th July, the mail had not then arrived, and we have another ship in yesterday that left Sincapore on the 2d of this month, and she had heard nothing of it; it is to come, I have heard, by a ship called the "John Brown," but whether this ship is a fast or a slow one nobody here knows.

Last Monday, the 7th, the barometer began to fall, though we had nothing that day, but in the course of Tuesday it fell from 29° 70′ to 29° 40′, and that night we had a most tremendous storm of thunder, lightning, and rain; the wind was so high that we were afraid a typhoon was coming on, so we got everything ready, but when the rain came the wind ceased, at least the extreme violence of it abated. It blew very hard all Wednesday and Thursday, with a very great deal of rain, which came through the roof in all directions; we had one place in the sitting-room, where we could sit round a table that was dry, and it did not come into my bed, nor into Cunynghame's, but all the rest of the house was running like a little river. It began to take up yesterday about noon, and the glass is now at 29° 60′, and on the rise, so we may consider it over for this time; it has not done much damage; it blew down a mat barracks of the 41st Madras N. I., and unroofed the officers' houses, also mat ones, of the 98th at Chuck-Choo; the boats all went over to the other side where it is more sheltered, and I have not heard of any harm to speak of having happened either to them or the ships. We heard yesterday that the "Samarang," Captain Belcher, a surveying ship, had got on shore near the island of Borneo, and the

"Vixen" steamer has started this morning to go to her assistance; they say she is high and dry near the mouth of some river,—that the crew have landed, and I have no doubt before the "Vixen" gets there, for the distance is about 1000 miles, they will have got so much out of her that they will easily get her off again. She has just come from England to complete a survey of part of these seas on which her Captain was employed some years back, in the "Sulphur," I believe.

Our great surveyor here, Captain Kellett, who has gone home in the "Ackbar," gave Cunynghame a kitten to help to keep our rats under, and by means of her and sundry dogs we have driven them quite out of the house; I have not seen one these two months, and before that, I used to see eight and ten a day. The said kitten has installed me as her feeder; I give her nothing but fish at breakfast and dinner, and she is very impatient, and makes more row and screaming till she gets her plate of it than even Tootles used to do, in consideration of which feeding she is now sitting on my shoulder making sundry attempts to get at the pen. Our dogs are excellent, and I believe a greater protection against the Chinese thieves, who are very expert, than the sentry is. At first we got a grown-up dog, but he was of no use, as the Chinamen spoke to him in Chinese, and he would not bark at them at all; so we sent into the market and got four or five of the dogs they sell there for food, which they do when they are quite young, just after they can see; these we have brought up, the servants have cut their tails and ears; we have brought them to kill rats, which they do as well as any English dog, and as they do not understand a word of Chinese, they will not let a Chinaman near the place.

I hear that Major Pottinger came here yesterday; he is the man you have read of in the Cabul business, and is a nephew of Sir Henry our Governor; I have not as yet seen him. I have no more news now; so goodbye for the present, my dear Mr. Dick.

22d.—You will see that I began this some days back, and we are still without any news of our mail from England, which is very provoking.

Major Pottinger dined here the other day; he is still suffering from the wound he got in Affghanistan; he is a pleasant conversible man, but older than I had put him down at, and not good-looking. Within this last month we have had a Mr. and Mrs. Halliday come over here from Macao to reside, she is an American, and rather a pretty woman; and we have also a Mr. and Mrs. Davidson, with her sister, a Miss Whittle, come from Sincapore for the same purpose, well-mannered people; and we have here also a nice elderly lady, a Mrs. Wilson, wife of Colonel Wilson our Paymaster-General; so I had them all to dinner yesterday, and considering that, except Mrs. Wilson, they were all entire strangers, the party went off very well. Grant could not dine, so we had no music for them; he has had the fever, but is better, and was out on horseback for the first time yesterday evening, but not well enough to face a dinner.

To-day I am going to dine with our Admiral, Sir W. Parker. Our little Admiral, as we call Sir T. Cochrane, has got so tired of the place that he is gone out on a cruise, and has been sailing about for this last month; he is, however, to come back early in next month, when Sir William is going for a lark to Macao and Canton, and after that he goes to Manilla, and as soon as the north-east monsoon is fairly set in, goes off to India to visit the different ports of his station, and leaves Cochrane to carry on the duty here. The "Vixen" steamer is expected back about the middle of September.

It seems that Sir E. Belcher had gone up the Sarawak river in Borneo, as far as a settlement made there by Mr. Brooke, an English gentleman, and in coming down, at high water, his ship took the ground, and when the water left her, fell over on her side. In order to give her air in the hold, she had air-holes from above the maindeck ports down the lining of the ship to the hold, the water got down these and filled her quite full, destroying everything in the shape of provisions, etc. etc., but I hear they saved the chronometers and other scientific instruments; they propose to build a dam round her to exclude the tide, and then pump her out, and if she has not knocked a hole in her bottom, or done herself any serious injury, they will most likely get her off, and at Sincapore she can be put all to rights.

23d.—No word of the mail, and although the "Petrel" leaves this to-day, she goes over to Macao and may not sail for a day or two yet; so if the mail comes in before she goes, I will send a line by her if possible; at all events I shall write again about the 1st of September, when, I hear, another clipper called the "Kelpie" is to go to Bombay, and our mail ought to be here by that time, if it is not lost. No more news; so, with love to Charles and Aunt Anne, to whom I wrote last packet, believe me, my dear Julia, yours affectionately,

S——.

CI.

Hong-Kong, 22d August 1843.

My dear Charles,—Here we are on the 22d, and as yet the June mail not come in, nor have we heard anything about it; we have a ship from Bombay that left that place on the 1st July, and the mail had not then arrived there; last year it reached this place on the 4th of August, but we have had very bad weather in the China seas this season, which has delayed it. Yesterday they sent word that a mail to Bombay would be made up at three o'clock to-morrow, to go direct by the "Petrel" clipper; so, although I have no sort of news to send from this, I write a few lines just to say that all is well, as we may not have another opportunity for some days, though I hear that something is to sail on or about the 1st of September, by which time I trust we shall have received our mail, and that I may have something certain to write about my return.

In my letter to Mr. Dick that goes with this, I have given an account of our gale of wind, and the weather is now fine again, and ever since the gale it has been cooler by four or five degrees than it was before. The sickness, however, continues: the 55th have 40 per cent. sick, and even the native troops have nearly 20; the 98th who are over at Chuck-Choo are more healthy, but they have two posts, for the protection of the inhabitants from pirates and robbers, that are more sickly, and in consequence the duty is very hard; and, from the way the roster is affected by men going into hospital, the healthy men sometimes have not two nights in bed.

The Commissary-General and his myrmidons have arrived, and the commissariat and pay departments are to be transferred to him on the 1st of September, but we can do nothing about the Ordnance, as no Ordnance storekeeper has as yet come out, nor do we hear of one coming, and it cannot be given over till one comes out.

The Indians are delighted at getting away, and I do not much wonder at it; to be sure, they love well-paid situations, but it is such a stupid place, to say nothing of the sickness at this time of the year, that a man ought to be well paid for staying here. .

They write from Canton that the Hong merchants, who were set aside by the Treaty of Peace, have combined, and are doing all they can to obstruct the trade, and at present nothing is doing; but then the teas are not yet come from the tea-country, nor will they come for three weeks or a month yet, and some people think when the tea merchants arrive they will be as ready to trade direct as our people are; however, others say the smaller Mandarins are at the bottom of this. Be this as it may, the trade in the north is going on most briskly, although the ports are not yet open, but will be shortly; and as the ports of Ningpo and Shanghai are not a third of the distance from the tea country that Canton is, if the Canton people do not take care the tea trade may leave them altogether, and be transferred to those ports, whereas now they have the whole of it.

Campbell was over here the other day from Chuck-Choo, he has been pretty well for some time, but still he has fever and ague every now and then; he begs me to remember him to you and Mr. Dick. I have no more news, so, with love to her and Aunt Anne, believe me, my dear Charles, yours very truly,

SALTOUN.

25th.—Our mail from England came in last night and brought me your letter of the 3d, as also one from Mr. Dick. I am very sorry for the poor old "Bull," but from your former letters I had very little hope for him. This case of Sir G. Berkley will give me a month or two more of this place. Our mail had been detained till this day at three o'clock, so I have opened this to say I have received your letters; I have also one from Aunt Anne. Love to Mr. Dick; yours truly, S——.

CII.

Hong-Kong, 4th September 1843.

MY DEAR CHARLES,—In my last, dated 22d of August, and which I opened after I had finished it to say that I had received your letter by the June mail, I mentioned either in my letter to you, or one to Mr. Dick, that I should write again by a ship that was to go on the 1st of this month, but my last letters to you and others did not actually sail till the 28th from Macao, and therefore I did not write anything to go by the 1st of this month, but I have just heard that the vessel that was intended to sail on the 1st was still at Whampoa, not having as yet discharged her cargo, and that she will not sail before the 7th, and very likely not before the 9th, by which time I hope we shall have our July mail in, and that I may be able to add something certain as to myself to the end of this letter.

Since my last things here remain in the same state; the trade at Canton stopped; and the Governor, Sir Henry, has gone over to Macao to be nearer at hand in the discussions that are taking place on this subject, and they expect it will be all set to rights very shortly. He, Sir Henry, has, however, sustained a great loss in arguing these matters, by the death of Mr. Morrison, which took place last week, from fever, as he was by far the best interpreter we have, and could be trusted to any extent as to his rendering our papers into Chinese, as he was perfectly well acquainted with all Chinese manners and customs, and a great favourite with every one. He had been in this country all his life, his father having been the missionary Morrison at the time of Lord Macartney's Embassy; I hardly know how Sir Henry will be able to supply his place.

As yet we have had no typhoon, but we had a very severe gale of wind which did some damage to our temporary buildings; I hope we may escape a typhoon this year, for I am certain if we have one that half the place will be laid smack smooth. I shall wait the event of our mail coming in before I add to this.

8th.—No mail as yet, but we know it is close by. However, the "Kelpie," which is to take this, sails to-day, so I cannot wait any longer, and shall probably write next by the "Anonima."

We yesterday heard from Pekin that the Emperor has confirmed the tariff and all the new consular regulations, and our Consuls, such as we have of them, are to go to the north on the 20th; this approval by the Emperor may have some effect on the Canton people.

The "Samarang," Sir E. Belcher, that I wrote in my last was on shore at Borneo, has been got off, I hear, with very little damage, but they lost all their provisions, and the men and officers all their clothes and other things, but they can be replaced. Most likely this letter and my next will go from Bombay at the same time; give my love to Mr. Dick and Aunt Anne, and believe me, my dear Charles, yours very truly, SALTOUN.

CIII.

Hong-Kong, 4th September 1843.

MY DEAR JULIA,—I have little or nothing to write about, at the same time I do not like to let an opportunity pass of sending a letter to Bombay, for the chance of its going by a different mail from the one by which my last letter, which left this on the 27th of last month, will go by. This ship, the "Kelpie," ought to have sailed on the 1st, but from the circumstance of something having gone wrong with the trade at Canton, she has not been able to discharge her cargo, and is therefore detained, and I am told not likely to sail till towards the end of the week,—this being Monday; so I write a few lines just to say that I have received your kind letter, No. 18, which came a day after I had sent my last to you to the post; but I opened my letter to Charles and mentioned this in my P.S. to his letter.

By the last mail I got no letter from Lord Fitzroy, but I heard otherwise that this command had been offered to Sir G. Berkley, and by a letter that Campbell had from the Horse Guards, they made certain there that he would take it. However, he has got a wife and family, which makes a difference in these matters. But we expect our next mail in every day, which will probably bring me something certain on this head, and I hope it may arrive before I am obliged to send this, in which case I will add all the intelligence I get.

A ship came in the other day from England, having on board Mrs. Ranier, the wife of a captain of the 98th; I have not as yet seen her, but my last ladies' party, of which I wrote you, went off so well that I have made a party for this lady, and some of the others dine here to-morrow, so she will be introduced to them regularly; I have also invited a Mrs. Sullivan, who, I hear, is a nice person; she and her husband came here in the "Warlock," a yacht, he having the charge of her; the said yacht has been sold to Jardine's house, to be employed here as a clipper in the opium trade, and in the meantime these Sullivans are, I conclude, waiting till they can get a good passage home, or he may be looking out for some ship that may become vacant.

I was delighted to find that you had got quite well again. I had a slight touch of fever myself yesterday was a week; it returned very slightly on the Tuesday, but on Thursday the doctor gave me quinine, and I have had none of it since, and the quinine is now reduced to two glasses a day: Grant has got the same fever, but it is more severe with him than with me; I suspect his stomach is more difficult to keep in order, which prevents the quinine from taking proper effect: as to Cunynghame, he has had none of it, and as we have now got through three of the bad months, he has a fair chance of escaping. The weather has changed a little, that is, the nights are cooler, and next month it will be much more so; still September and the first part of October are not healthy in this climate; the tremendous vegetation which the rains produce is then dying, and that in all countries is a bad time of the year. I have no more to say just now, so good-bye for the present, my dear Mr. Dick.

8th.—No mail as yet come in, and this letter must go to the post this forenoon, or it will be too late. We know the mail must be somewhere close by, for the "Spiteful" came in from Sincapore yesterday, and the mail in the "Anonima" had sailed from that place four days before she did, but these merchants often play these tricks whenever they expect a rise or fall in the price of the great staple here, the opium, so I shall not be able to write to you again till the "Anonima" returns, and that, I hear, will be in a few days after she has come in here, and in all probability you will get this letter and the one by the "Anonima" at the same time.

We have heard all the general news, for Captain Maitland of the "Spiteful" steamer brought a paper of the 6th July from Sincapore; so we know that old Lord Cathcart is dead, and that Earl Grey has had a paralytic attack, also that Napier has been made a G.C.B. and got a regiment, both of which he deserves: also about this duel in which Colonel Fawcett was killed, perhaps when the letters come some of the officers of this regiment may hear what was the cause of these brothers-in-law fighting, for the papers say nothing about it. I must finish now, my dear Mr. Dick; so, with love to Charles and Aunt Anne, believe me, my dear Julia, yours affectionately, S——.

CIV.

Hong-Kong, 15th September 1843.

MY DEAR JULIA,—My last letter to you was sent from this on the 8th inst., and the next day the "Anonima" came in with the July mail, and brought me your letter, with the supplement to it, and a song on what they call here imperial coloured paper. I hear that the "Anonima" is to return to Bombay in a few days, but as yet no day has been fixed; so I write a few lines to thank you for your nice long letter, with so much in it of your every-day going-on; but I can send you nothing of that sort in return, for every day passes here so much like the previous one that it is impossible to fancy anything more dull than this place is at this season. The only news is that one sick officer is a little better, and another a little worse; I hope, however, that we have got over the worst of it for this year, as the weather has become cooler by from five to six degrees during the day, and from eight to ten during the night, and in about six weeks from this we shall have it cool and pleasant enough.

I wrote you in my last that I was to have another ladies' party, and it went off very well. Mrs. Ranier, the new lady, and wife of a captain of the 98th, is a pleasant conversable person; poor lady, she is badly off for wardrobe, for all her ornaments and new dresses were in a large tin chest which is not to be found, and they suppose that the outfit-man at home, who undertook to see it embarked, neglected to do so, and that it has never been sent; if so, she may get it out by another ship, but in the meantime the inconvenience is as great as if it had been lost. Another lady has arrived within these few days, I hear a very nice pretty person, but I have not seen her, nor am I likely for some time; she is the wife of Dr. Burritt, and comes from Madras; he is surgeon to the 41st Madras N. Infantry, and, poor fellow, is suffering severely from fever, and is still in considerable danger, but the doctors hope to get him through, although medical men are much the worst patients; they know too much, and are generally very apt to despond.

I wish I could anticipate the next mail from England, but that cannot be, and so I must have patience for seven or eight weeks at least before it can come. I heard by the last that D'Aguilar was to relieve me, but not a word about when he was likely to come, as he was only just appointed, and was on the staff in Ireland; but the next mail will most likely tell me when and how he comes out, and then I shall be able to calculate the probable time when I am likely to reach home; but we have now got to the time of the year when our communication from home is long, and last year our August mail did not come till the 4th November, and we have no right to expect it sooner this year.

Campbell came over yesterday from Chuck-Choo; he has a bed here whenever he comes; he has been remarkably well for some time, and begs to be kindly remembered to you and Charles. Grant had so much fever here for some days that I sent him over to Chuck-Choo for change of air, and Campbell, in whose house he stays there, tells me he is better, but that he still has occasional fever; I expect him back about the 20th. I heard yesterday from Chusan, they have had there a sort of typhoon, which has done much damage; but I will give Charles the history of that, and not bother you with it.

You seem to have in England a nice funny publication called *Punch;* I have read in the papers many extracts from it, and it seems to be written with a great turn of wit, and very little ill-nature. The difficulty of getting anything here in the shape of books is one of the greatest drawbacks to this place; the recent settlement, and the uncertainty in which all parties (I mean military) are as to the length of time they may stay here, has prevented anything like libraries or book-clubs being formed; whereas at every station in India, and in every regiment, they have societies of this kind, and they get everything out that is published in London; but I do not believe a single venture of books has ever been sent to this place. Now and then, when a man dies and his effects are sold, some books are put up, but for the most part they consist of old standard works that most people have read years back. At Macao they have a very fair book society provided from Calcutta, but it is of course confined to their own members, and we get no good of it here. I have read all my books except the second volume of Hallam's *Europe in the Middle Ages,* and I shall most likely finish that before the mail comes, but I read every bit of trash I can pick up by way of passing time, and keeping something for a last resource.

Since Grant has been ill I have had no music with him, and the weather has been so hot that I have not done much on the guitar by myself; however, I pass from half an hour to an hour at it most days, just enough to prevent the fingers getting soft, but the dry weather will soon set in now, and I can then string the instrument properly again, and it will serve to pass more time than it has done for the last two months; but with the cool weather the musquitos will come again, and they bite me when playing, as bad as the midges used to do you at the Hill; but perhaps when they come again (for in this hot weather we have few or none of them), I shall be more used to them, or they to me, and I hope the bites will not swell so much as they did last year. I am going to ride part of the way back with Campbell, who returns to Chuck-Choo this afternoon as soon as the sun gets a little lower, so I must put this by for the present, my dear Mr. Dick.

24th Sept.—The mail closes to-day, and goes over this evening in the "Driver" steamer to Macao, to be put on board the "Anonima," that sails for Bombay to-morrow.

Grant has come back this morning, and is much better, but still weak; however, the change of weather has made things better. Yesterday was the new moon, when they expected my fever to return, but I had none of it, nor have I any of it to-day, so I conclude I have beat it; with those who are subject to it, both here and in India, it comes as regularly as the new moon does till the wet weather sets in, and many have it all the year round.

I had both the Admirals to dinner yesterday, but they had no news. Sir W. Parker talks of going up to Canton shortly, and I intend to send Cunynghame with him, for I have had a letter from General Grey, your Moorish friend, and he wants me to send him some China crape, so I send Cunynghame to Canton to get it, and some for myself; also another manufacture they call here grass-cloth, it is a very nice article, like cambric and very fine. I shall bring some of it home, or rather send it with my other things, when I make a start, of which I hope to be able to give you some notion, if not in my next letter, in the one after the next mail comes; and now, with love to Charles and Aunt Anne (to whom I have written), believe me, my dear Julia, yours affectionately, S——.

CV.

Hong-Kong, 23d September 1843.

MY DEAR CHARLES,—Our mail from England reached this on the 9th, but I did not get any letter from you by this one, although I know you wrote me, because Mr. Dick in her letter to me mentions that you have done so; I have no doubt it has been mislaid in sorting at Bombay, and that it will come by the next conveyance from that place; the same thing happened before to a letter from my mother, and one from Cox and Co., but I got them both by the next mail.

I wrote you last by the "Kelpie" on the 4th of this month, but I was obliged to send that letter off before the last mail came in, by which I have heard that

Major-General D'Aguilar is to succeed me here, but not a word about when he is to set out, and until I know that I can give no sort of guess about the time of my getting home; and what makes it more provoking is, that the time of our hearing quickly from home is passed, as the monsoon has already changed in the distant seas, and will shortly change here, so we cannot expect our next mail before the end of October or beginning of November; last year it came on the 4th November.

As yet, thank God, we have escaped a typhoon, and in about five weeks more we may think ourselves safe for this year; the destruction amongst our temporary buildings, and the loss of life would be awful. I have just heard from Chusan, where they have had something very like one; it came on the afternoon of the 1st inst., and has destroyed the whole of the barracks, or nearly so, and they report one soldier and two or three followers killed, and a large number of men more or less seriously hurt; it is very seldom that a gale of this severity takes place so far to the north as that island lies; they say the typhoons do not extend beyond 26° north latitude, but the gale they have had there has done as much damage as any typhoon could, and was very much of the same character, beginning at the north-east and finishing at south-west. The expense of the repairs will be great, six or seven thousand dollars, and they must make great exertions to get them done, or they will not have cover for their men before winter comes, and it is as cold there as in England.

A singular thing took place here the other day, a Mr. Hay, quartermaster of the 41st Madras N. Infantry, was ill of the fever, which, when the fit is on, produces delirium with many people, and when in this state he found a pistol belonging to his Colonel, who lived in the same house, put it into his mouth and discharged it; strange to say it did not kill him, it is now ten days since, and the surgeon told me yesterday he was doing as well as could be expected. The Colonel says he put in a very small charge, as in case of robbers, he only wanted to wound, not to kill them; I think most likely the ball had fallen out of the pistol before he fired it, but the doctors do not think so; however, they cannot find the ball, nor have they any notion where it is lodged. The unfortunate part of the case is, that although the young man is quite sane, and it can be traced to the fever-delirium, it will be difficult hereafter to persuade the world of this.

Our paper here writes very gloomily about trade and things in general; but I have found out that the Editor applied for one of the Consulships, which Sir Henry refused, so now he writes all against him, and I yesterday saw a Mr. Burns, one of the large merchants here, come over from Macao for a few days, and he told me he had cleared out and sold the cargoes of five large ships from Bombay without any difficulty, and taking into consideration the great change that had to be effected here, what surprised him was that the difficulties were not much greater.

I hope you had a pleasant trip to the North, they would all be delighted to see you.

I suppose I shall get home some time during next spring, but I hope to be able to write you with greater certainty by our November opportunity. Love to Mr. Dick and all friends, and believe me, my dear Charles, yours very truly,

SALTOUN.

CVI.

Hong-Kong, 9th November 1843.

MY DEAR CHARLES,—We heard yesterday that our mail had reached Macao, and we are expecting it in every hour; I am anxious for it, as it will probably bring me some news from home about when General D'Aguilar starts.

In the meantime since I last wrote to you on the 23d September (since which time no opportunity has offered), we have been going on but badly, I mean on the head of sickness, for in all other respects the conduct of the troops has been most excellent: I trust, however, that now the sickness may be considered as over, although many deaths must still take place, for of the men who get dysentery after the fever very few live. Poor Dr. Graham, who attended me in my accident, after holding out a long time, died on Sunday last; and I heard yesterday that Lieutenant-Colonel Knowles was dead at Macao, where he had been sent for change of air and to get a passage home; he is the last of the artillery that were here when I came: Greenwood and Anderson sent home from sickness, and Freese sent to Sincapore for the same reason, the other two, Spencer and Young, gone home to join the Horse Brigade. It is high time that we began to get more healthy, for our doctors are getting very scarce: Graham dead, the surgeon and an assistant-surgeon of the 98th sent home sick; the surgeon of the 18th, on his way to Macao to get a passage home, was murdered by pirates; and his successor, a Dr. Alman of the 78th, who came here with a detachment, and wished to remain, is dead: the surgeon of the 41st Madras N. I. has done no duty for two months from fever. All this brings the work very hard upon the others; however, I am happy to say that at Chusan they have had little or no sickness to speak of; I got the half-monthly returns yesterday to 15th October, and they had not more than 342 in hospital in a force of 1900 strong.

They had a typhoon at Chusan on the 1st September, of which I wrote you, and they had another severe gale and rain on the 30th, which did a great deal of harm, so I have sent up Major Aldridge, the chief engineer, to put things to rights, not that we can very well do without him here, but as he goes by steam, and returns by the same, I thought it for the advantage of the service to send him.

10th.—Our mail came in last night, and I have got your letter of the 2d August, and am delighted to find you and Mr. Dick are so well, and that you enjoyed your trip to the north; but I am sorry you intend to send the next letter to Bombay, for General D'Aguilar cannot be here before the very end of the year, and most likely not till January, and long before that we shall have our September mail and very likely the October one: as to me it is impossible I can be at Bombay sooner than February, and most likely not before March or it may be April.

I fear you will never get my missing letters, for we have heard that the "Memnon" steamer was lost between Bombay and Suez, and I suspect all my letters written between the 8th of March and the 21st of April, as also those written between the 11th of May and the 9th of June, amounting in number to 39 letters to various people, were on board of her, and therefore you will never receive my letters between Nos. 30 and 40, except the two 35 and 36 which you have got, embracing a space of time from the 8th of March to the 17th of June, the dates of Nos. 31 and 40, which last was written at Macao and sent viâ Calcutta, and it therefore may have gone in the steamer from that place, and you may therefore receive that one. It is very provoking to lose so many letters, for one half of the people that I wrote to will never believe that I have done so.[1]

If the Admiral goes soon to Manilla I shall go with him, so you will not hear

---

[1] The loss, as regarded the letters to Colonel and Mrs. Charles Ellis, was not so great as he anticipated. Nos. 31, 32, and 33 were lost; but how many of the thirty-nine letters to various people shared that fate cannot be ascertained.

from me again from this till my return from that place; he is to take me with him in the "Cornwallis," and takes the "Dido" over to bring me back, as he goes from that on to India; so I must brush up my Spanish for the Donnas there.

Give my love to Mr. Dick, and say I have received her letter No. 20, which I shall answer by the same ship this goes by. Believe me, my dear Charles, yours very truly, SALTOUN.

CVII.

Manilla, 14th December 1843.

MY DEAR JULIA,—The last time I took a trip of pleasure, when I went to Macao and Canton, I wrote to Charles, so it is your turn to have the extra letter now, and I would rather have been a few days longer here before I wrote it, but that cannot be, as the ship is to sail for Bombay to-night, and I am not likely to get another opportunity.

This ship has been waiting here for some time for a dress, a present from the great Parsee merchant of Bombay, Sir Jamsetjee Jejeebhoy, to our Queen, and it was only finished yesterday and brought here for us to see; it is certainly a very beautiful thing, and I hear cost 4000 dollars, or about a thousand pounds; the groundwork of the dress is beautifully fine, of a thread they make here from the pine-apple, and worked in cotton after the manner of the Perth work, but much more elaborate; one of the mantelets took forty women four months to execute, and all the dress is in the same proportion, and dresses of the same sort are sent for the Prince of Wales and Princess Royal. I fear, however, that they have made the dress for a much taller person than our Queen.

My last letter to you and also one to Charles sailed from Hong-Kong on the 1st of this month by the "Spiteful" steamer, and on the 4th the Admiral, Sir W. Parker, got under weigh and brought me with him, as also Cunynghame and Grant, whom the doctors advised to take the trip, and I think upon the whole it has done him good, although he had a sharp touch of fever coming over, so we were only able to give the Admiral two fiddlings on the passage. We had a strong breeze of wind at first and some sea, but after that it got light weather and we anchored here on the afternoon of the 12th, and landed yesterday with all the honours of war, and had escorts and carriages to take us to pay our visit of ceremony to the Governor, a fine gentleman-like old Spaniard, by name Don

Francisco Alcalar; he had been one of Espartero's captains in the Carlist war, and got this Government as a reward, and has not been here more than six months. He received us in great state, and ordered guards of honour of infantry and cavalry to mount over our house; but, as you may suppose, we dispensed with these, and after our interview was over, we drove to the house where we were to stay, that of the principal English merchant here, Signor Othadin; he himself spoke perfect English, and has been in London, and all that, but his lady can only speak Spanish; the family have been settled here for some generations, and I have no doubt came originally from Ireland, and were called O'Thady. He has put us up very comfortably, that is, the Admiral and me, and Cunynghame is at the house of a Mr. Diggle, another merchant, who acts as a sort of Consul here, although we have no regular one at the place, and he offered to put me up also, but I did not think it worth while to change, particularly as the Admiral and I intend to go and see all the sights together. The Admiral has gone out to ride this morning, but I hate getting up by candle-light for that purpose, and never do it except when duty requires it; the fact is, I like to wash and dress comfortably when I get out of bed, and not after I have been up an hour or two, so I am now before breakfast writing this to you, having written a letter to my mother, the only two I mean to send from this place, and I am in hopes they will be in time at Bombay to go on by the February mail and reach England in March.

Yesterday, after we had done with the Governor and had come here, we were called upon by various people, and amongst the rest the Commandant, who brought with him all the officers of the garrison, so we had a regular levee that lasted about three hours, and I was heartily glad when I got the fine coat off, for at this hot place it is no joke. To-day we are to return the Commandant's visit, and after that we are to go and see the tobacco manufactory, the principal feature of which I am told is that we shall see 8000 women in one large building making cigars; and after that we are to go and see the rope-works, which last is more in the Admiral's line than in mine, and this, I think, will be our day's work, for they dine here at four, and after that drive, and return to tea.

The town is a large place, and the houses are good, with fine rooms, but it makes no appearance from the sea, for as the place is subject to earthquakes, the houses are only of one story, that is, they have cellars and offices on the ground, and the living rooms over them. The place is very hot, only 14 degrees from the line, and now in the winter the thermometer is never below 85°, but for all that it is very healthy, and no bad fevers known in it, though a long residence wears out Europeans much the same as Sincapore does, which it very much resembles in climate. I hear they are to give us several balls, and I hope they will let us know to-day when they are to take place, for I want to go up the river about four-and-twenty miles, to where there is a great lake that has hot and cold springs in it, and several natural curiosities, besides some beautiful scenery.

I have as yet seen no lady but our hostess; she can only speak Spanish, at which I do not find myself so much at home as I used to be in Spain; she is a lady-like person, not very young, and much fairer than one Spanish lady out of a hundred is in Spain; but as this letter must go on board to-day, it must be my next before I can give you any account of the beauties here. I hope to get back in less than ten days, and after that, not to wait long for General D'Aguilar, and as soon as he comes, to turn my head in the direction of England; so, with love to Charles and Aunt Anne, believe me, my dear Julia, yours affectionately,

S——.

P.S.—Just come back from the manufactory of cigars, and our visit to the Commandant, or, as they call him here, the second Governor.

They have an odd custom here which they have never changed; that is, they are one day in the week behind us. The original people came here west about, and accordingly they lost a day, our Monday being Sunday with them, and it still remains so.

It is a fine country, very rich and populous, and they have villages in the interior with populations of from 10,000 to 40,000, very easily managed, mostly by the Padres for they are all Christians, and each town elects an officer every year, who administers justice and settles disputes. They have a large revenue which pays all expenses, and they have 10,000 troops, and good-looking troops also, and they can send home to Spain about 3,000,000 of dollars in most years, but that varies according to the season being good or otherwise.

We are to dine to-morrow with the Governor, which will be a hot job, for I suppose we must be in full dress, and then I hope we shall settle our trip to the lake; for the second Governor, who also has just come from Spain, told us to-day he meant to go with us, as he had never seen it; so we shall have all right up the country: the inhabitants of the back country beyond where civilisation has penetrated are regular savages, and live without houses or cultivation. No more time now, so God bless you, my dear Mr. Dick.—Believe me, yours affectionately,

S——.

CVIII.

Hong-Kong, 20th January 1844.

MY DEAR CHARLES,—I wrote last to Mr. Dick from Manilla, dated 14th December.

We remained there and were treated with the greatest kindness and hospitality till the 31st, and saw everything worth seeing in the island, and on the 1st of this month I came back here in the "Dido," got here on Sunday the 7th, and found that General D'Aguilar had come, and on the 11th I gave over everything to him, and he took the command, which I put in orders to begin from the 1st, so as to make no broken period about accounts.

The "Dido" is taking in money at Whampoa, and as soon as she has got it, comes here, and I go in her with Cunynghame and Grant to Calcutta, which place we expect to reach by the 1st of March. The "Bentick" steamer sails from that on the 15th, and I shall take my passage in her with Cunynghame for Suez, and Grant will join his regiment. The "Bentick" will reach Suez about, or rather before, the time that the steamer from Bombay of the 1st April gets there, and we all come down the Mediterranean in the one that will reach home by the beginning of May.

We have a ship here, a little clipper called the "Louisa," which sails in a day or two for Bombay direct, and as it is just possible that she may reach Bombay in time for the March mail, I send this by her, as if she does, you will receive this in April, and you may look out for me in May; but as the chances are against her, you are more likely to get this in May, and you may look out for me a few days afterwards: I should have gone in this clipper for the chance, had I not settled to go by the "Dido," and I shall see Calcutta, Madras, and Ceylon, besides being more comfortable in a good ship-of-war, with a good fellow, which Keppel[1] is, who commands her.

I have no news to send from this; everything here is quiet, and now all are

[1] Now Admiral of the Fleet, the Honourable Sir Henry Keppel, G.C.B.

healthy, and I am eating my way out as fast as I can, for everybody is giving me farewell dinners. Give my best love to Julia and Aunt Anne, and believe me, my dear Charles, yours very truly, SALTOUN.

P.S.—I find the "Louisa" has no chance of getting in time to Bombay, but that a good ship is going to Madras, and if she gets there before the 23d of February, this will be in time for the Government express to catch the March mail at Bombay, so I send it that way for the chance. I expect the "Dido" here by the end of the week, and we shall then make a start. S.

CIX.

Alexandria, 19th April 1844.

MY DEAR CHARLES,—I wrote you last on the 20th of January from Hong-Kong, and by a letter I have this moment received from my mother, letters sent by that mail have reached England, so I conclude you have received it.

I began a letter to Mr. Dick at Calcutta and carried it on, but finding at Suez that it might be in time for the French mail, I sent it with the ship letters, and suppose it will all come right; but as I have got here before the departure of said French mail I write you this stave, because, with all the care one can take, things will sometimes go wrong, and if my letter to Mr. Dick has been sent to the English Consul instead of the French Consul, it will not go till we do, but I will take this to the French office myself.

We landed at Suez on the night of the 13th; left by the vans that night at two o'clock, and got to Cairo the next night at one o'clock. Saw all that was to be seen; Mahomet Ali the Pacha, who gave me an audience of about forty minutes, included. On the 15th went to the Pyramids, a business of about seven hours on a donkey. Left Cairo in steamboats on the 16th at ten A.M., and got here on the 17th at about twelve o'clock, and found our old Guardsman, Dick Burnett, here as Consul-General. Yesterday the "Great Liverpool" came in with the mail from England, which is our first step towards moving. The mail and passengers were sent off last night to Cairo, and as soon as they can get to Suez, which must take three days, the mail from Bombay (which our boat from Calcutta beat at least four days) will be sent over here, and as soon as it arrives we sail for England. This can hardly be before the 25th, and then we reckon twenty-one days, including the quarantine, which will make it the 15th or 16th of May before I can get on shore at Southampton, as they require twenty-one days' quarantine from this place, but in these days they include the passage, which takes up some sixteen or seventeen of them; but when I write from Malta, which I will do, I shall be able to tell you to a day, that is, if the ship is all healthy when we arrive.

As yet I have seen nothing here, but we have Pompey's Pillar, Cleopatra's Needle, the field of battle of the 21st March, and the landing-place on the 8th of that month in 1801, also the Dockyard and the Pacha's fleet, so we have something to do. Give my best love to Mr. Dick and to Aunt Anne, and believe me, my dear Charles, yours very truly, SALTOUN.

P.S.—I wrote to Bombay about sending my letters here, but they have not come as yet.

CX.

"Great Liverpool," at Sea, 26th April 1844.

MY DEAR JULIA,—My last to you[1] was begun at Calcutta, but was not finished and sent till we got to Suez, from which place they told me it would be in time for the French steamer; but as we reached Alexandria before the said steamer sailed, I found out there, unless it had been taken to the French post-office, it would not go by that ship, so I wrote to Charles and put that into the French Consul's post-office myself; and I conclude you will have received that letter.

After I had sent it off, our mail from Bombay reached us, and by it I got your letter sent in September last to China, and also Charles's letter of the 5th September; these letters reached Hong-Kong after I had left, and were sent back to Bombay by the "Sesostris" steamer. 1 had written to the postmaster at Bombay to send all letters that might be there to Alexandria, but I got none but those that had been returned from China; so, as I know some of you must have written either in October or November, I fear, instead of sending them to the post-office, you have sent them to the care of some person there, and I, not knowing that, have missed them, as I could only write to the postmaster.

[1] This letter has been lost.

We were at Alexandria just one week, and saw everything worth seeing, and I got there a letter from my mother, by which I heard that every one was well, but that William had the gout; her letter was dated 6th of April and came by the ship I am now aboard of.

We sailed on the 24th: shall reach Malta, from which place this letter will go, on the 28th, and we shall probably reach Southampton on the 9th or 10th of May; but as they make us keep twenty-one days' quarantine, including the passage, we shall not be permitted to land before the 14th, on which day I hope to get to London to dinner.

I have got a very nice cabin on the poop, where you feel the motion of the ship most; that I personally do not care about, but it makes it very difficult to write, so I hope you may be able to decipher this. We are very much crowded, as, besides what we brought from Calcutta, the Bombay boat brought fifty passengers, and such a lot of squalling children as never were heard before. I shall finish this near Malta; so no more now, my dear Mr. Dick.

28th.—Malta in sight, and we shall be there in half an hour; we are not permitted to land, being in quarantine; but all well, and this goes on shore to be fumigated: my next will be from the Mother Bank. Love to Charles and Aunt Anne, and believe me, my dear Julia, yours affectionately, S——.

CXI.

Letter to Mrs. George Ellis.

"Great Liverpool," 10th May 1844.

My dear Aunt Anne,—After our letters home had been sent from Malta, they brought us those from England, and I received yours of the 13th February, and also several newspapers, which helped to pass the time, for steaming is very dull work; however, I have no right to complain, for we have had an excellent passage, having left Calcutta this day eight weeks, and we are now about forty miles from Portland, and expect to anchor some time to-night at the Mother Bank, which is the reason I am writing now, for as the mail is immediately taken out by the quarantine people, if my letter was not ready I should lose a post, so you will know that although this letter is dated at sea, we have come to anchor in Old England before it could be sent off.

As soon as we anchor at the Motherbank, we are put under quarantine, and are to remain so, they tell me, till Tuesday morning, that being twenty-one days from Alexandria; but when we signalise to Southampton, a steamer comes off with supplies and all our letters, which we get through the quarantine ship, so I shall expect to hear from some of you there at all events.

This quarantine is a most horrid bore, and what is worse, I may still be kept a day after it is over at Southampton, as they will not allow us to take anything on shore, but all is sent to the Custom-house and examined according to a list sent from the ship, which is made out according to the order in which we took our passages. However, I hope to get through on Tuesday, and if I can persuade them to let me have a carpet-bag, I shall leave the rest to follow at their leisure; these regulations are bores that we cannot prevent, so it is no use minding them.

We have had, and still have, beautiful weather, and are going on at about ten knots an hour; indeed, we have not had a single bad day since we left Hong-Kong, and as the distance is more than 10,000 miles, and all of it, excepting about eighty, by sea, I think we have been very fortunate, particularly since we came into these European seas, where the weather is not so steady as it is in the East. Land just reported in sight. Believe me, my dear Aunt Anne, yours affectionately,
SALTOUN.

LETTERS of later dates to LIEUTENANT-COLONEL and MRS. CHARLES ELLIS.

CXII.

Lees, 29th January 1849.

MY DEAR JULIA,—I little thought, when I wrote to Charles on Friday last, to have to write you such melancholy information as this must contain; our poor Willy, who was quite well on Saturday (we were out hunting all that day), and who read the prayers yesterday morning to all of us as well as ever he did in his life, was attacked just at dinner-time with cholera, and died at three o'clock this morning. He, poor fellow, had very little suffering, and was sensible to the last, but I never before saw such a sudden prostration of strength, even when men have died of severe mortal wounds. Poor Eleanor and Fanny were with him, May had fainted and been taken away, and he actually, if I may use the expression, went *to sleep* in their arms, and knew me as long as his eye had life in it.[1] I need not try to describe to you the state that this house is in; I have no one here but young Menzies,[2] the rest are all women. Poor Fanny bears up well, and is helping me to write to those who ought to be informed at once of this painful loss, and I know none who will feel and deplore our present melancholy situation more than you and Charles will. I have just seen Eleanor, who is as composed as it is possible to be under these circumstances. As to me, to say nothing of the relationship, I feel I have lost a dear and valued friend, on whom, under any circumstances, I could rely as firmly as I can on Charles, and that is saying a great deal. Pray tell Aunt Anne, as I fear I may not be able to write to her to-day; and believe me, with love to Charles, yours affectionately,

S——.

CXIII.

London, 22d June 1850.

MY DEAR CHARLES,—Many thanks for your letter, and I am glad that by next Saturday you feel that you will be well enough for my visit, and I shall come down as I proposed by the quarter-past ten in the morning, which gets to Clevedon in good time for your dinner-hour, and the train the next day will bring me back to London about eleven at night.

I am going to dine with Brown[3] to-morrow at Bromley, and will bring word how he is. On Sunday last I went to Portsmouth, and Lord Frederick Fitz-Clarence gave a grand dinner, and the next day we had the christening at three o'clock, and about four sat down to a *déjeûner* at the George, where we had about forty people, ladies and gentlemen, and Lord Frederick proposed the health of the father and mother and the little child, which was drunk with all the honours, and the baby was carried round the table, and did not cry, but behaved perfectly well.[4] I came back to town by the morning train to dine at the Waterloo dinner.

My best love to Mr. Dick, and believe me, my dear Charles, yours very truly,

SALTOUN.

---

[1] Mr. Grant Macdowall of Arndilly his brother-in-law, Mrs. Grant Macdowall, and their two daughters.

[2] The late Ronald Steuart Menzies of Culdares, husband of May, the elder daughter.

[3] General Samuel Brown, who married Miss Caroline Thurlow, Lady Saltoun's sister.

[4] The "baby" is the Honourable Mrs. William Keppel, eldest daughter of the present Lord Saltoun, and grand-niece of the writer of the letter.

CXIV.

Auchinroth, 31st August 1851.

MY DEAR JULIA,—I wrote to Aunt Anne on Friday, and I have just received a letter from her, in which she says you were not sorry at the mistake that Mrs. Phillips had made about the direction of the grouse; not that any mistake was made, for they were as much intended for you as for Aunt Anne.

But my writing to you now is because I know no person in the world who would be more happy at any advantage happening to me than you would; not that I am to get any increase of fortune by this, but an additional honour. I yesterday received a letter from Lord John Russell, informing me that her Majesty had been graciously pleased to confer on me the Order of the Thistle, vacant by the death of the late Lord Melville. I had heard several days back from Lord Fitzroy Somerset that this was to be the case, for, Lord Fitzroy having met Lord John at Court, Lord John had told him he did not think these marks of distinction should be exclusively given to the friends of the Ministry, but should be given to Peers or others who had in any way distinguished themselves in the service of the country, and that it was his intention to recommend me to her Majesty for this honour, in consequence of my meritorious service in the army; and he wrote a letter to Lord Fitzroy, in which he further added that it was done without reference to politics, and that he did not expect me to alter my conduct as a Member of Parliament, nor did he expect any support from me in consequence. Lord Fitzroy sent me this letter in one from himself, to which I sent a proper answer, and yesterday I received the official communication which, coming from the head of a party against which I have voted for forty-three years—and against which I intend to vote in future—cannot but be considered as a very high compliment, and certainly most unexpected on my part.

We have still the same beautiful weather and fair sport, and I yesterday killed a very fine salmon of 26 lbs., and four grilse.

Give my love to Aunt Anne, and believe me, my dear Julia, yours affectionately,

S——.

CXV.

Auchinroth, 6th August 1853.

My dear Julia,—This is the day you mention in your kind letter that you were to go to Bath, so I write, as most likely this letter will reach you before you quit that place.

I got down here better and less tired than I expected, but I am not much better, though not worse, than I was in London, except the swelled legs; but by rubbing them night and morning, they do not at all events get worse, and neither Wilson[1] nor I expect anything worse from them than some trouble. I took great care of myself on the way down, and saw a doctor at every place, and Wilson is in correspondence with the Aberdeen one, Mr. Pirie, who is Professor of Surgery at the College there.

Gilmour[2] is here, as also Wilson, and it has been the finest fishing year that ever was known on the Spey: fancy Gilmour to his own rod killing 111 salmon in eleven days' fishing; but I can take no part in it. I began little walks yesterday, and shall go on with them, as I think they do more good than anything. I pass the evening pleasantly enough: Gilmour comes up after fishing and then we dine, and I go to bed at eleven, and as yet have slept very fairly; and during the day I read and write, but somehow writing tires me. I cannot expect much good for some days, so I shall not write to you again till I hear you are gone on to Devonshire. Believe me, my dear Julia, yours affectionately, S——.

CXVI.

Auchinroth, 11th August 1853.

My dear Julia,—When I wrote you from this to Bath, neither I nor Dr. Wilson knew what was really the matter, although the doctor at Edinburgh and the one at Aberdeen had hinted it to Phillips; but on Sunday, as, instead of getting better, I had gone downwards like a cow's tail, Wilson got anxious, and sent for a very excellent man at Elgin, a Doctor Paul, who came, and, having

---

[1] The late Dr. Wilson, an old acquaintance.
[2] Mr. Little Gilmour, his co-partner in the fishings on the Spey.

examined me, said there was no doubt about it but that I had water in both legs, and also in the stomach. He came over to see me this morning, but as yet, he said, no time had been given to say whether I was better or not, as, until the medicine began to work on the system, it would have no effect on the water. I have a great deal of oppression and difficulty of breathing, but no absolute pain, although I can feel the water.

This is the day you are to leave Bath, and I shall send this to Abbeville[1] to meet you there; and now, as writing is disagreeable from the way I must sit to do it, I will stop, but will write you again as soon as I have seen my doctor, which will be Sunday.

Robertson came yesterday, having had a crash on the road near Montrose, and hurt his head, but not much. He and Wilson are to shoot grouse together, and then I get a couple of hours' talk after dinner, and then go to bed. Believe me, my dear Julia, yours affectionately,   S——.

LETTER from Mr. ROBERTSON of Ladykirk (the late LORD MARJORIBANKS), announcing Lord Saltoun's death.

CXVII.

Auchinroth, Thursday Night,
[August 18th, 1853].

MY DEAR MRS. CHARLES ELLIS,—I should have written to Mrs. Ellis[2] or to you before this, but I had not heart to do so since my arrival here a week ago, as the instant I saw him I took a much more gloomy view of our poor dear old friend's state (which, alas, has been too truly and too sadly realised by the closing event of this day) than any one else but his faithful excellent old servant Phillips.

I did not consequently write to you or to any one, knowing well how deep the wound would be both to Mrs. Ellis and yourself in learning that the days and hours of your affectionate old friend appeared too plainly to me to be numbered.

I also thought and think that from the first moment I saw him, he was well aware, as we were, at least as I was, how ill he had become.

[1] Abbeville House, near Exeter.
[2] Mrs. George Ellis, the Aunt Anne of former letters

This I gathered at once from many observations he made to me, yet, with his usual consideration and kindness, he threw a veil over what he felt that he had no power to remedy, not unnecessarily to distress others and, it may be, himself.

But every day there was a sensible change for the worse. Medicine, from which much was expected, had no influence whatever on the fatal disease which hurried him on to his end more visibly and more rapidly than anything I ever saw in my life.

He retained his strong mind in its fullest vigour to the last. The machinery of his iron frame was worn out, and he died in the softest and most impressive manner, sitting in his arm-chair, with but a little short breathing, and without a murmur or a sigh.

He spoke to us all about his danger the last two days, and with his approval, Sir John Bayley[1] and Fraser[2] were sent for.

It will be a consolation to Mrs. Ellis and to yourself to learn that his affectionate attachment to you both remained to the last. On receiving your last letter (Wilson gave it to him), he was deeply affected, he held it in his hand a few minutes with tears in his eyes and an effort to breathe, and then summoned courage to open it and seemed much gratified.

I need not add that I shall remain here with Wilson till Fraser and Sir John come, and shall attend his funeral at Philorth. Hay Macdowall[3] has been here these three or four days, and words cannot convey a just impression of his kindness, unwearied attention, and judicious conduct.

With my most sincere and kindest regards to Mrs. Ellis and to yourself, believe me, my dear Mrs. Charles Ellis, yours most sincerely,

DAVID ROBERTSON.

[1] A friend from boyhood, and his executor. [2] The present Lord Saltoun.
[3] The late Mr. Macdowall-Grant of Arndilly.

Index of Persons.

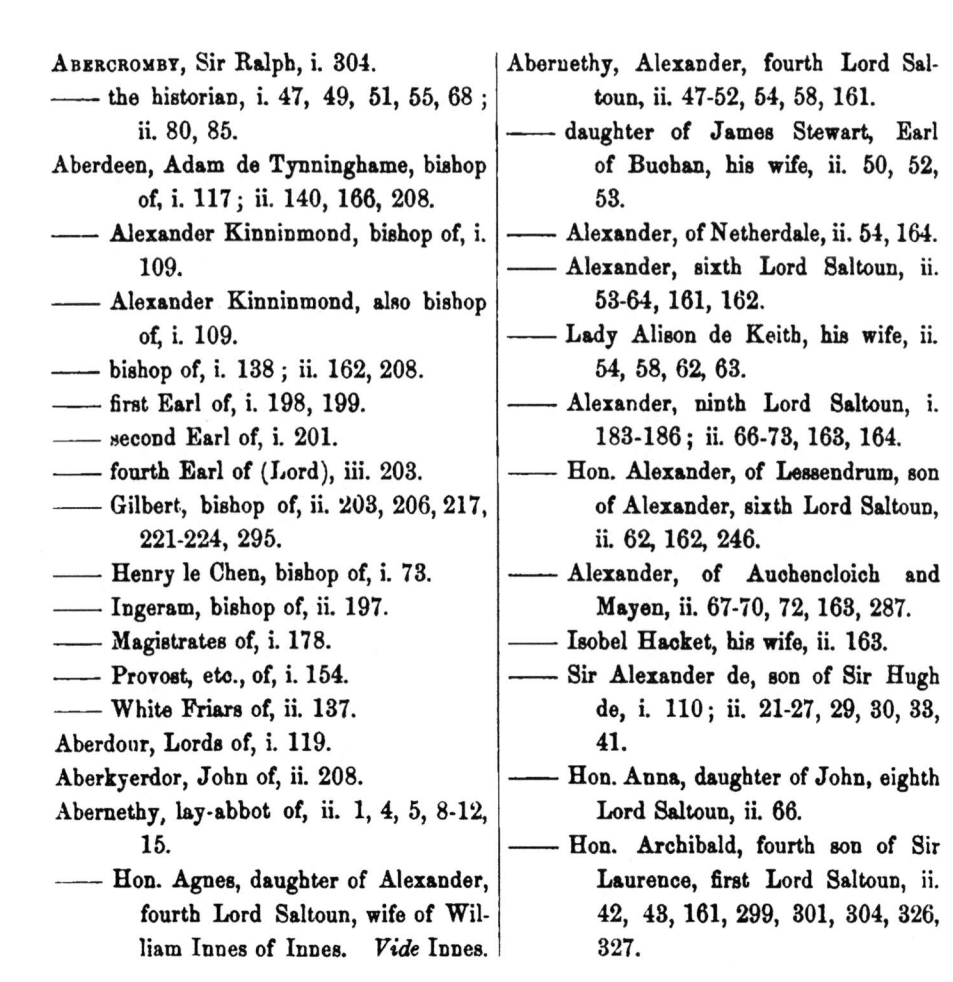

ABERCROMBY, Sir Ralph, i. 304.
—— the historian, i. 47, 49, 51, 55, 68; ii. 80, 85.
Aberdeen, Adam de Tynninghame, bishop of, i. 117; ii. 140, 166, 208.
—— Alexander Kinninmond, bishop of, i. 109.
—— Alexander Kinninmond, also bishop of, i. 109.
—— bishop of, i. 138; ii. 162, 208.
—— first Earl of, i. 198, 199.
—— second Earl of, i. 201.
—— fourth Earl of (Lord), iii. 203.
—— Gilbert, bishop of, ii. 203, 206, 217, 221-224, 295.
—— Henry le Chen, bishop of, i. 73.
—— Ingeram, bishop of, ii. 197.
—— Magistrates of, i. 178.
—— Provost, etc., of, i. 154.
—— White Friars of, ii. 137.
Aberdour, Lords of, i. 119.
Aberkyerdor, John of, ii. 208.
Abernethy, lay-abbot of, ii. 1, 4, 5, 8-12, 15.
—— Hon. Agnes, daughter of Alexander, fourth Lord Saltoun, wife of William Innes of Innes. *Vide* Innes.
Abernethy, Alexander, fourth Lord Saltoun, ii. 47-52, 54, 58, 161.
—— daughter of James Stewart, Earl of Buchan, his wife, ii. 50, 52, 53.
—— Alexander, of Netherdale, ii. 54, 164.
—— Alexander, sixth Lord Saltoun, ii. 53-64, 161, 162.
—— Lady Alison de Keith, his wife, ii. 54, 58, 62, 63.
—— Alexander, ninth Lord Saltoun, i. 183-186; ii. 66-73, 163, 164.
—— Hon. Alexander, of Lessendrum, son of Alexander, sixth Lord Saltoun, ii. 62, 162, 246.
—— Alexander, of Auchencloich and Mayen, ii. 67-70, 72, 163, 287.
—— Isobel Hacket, his wife, ii. 163.
—— Sir Alexander de, son of Sir Hugh de, i. 110; ii. 21-27, 29, 30, 33, 41.
—— Hon. Anna, daughter of John, eighth Lord Saltoun, ii. 66.
—— Hon. Archibald, fourth son of Sir Laurence, first Lord Saltoun, ii. 42, 43, 161, 299, 301, 304, 326, 327.

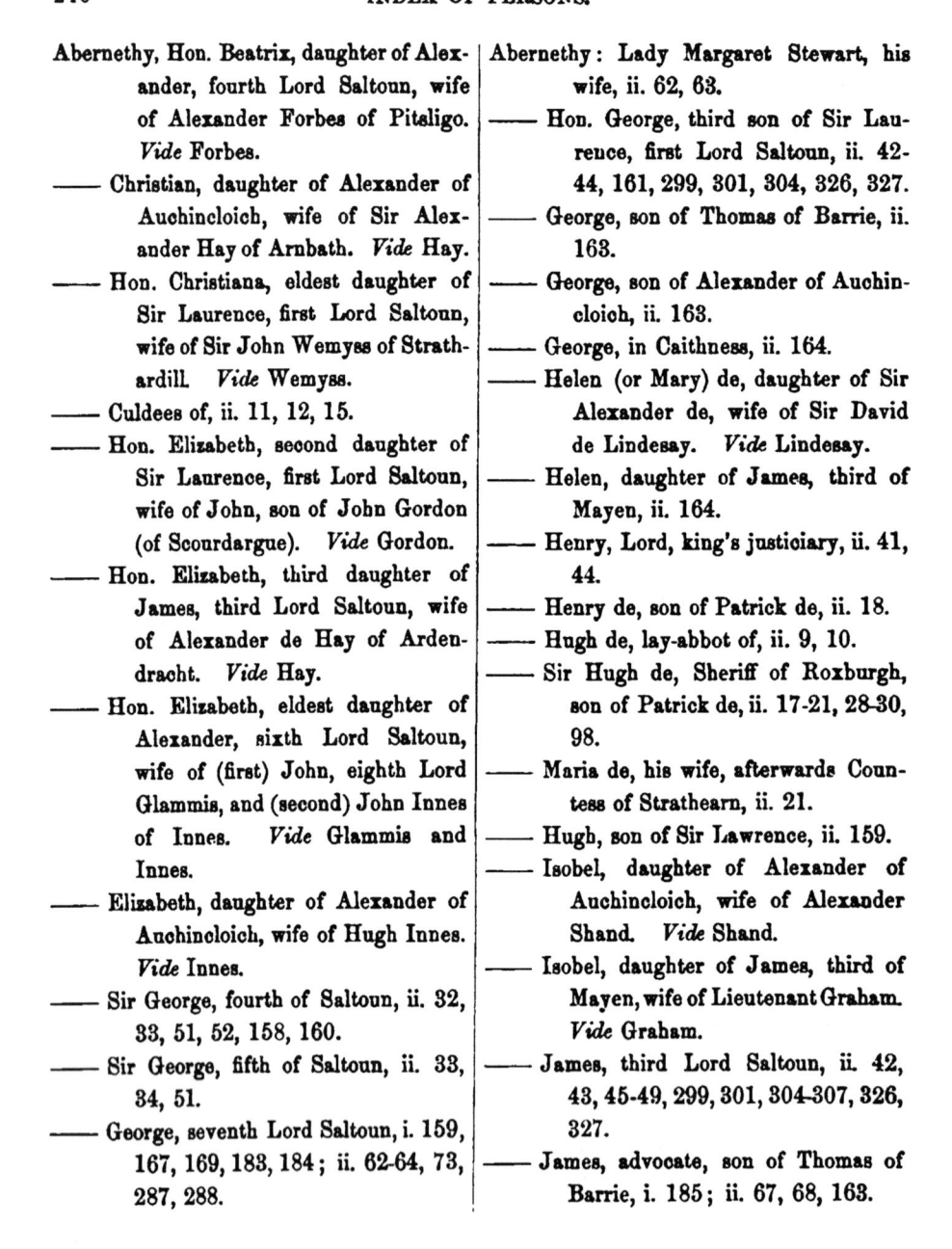

Abernethy, Hon. Beatrix, daughter of Alexander, fourth Lord Saltoun, wife of Alexander Forbes of Pitsligo. *Vide* Forbes.

—— Christian, daughter of Alexander of Auchincloich, wife of Sir Alexander Hay of Arnbath. *Vide* Hay.

—— Hon. Christiana, eldest daughter of Sir Laurence, first Lord Saltoun, wife of Sir John Wemyss of Strathardill. *Vide* Wemyss.

—— Culdees of, ii. 11, 12, 15.

—— Hon. Elizabeth, second daughter of Sir Laurence, first Lord Saltoun, wife of John, son of John Gordon (of Scourdargue). *Vide* Gordon.

—— Hon. Elizabeth, third daughter of James, third Lord Saltoun, wife of Alexander de Hay of Ardendracht. *Vide* Hay.

—— Hon. Elizabeth, eldest daughter of Alexander, sixth Lord Saltoun, wife of (first) John, eighth Lord Glammis, and (second) John Innes of Innes. *Vide* Glammis and Innes.

—— Elizabeth, daughter of Alexander of Auchincloich, wife of Hugh Innes. *Vide* Innes.

—— Sir George, fourth of Saltoun, ii. 32, 33, 51, 52, 158, 160.

—— Sir George, fifth of Saltoun, ii. 33, 34, 51.

—— George, seventh Lord Saltoun, i. 159, 167, 169, 183, 184; ii. 62-64, 73, 287, 288.

Abernethy: Lady Margaret Stewart, his wife, ii. 62, 63.

—— Hon. George, third son of Sir Laurence, first Lord Saltoun, ii. 42-44, 161, 299, 301, 304, 326, 327.

—— George, son of Thomas of Barrie, ii. 163.

—— George, son of Alexander of Auchincloich, ii. 163.

—— George, in Caithness, ii. 164.

—— Helen (or Mary) de, daughter of Sir Alexander de, wife of Sir David de Lindesay. *Vide* Lindesay.

—— Helen, daughter of James, third of Mayen, ii. 164.

—— Henry, Lord, king's justiciary, ii. 41, 44.

—— Henry de, son of Patrick de, ii. 18.

—— Hugh de, lay-abbot of, ii. 9, 10.

—— Sir Hugh de, Sheriff of Roxburgh, son of Patrick de, ii. 17-21, 28-30, 98.

—— Maria de, his wife, afterwards Countess of Strathearn, ii. 21.

—— Hugh, son of Sir Lawrence, ii. 159.

—— Isobel, daughter of Alexander of Auchincloich, wife of Alexander Shand. *Vide* Shand.

—— Isobel, daughter of James, third of Mayen, wife of Lieutenant Graham. *Vide* Graham.

—— James, third Lord Saltoun, ii. 42, 43, 45-49, 299, 301, 304-307, 326, 327.

—— James, advocate, son of Thomas of Barrie, i. 185; ii. 67, 68, 163.

INDEX OF PERSONS.

Abernethy, James, son of George of Barrie, ii. 163.
—— James, third of Mayen, son of John, second of Mayen, ii. 163.
—— Jane Duff, his wife, ii. 163.
—— James, their son, fourth of Mayen, ii. 164.
—— Jane, daughter of James, third of Mayen, wife of Alexander Duff. *Vide* Duff.
—— Hon. Janet, second daughter of James, third Lord Saltoun, wife of Alexander Ogilvie of Deskford. *Vide* Ogilvie.
—— Janet, daughter of Alexander of Auchincloich, ii. 163.
—— Hon. Jean, daughter of George, seventh Lord Saltoun, wife of (first) Sir John Lindsay of Kinfauns, and (second) . . . Gordon, Laird of Gight. *Vide* Lindsay and Gordon.
—— Joan, daughter of Alexander of Auchincloich, wife of James Moir of Stoneywood. *Vide* Moir.
—— Joan, daughter of John, second of Mayen, wife of William Moir. *Vide* Moir.
—— John, eighth Lord Saltoun, i. 184, 185; ii. 63-68, 72, 163, 246, 251-254, 320.
—— Lady Mary Stewart, his first wife, ii. 64.
—— Hon. Anne Stewart, his second wife, ii. 64-67, 72.
—— Sir John, son of Sir George, fourth of Saltoun, ii. 33, 160, 219.

Abernethy, John, son of Sir William, sixth of Saltoun, ii. 35, 39, 160, 161.
—— John of Barrie, son of Alexander, sixth Lord Saltoun, ii. 62, 162, 163, 164.
—— John, second of Mayen, son of Alexander of Auchencloich and Mayen, ii. 70, 163.
—— John, son of Oswald, ii. 43, 161, 299, 301, 304, 326, 327.
—— Mr. John, ii. 54.
—— Lancelot de, ii. 41, 44.
—— Sir Laurence, second son of Sir William, second of Saltoun, ii. 31, 32, 158, 159.
—— Sir Laurence, first Lord Saltoun, ii. 39-42, 44, 45, 48, 51, 161, 162, 297, 298, 325.
—— Margaret, Lady Saltoun, his wife, ii. 41.
—— Sir Laurence de, son of Orm de, last lay-abbot of Abernethy, ii. 10-17.
—— Devorguile de, his wife, ii. 16.
—— Hon. Laurence, son of Alexander, fourth Lord Saltoun, ii. 52, 55, 161, 162.
—— Lord of, ii. 9.
—— Major, ii. 164.
—— Margaret de, daughter of Sir Alexander de, Countess of Angus, wife of John Stewart, Earl of Angus. *Vide* Angus.
—— Hon. Margaret, daughter of George, seventh Lord Saltoun, first wife of Alexander Fraser, ninth of Philorth. *Vide* Fraser.

INDEX OF PERSONS.

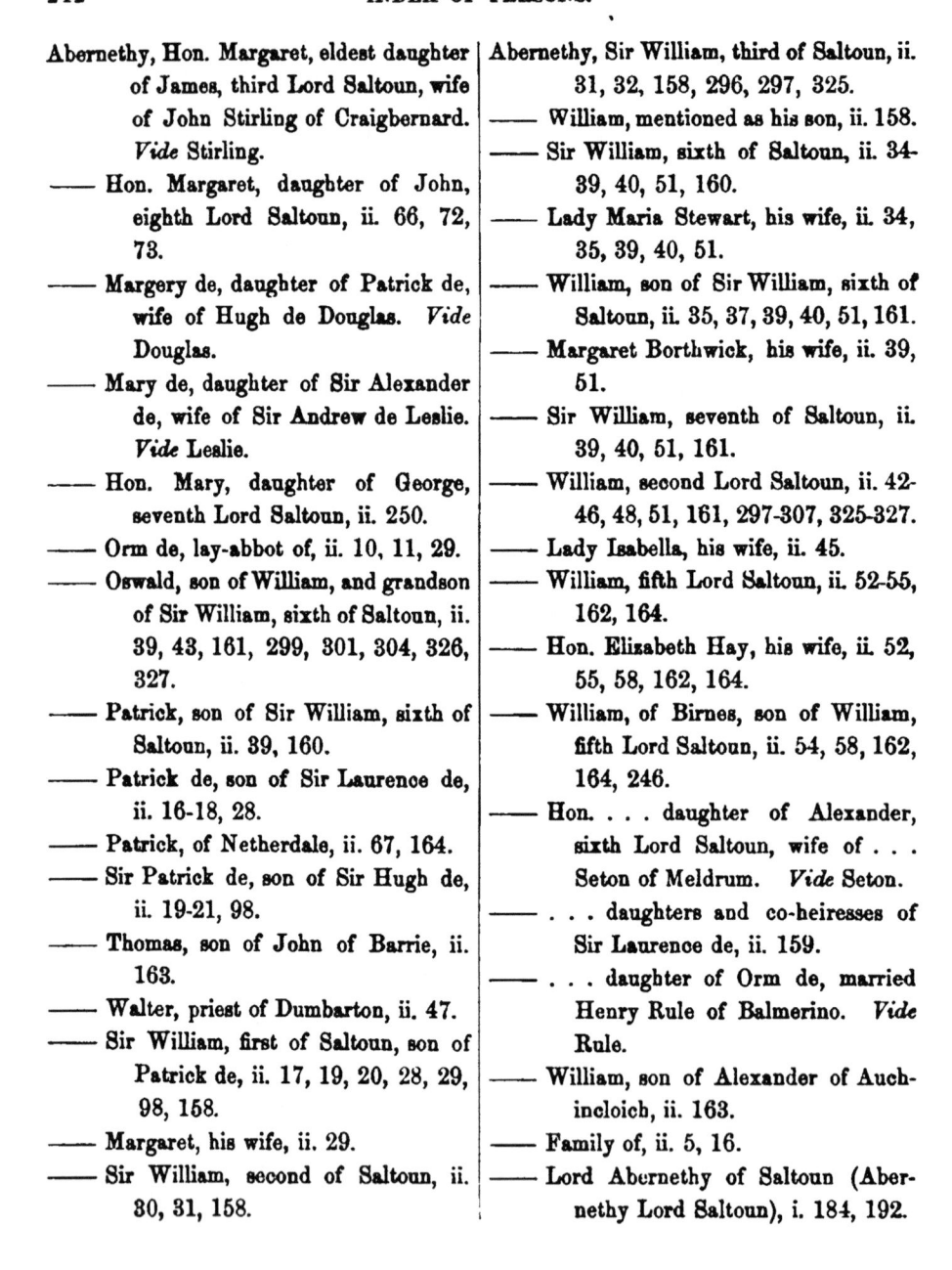

Abernethy, Hon. Margaret, eldest daughter of James, third Lord Saltoun, wife of John Stirling of Craigbernard. *Vide* Stirling.
—— Hon. Margaret, daughter of John, eighth Lord Saltoun, ii. 66, 72, 73.
—— Margery de, daughter of Patrick de, wife of Hugh de Douglas. *Vide* Douglas.
—— Mary de, daughter of Sir Alexander de, wife of Sir Andrew de Leslie. *Vide* Leslie.
—— Hon. Mary, daughter of George, seventh Lord Saltoun, ii. 250.
—— Orm de, lay-abbot of, ii. 10, 11, 29.
—— Oswald, son of William, and grandson of Sir William, sixth of Saltoun, ii. 39, 43, 161, 299, 301, 304, 326, 327.
—— Patrick, son of Sir William, sixth of Saltoun, ii. 39, 160.
—— Patrick de, son of Sir Laurence de, ii. 16-18, 28.
—— Patrick, of Netherdale, ii. 67, 164.
—— Sir Patrick de, son of Sir Hugh de, ii. 19-21, 98.
—— Thomas, son of John of Barrie, ii. 163.
—— Walter, priest of Dumbarton, ii. 47.
—— Sir William, first of Saltoun, son of Patrick de, ii. 17, 19, 20, 28, 29, 98, 158.
—— Margaret, his wife, ii. 29.
—— Sir William, second of Saltoun, ii. 30, 31, 158.
Abernethy, Sir William, third of Saltoun, ii. 31, 32, 158, 296, 297, 325.
—— William, mentioned as his son, ii. 158.
—— Sir William, sixth of Saltoun, ii. 34-39, 40, 51, 160.
—— Lady Maria Stewart, his wife, ii. 34, 35, 39, 40, 51.
—— William, son of Sir William, sixth of Saltoun, ii. 35, 37, 39, 40, 51, 161.
—— Margaret Borthwick, his wife, ii. 39, 51.
—— Sir William, seventh of Saltoun, ii. 39, 40, 51, 161.
—— William, second Lord Saltoun, ii. 42-46, 48, 51, 161, 297-307, 325-327.
—— Lady Isabella, his wife, ii. 45.
—— William, fifth Lord Saltoun, ii. 52-55, 162, 164.
—— Hon. Elizabeth Hay, his wife, ii. 52, 55, 58, 162, 164.
—— William, of Birnes, son of William, fifth Lord Saltoun, ii. 54, 58, 162, 164, 246.
—— Hon. . . . daughter of Alexander, sixth Lord Saltoun, wife of . . . Seton of Meldrum. *Vide* Seton.
—— . . . daughters and co-heiresses of Sir Laurence de, ii. 159.
—— . . . daughter of Orm de, married Henry Rule of Balmerino. *Vide* Rule.
—— William, son of Alexander of Auchincloich, ii. 163.
—— Family of, ii. 5, 16.
—— Lord Abernethy of Saltoun (Abernethy Lord Saltoun), i. 184, 192.

INDEX OF PERSONS.

Abernethy of Birnes, Family of, ii. 162.
Achar, a black servant, iii. 163.
Achintowill, laird of, ii. 284-286.
Achmacoy, laird of, ii. 285.
A'Court (Miss), second wife of Sir John Fraser of Park. *Vide* Fraser.
Ada (natural daughter of William the Lion). *Vide* Dunbar.
Adair, Captain, i. 272; iii. 63.
Adam (son of Udard). *Vide* Fraser.
—— son of Alden, i. *inter* 12 and 13.
—— son of Edgar, i. *inter* 12 and 13.
—— son of Gilbert, i. 25.
—— son of Kylvert, i. 15, 31.
—— son of Muryn, i. 27.
Adamnan, ii. 1, 3.
Adams, General, i. 268, 269; iii. 82, 83.
Adamson, John, ii. 236.
—— William, Edinburgh, i. 146.
Admiral, The, commanding at the Cape of Good Hope, iii. 101.
Aguilar, D', Major-General, i. 303; iii. 220, 223-225, 228, 229.
Alava, General, iii. 78.
Albany, Robert Stewart, Regent, Duke of, i. 81, 123-125; ii. 34-36, 38-40, 51, 160, 172, 176, 201, 202, 206, 219, 295, 311.
—— Lady Margaret de Mentoith, his first wife, i. 81.
—— Murielle de Keith, his second wife, i. 81, 124, 125.
Alcalar, Don Francisco, iii. 227.
Aldborough, Ivo de, ii. 120.
Alden, i. *inter* 12 and 13.
Aldourie, family of. *Vide* Fraser.

Aldridge, Major, iii. 189, 208, 225.
Alerdes, John, ii. 203.
Alexander I., King, i. 10; ii. 5, 8, 9.
—— II., King, i. 13, 18, 21-26; ii. 16, 74.
—— III., King, i. 24, 35, 38, 105; ii. 18, 19, 74, 75, 77, 78, 97-99, 107, 108, 112, 167.
—— Prince of Scotland, son of Alexander III., ii. 77.
—— the Steward of Scotland. *Vide* Scotland.
Ali, Mahomet, Pacha of Egypt, i. 303; iii. 230.
Alison, the historian, iii. 89, 103.
Allan, Patrick, ii. 276.
Allan, "dapifer" to King William the Lion, i. 16, 18.
Alman, Dr., iii. 225.
Alpin, King of Scots, ii. 2.
Alva, Duke of, ii. 59.
Alvanley, Lady, iii. 48.
Amory, Mr., i. 218
Anabell, daughter of Samuel, i. 24.
Anderson, John, author of History of the Family of Fraser, i. 23, 41, 44, 45, 49, 50, 89-96, 158, 169, 191; ii. 90, 96, 117, 120, 121, 125-127, 130, 131, 133, 147-150, 168, 169, 171, 175-179.
—— Mr., or Captain, R.A., iii. 224.
—— Sir Alexander, I. xii.
—— Alexander, of Cundacraig, i. 215.
—— Alexander, junior, ii. 277.
—— Dr., Editor of "The Bee," i. 221-223.
—— Hugh, ii. 277.
—— Dr. James, of Moonie, i. 215.

Anderson, William, ii. 283, 284.
Andrew, of the Culdees, ii. 14.
Anglo-Danes, The, i. 2.
Angouleme, Aymery, Count of, i. 3.
—— D', Duke, i. 247.
Anguish, C., iii. 19.
Angus, Archibald Douglas, sixth Earl of, ii. 50.
—— Archibald Douglas, eighth Earl of, ii. 62.
—— Douglas, Earls of, ii. 27, 41.
—— Gilbert de Umphraville, Earl of, ii. 84.
—— Gilchrist, Thane of, i. 23.
—— John Stewart, Earl of, ii. 27.
—— Margaret de Abernethy, his wife, i. 107; ii. 26, 27, 41.
—— King of the Picts, son of Fergus, ii. 2.
—— Thomas Stewart, second Earl of, ii. 27.
—— William Douglas, tenth Earl of, i. 159.
Anjou, Henry of. *Vide* Henry II.
Annand, Alexander, younger of Auchtirallane (Ochterellon), i. 151; ii. 251, 252.
—— Margaret Fraser, his wife, i. 151.
Anne of Denmark, Queen of James VI. *Vide* James VI.
—— Aunt. *Vide* Ellis, Mrs. George.
Anstruther, Major, R.A., iii. 125, 126.
Antrim, Earl of, i. 157.
Aquitaine, Edward, Duke of. *Vide* Edward I.
Arbroath (Aberbrothok), abbot of, i. 116; ii. 136, 292.
—— Bernard, abbot of, i. 50, 65, 66; ii. 165.
—— John, abbot of, i. 66; ii. 140, 141, 291.

Arbroath, monks of, i. 65; ii. 12.
—— Walter, abbot of, ii. 292.
Arbuthnot, Lord of, i. 146, 156.
—— Lords, i. 85.
—— Philip de, i. 85.
—— Janet de Keith, his first wife, i. 85.
—— Margaret de Douglas, his second wife, i. 85.
Ard (Airde), Margaret de la, of Ercles, ii. 35.
—— family of, ii. 172.
Ardendracht, family of. *Vide* Fraser.
Arderne, Sir Thomas de, ii. 83.
Aremberg, Duke de, iii. 55.
Argyll, Alexander of. *Vide* Macdougal.
—— Colin, Earl of, ii. 300, 302.
—— Earl of, ii. 56, 61.
—— Marquis of, i. 173, 175, 177.
Arispe, General, iii. 26.
Arran, Earl of, Governor of Scotland, i. 149; ii. 55-58.
Askew, Colonel, i. 255, 257, 272; iii. 63.
Aslowin, laird of, ii. 286.
Atang, Chinese servant, iii. 121.
Atholl, Countess of, ii. 26.
—— Duke of, i. 200.
—— David de Strathbogie, Earl of, ii. 25, 31, 121, 296.
—— James, Earl of, i. 185; ii. 64.
—— John, first Marquess of, i. 195, 196.
—— John de Strathbogie, Earl of, ii. 102, 195.
—— John Stewart, Earl of, ii. 61-63.
Auchanayouche, John of, ii. 41.
—— Philip, his father, ii. 41.
Auchnagairn, family of. *Vide* Fraser.

Augustine, priest of the Culdees, ii. 8.
Austria, Emperor of, i. 301.
Austrians, The, i. 277; iii. 64.
Avandale, Andrew, Lord, ii. 300, 302.
Avenel, Roger, Lord of Eskdale, i, 34.

BAILLIE, General, i. 191.
—— Leslie, wife of Robert Cumming of Logie. *Vide* Comyn.
—— Sir William de, ii. 83.
Baillo, John de, i. 69.
Baird (Bard), of Auchmedden, i. 168; ii. 284, 285.
—— Mary Fraser, his wife, i. 168, 181.
—— General Sir David, i. 235.
—— George, of Stichell, ii. 150.
—— George, of Ordinschivas, i. 136.
—— Janet Fraser, his wife, i. 136.
—— Sir James, of Auchmedden, ii. 287, 288.
—— Mr. James, ii. 284.
—— Thomas, of Ordinhuch, ii. 305.
—— Walter, of Ordinghuffis, ii. 252.
Balcarres, Colin, Earl of, i. 201; ii. 155.
Balfour, Sir James, Lyon King-of-Arms, i. 177.
—— of Burley, i. 193.
Baliol, Sir Alexander de, i. 37; ii. 83.
—— Edward de, son of King John Baliol, i. 75, 77, 79, 100, 107; ii. 31, 129, 159.
—— Henry de, ii. 129.
—— King John, i. 35, 36, 38, 43, 44, 51, 75, 110; ii. 21, 22, 78, 80, 90, 92, 102, 104-114, 196.

Ball, musical composer, iii. 210.
Balmanoch, Robert of, ii. 230, 231.
Balnain, family of. *Vide* Fraser.
Bamfield, Mrs., iii. 192.
Banff, George, Lord, ii. 287.
—— Sheriff of, i. 149.
Bannatine, Sir Lewis, of Brochtoun, ii. 72.
Bannerman, Alexander, of Watertoun, ii. 236.
—— Alexander, of Alesick, burgess of Aberdeen, i. 117; ii. 200.
—— Dr. Alexander, of Kirkhill, i. 215.
—— John, of Watertoun, ii. 230.
—— Miss, of Crimonmogate, i. 115.
—— Simon, ii. 225.
Barbour, Alexander, archdeacon of Caithness, ii. 221.
—— John, author of "The Bruce," i. 51-56, 58-60, 62, 67, 74, 78; ii. 24, 124, 125, 166, 183-194.
Barclay (Berclay, Berkley, Berkeley), Alexander, of Kercow, ii. 160, 294.
—— Alexander, ii. 203.
—— General Sir G., iii. 216, 218.
—— Sir Hugh de, Justiciar of Lothian, i. 35; ii. 18, 75.
—— John, of Towy, ii. 305.
—— Katherine, of Gairntully, i. 143.
—— Patrick, of Grantuly, ii. 305.
—— Patrick, sheriff-depute of Kincardine, ii. 203.
—— Robert de, ii. 11.
—— William, advocate, ii. 276, 277.
—— William de, Lord of Tolly, ii. 294.
—— William, of Kerkhou, ii. 160.

Barnard, Lieut.-Colonel (General Sir Andrew), iii. 41, 42, 69, 75.
Barnes, Adjutant-General, i. 282; iii. 71, 72.
Barrington, Ensign, i. 272; iii. 63.
Bartlay, Mr. Consul, iii. 85.
Bartley, Major-General, i. 295; iii. 122, 125.
Barton, Ensign, i. 272; iii. 63.
Batty, Ensign, i. 272; iii. 63.
Baty (Beattie), John, of the Corss, i. 157.
Baxter, William, ii. 270.
Bayley, Mr. Francis, i. xi.
—— Sir John, Bart., i. 311; iii. 238.
—— Mr. Lyttleton H., i. 311.
Beatrix, wife of Oliver, son of Kylvert, i. 26.
Beauly, Robert, prior of, ii. 233.
—— monks of, ii. 173.
Beaumont (Belmont), Henry de, i. 78; ii. 25, 26.
Bede, the historian, ii. 2.
Bedford, Duchess of, iii. 44.
Belcher, Captain Sir E., iii. 212, 214, 217.
Belhelvie, Patrick, Lord of Glamis and, ii. 141.
Bell, Captain, ii. 60, 61.
Belladrum, family of. *Vide* Fraser.
Bengilloune, John, of Saltoun, ii. 30.
Bentinck (first Earl of Portland). *Vide* Portland.
Benvoin, John, ii. 126, 198.
Beollan, father of Malnethte, priest of Abernethy, ii. 8.
Berbeadh, rector of Abernethy, ii. 7, 8.
Bergmuller, Frederick, musical composer, iii. 113.

Berri, Julius de (or de Fraise), i. 1, 2.
Berwick, garrison of, ii. 82, 83.
—— Governor of, ii. 82, 83.
—— Sheriff of, i. 38.
Bethune, Captain, iii. 116, 122.
Beton, Sir David de, i. 44.
Bey, Vice-Admiral Mahomet, i. 304.
Binge, Captain, of Jersey, i. 178.
Birnie, William, ii. 270, 274.
Bisset, Alexander, of Lessendrum, i. 213.
—— Cecilia, daughter of John, wife of Sir William de Fentoun. *Vide* Fentoun.
—— Elizabeth, daughter of John, wife of Sir Andrew de Bosco. *Vide* Bosco.
—— Rev. John, Aberdeen, i. 202.
—— John, of Lovat, ii. 167, 172.
—— John, of Lovat, his son, ii. 172.
—— John, of Lovat, his son, ii. 172.
—— Muriel, daughter of John, wife of Sir David de Graham. *Vide* Graham.
—— Walter, ii. 203.
—— William, of Hovthyrlys, ii. 208.
—— William, Sheriff of Clackmannan, ii. 22.
Bissets of Lovat, ii. 75, 172.
Blair, Bryce, of Muir Hall, ii. 159.
—— Sir D. H., iii. 16.
—— Mr. Hunter, Lord Provost of Edinburgh, i. 215, 216.
Blakeburn, i. 5.
Blakemore, iii. 57.
Blaktoun, laird of, ii. 286.
Blantyre, Walter Stewart, first Lord, ii. 64, 66.

Blantyre, William, second Lord, ii. 67.
Bloomfield, General Sir John, R.H.A., i. 261.
—— Mr., iii. 203.
Blucher, Marshal, iii. 46, 48, 103.
Bois, Aubert des, genealogist, i. 7.
Boethius (Hector Boece), the historian, i. 98, 100; ii. 6.
Bohun, Edward de, ii. 121.
Bombelles, Count Henry Francis, ii. 154.
—— Sophia Mary Jane Fraser, his wife, ii. 154.
Bonar, Ninian, ii. 45.
—— Robert, ii. 45.
Bondington, William de, Chancellor and Bishop of Glasgow, i. 18, 24-26.
Bonham, Mr., iii. 104, 106.
Bonville, John de, father and son, Lords of Balhelvy-Bonville, ii. 140, 293, 294, 324.
Bootle, Edward Wilbraham, first Lord Skelmersdale, i. 224.
Borthwick, Margaret, daughter of Sir William, wife of (first) William Abernethy, son of Sir William, sixth of Saltoun; and (second) Sir James Douglas of Dalkeith. *Vide* Abernethy and Douglas.
—— Thomas, ii. 298.
—— William, Lord, ii. 305.
—— Sir William, ii. 39, 51, 221, 224.
—— William, his son, ii. 221, 224.
Bosco, Sir Andrew de, ii. 172.
—— Elizabeth Bisset, his wife, ii. 172.
—— Maria de, their daughter, wife of Hugh de Rose. *Vide* Rose.

Bothwell, Earl of, i. 159.
—— James, Earl of, ii. 58.
—— Patrick, Earl of, ii. 48.
Bouer, John, monk, ii. 291.
Boulmer, Sir Rauffe, ii. 57.
Bower (Bowyer), Walter, the historian, i. 76, 98; ii. 5-7, 39, 124, 134, 185, 194.
Bowes, Sir Robert, ii. 56.
Boyd, Sir Alexander, of Drumcoll, ii. 44, 300.
—— Mr., iii. 87.
Boys (Boyis), Sir Thomas de, ii. 88.
—— William, ii. 212, 216.
Boysy, John de, i. 69.
Brabazon, Roger de, ii. 103.
Bradford, Lieut.-Colonel, i. 272; iii. 63.
Bradly, Mr., iii. 93, 94.
Breadalbane, Earl of, i. 199.
Brebner (Brebuner), John, i. 146.
—— William, of Lairnie, i. 214.
Brechin, bishop of, ii. 20.
—— Sir David de, i. 56, 57, 59, 60; ii. 24, 89, 184.
—— George, bishop of, ii. 227.
—— George of Schoriswood (Schorswald), bishop of, and Chancellor of Scotland, ii. 40, 41.
—— Patrick, bishop of, Chancellor of Scotland, ii. 208.
—— Walter, bishop of, ii. 221, 223, 224.
Bricius, bishop of Moray. *Vide* Moray.
—— a Culdee, ii. 13, 14.
—— the judge, ii. 11.
Bridgeman, Ensign, afterwards Captain, i. 242, 272; iii. 17, 63.

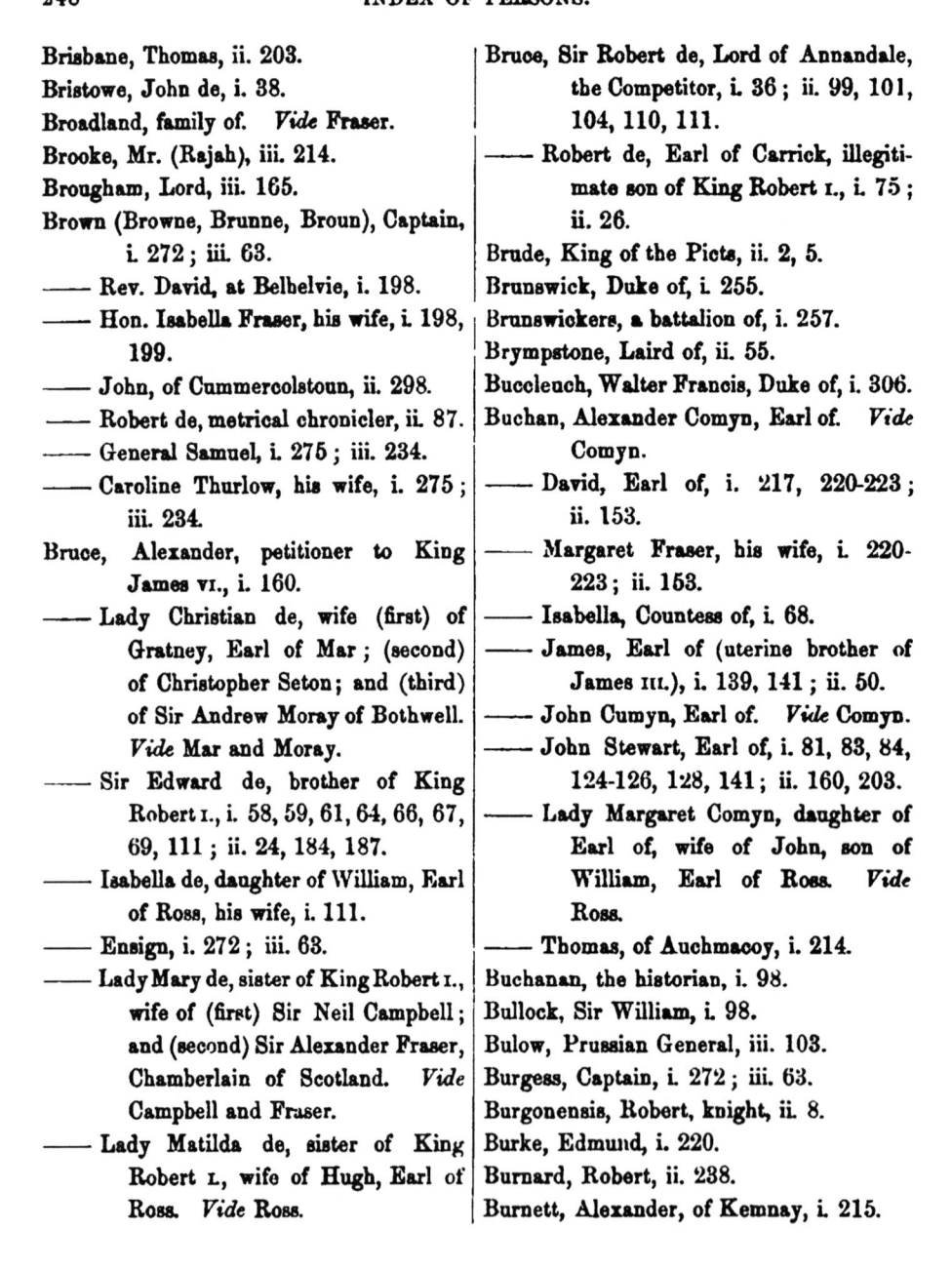

Brisbane, Thomas, ii. 203.
Bristowe, John de, i. 38.
Broadland, family of. *Vide* Fraser.
Brooke, Mr. (Rajah), iii. 214.
Brougham, Lord, iii. 165.
Brown (Browne, Brunne, Broun), Captain, i. 272; iii. 63.
—— Rev. David, at Belhelvie, i. 198.
—— Hon. Isabella Fraser, his wife, i. 198, 199.
—— John, of Cummercolstoun, ii. 298.
—— Robert de, metrical chronicler, ii. 87.
—— General Samuel, i. 275; iii. 234.
—— Caroline Thurlow, his wife, i. 275; iii. 234.
Bruce, Alexander, petitioner to King James VI., i. 160.
—— Lady Christian de, wife (first) of Gratney, Earl of Mar; (second) of Christopher Seton; and (third) of Sir Andrew Moray of Bothwell. *Vide* Mar and Moray.
—— Sir Edward de, brother of King Robert I., i. 58, 59, 61, 64, 66, 67, 69, 111; ii. 24, 184, 187.
—— Isabella de, daughter of William, Earl of Ross, his wife, i. 111.
—— Ensign, i. 272; iii. 63.
—— Lady Mary de, sister of King Robert I., wife of (first) Sir Neil Campbell; and (second) Sir Alexander Fraser, Chamberlain of Scotland. *Vide* Campbell and Fraser.
—— Lady Matilda de, sister of King Robert I., wife of Hugh, Earl of Ross. *Vide* Ross.

Bruce, Sir Robert de, Lord of Annandale, the Competitor, i. 36; ii. 99, 101, 104, 110, 111.
—— Robert de, Earl of Carrick, illegitimate son of King Robert I., i. 75; ii. 26.
Brude, King of the Picts, ii. 2, 5.
Brunswick, Duke of, i. 255.
Brunswickers, a battalion of, i. 257.
Brympstone, Laird of, ii. 55.
Buccleuch, Walter Francis, Duke of, i. 306.
Buchan, Alexander Comyn, Earl of. *Vide* Comyn.
—— David, Earl of, i. 217, 220-223; ii. 153.
—— Margaret Fraser, his wife, i. 220-223; ii. 153.
—— Isabella, Countess of, i. 68.
—— James, Earl of (uterine brother of James III.), i. 139, 141; ii. 50.
—— John Cumyn, Earl of. *Vide* Comyn.
—— John Stewart, Earl of, i. 81, 83, 84, 124-126, 128, 141; ii. 160, 203.
—— Lady Margaret Comyn, daughter of Earl of, wife of John, son of William, Earl of Ross. *Vide* Ross.
—— Thomas, of Auchmacoy, i. 214.
Buchanan, the historian, i. 98.
Bullock, Sir William, i. 98.
Bulow, Prussian General, iii. 103.
Burgess, Captain, i. 272; iii. 63.
Burgonensis, Robert, knight, ii. 8.
Burke, Edmund, i. 220.
Burnard, Robert, ii. 238.
Burnett, Alexander, of Kemnay, i. 215.

INDEX OF PERSONS.

Burnett, John, of Elrick, i. 215.
—— Richard (Consul-General at Alexandria), iii. 230.
—— Sir Robert, of Leys, i. 215.
Burns, Mrs., iii. 198.
—— Mr., iii. 224.
—— Robert, the poet, i. 220; ii. 157.
Burrard, son of Sir H. Burrard, an officer 1st Guards, i. 242; iii. 17.
Burritt, Dr., iii. 220.
Burroughs, Captain, i. 246; iii. 32.
Burton, Mr. Hill, i. viii, ix.
Bushby, Captain, R.N., iii. 87.
Butt, Captain, iii. 165.
Bykyrton, Walter de, i. 66.
Byng, General Sir John, i. 254, 259, 261, 263, 264, 273, 274, 279; iii. 66.

CADELA, John de, i. 28.
Cadogan, first Earl, iii. 14.
—— Hon. Henry, Lieut.-Colonel, his son, iii. 14.
Cadzow, Family of Hamilton of, i. 120.
Cain, Major, iii. 163.
Caithness, Alan, bishop of, ii. 100.
—— Earl of, ii. 169.
—— Isabella, daughter of Magnus, Earl of, wife of Malise, Earl of Strathearn. *Vide* Strathearn.
—— Margaret, daughter of Magnus, Earl of, wife of Sir Simon Fraser, brother of the Chamberlain. *Vide* Fraser.
—— John, Earl of Orkney and, ii. 128.
—— Magnus, Earl of, ii. 125, 128, 174.

Calder (Cawdor), Captain, ii. 60, 61.
—— Margery, daughter of Thane of, i. 137, 138.
—— Thanes of, i. 138.
—— William, Thane of, i. 137, 138; ii. 178.
Caldwell, Robert de, Lord of Todrig, i. 101.
Calentyr, M., thane of, ii. 17.
Callander, Earl of, i. 176.
Calonne, Mr., i. 223.
Cambhow, Walter de, ii. 109.
Cambronne, French General, i. 269.
Camera. *Vide* Chalmers.
Cameron, Captain, i. 272; iii. 63.
Camoens, the poet, iii. 201.
Campania, Patrick de, ii. 109.
Campbell, Colin (Lord Clyde), i. 291; iii. 92, 95, 100, 105, 121, 122, 130, 136, 138, 141, 155, 160, 163, 172, 183, 188, 190, 193, 202, 216, 218, 221, 222.
—— Sir Colin, of Lochaw, i. 23.
—— Fenella Fraser, mentioned as his wife, i. 23.
—— Lieut.-General Duncan, of Lochnell, i. 206, 219.
—— Hon. Eleanor Fraser, his wife, i. 206, 219.
—— John, second son to Earl of Breadalbane, i. 199.
—— Lady John, iii. 48.
—— Major, iii. 16.
—— Sir Nigel or Neil, i. 66, 67, 69, 93.
—— Lady Mary de Bruce, his widow, afterwards wife of Sir Alexander Fraser, the Chamberlain. *Vide* Fraser.

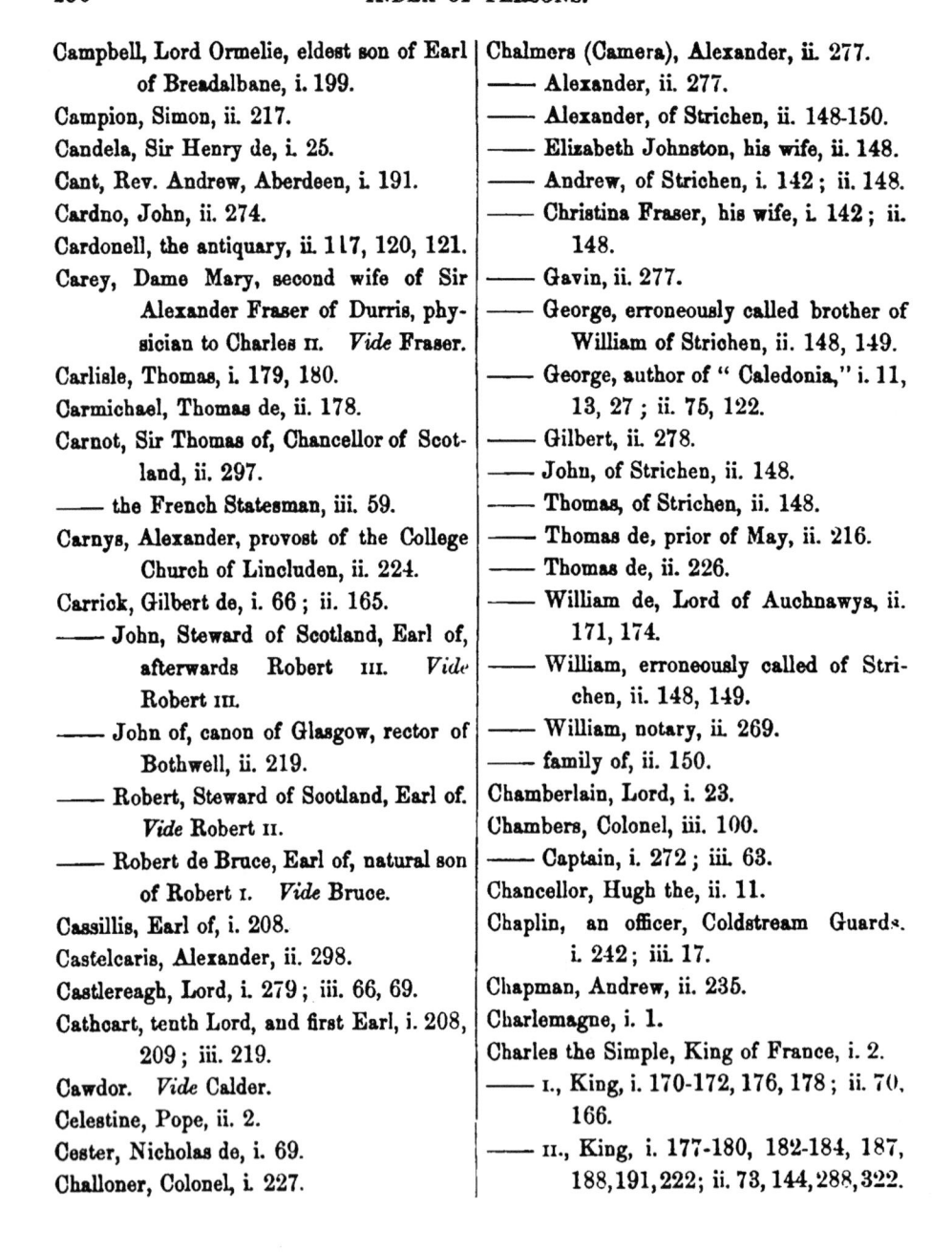

Campbell, Lord Ormelie, eldest son of Earl of Breadalbane, i. 199.
Campion, Simon, ii. 217.
Candela, Sir Henry de, i. 25.
Cant, Rev. Andrew, Aberdeen, i. 191.
Cardno, John, ii. 274.
Cardonell, the antiquary, ii. 117, 120, 121.
Carey, Dame Mary, second wife of Sir Alexander Fraser of Durris, physician to Charles II. *Vide* Fraser.
Carlisle, Thomas, i. 179, 180.
Carmichael, Thomas de, ii. 178.
Carnot, Sir Thomas of, Chancellor of Scotland, ii. 297.
—— the French Statesman, iii. 59.
Carnys, Alexander, provost of the College Church of Lincluden, ii. 224.
Carrick, Gilbert de, i. 66; ii. 165.
—— John, Steward of Scotland, Earl of, afterwards Robert III. *Vide* Robert III.
—— John of, canon of Glasgow, rector of Bothwell, ii. 219.
—— Robert, Steward of Scotland, Earl of. *Vide* Robert II.
—— Robert de Bruce, Earl of, natural son of Robert I. *Vide* Bruce.
Cassillis, Earl of, i. 208.
Castelcaris, Alexander, ii. 298.
Castlereagh, Lord, i. 279; iii. 66, 69.
Cathcart, tenth Lord, and first Earl, i. 208, 209; iii. 219.
Cawdor. *Vide* Calder.
Celestine, Pope, ii. 2.
Cester, Nicholas de, i. 69.
Challoner, Colonel, i. 227.

Chalmers (Camera), Alexander, ii. 277.
—— Alexander, ii. 277.
—— Alexander, of Strichen, ii. 148-150.
—— Elizabeth Johnston, his wife, ii. 148.
—— Andrew, of Strichen, i. 142; ii. 148.
—— Christina Fraser, his wife, i. 142; ii. 148.
—— Gavin, ii. 277.
—— George, erroneously called brother of William of Strichen, ii. 148, 149.
—— George, author of "Caledonia," i. 11, 13, 27; ii. 75, 122.
—— Gilbert, ii. 278.
—— John, of Strichen, ii. 148.
—— Thomas, of Strichen, ii. 148.
—— Thomas de, prior of May, ii. 216.
—— Thomas de, ii. 226.
—— William de, Lord of Auchnawys, ii. 171, 174.
—— William, erroneously called of Strichen, ii. 148, 149.
—— William, notary, ii. 269.
—— family of, ii. 150.
Chamberlain, Lord, i. 23.
Chambers, Colonel, iii. 100.
—— Captain, i. 272; iii. 63.
Chancellor, Hugh the, ii. 11.
Chaplin, an officer, Coldstream Guards, i. 242; iii. 17.
Chapman, Andrew, ii. 235.
Charlemagne, i. 1.
Charles the Simple, King of France, i. 2.
—— I., King, i. 170-172, 176, 178; ii. 70, 166.
—— II., King, i. 177-180, 182-184, 187, 188, 191, 222; ii. 73, 144, 288, 322.

Charles III., King of Spain, ii. 153.
—— Archduke of Austria, i. 301.
Charrun, Guischard de, i. 35; ii. 99.
Charters, Patrick de, ii. 120, 121.
—— Margaret Corbet, his wife, ii. 120, 121.
Chatham, William Pitt, Earl of, i. 236, 237.
Chen (Cheyne), Alexander, ii. 277.
—— Henry le, bishop of Aberdeen. *Vide* Aberdeen.
—— Patrick, of Esselmont, i. 166.
—— Magdalen Fraser, his wife, i. 166.
—— Sir Reginald le (junior), i. 45, 46, 66; ii. 127.
—— Lady Mary de Moravia, of Duffus, his widow, i. 45, 46, 50, 66; ii. 127.
—— Sir Reginald le, Lord of Duffus, probably the grandson of Lady Mary, i. 46.
—— Sir Reginald le (senior), i. 46.
—— Eustachia de Colville, his wife, i. 46.
—— William, i. 138.
—— William, servant to Sir A. Fraser, eighth of Philorth, i. 160.
Chesney, General, ii. 156.
—— Evorilda Fraser, his wife, ii. 156.
Chessors, John (elder), i. 175.
—— John (younger), i. 175.
China, Emperor of, i. 292; iii. 97, 109-111, 120, 124, 128, 132-134, 136, 150, 157, 160, 171, 175, 178, 184, 185, 204, 217.
Chisholm (Chesehelme), Alexander de, ii. 173, 238.
—— Helen, ii. 65.

Chisholm, Sir Robert de, ii. 130.
—— Thomas de, ii. 35, 171.
—— Family of, ii. 51, 172.
Christiana, daughter of Adam, son of Gilbert, i. 25.
Christiani, French General, i. 267.
Christie, Colonel, iii. 74.
Clarendon, Lord, statesman and historian, i. 177, 180.
Clarke, Dr., iii. 138.
Clement V., Pope, ii. 25, 26.
Clements, Captain, i. 272; iii. 55, 63.
Clephane, George, of Carslogie, ii. 53.
Clerksone, James, vicar of Pencaitland, ii. 298.
Clifford, Sir Robert de, ii. 84, 88, 186, 188, 190.
Clinton, Lord, i. 194.
Cochrane, Sir Thomas, Rear-Admiral, iii. 146, 147, 150, 154-158, 160, 164, 165, 169, 171, 175, 178, 179, 181, 214, 222.
—— William de, ii. 203.
Cockburn, Alexander de, ii. 33.
—— John de, his son, ii. 33.
—— James de, son of Patrick de, of Newbigging, ii. 298.
—— Patrick de, of Newbigging, ii. 42, 297, 298.
Cockburns, The, ii. 45.
Coffin, Sir . . . Commissary-General, iii. 205, 206, 208, 210, 215.
Colban, Earl of Fife. *Vide* Fife.
Colby, an officer, 98th Regiment, iii. 112.
Coldinghame, monks of, i. 13; ii. 75.

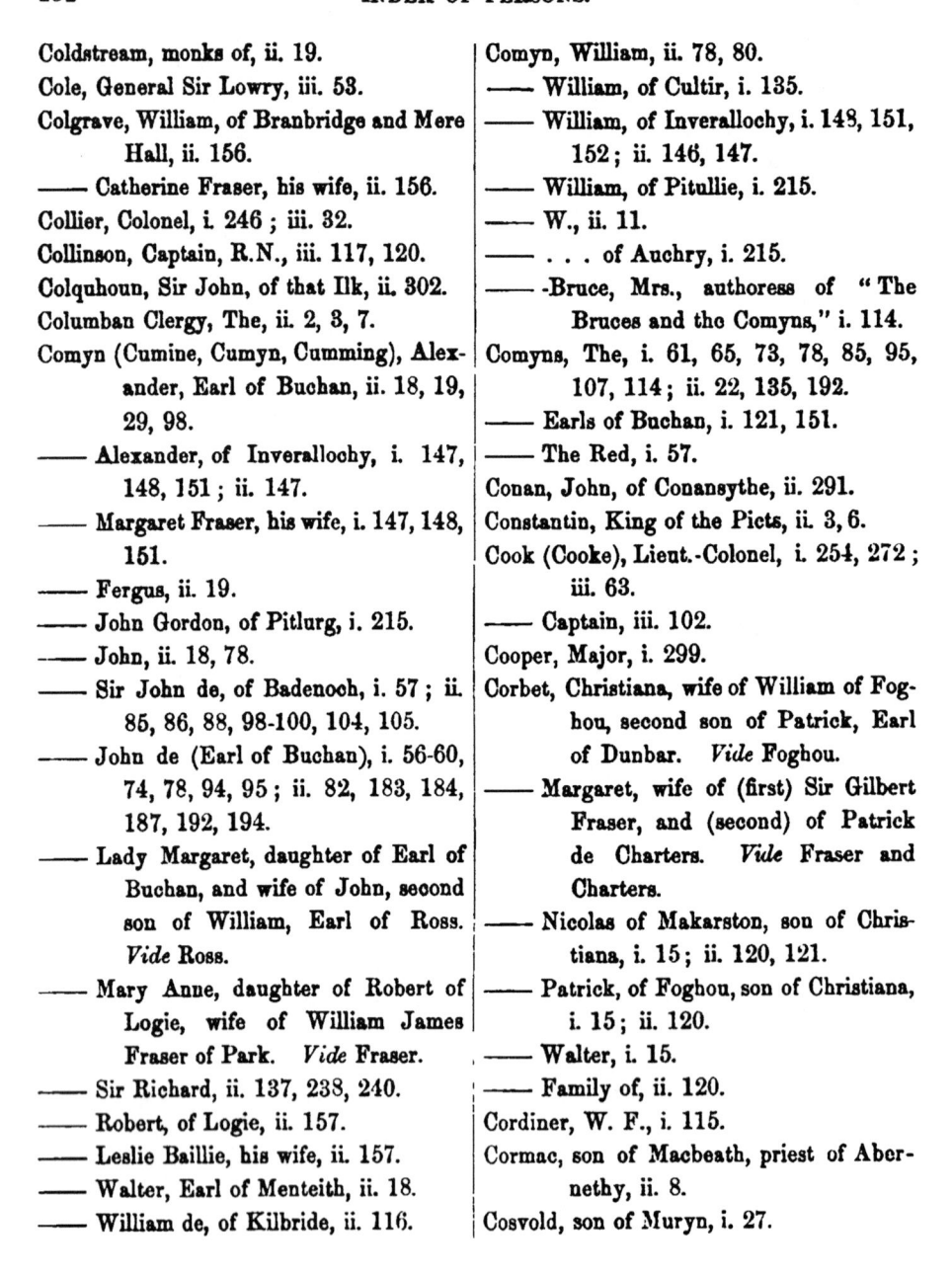

Coldstream, monks of, ii. 19.
Cole, General Sir Lowry, iii. 53.
Colgrave, William, of Branbridge and Mere Hall, ii. 156.
—— Catherine Fraser, his wife, ii. 156.
Collier, Colonel, i. 246 ; iii. 32.
Collinson, Captain, R.N., iii. 117, 120.
Colquhoun, Sir John, of that Ilk, ii. 302.
Columban Clergy, The, ii. 2, 3, 7.
Comyn (Cumine, Cumyn, Cumming), Alexander, Earl of Buchan, ii. 18, 19, 29, 98.
—— Alexander, of Inverallochy, i. 147, 148, 151; ii. 147.
—— Margaret Fraser, his wife, i. 147, 148, 151.
—— Fergus, ii. 19.
—— John Gordon, of Pitlurg, i. 215.
—— John, ii. 18, 78.
—— Sir John de, of Badenoch, i. 57 ; ii. 85, 86, 88, 98-100, 104, 105.
—— John de (Earl of Buchan), i. 56-60, 74, 78, 94, 95; ii. 82, 183, 184, 187, 192, 194.
—— Lady Margaret, daughter of Earl of Buchan, and wife of John, second son of William, Earl of Ross. *Vide* Ross.
—— Mary Anne, daughter of Robert of Logie, wife of William James Fraser of Park. *Vide* Fraser.
—— Sir Richard, ii. 137, 238, 240.
—— Robert, of Logie, ii. 157.
—— Leslie Baillie, his wife, ii. 157.
—— Walter, Earl of Menteith, ii. 18.
—— William de, of Kilbride, ii. 116.

Comyn, William, ii. 78, 80.
—— William, of Cultir, i. 135.
—— William, of Inverallochy, i. 148, 151, 152; ii. 146, 147.
—— William, of Pitullie, i. 215.
—— W., ii. 11.
—— . . . of Auchry, i. 215.
—— -Bruce, Mrs., authoress of "The Bruces and the Comyns," i. 114.
Comyns, The, i. 61, 65, 73, 78, 85, 95, 107, 114 ; ii. 22, 135, 192.
—— Earls of Buchan, i. 121, 151.
—— The Red, i. 57.
Conan, John, of Conansythe, ii. 291.
Constantin, King of the Picts, ii. 3, 6.
Cook (Cooke), Lieut.-Colonel, i. 254, 272 ; iii. 63.
—— Captain, iii. 102.
Cooper, Major, i. 299.
Corbet, Christiana, wife of William of Foghou, second son of Patrick, Earl of Dunbar. *Vide* Foghou.
—— Margaret, wife of (first) Sir Gilbert Fraser, and (second) of Patrick de Charters. *Vide* Fraser and Charters.
—— Nicolas of Makarston, son of Christiana, i. 15; ii. 120, 121.
—— Patrick, of Foghou, son of Christiana, i. 15; ii. 120.
—— Walter, i. 15.
—— Family of, ii. 120.
Cordiner, W. F., i. 115.
Cormac, son of Macbeath, priest of Abernethy, ii. 8.
Cosvold, son of Muryn, i. 27.

INDEX OF PERSONS.

Cotton, Sir Stapleton, iii. 26.
Coupeland, William de, i. 69.
Courtenay, de, Family of, i. 15.
Courteys, Peter de, i. 69.
Coventry, bishop of, ii. 84.
Cowie, Durris, and Philorth, family of. *Vide* Fraser.
Cox and Co., iii. 155, 222.
Crag, John of, ii. 126, 197, 198.
Craig, Sir William Gibson-, Lord Clerk-Register of Scotland, ii. 165.
Craigheid, Margaret, ii. 65.
Craigie, Lieut.-Colonel, iii. 115.
Cranstoun, Lord, i. 208; ii. 66.
—— Sarah, his wife, ii. 66.
Craven, Mr. Fuller, i. 292; iii. 99.
—— his son, naval officer, i. 292; iii. 99.
Crawford (Crawfurd, Crauford), Alexander, ii. 253.
—— Alexander, ancestor of Alexander in Rathen, i. 194.
—— Alexander, in Rathen, i. 194.
—— Andrew, ii. 240.
—— David, Earl of, ii. 302, 305.
—— Earls of, ii. 27.
—— George, of Fedderat, i. 150.
—— George, the historian, i. 13, 23, 24, 38, 46, 48, 53, 62, 72, 102-104, 122, 128, 129, 136, 142, 143, 148, 153, 156, 165, 166, 172; ii. 97, 121, 125, 147, 150, 151.
—— Henry Lindsay, twelfth Earl of, ii. 63.
—— Hugh, of Qubythill, ii. 270, 276.
—— John of, keeper of the Privy Seal, ii. 218.
—— Margaret, in Rathen, i. 194.

Crawford, Patrick, of Fedreth, ii. 235.
—— Sir William, of Ferme, ii. 224.
—— William, of Federat, i. 134, 150, 151; ii. 235.
—— Christiana Fraser, his wife, i. 150, 151.
—— William, ii. 240.
Crichton, Hon. Agnes, daughter of William, Lord, wife of Alexander, second Lord Glamis. *Vide* Glamis.
—— George, of Conzie, ii. 54.
—— Elizabeth de, third wife of Alexander de Seton Gordon, first Earl of Huntly. *Vide* Huntly.
—— James, i. 54.
—— John de, ii. 219.
—— Robert, ii. 54.
—— William Lord, Chancellor of Scotland, ii. 179.
—— William, brother of Viscount Frendraught, i. 173, 174.
Crichtons of Frendraught, ii. 54.
Croft, Ensign, i. 272; iii. 63.
Crofton, Captain, i. 246; iii. 32.
Cromarty, Earl of, i. 200.
Cromwell, Oliver, i. 177, 179, 180; ii. 67.
Cruickshank, David, ii. 203.
Cruz Mourgeon, Spanish General, i. 238, 239.
Cryne, William, ii. 295.
Cuille, Captain, French Navy, iii. 170, 171.
Culbockie, family of. *Vide* Fraser.
Culdees, ii. 1, 3-5.
—— Irish, ii. 3.
Culduthel, Family of. *Vide* Fraser.
Cullen, Alexander, ii. 277.
—— Gilbert, ii. 277.

254

INDEX OF PERSONS.

Cumberland, Duke of, iii. 1.
—— barons of, ii. 103.
Cunigburg, Alicia de, wife of John Fraser. *Vide* Fraser.
—— William de, Lord of Stapilgorton, i. 34; ii. 117.
Cunningham (Cunynghame), Captain, afterwards General Sir Arthur, G.C.B., i. 291, 305; iii. 86, 87, 92, 99, 100, 104, 112, 138, 141, 144, 146, 148, 155, 164, 166, 171, 172, 194, 198, 210, 212, 213, 219, 222, 226, 227, 229.
—— Marion, Countess of Findlater, second wife of Alexander Fraser, Master of Saltoun, son of Alexander, tenth of Philorth, and tenth Lord Saltoun. *Vide* Fraser.
—— Mrs., sister of Catherine Thurlow, Lady Saltoun, iii. 47.
—— Sir Walter Montgomery, of Corsehill, Lord Lyle, i. 208.
—— Sir William, of Kilmaurs, ii. 218.
Currie, Walter, i. 98, 99.
Currour, Alexander, ii. 245.
—— John, ii. 45.

DALGARNOCK, Sir John de, i. 106, 116; ii. 139, 289.
Dalhousie, Earl of, i. 208.
Dallirdase, David, ii. 203.
Dalmahoy, William, of Ravelrig, i. 198.
—— Hon. Mary Fraser, his wife, i. 198.
Dalrymple, Sir James, ii. 50.
Dalzell, Robert de, ii. 225.

Danes, The, i. 2; ii. 3, 7.
Darnley, John Lord, ii. 300, 302.
Dartmouth, Lord, i. 224.
David I., King, i. 7, 8, 10; ii. 5, 8, 9, 106, 185.
—— II., King, i. 45, 46, 74, 75, 77, 78, 85, 93, 97, 100-104, 106-109, 111-113, 115, 125, 134, 206; ii. 27, 31-33, 36, 116, 118, 121, 123, 129, 130, 132, 134, 159, 160, 200, 206, 208, 209, 296.
Davidson, Mr. and Mrs., iii. 213.
—— Sir Robert, Provost of Aberdeen, ii. 37, 38.
Davis, an officer 1st Guards, iii. 39.
Davoust, Marshal, i. 282; iii. 64, 71.
Deer, abbot of, ii. 41, 162.
—— monks of, ii. 41.
—— William, abbot of, ii. 230, 231.
Delisle, M. Leopold, i. 8.
Dempster, John, of Auchterless, i. 144.
—— the historian, ii. 150, 151.
Dent, Mr., iii. 197.
Dent and Co., iii. 192, 196, 198.
Derby, Earl of, i. 179.
Devorguile, wife of Sir Laurence de Abernethy. *Vide* Abernethy.
Dewar, David, ii. 217.
Dick, Mr. *Vide* Ellis, Mrs. Charles.
Dickson, Mr. Thomas, I. xii.
Dickysone, Ninian, ii. 298.
Diggle, Mr., iii. 227.
Dingwall, John, of Ranniston, i. 214.
—— William, of Brucklaw, i. 214.
—— William de, Dean of Ross, ii. 238, 240.

Dingwall Fordyce. *Vide* Fordyce.
Dirom, Alexander, of Muiresk, i. 214.
Disschyngtoun, Sir William de, ii. 207, 210, 215, 291.
—— William de, his son, ii. 291.
Dochty, Elizabeth, first wife of Sir Alexander Fraser of Durris, physician to Charles II. *Vide* Fraser.
Dompnach, father of King Garnard, ii. 5.
Donaldsone, Alexander, ii. 210.
Douglas, Andrew, ii. 123.
—— Archibald, third Earl of, Lord of Galloway and of Bothwell, i. 104, 117, 119, 120, 122; ii. 160, 201, 206, 207, 210, 215, 218, 219, 295, 314.
—— Johanna or Jean Moray of Bothwell, his wife, i. 104, 119, 120; ii. 218, 219.
—— Archibald, fourth Earl of, Lord of Galloway and of Bothwell, i. 104, 119, 120, 122, 123; ii. 34, 35, 221-224, 315.
—— Archibald, brother of the "good" Sir James, ii. 129.
—— Archibald, Earl of Moray, ii. 178.
—— Elizabeth, Countess of Moray, his widow, ii. 178.
—— Lady Janet, their daughter, ii. 178.
—— Archibald, of Kilspindie, ii. 50.
—— Elinor de, natural daughter of James, second Earl of, and first wife of Sir William Fraser of Cowie and Durris, second of Philorth. *Vide* Fraser.
—— Sir George, ii. 55.

Douglas, George of, brother of Earl of Angus, ii. 50.
—— Hugh, son of Sir William, Lord of, ii. 18, 19.
—— Margery Abernethy, his wife, ii. 18, 19.
—— Isabella de, Countess of Mar, i. 122; ii. 224, 316.
—— James, second Earl of, and Earl of Mar, i. 117, 118, 122; ii. 34, 201.
—— James, ninth Earl of, ii. 41, 44, 129.
—— James de, Lord of Abercorn, Aberdour, and Balvenie, son of Archibald, third Earl of, i. 104, 119, 120, 122, 124, 127; ii. 220-225, 315.
—— the "good" Sir James of, i. 57, 61-63, 66, 67, 69, 71, 74, 75; ii. 94, 128, 129, 158, 186-190.
—— Sir James de, Lord of Dalkeith, i. 85; ii. 34, 39, 171, 206, 295.
—— Margaret Borthwick, his wife, ii. 39.
—— James, of Pittendreich, ii. 305.
—— Margaret, daughter of Sir James de, of Dalkeith, second wife of Philip de Arbuthnot. *Vide* Arbuthnot.
—— Mr., minister of Forgie, i. 173.
—— Sir William de, Lord of, i. 37; ii. 18-20, 29, 30, 118, 128.
—— Sir William de, i. 77, 98, 99, 101, 102; ii. 130.
—— Sir William de, ii. 159.
—— William, first Earl of, and Earl of Mar, ii. 207, 210, 215, 219.
—— William, eighth Earl of, i. 128.
—— family or House of, i. 102-104, 122, 129; ii. 169.

Douglas, Earl of Angus. *Vide* Angus.
Downy, William, i. 144.
Drumelzier, family of. *Vide* Fraser.
Drummond, Mr., iii. 1.
—— Hon. Mr., son of Lord Strathallan, iii. 196.
Dryburgh, abbot of, ii. 13.
—— Mr. Peter of, ii. 14.
—— monks of, ii. 30.
Dublin, Archbishop of, ii. 157.
Duff, Adam, of Drummuir, i. 185.
—— Hon. Alexander, of Echt, i. 214.
—— Alexander, of Drummuir, i. 186.
—— Alexander, of Braco, i. 186, 194; ii. 70.
—— Major Alexander, ii. 164.
—— Jane Abernethy, his wife, ii. 164.
—— Jane, wife of James Abernethy, third of Mayen. *Vide* Abernethy.
—— John, of Hatton, i. 214.
—— Admiral Robert, of Logie, i. 215.
—— William, of Corsindae, i. 214.
—— of Crombie, ii. 163.
Duffus, Mr. Adam, i. 147.
—— John, notary, ii. 211.
—— Lady Mary de Moravia, of. *Vide* Chen.
Dumfries, Sheriff of, i. 38.
—— Earl of, i. 208.
Dunbar, Ada, daughter of Patrick, Earl of. *Vide* Home.
—— Aelina, Countess of, i. *inter* 12 and 13.
—— Sir Alexander, of Westfield, i. 132; ii. 305.
—— Alexander, second son of John, Earl of Moray, ii. 138.

Dunbar: Mauld Fraser, his wife, ii. 138.
—— Archibald, of Newton, ii. 163.
—— Elizabeth Hacket, his wife, ii. 163.
—— Earls of, i. 7, 11, 14, 15, 21, 29.
—— Edward, uncle of Waldeve, Earl of, i. *inter* 12 and 13.
—— Edward Dunbar, ii. 72, 164.
—— Gospatrick, first Earl of, i. 9, 11.
—— Gospatrick, last Earl of that name, i. 9, 13.
—— James, of Cumnock, ii. 305.
—— James, of Frendraught, ii. 138, 178.
—— Janet de, Countess of Moray. *Vide* Moray.
—— Patrick (first of that name), Earl of, i. 15, 16, 18, 20, 21, 23, 27, 28; ii. 120.
—— Ada, Countess of, natural daughter of William the Lion, his wife, i. 15, 20, 27.
—— Patrick, brother of Waldeve, Earl of, i. *inter* 12 and 13, 15.
—— Cecilia, his wife, i. 15.
—— Patrick (second of that name), Earl of, i. 18, 28.
—— Patrick de, Earl of March and Moray. *Vide* March and Moray.
—— Robert de, ii. 291.
—— Thomas, Earl of Moray. *Vide* Moray.
—— Waldeve, Earl of, i. 9, *inter* 12 and 13, 13, 15.
—— Earl of Moray (1388), i. 117-119.
—— a sailor, iii. 93.
Dunbreck, Philip de, i. 108.
Duncan, Earl, justiciar. *Vide* Fife.
—— George, ii. 245.

INDEX OF PERSONS.

Duncanson, Laurence, ii. 198.
Dundas, James, i. 176.
—— Sir Thomas, i. 224.
Dunfermline, abbot of, ii. 137.
—— Archibald, abbot of, ii. 11.
Dunkeld, bishop of, ii. 109.
—— Hugh, bishop of, i. 28.
—— James, bishop of, ii. 305.
—— John of Leicester, bishop of, i. 20, 28.
—— John Peebles, bishop of, ii. 200, 219.
—— Richard, bishop of, Chancellor, ii. 18, 297.
—— Robert, bishop of, ii. 221, 223, 224.
Dunmore, Earl of, i. 200.
Duns, Hugh of, i. *inter* 12 and 13.
D'Urban, Sir B., former Governor of Cape Colony, iii. 101.
Durham, Antony Beck, bishop of, ii. 100, 102.
—— bishop of, i. 118 ; ii. 84, 196.
—— Simeon of, i. 14.
Durris, family of. *Vide* Fraser.
Durward, Allan, high justiciary, ii. 18.
Dustah, abbot of Lochleven, ii. 8.
Dyce, John, of Tillygreig, i. 215.
Dysart, Earl of, i. 208.

Eady, Captain, iii. 136.
Edgar, King of Scotland, ii. 5.
Edinburgh Castle, governor of, i. 99.
—— Sheriff of, i. 38.
Edintun, Adam of, i. *inter* 12 and 13.
Edname, Thomas, canon of Aberdeen, ii. 198.

Edward I., King, i. 4, 5, 11, 35-44, 47-49, 51-53, 55, 64, 67, 71, 74, 90, 93-96 ; ii. 20-24, 29, 30, 78-85, 87-94, 99-115, 117, 118, 120, 122, 126, 158, 165, 166, 173, 185-190, 194-196.
—— Eleanor, his Queen, ii. 102.
—— II., King, i. 55, 56, 64, 72, 78 ; ii. 23-27, 92, 99, 100, 113, 187, 189, 190-192, 194.
—— III., King, i. 75, 77, 101 ; ii. 32, 120, 159, 173 ; iii. 61.
—— IV., King, i. 133, 134.
—— chaplain of the bishop of St. Andrews, ii. 14.
—— Prince of Wales or of England. *Vide* Edward II.
Edwards, L. M., Captain, i. 303.
Eglinton, Earl of, i. 208.
Elcho, Lord, i. 306.
Eleanor, Queen of Edward I. of England. *Vide* Edward.
Elipoo, Chinese Commissioner, i. 296 ; iii. 133, 134, 155, 159, 171, 178, 184, 188, 194.
Elizabeth, Queen of England, i. 8, 212 ; ii. 58, 61.
Ellis, Lieut.-Colonel (Captain) Charles, i. x, 250, 251, 256, 264, 272, 306 ; iii. 63, 83, 84, 86-88, 91-96, 100-106, 109-111, 115-120, 125-128, 132-141, 144-149, 151-160, 163, 165-168, 173-179, 182-185, 188-191, 193, 195-198, 203-208, 212, 214-219, 221-226, 228-234.

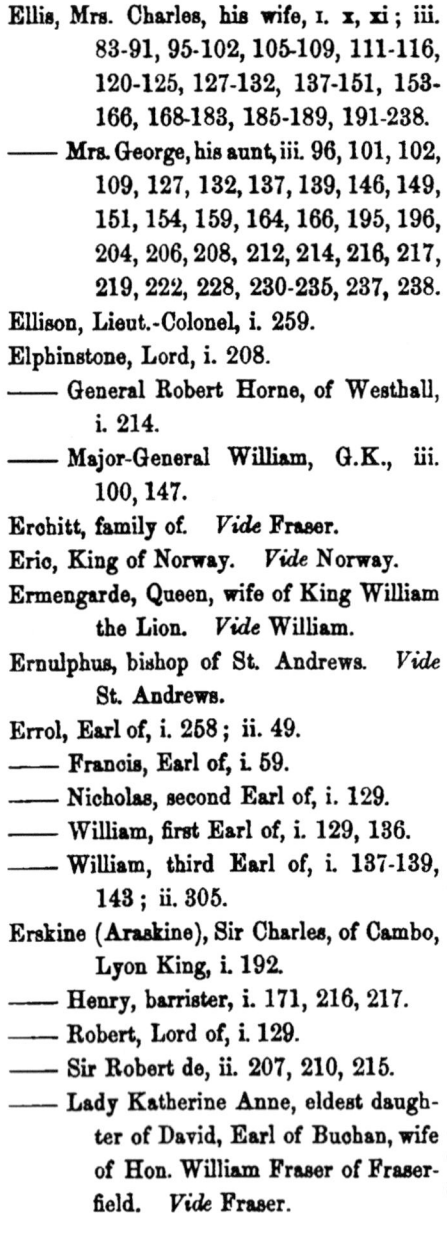

Ellis, Mrs. Charles, his wife, i. x, xi; iii. 83-91, 95-102, 105-109, 111-116, 120-125, 127-132, 137-151, 153-166, 168-183, 185-189, 191-238.
—— Mrs. George, his aunt, iii. 96, 101, 102, 109, 127, 132, 137, 139, 146, 149, 151, 154, 159, 164, 166, 195, 196, 204, 206, 208, 212, 214, 216, 217, 219, 222, 228, 230-235, 237, 238.
Ellison, Lieut.-Colonel, i. 259.
Elphinstone, Lord, i. 208.
—— General Robert Horne, of Westhall, i. 214.
—— Major-General William, G.K., iii. 100, 147.
Erchitt, family of. *Vide* Fraser.
Eric, King of Norway. *Vide* Norway.
Ermengarde, Queen, wife of King William the Lion. *Vide* William.
Ernulphus, bishop of St. Andrews. *Vide* St. Andrews.
Errol, Earl of, i. 258; ii. 49.
—— Francis, Earl of, i. 59.
—— Nicholas, second Earl of, i. 129.
—— William, first Earl of, i. 129, 136.
—— William, third Earl of, i. 137-139, 143; ii. 305.
Erskine (Araskine), Sir Charles, of Cambo, Lyon King, i. 192.
—— Henry, barrister, i. 171, 216, 217.
—— Robert, Lord of, i. 129.
—— Sir Robert de, ii. 207, 210, 215.
—— Lady Katherine Anne, eldest daughter of David, Earl of Buchan, wife of Hon. William Fraser of Fraserfield. *Vide* Fraser.

Erskine, Lady Sophia, sister to Earl of Kellie, third wife of Alexander Fraser, Master of Saltoun, son of Alexander, tenth of Philorth and tenth Lord Saltoun. *Vide* Fraser.
—— Thomas, Lord, i. 129; ii. 228, 305.
—— Sir Thomas de, ii. 201, 206, 295.
Ethelred, brother of Alexander I. and David I., ii. 8.
Ettal, Thomas, ii. 198.
Eugene, son of Anabell, daughter Samuel, i. 24.
Eugenius the Third, Pope, ii. 12.
—— the Fourth, Pope, ii. 216.
Exeter, Walter of, ii. 84, 95.

Farde, Gerard de la, i. 69.
Farquhar, Dr., i. 226.
Farquharson, Alexander, of Haughton, i. 215.
—— Francis, of Finzean, i. 213.
—— James, of Invercauld, i. 213.
—— William, of Bruxie, i. 214.
Farraline, family of. *Vide* Fraser.
Faucon, Seigneur de, ii. 84.
Fawcett, Colonel, iii. 219.
Fayrle, William, Lord of Brade, ii. 223.
Fead, Lieut.-Colonel, i. 272.
Fearn (Fern), Donald, abbot of, ii. 233.
—— monks of, i. 110.
Fedreth, William de, i. 46.
—— Christian de Moravia, his wife, i. 46.
Feldew, John, ii. 216.
Felton, Robert de, ii. 173.

INDEX OF PERSONS.

Fentoun, Sir William de, of Beaufort, ii. 173.
—— William de, of Baky, ii. 35, 171, 172.
—— Cecilia Bisset, his wife, ii. 172.
—— William, of that Ilk, ii. 223, 224.
—— Family of, of Baky, ii. 51.
—— Family of, ii. 172.
Ferdinand the Fourth, iii. 4.
Fergus, father of Angus, King of the Picts, ii. 2.
Ferguson, James, of Pitfour, i. 213-215.
—— of Kinmundy, i. 215.
Fife, Colban, Earl of, son of Malcolm, Earl of (1266), i. 43; ii. 107, 108.
—— Constantine, Earl of, ii. 8.
—— Duncan, justiciar, Earl of (1165-1171), ii. 10, 11.
—— Duncan, Earl of (1227), ii. 16.
—— Duncan, Earl of, son of Colban (1288), ii. 19, 20, 22, 29, 30, 98, 99, 107, 108.
—— Duncan his son, Earl of, ii. 99, 107-109.
—— (present) Earl of, i. 186, 194; ii. 70.
—— Earls of, ii. 8, 9, 163.
—— Isabella, Countess of, ii. 133.
—— James, Earl of, i. 214.
—— Macduff, son of Malcolm, Earl of (1266). *Vide* Macduff.
—— Macduff, thane of, i. 8, 9.
—— Malcolm, Earl of (1266), i. 1, 3; ii. 107, 108.
—— Malcolm, son of Duncan, Earl of. *Vide* Malcolm.

Fife and Menteith, Robert, Earl of. *Vide* Albany, Robert, Duke of.
Filmer, Sir Robert, i. 220.
Findlater, Earl of, i. 199; ii. 155.
—— Mr., i. 222, 223.
Findlay, Alexander, ii. 270.
Finlayson, Matthew, of Killeith, ii. 246, 253, 254.
Findrack, family of. *Vide* Fraser.
Fitzallan, Sir Brian, i. 37; ii. 104, 105.
Fitzclarence, Lord Frederick, iii. 234.
Fitz-Roger, Robert, ii. 84.
Fitz-William, Radulph, ii. 84.
Fleetwood, General, i. 180.
Fleming, Sir David, of Biggar, ii. 218.
—— John, Earl of Wigton, Lord, i. 91.
—— Malcolm, Earl of Wigton, ii. 297.
—— Sir Patrick, i. 91; ii. 94.
—— Patrick, ii. 94.
Fletcher, Sir Andrew, of Inverpeffer and of Saltoun, i. 185; ii. 67.
—— Andrew, of Saltoun, i. 221.
—— Mr., iii. 173.
Fletchers, The, ii. 70.
Fludyer, Ensign, i. 272; iii. 63.
Foghou, Adam of, i. *inter* 12 and 13.
—— William of, second son of Patrick, Earl of Dunbar, i. 15, 18, 23, 28; ii. 120.
—— Christiana Corbet, his wife, i. 15, 18; ii. 120.
Forbes, Alexander, first Lord, i. 123-125, 127.
—— Alexander, of Blacktoun, ii. 163.
—— Isobel Hacket, his wife, ii. 163.
—— Alexander, of Brux, i. 144.

Forbes, Alexander, of Pitsligo (1544), ii. 52.
—— Hon. Beatrix Abernethy, his wife, ii. 52.
—— Alexander, of Pitsligo (1630), i. 170.
—— Sir Alexander, of Tolquhon, ii. 287.
—— Arthur, of Brux, i. 186.
—— Arthur, of Echt, i. 186; ii. 68, 70-73.
—— Duncan, of Balgounie, ii. 155.
—— Elizabeth, daughter of Thomas of Ballogie, wife of Erskine Fraser. *Vide* Fraser.
—— Hugh, of Schivas, i. 214.
—— Isabel, wife of (first) Thomas Fraser of Strichen (Philorth), and (second) Thomas Fraser of Knockie (Lovat). *Vide* Fraser.
—— James, of Blacktoun, i. 168.
—— Magdalen Fraser, his wife, i. 168.
—— John Lord of, i. 117; ii. 140, 166.
—— John, Lord, i. 144.
—— John, Master of, his eldest son, i. 144.
—— Sir John Stuart, i. 194.
—— Sir John, of Craigievar, i. 186.
—— John, of Pitsligo, i. 150; ii. 270, 273, 275-277.
—— John de, Lieutenant to Vicecomes of Aberdeen, i. 109.
—— John, of Skellater, ii. 153.
—— John, Sheriff-depute of Aberdeen, i. 186.
—— Laird of Blacktoun, ii. 68, 71.
—— Lord (1468), ii. 45.
—— Lord, i. 199, 208.

Forbes, Mary Christina, daughter of John of Skellater, wife of Henry David Fraser. *Vide* Fraser.
—— Master of, i. 176.
—— -Mitchell, Duncan, of Thainstoun, ii 153, 155.
—— Katherine A. Fraser, his wife, ii. 153.
—— Henry David, his sixth son, ii. 153, 155.
—— Margaret Fraser, of Fraserfield, his wife, ii. 153-155.
—— Richard, Keeper of the Rolls, ii. 228.
—— Robert, tutor of Craigievar, i. 186.
—— Thomas of Ballogie, ii. 154.
—— Walter, of Blacktoun, ii. 287.
—— William, Master of, ii. 287.
—— Sir William, of Pitsligo, i. 214.
—— Sir William, of Craigievar, i. 215, 224.
—— William, of Camphoe, i. 186.
—— William de, of Kinaldie, i. 125-128.
—— Agnes Fraser, his wife, i. 125-128.
—— William, of Tolquhoun, i. 162, 169, 170.
—— his daughter, first wife of Alexander Fraser, tenth of Philorth. *Vide* Fraser.
—— William, of Corsindae, ii. 149.
—— Katherine Fraser, his wife, ii. 149.
—— William, minister at Fraserburgh, i. 164, 165.
—— William, advocate, i. 171; ii. 287.
—— of Balgounie, family of, ii. 155.
—— of Corfurdie, ii. 147.
—— of Pitsligo, family of, i. 127.

Fordun, the historian, i. 20, 25, 27, 64, 104; ii. 1, 2, 4-6, 18-20, 29, 85, 86, 98, 124, 129, 130, 134, 183-186, 188-194.
Fordyce, Arthur Dingwall, of Culsh, i. 214.
Forest, family of. *Vide* Fraser.
Forester (Forster), Adam, ii. 171.
—— Sir John, chamberlain to James I., ii. 206.
Forglen, Robert, rector of, ii. 208.
Forglen and Ardendracht, family of. *Vide* Fraser.
Forgue, Christian, vicar of, ii. 208.
Forman, Martin, ii. 245.
Formartine, Henry de Preston, Lord of, ii. 140.
Forton, "Ness," mentioned as Lord of, i. 19.
Fotheringham, (Fodryngham), William de, ii. 171.
Fouché, French statesman, iii. 59.
Foulis, Sir James, i. 176.
—— William, Keeper of the Privy Seal, ii. 206.
Fowlarton, Walter, ii. 198.
Fox, Charles James, i. 223.
Foy, French General, i. 261.
Foyers, family of. *Vide* Fraser.
France, King of, i. 4, 37, 42, 47, 101; ii. 80, 88, 193.
Fraise, Julius de (or de Berri), i. 2.
—— Philip, King of, i. 64, 65; ii. 25, 26, 109.
Fraser (Frasel, Frasier, Fresel, Fresell, Freser, Freseyle, Freshell, Fresille, Freysel, Frezeau, Frezel, Frisel, Frisell, Frissell, Frysel, Frysell), Ada, prioress de Eccles, ii. 122.

Fraser, Adam (son of Udard), i. 14-16, 24, 26-31; ii. 116.
—— Constantia, his wife, i. 28; ii. 116.
—— Agnes, daughter of Sir William, second of Philorth, wife of William de Forbes of Kinaldie. *Vide* Forbes.
—— Sir Alexander, of Cowie and Durris, Sheriff of Aberdeen and first of Philorth, i. 93, 100, 103, 104, 106-110, 113, 116-122, 124, 127-129, 140; ii. 36, 136, 139-143, 145, 160, 166, 169, 180, 200, 201, 203-205, 209-215, 217-223, 289, 290, 293, 294, 310, 311, 313-316, 323.
—— Lady Johanna de Ross, his first wife, i. 103, 110-114, 116, 119-121, 125-127, 132, 134, 206; ii. 140, 143, 207, 209-211, 214, 215, 218, 219.
—— Lady Elizabeth de Hamilton, his second wife, i. 120, 122, 124; ii. 141-143, 201, 204, 205, 221, 311, 315.
—— Sir Alexander, third of Philorth, i. 126-136, 139, 140; ii. 141, 143, 145, 146, 157, 170, 179, 203, 210, 211, 213, 225-235, 313, 316-318.
—— Marjorie Menzies, his wife, i. 127, 128, 135; ii. 225, 226, 229.
—— Alexander, fourth of Philorth, i. 135, 136, 139, 140; ii. 146, 211, 212, 228, 229, 235, 313, 318.
—— Lady Margaret de Hay, his wife, i. 136, 139.

Fraser, Alexander, fifth of Philorth, i. 136-140; ii. 235, 236, 318.
—— Alexander, seventh of Philorth, i. 142-152, 157; ii. 146-151, 240-246, 319, 320.
—— Katherine Menzies, his wife, i. 142-144, 147, 150.
—— Sir Alexander, eighth of Philorth, founder of Fraserburgh, i. 150, 152-167, 169, 170, 181, 194; ii. 144, 147, 150-152, 243-284, 320, 322.
—— Magdalen Ogilvie, his first wife, i. 152, 161, 166, 167.
—— Lady Elizabeth Maxwell, his second wife, i. 152, 161, 163, 164, 168.
—— Alexander, ninth of Philorth, i. 159, 161-163, 165-170, 192; ii. 63-65, 144, 246-253, 277-284, 320, 322.
—— Hon. Margaret Abernethy, his first wife, i. 159, 163, 167-169, 183, 192; ii. 63-65, 246-254, 320.
—— Isabella Gordon, his second wife, i. 167, 168.
—— Alexander, tenth of Philorth, tenth Lord Saltoun, i. 163, 164, 167-194; ii. 65, 72, 73, 145, 152, 284-288, 322.
—— . . . Forbes, daughter of William Forbes of Tolquhoun, his first wife, i. 169, 170, 190.
—— Elizabeth Seton, his second wife, i. 169, 170, 191.
—— Alexander, twelfth of Philorth, twelfth Lord Saltoun, i. 195-205; ii. 153.

Fraser: Lady Mary Gordon, his wife, i. 197-199; ii. 153.
—— Alexander, thirteenth of Philorth, thirteenth Lord Saltoun, i. 203-205; ii. 153.
—— Alexander, fifteenth of Philorth, fifteenth Lord Saltoun, i. 206-226, 312; ii. 155, 231.
—— Marjory Fraser, his wife, i. 207, 209, 210, 219, 221-227, 233, 234, 240, 245, 276, 283, 285, 310; iii. 1-8, 13, 15, 27, 29, 37, 41, 67, 73, 74, 91, 109, 128, 138, 149, 159, 161, 162, 174, 179.
—— Alexander George, sixteenth of Philorth, sixteenth Lord Saltoun, i. x-xii, 226-313; ii. 146; iii. 1-238.
—— Catherine Thurlow, his wife, i. 226, 241, 245, 247, 251-253, 269, 270, 274-276, 283, 288; iii. 8-75.
—— Alexander, seventeenth of Philorth, seventeenth Lord Saltoun, i. ix, 313.
—— Alexander, eldest son of Alexander, seventh of Philorth, i. 147, 148, 150-152.
—— Lady Beatrice de Keith, his wife, i. 148, 150.
—— Alexander, Master of Saltoun, only son of Alexander, tenth Lord Saltoun, i. 170, 181, 185-191, 193; ii. 73, 284.
—— Lady Ann Kerr, his first wife, i. 181, 187, 193.
—— Lady Marion Cunningham, Countess of Findlater, his second wife, i. 187.

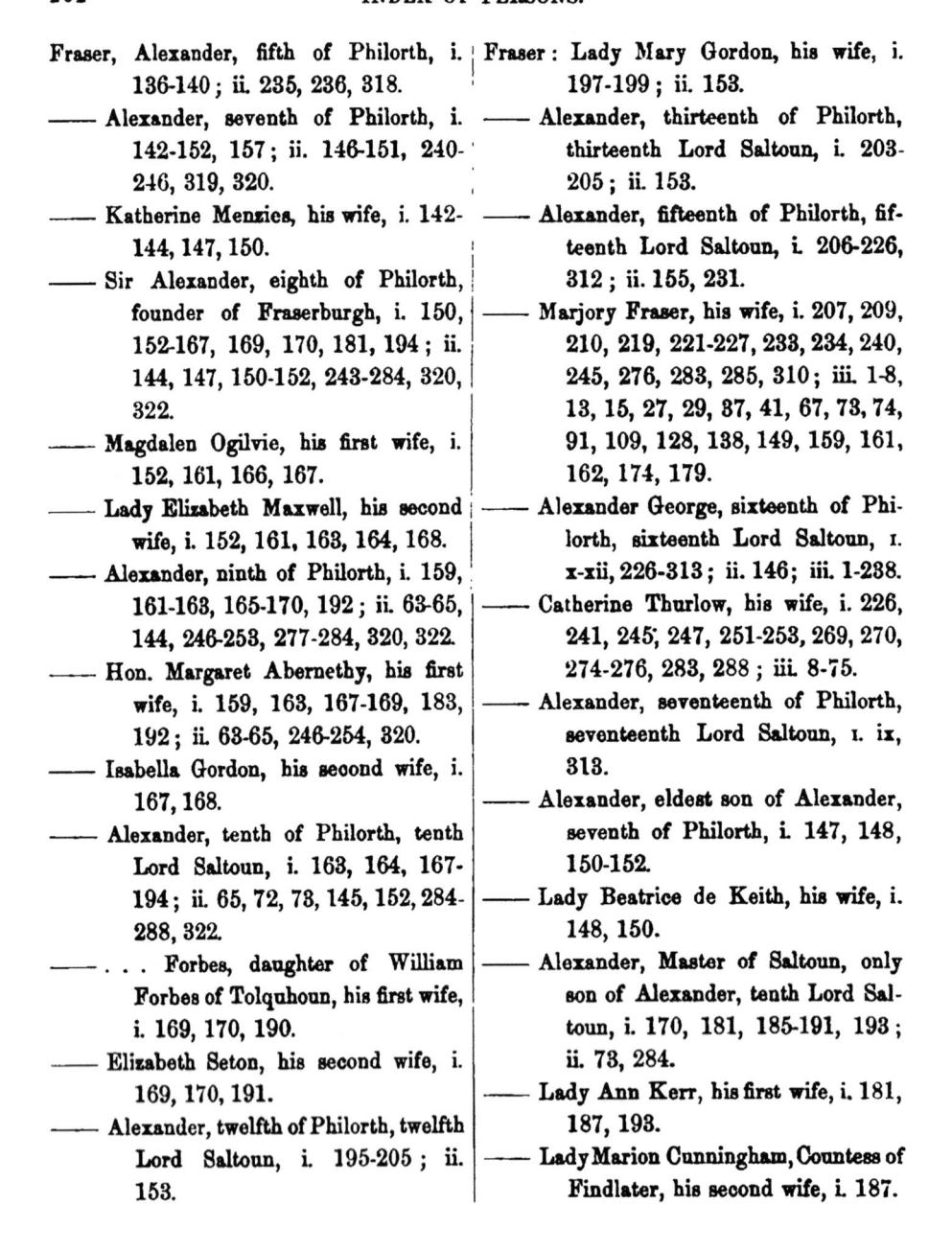

Fraser: Lady Sophia Erskine, his third wife, i. 187, 188.
—— Alexander, his elder son, i. 187, 189, 193.
—— Alexander, of Bogheid, ii. 270.
—— Alexander, of Fraserdale (Mackenzie of Prestonhall), i. 197, 200.
—— Alexander, of Strichen, i. 214, 216.
—— Alexander, probably the son of Sir Simon, the Chamberlain's brother, i. 104, 131; ii. 130-133, 169, 174.
—— daughter of Sir Andrew Moray of Bothwell, his wife, ii. 131, 169, 174.
—— Sir Alexander, probably the son of Adam, i. 49, 93-96; ii. 117, 118.
—— Sir Alexander, of Touchfraser, Cowie, etc., Chamberlain of Scotland, i. vi, viii, ix, xi, 79-82, 87, 90, 92-98, 106, 107, 109, 130, 131; ii. 25, 89, 96, 124-129, 131, 133-135, 144, 165, 166, 168, 180, 183, 187, 196-199, 309, 310.
—— Lady Mary de Bruce, sister of Robert I., his wife, i. 49, 50, 67-69, 72, 76, 93, 98, 108; ii. 198, 199, 309.
—— Sir Alexander, of Cornetoun, probably the son of John, son of Sir Gilbert Fraser, i. 34, 49, 50, 52, 96, 97, 104, 132; ii. 165, 166.
—— Alexander, of Tyrie, ii. 152, 285, 287.
—— Alexander, of Durris, natural son of Sir Alexander, first of Philorth, i. 120, 124; ii. 141-143, 204, 205.
Fraser, Alexander, of Durris (1461), ii. 203, 230, 231.
—— Alexander, of Durris (1616), i. 162, 163, 181; ii. 144, 251, 270.
—— Sir Alexander, of Durris, physician to Charles II., i. 191; ii. 144.
—— Elizabeth Dochty, his first wife, ii. 144.
—— Dame Mary Carey, his second wife, ii. 144.
—— Alexander, younger of Durris, ii. 144.
—— Alexander, kinsman (?) of Alexander, third of Philorth, i. 135.
—— Alexander, son of Duncan of Tulifour, and cousin of John of Forglen or Ardendracht, i. 131; ii. 133, 141, 170, 295, 324.
—— Alexander, of Techmuiry, i. 190; ii. 147, 287.
—— Janet Fraser, his wife, i. 190.
—— Alexander, of Forest, ii. 145.
—— Alexander, in Ardmacron, ii. 146.
—— Alexander, in Memsie, ii. 146.
—— Alexander, of Fraserfield, ii. 153, 154.
—— Mary Christina Moir, his wife, ii. 154.
—— Alexander, second of Lovat, ii. 171, 175-177.
—— Elizabeth de Keith, his wife, ii. 176.
—— Alexander, his second son, erroneously called elder son of Hugh, third of Lovat, ii. 175-177.
—— Alexander, fourth Lord Lovat. *Vide* Lovat.

INDEX OF PERSONS.

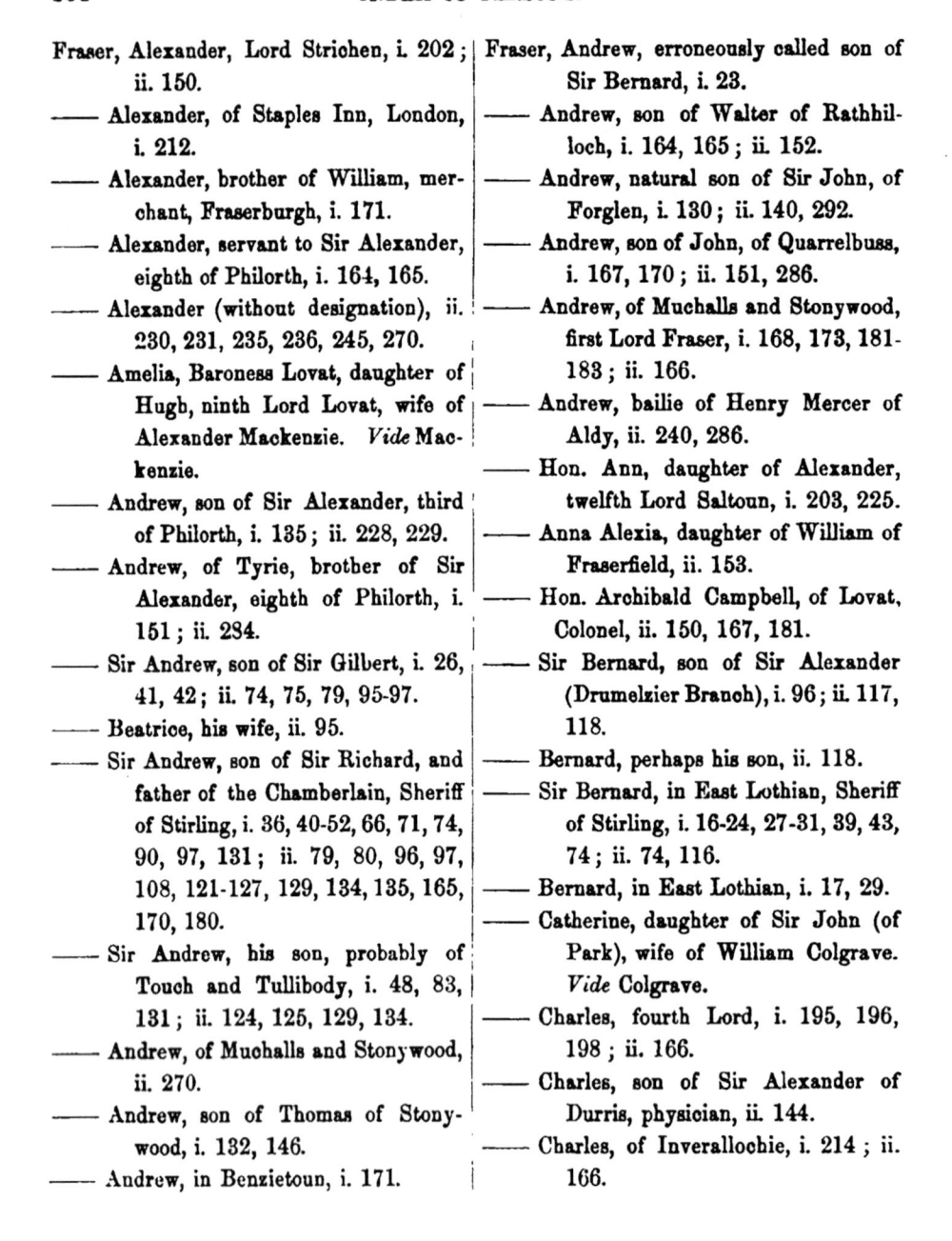

Fraser, Alexander, Lord Strichen, i. 202; ii. 150.
—— Alexander, of Staples Inn, London, i. 212.
—— Alexander, brother of William, merchant, Fraserburgh, i. 171.
—— Alexander, servant to Sir Alexander, eighth of Philorth, i. 164, 165.
—— Alexander (without designation), ii. 230, 231, 235, 236, 245, 270.
—— Amelia, Baroness Lovat, daughter of Hugh, ninth Lord Lovat, wife of Alexander Mackenzie. *Vide* Mackenzie.
—— Andrew, son of Sir Alexander, third of Philorth, i. 135; ii. 228, 229.
—— Andrew, of Tyrie, brother of Sir Alexander, eighth of Philorth, i. 151; ii. 284.
—— Sir Andrew, son of Sir Gilbert, i. 26, 41, 42; ii. 74, 75, 79, 95-97.
—— Beatrice, his wife, ii. 95.
—— Sir Andrew, son of Sir Richard, and father of the Chamberlain, Sheriff of Stirling, i. 36, 40-52, 66, 71, 74, 90, 97, 131; ii. 79, 80, 96, 97, 108, 121-127, 129, 134, 135, 165, 170, 180.
—— Sir Andrew, his son, probably of Touch and Tullibody, i. 48, 83, 131; ii. 124, 125, 129, 134.
—— Andrew, of Muchalls and Stonywood, ii. 270.
—— Andrew, son of Thomas of Stonywood, i. 132, 146.
—— Andrew, in Benzietoun, i. 171.

Fraser, Andrew, erroneously called son of Sir Bernard, i. 23.
—— Andrew, son of Walter of Rathhilloch, i. 164, 165; ii. 152.
—— Andrew, natural son of Sir John, of Forglen, i. 130; ii. 140, 292.
—— Andrew, son of John, of Quarrelbuss, i. 167, 170; ii. 151, 286.
—— Andrew, of Muchalls and Stonywood, first Lord Fraser, i. 168, 173, 181-183; ii. 166.
—— Andrew, bailie of Henry Mercer of Aldy, ii. 240, 286.
—— Hon. Ann, daughter of Alexander, twelfth Lord Saltoun, i. 203, 225.
—— Anna Alexia, daughter of William of Fraserfield, ii. 153.
—— Hon. Archibald Campbell, of Lovat, Colonel, ii. 150, 167, 181.
—— Sir Bernard, son of Sir Alexander (Drumelzier Branch), i. 96; ii. 117, 118.
—— Bernard, perhaps his son, ii. 118.
—— Sir Bernard, in East Lothian, Sheriff of Stirling, i. 16-24, 27-31, 39, 43, 74; ii. 74, 116.
—— Bernard, in East Lothian, i. 17, 29.
—— Catherine, daughter of Sir John (of Park), wife of William Colgrave. *Vide* Colgrave.
—— Charles, fourth Lord, i. 195, 196, 198; ii. 166.
—— Charles, son of Sir Alexander of Durris, physician, ii. 144.
—— Charles, of Inverallochie, i. 214; ii. 166.

Fraser, Christina, daughter of William, sixth of Philorth, wife of Andrew Chalmers. *Vide* Chalmers.
—— Christiana, daughter of Alexander, seventh of Philorth, wife of William Crawford. *Vide* Crawford.
—— Hon. David M., Captain (now Colonel) R.H.A., brother of seventeenth Lord Saltoun, i. 311.
—— Duncan, of Tulifour, i. 131 ; ii. 132, 133, 141, 170, 180, 295.
—— Christiana, daughter of Margaret Gelibrande, his wife, ii. 132.
—— Eda, daughter of Simon, wife of Hugh Lorens. *Vide* Lorens.
—— Hon. Eleanor, daughter of George, fourteenth Lord Saltoun, wife of (first) Sir George Ramsay, and (second) Lieut.-General Duncan Campbell. *Vide* Ramsay and Campbell.
—— Hon. Eleanor, daughter of Alexander, fifteenth Lord Saltoun, wife of William Macdowall Grant of Arndilly. *Vide* Grant.
—— Eleanor, daughter of Sir John of Park, ii. 156.
—— Eleanor, daughter of William of Park, ii. 156.
—— Eliza, daughter of William James Fraser of Park, ii. 157.
—— Elizabeth, daughter of Sir Alexander, eighth of Philorth, wife of Sir R. Keith. *Vide* Keith.
—— Elizabeth (Mrs. Leslie), daughter of William, last of Memsie, ii. 146.

Fraser, Elizabeth, daughter of William of Woodhill, ii. 154.
—— Erskine, Colonel, of Woodhill, son of William of Fraserfield, ii. 154.
—— Elizabeth Forbes, his wife, ii. 154.
—— Erskine William, son of Hugh, Rector of Woolwich, ii. 154.
—— Evorilda, daughter of Sir John (of Park), wife of General Chesney. *Vide* Chesney.
—— Evorilda Eliza Maria, daughter of William James Fraser of Park, wife of John G. G. Stuart. *Vide* Stewart.
—— Fenella, said to be daughter of Sir Bernard, wife of Sir Colin Campbell. *Vide* Campbell.
—— Frederick Mackenzie, of Castle Fraser, Colonel, ii. 166, 181.
—— Galfridus, i. 5.
—— Geoffry, Chevalier, i. 7.
—— George, son of Sir Alexander, third of Philorth, i. 135 ; ii. 228, 229.
—— George, son of Alexander, fourth of Philorth, i. 136, 137.
—— George, fourteenth of Philorth, fourteenth Lord Saltoun, i. 203-207 ; ii. 155, 156.
—— Eleanor Gordon, his wife, 204-207 ; ii. 156.
—— Hon. George, their second son, i. 206.
—— Hon. George, their fourth son, i. 206.
—— George, second of Park, son of William of Park, ii. 156, 157.

INDEX OF PERSONS.

Fraser, George, fourth of Park, son of William James Fraser of Park, ii. 157.
—— Angusina Macdonald, his wife, ii. 157.
—— Gilbert, in East Lothian, i. *inter* 12 and 13, 13, 14, 19, 29.
—— Gilbert, erroneously called son of Sir Bernard, i. 23.
—— Sir Gilbert, Sheriff of Traquair and Peebles, i. 16, 22-26, 29-35, 39, 41, 42; ii. 74, 75, 95, 97, 121, 122.
—— Christiana, his wife, i. 26, 33.
—— Sir Gilbert, of Mackarstoun, ii. 120, 121.
—— Margaret Corbet, Lady of Mackarstoun, his wife, ii. 120, 121.
—— Grace Louisa, daughter of William James Fraser of Park, wife of Thomas G. R. Innes. *Vide* Innes.
—— Helen, a nun, said to be daughter of Sir Bernard, i. 23.
—— Hon. Helen, daughter of William, eleventh Lord Saltoun, wife of James Gordon of Park. *Vide* Gordon.
—— Hon. Henrietta, daughter of William, eleventh Lord Saltoun, wife of John Gordon of Kinellar. *Vide* Gordon.
—— Hon. Henrietta, daughter of George, fourteenth Lord Saltoun, i. 206.
—— Henrietta, daughter of William of Park, wife of John M'Bean. *Vide* M'Bean.
—— General Henry David, son of William of Fraserfield, ii. 153.

Fraser: Mary Christina Forbes, his wife, ii. 153.
—— Herbald, ii. 232.
—— Highland Clan, i. vi, vii.
—— Hugh, first of Lovat, i. 2, 45, 85, 91, 131; ii. 133, 168-177, 180, 182.
—— Hugh, third of Lovat, ii. 175-179.
—— Janet de Fentoun, his wife, ii. 175, 176, 178.
—— Hugh, fifth of Lovat, and first Lord. *Vide* Lovat.
—— Hugh, seventh Lord Lovat. *Vide* Lovat.
—— Hugh, ninth Lord Lovat. *Vide* Lovat.
—— Hugh, erroneously called only son, and second son, of Hugh, third of Lovat, i. 175-177.
—— Hugh, erroneously called fourth of Lovat, ii. 176, 178.
—— Hugh, of Easter Tyrie, i. 174.
—— Hugh, of Fraserdale, i. 200, 201.
—— Hugh, second son of Thomas, second of Strichen, ii. 145.
—— Hugh, Mr., i. xii.
—— Hugh, erroneously mentioned as son of Sir Simon, the Chamberlain's brother, ii. 130, 168.
—— Hugh, son of William of Fraserfield, ii. 153.
—— Hugh, rector of Woolwich, son of William of Fraserfield, ii. 154.
—— Miss Lloyd, his wife, ii. 154.
—— Isabella, daughter of William, second of Philorth, wife of Gilbert Menzies. *Vide* Menzies.

INDEX OF PERSONS.

Fraser, Hon. Isabella, daughter of eleventh Lord Saltoun, wife of Rev. David Brown at Belhelvie. *Vide* Brown.
—— Isabella, probably daughter of John Fraser of Quarrelbus, ii. 286.
—— James, escheator for Henry III., i. 5.
—— James, of Bledelaw, i. 5.
—— Sir James, brother of Sir Alexander, the Chamberlain, i. 41, 48, 87, 131; ii. 124, 129, 134-136, 180.
—— Margaret Stewart, his wife, i. 87; ii. 134-136.
—— Sir James, of Frendraught, his son, i. 86, 90, 110; ii. 135, 136-138, 294.
—— James, of Frendraught, ii. 86, 137, 138.
—— James, of Tyrie, third son of Sir Alexander, eighth of Philorth, i. 166; ii. 152, 270, 277, 285.
—— Hon. James, of Lonmay, third son of William, eleventh Lord Saltoun, i. 198; ii. 155.
—— Lady Eleanor Lindesay, his wife, ii. 155.
—— James, of Cairness, ii. 270.
—— James, of Memsie, second son of Alexander, third of Philorth, i. 135, 136, 140; ii. 146, 228, 229.
—— James, of Hospitalfield, ii. 157.
—— James, the Bailie, i. 140.
—— Mr. James, i. 216.
—— Jane, daughter of Alexander of Techmuiry, wife of James Gordon. *Vide* Gordon.

Fraser, Janet, daughter of Alexander, fourth of Philorth, wife of George Baird of Ordinschivas. *Vide* Baird.
—— Janet, daughter of Alexander, tenth of Philorth, wife of Alexander of Techmuiry. *Vide* Alexander Fraser.
—— Jean, daughter of James Fraser of Tyrie, ii. 152, 285.
—— John, of Ardglassie, son of Sir Alexander, third of Philorth, i. 135, 137, 140, 143; ii. 228, 229, 240.
—— John, rector of the University of Paris, fourth son of Alexander, seventh of Philorth, i. 151; ii. 150, 151.
—— John, second son of Alexander, ninth of Philorth, by Isabella Gordon, i. 167, 168, 170.
—— Hon. John, third son of George, fourteenth Lord Saltoun, i. 206.
—— Sir John, of Forglen and Ardendracht, second son of Sir William of Cowie and Durris, i. 102-104, 106, 109, 116, 117, 121, 128, 130, 131, 140; ii. 139-141, 143, 166, 169, 180, 289-294.
—— Marjory, daughter of Sir John of Monymusk, his wife, ii. 139, 140.
—— John, of Forglen and Ardendracht, his son, i. 130, 131; ii. 133, 140, 141, 170, 180, 292, 293, 295.
—— John, of Memsie, i. 194.
—— John, of Quarrelbuss and Crechie, brother of Sir Alexander, eighth of Philorth, i. 151, 167, 196; ii. 151, 252, 286.

Fraser, John, fourth son of Thomas of Durris, ii. 144.
—— General Sir John, G.C.H., ii. 156, 157; iii. 74, 75, 77, 78.
—— Evorilda Hamer, his first wife, ii. 156; iii. 75.
—— (Miss) A'Court, his second wife, ii. 157; iii. 75.
—— John, of Touchfraser, eldest son of the Chamberlain, i. 51, 73, 76-80, 84, 86, 97, 106; ii. 199.
—— John, erroneously styled Sheriff of Tweeddale, i. 33.
—— John, eldest son of Sir Gilbert, i. 26, 31-35, 39, 41, 42; ii. 75.
—— Alicia de Cunigberg, his wife, i. 33, 34.
—— John Henry David, son of General Henry David, ii. 154.
—— John, vicar of Houghton, Norfolk, i. 5.
—— John (Cambridgeshire), i. 5.
—— John, of Forest, Unicorn Pursuivant, i. 144; ii. 145, 211.
—— Mr. John, i. 147.
—— John, archdeacon of St. Andrews, ii. 122.
—— Katherine, daughter of Thomas of Strichen (Philorth line), wife of William Forbes of Corsindae. *Vide* Forbes.
—— Katherine Anne, wife of Duncan Forbes-Mitchell of Thainstoun. *Vide* Forbes.
—— Katherine Isabella, daughter of Alexander of Fraserfield, ii. 154.

Fraser, Kennedy, son of William of Fraserfield, ii. 154.
—— Lady, grandmother of the present Sir William Fraser, Bart., iii. 47.
—— Lancelot, i. 7.
—— Sir Lawrence, of Drumelzier and Hales, i. 28, 30, 31; ii. 79, 116-120.
—— Lawrence, probably his son, ii. 117, 118.
—— Leslie Anne, daughter of William James of Park, wife of Rev. Edward Whately. *Vide* Whately.
—— Lord, I. ix.
—— Magdalene, daughter of Sir Alexander, eighth of Philorth, wife of Patrick Cheyne. *Vide* Cheyne.
—— Magdalene, daughter of Alexander, ninth of Philorth, wife of James Forbes of Blackton. *Vide* Forbes.
—— Magnus, ii. 270.
—— Margaret, daughter of Alexander, seventh of Philorth, wife of (first) Alexander Cumming of Inverallochy, and (second) Alexander Annand of Auchtirallane. *Vide* Cumming and Annand.
—— Margaret, daughter of Sir Alexander, eighth of Philorth, wife of Hay of Ury. *Vide* Hay.
—— Hon. Margaret, daughter of Alexander, fifteenth Lord Saltoun, i. 226, 283, 310; iii. 74, 159, 161, 183.
—— Margaret, daughter of William of Fraserfield, wife of David, Earl of Buchan. *Vide* Buchan.

INDEX OF PERSONS.

Fraser, Margaret, of Fraserfield, daughter of Alexander of Fraserfield, wife of Henry David Forbes. *Vide* Forbes.
—— Margaret Alexia, daughter of General Henry David, wife of the Marquis de Garzallo. *Vide* Garzallo.
—— Margaret, wife of Egidius Peche, i. 5.
—— Margaret, daughter of John of Touchfraser, and grand-daughter of the Chamberlain, wife of Sir William de Keith, the Marischal. *Vide* Marischal.
—— Margaret, Lady of Ardendracht and Auchluchries, ii. 141, 295, 296, 325.
—— Margaret, Lady of Mackarstoun, ii. 121.
—— Marjory, daughter of Simon of Ness Castle, wife of Alexander, fifteenth Lord Saltoun. *Vide* Alexander Fraser.
—— Mary, daughter of Alexander, ninth of Philorth, wife of . . . Baird of Auchmedden. *Vide* Baird.
—— Hon. Mary, daughter of William, eleventh Lord Saltoun, wife of William Dalmahoy of Ravelrig. *Vide* Dalmahoy.
—— Hon. Mary, daughter of George, fourteenth Lord Saltoun, i. 206.
—— Mary, daughter of Alexander of Fraserfield, wife of William Urquhart of Craigstoun. *Vide* Urquhart.
—— Mary Ann, daughter of General Henry David, ii. 154.

Fraser, Mauld, heiress of Frendraught, wife of Alexander Dunbar, second son of John Dunbar, Earl of Moray. *Vide* Dunbar.
—— Michael, of Techmuiry, ii. 146, 147.
—— Mr., of Gortuleg, i. 218.
—— Sir Nesius, i. 25; ii. 121-123.
—— Sir Peter, of Durris, i. 191; ii. 144.
—— Pierre, i. 1, 7.
—— Rachel, daughter of William of Fraserfield, ii. 153.
—— Rachel, daughter of Erskine of Woodhill, ii. 154.
—— Rachel, daughter of Alexander of Fraserfield, wife of William Maxwell. *Vide* Maxwell.
—— Sir Radulph, i. 4, 8.
—— René, i. 7.
—— René, his son, i. 7.
—— Sir Richard, of Touchfraser, etc., Sheriff of Berwick, i. 3, 31, 34-43, 48, 50, 71, 90; ii. 75, 78, 80, 99, 121, 125-127, 166.
—— Richard, i. 5.
—— Robert, ii. 231.
—— Robert, son and heir of Alexander of Durris, i. 162, 163; ii. 270.
—— Robert, ii. 122.
—— Robert, of Overtoun, ii. 123.
—— Sarah, daughter of Thomas, ii. 122.
—— Seiree. *Vide* Sir Simon (filius).
—— Simon, son of René, i. 7.
—— Simon, of Keith, i. 12, 13, 17, 29, 86.

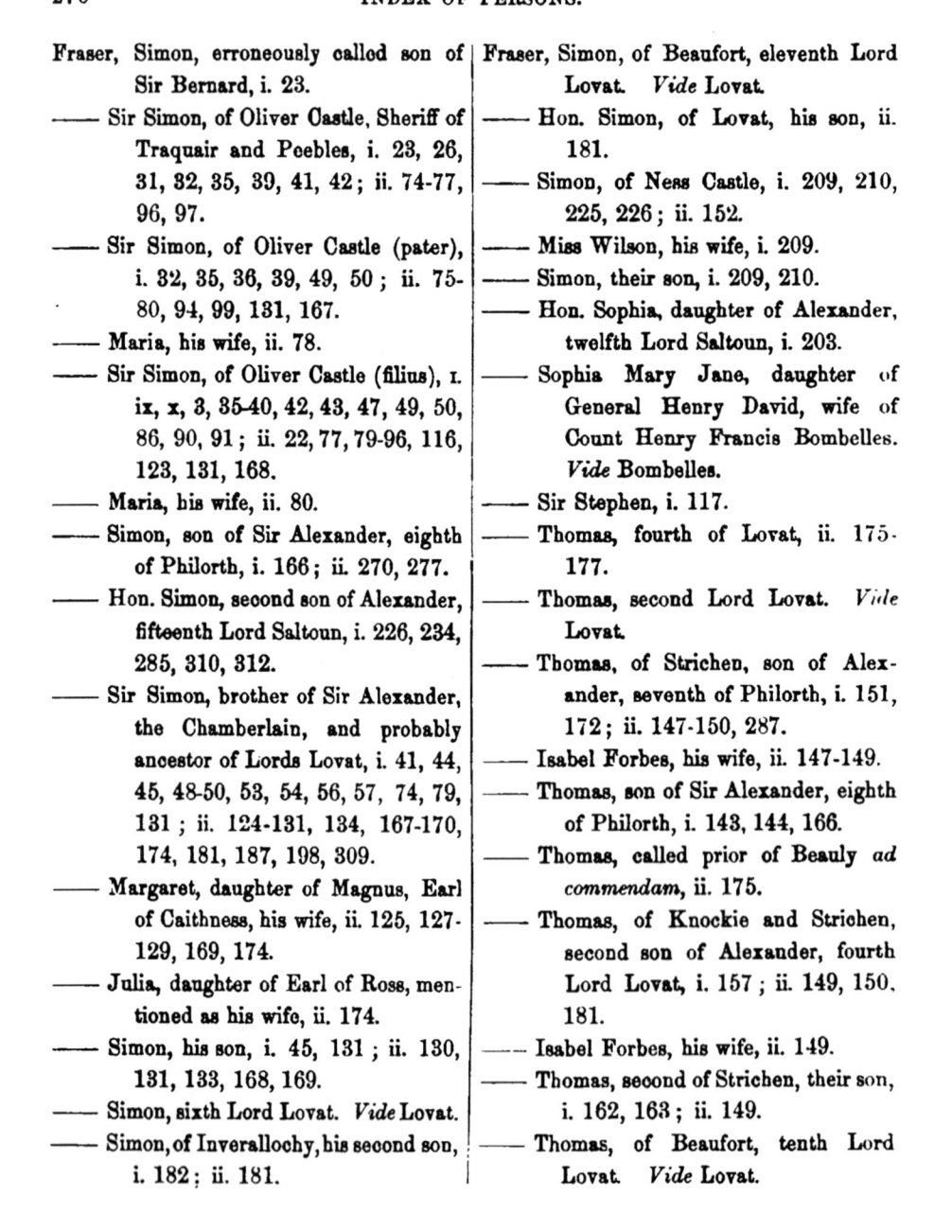

Fraser, Simon, erroneously called son of Sir Bernard, i. 23.
—— Sir Simon, of Oliver Castle, Sheriff of Traquair and Peebles, i. 23, 26, 31, 32, 35, 39, 41, 42; ii. 74-77, 96, 97.
—— Sir Simon, of Oliver Castle (pater), i. 32, 35, 36, 39, 49, 50; ii. 75-80, 94, 99, 131, 167.
—— Maria, his wife, ii. 78.
—— Sir Simon, of Oliver Castle (filius), i. ix, x, 3, 35-40, 42, 43, 47, 49, 50, 86, 90, 91; ii. 22, 77, 79-96, 116, 123, 131, 168.
—— Maria, his wife, ii. 80.
—— Simon, son of Sir Alexander, eighth of Philorth, i. 166; ii. 270, 277.
—— Hon. Simon, second son of Alexander, fifteenth Lord Saltoun, i. 226, 234, 285, 310, 312.
—— Sir Simon, brother of Sir Alexander, the Chamberlain, and probably ancestor of Lords Lovat, i. 41, 44, 45, 48-50, 53, 54, 56, 57, 74, 79, 131; ii. 124-131, 134, 167-170, 174, 181, 187, 198, 309.
—— Margaret, daughter of Magnus, Earl of Caithness, his wife, ii. 125, 127-129, 169, 174.
—— Julia, daughter of Earl of Ross, mentioned as his wife, ii. 174.
—— Simon, his son, i. 45, 131; ii. 130, 131, 133, 168, 169.
—— Simon, sixth Lord Lovat. *Vide* Lovat.
—— Simon, of Inverallochy, his second son, i. 182; ii. 181.
—— Fraser, Simon, of Beaufort, eleventh Lord Lovat. *Vide* Lovat.
—— Hon. Simon, of Lovat, his son, ii. 181.
—— Simon, of Ness Castle, i. 209, 210, 225, 226; ii. 152.
—— Miss Wilson, his wife, i. 209.
—— Simon, their son, i. 209, 210.
—— Hon. Sophia, daughter of Alexander, twelfth Lord Saltoun, i. 203.
—— Sophia Mary Jane, daughter of General Henry David, wife of Count Henry Francis Bombelles. *Vide* Bombelles.
—— Sir Stephen, i. 117.
—— Thomas, fourth of Lovat, ii. 175-177.
—— Thomas, second Lord Lovat. *Vide* Lovat.
—— Thomas, of Strichen, son of Alexander, seventh of Philorth, i. 151, 172; ii. 147-150, 287.
—— Isabel Forbes, his wife, ii. 147-149.
—— Thomas, son of Sir Alexander, eighth of Philorth, i. 143, 144, 166.
—— Thomas, called prior of Beauly *ad commendam*, ii. 175.
—— Thomas, of Knockie and Strichen, second son of Alexander, fourth Lord Lovat, i. 157; ii. 149, 150, 181.
—— Isabel Forbes, his wife, ii. 149.
—— Thomas, second of Strichen, their son, i. 162, 163; ii. 149.
—— Thomas, of Beaufort, tenth Lord Lovat. *Vide* Lovat.

INDEX OF PERSONS.

Fraser, Thomas Alexander, tenth of Strichen, and fourteenth Lord Lovat. *Vide* Lovat.
—— Thomas, of Cornetoun, i. 117 ; ii. 166, 291, 294.
—— Thomas, of Muchalls and Stonywood, his grandson, i. 132 ; ii. 166, 230, 231, 235.
—— Thomas, brother of Sir Simon (filius), ii. 79, 94.
—— Thomas, ii. 122.
—— Thomas, of Durris, ii. 144.
—— Thomas (Southton), i. 5.
—— Thomas, in East Lothian, i. 16, 29.
—— Udard (Odoard), in East Lothian, i. 14-16, 27, 28, 30.
—— Violet, daughter of Thomas of Strichen (Philorth line), wife of James Sutherland of Duffus. *Vide* Sutherland.
—— Walter, of Rathhilloch, brother of Sir Alexander, eighth of Philorth, i. 150, 164 ; ii. 151, 152.
—— Walter, i. 5.
—— William, of Aytoune, ii. 245.
—— Sir William, of Cowie and Durris, second son of the Chamberlain, i. 51, 76, 92, 93, 97-104, 106, 107, 110, 116, 120, 130 ; ii. 139, 169.
—— Margaret Moray, his wife, i. 92, 97, 100-102, 104, 107, 120, 122; ii. 169.
—— Sir William, of Cowie and Durris, second of Philorth, i. 103, 116, 119, 121-129, 150 ; ii. 140, 143, 201, 202, 218, 220, 222, 224-226, 289, 290, 311-316.

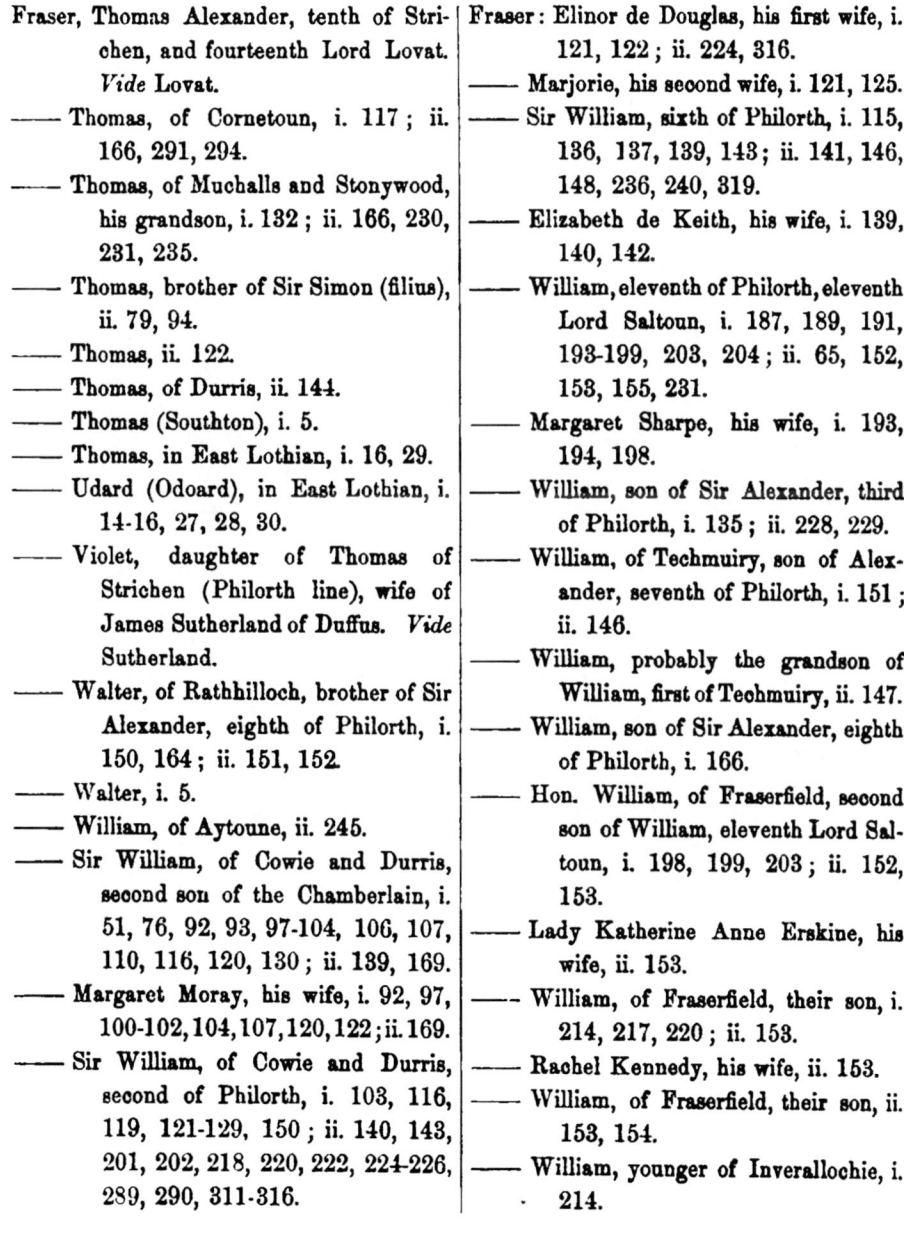

Fraser: Elinor de Douglas, his first wife, i. 121, 122 ; ii. 224, 316.
—— Marjorie, his second wife, i. 121, 125.
—— Sir William, sixth of Philorth, i. 115, 136, 137, 139, 143 ; ii. 141, 146, 148, 236, 240, 319.
—— Elizabeth de Keith, his wife, i. 139, 140, 142.
—— William, eleventh of Philorth, eleventh Lord Saltoun, i. 187, 189, 191, 193-199, 203, 204 ; ii. 65, 152, 153, 155, 231.
—— Margaret Sharpe, his wife, i. 193, 194, 198.
—— William, son of Sir Alexander, third of Philorth, i. 135 ; ii. 228, 229.
—— William, of Techmuiry, son of Alexander, seventh of Philorth, i. 151 ; ii. 146.
—— William, probably the grandson of William, first of Techmuiry, ii. 147.
—— William, son of Sir Alexander, eighth of Philorth, i. 166.
—— Hon. William, of Fraserfield, second son of William, eleventh Lord Saltoun, i. 198, 199, 203 ; ii. 152, 153.
—— Lady Katherine Anne Erskine, his wife, ii. 153.
—— William, of Fraserfield, their son, i. 214, 217, 220 ; ii. 153.
—— Rachel Kennedy, his wife, ii. 153.
—— William, of Fraserfield, their son, ii. 153, 154.
—— William, younger of Inverallochie, i. 214.

272   INDEX OF PERSONS.

Fraser, Sir William (Drumelzier branch), son of Sir Alexander Fraser, i. 90, 93-96; ii. 117-119.
—— William, of Durris, ii. 143.
—— Hon. William, second son of Alexander, twelfth Lord Saltoun, i. 203, 205.
—— Hon. William, third son of Alexander, fifteenth Lord Saltoun, i. 221, 226, 283, 310, 312, 313; iii. 7, 35, 37, 39-41, 43, 46, 68, 74, 78, 88, 138, 146, 149, 155, 159, 161, 174, 176, 186, 232.
—— Elizabeth Graham Macdowall Grant, his wife, i. 313.
—— William, of the Kirktoun, i. 140.
—— William, laird of Newforest (Forest), ii. 235.
—— William, lord of Fruid, ii. 118.
—— William, natural son of Sir John of Forglen, i. 130; ii. 140, 292.
—— William, de Saxham, i. 5.
—— William, erroneously called son of Sir Bernard, i. 23.
—— William, bishop of St. Andrews and Regent of Scotland, son of Sir Gilbert, i. 23, 26, 32, 35, 41-43, 90; ii. 75, 78, 80, 82, 91, 96-115, 195, 196, 308.
—— Sir William D., of Leadclune and Morar, Bart., iii. 47.
—— William, of Memsie, son of Michael of Techmuiry, ii. 146, 147.
—— William, last of Memsie, ii. 146.
—— William, of the county of Edinburgh, ii. 122.

Fraser, William John, son of General Henry David, ii. 154.
—— William, Colonel, of Woodhill, ii. 154.
—— Mary Elizabeth Shuttleworth, his wife, ii. 154.
—— William, son of Hon. James of Lonmay, ii. 155.
—— William, first of Park, ii. 155.
—— Catherine Gordon, his wife, ii. 155.
—— William James, third of Park, son of Sir John, and grandson of William of Park, ii. 156, 157.
—— Mary Ann Cumming, his wife, ii. 157.
—— William James, fifth of Park, son of George, ii. 157.
—— William, merchant, Fraserburgh, i. 171.
—— William, author of "The Book of Carlaverock," i. xii, 35; ii. 75.
Frasers of Aldourie, ii. 181.
—— family of Anjou, i. 6, 7.
—— of Ardendracht. Vide Frasers of Forglen.
—— of Auchnagairn, ii. 181.
—— of Balnain, ii. 281.
—— of Belladrum, ii. 181.
—— of Broadland, ii. 157.
—— of Cowie, Durris, and Philorth, 92-168.
—— of Culbockie, ii. 181.
—— of Culduthel, ii. 181.
—— of Drumelzier, i. 31, 32; ii. 116-119.
—— of Durris, i. 120, 192; ii. 141-145.
—— of Erchitt, ii. 181.
—— of Farraline, ii. 181.
—— of Findrack, ii. 144.
—— of Forest, ii. 145.

INDEX OF PERSONS.

Frasers of Forglen and Ardendracht, i. 103, 131; ii. 139-141; ii. 289-296, 323.
—— of Foyers, ii. 181.
—— of Fraserfield, ii. 152-155.
—— of Frendraught, i. 87; ii. 134-138.
—— of Fruid, i. 117; ii. 118.
—— of Gortuleg, ii. 181.
—— of Hospitalfield, ii. 157.
—— of Inverallochie, ii. 166, 181.
—— of Leadclune, ii. 181.
—— of Lonmay, ii. 155.
—— in Lothian, East, i. 12-32.
—— Lords Lovat (Lords Fraser of Lovat), i. vii, ix, 89-91, 163, 192; ii. 119, 167-182.
—— of Makarston, i. 38; ii. 120, 121.
—— of Memsie, ii. 146, 147.
—— of Moniack, ii. 181.
—— of Oliver Castle, i. 31, 32, 38, 39, 49, 86; ii. 74-97, 165, 168.
—— of Overtoun, ii. 123.
—— of Park, ii. 155-157.
—— of Phopachy, ii. 119.
—— of Quarrelbuss, ii. 151.
—— of Rathillock, ii. 151.
—— of Relig, ii. 181.
—— Lords Saltoun, i. 1, 169-313.
—— of Strichen, i. 163; ii. 145, 147-150, 181.
—— of Struy, ii. 181.
—— of Techmuiry, ii. 146, 147.
—— of Touchfraser, etc., and Cowie, i. 31-92.
—— of Tulifour, ii. 132, 133.
—— of Tyrie, i. 166; ii. 152.
Fraserburgh, feuars of, i. 154, 166, 311.
Frederick the Great, i. 241.

Frederick, Captain, R.N., iii. 90, 99.
Freese, officer, R. A., iii. 224.
Frendraught (Ferendrache), Sir Duncan de, ii. 135.
—— Viscount, i. 173.
—— Henry de, ii. 137.
—— Barons of, ii. 135.
—— Crichtons of, ii. 54.
—— Family of. *Vide* Fraser.
Frere, General, i. 242; iii. 17.
Freslay (Freslye), William de, ii. 122, 123.
—— Family of, i. 117; ii. 122, 123.
Fresle, Richard, i. 9.
Frezelière, Duke de la, i. 6, 7.
Friant, French General, Count, i. 267.
Froissart, the historian, i. 98, 117, 118; ii. 34, 128, 130.
Fruid, family of. *Vide* Fraser.
Fullarton, General Robert, of Dudwick, i. 218.
Futhas, John, of Rothebyrsbane, ii. 211.
—— Lanslot, i. 135.
Fyvie, Lord, i. 183.

Gagin, Stephen, i. 287.
Galloway (Gallwie), Alexander, rector of Kinkell, i. 147.
—— Lords of, ii. 29.
Gamery, John, canon of Caithness, ii. 208.
Garden (Gardyne), John, vicar of Kellymoir, ii. 217.
—— William, of Drumely, ii. 203.
Gardenstone, Francis Garden, Lord, i. 215, 218.
Garioch, Mr. William, i. 203.

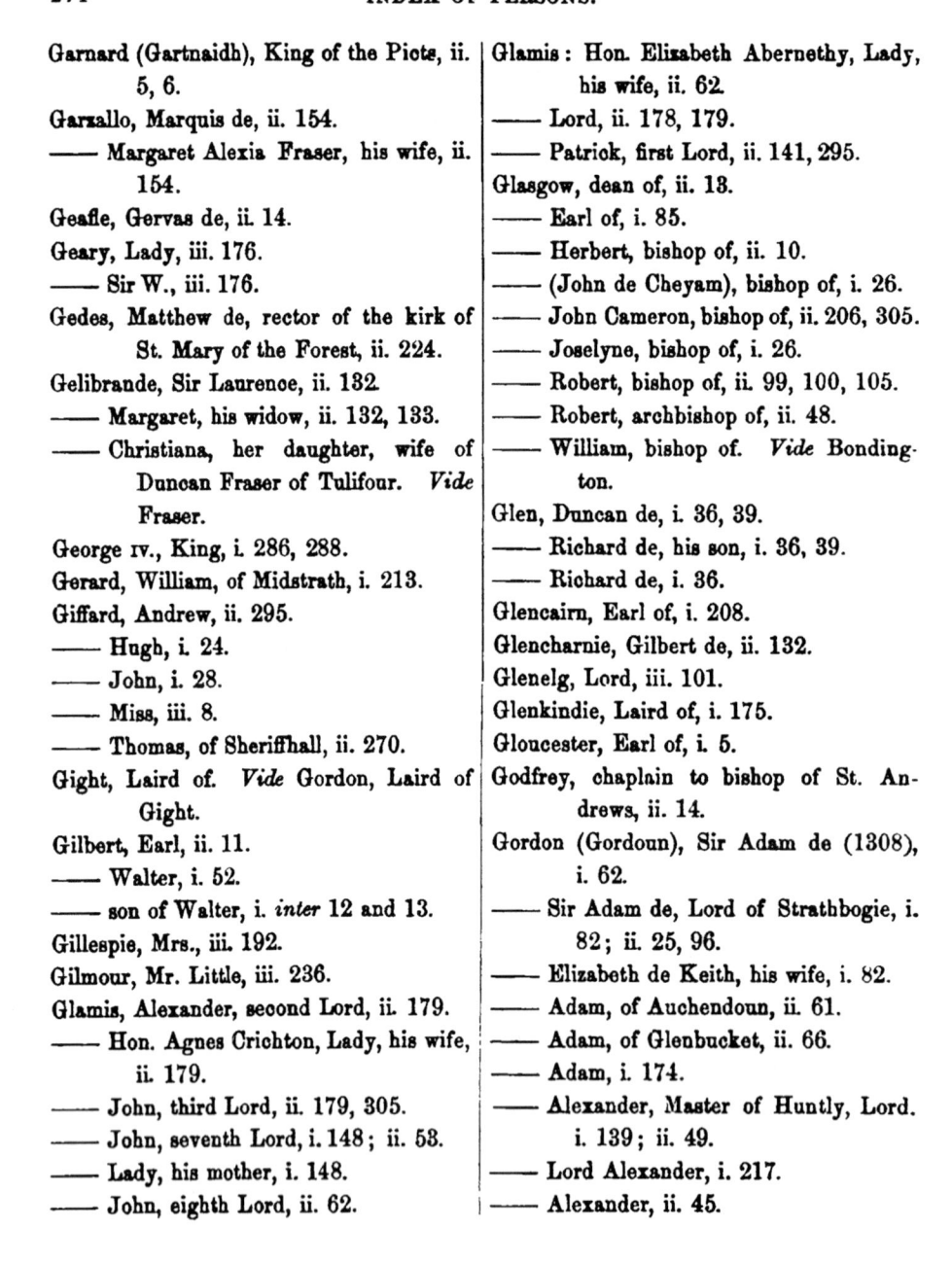

Garnard (Gartnaidh), King of the Picts, ii. 5, 6.
Garzallo, Marquis de, ii. 154.
—— Margaret Alexia Fraser, his wife, ii. 154.
Geafle, Gervas de, ii. 14.
Geary, Lady, iii. 176.
—— Sir W., iii. 176.
Gedes, Matthew de, rector of the kirk of St. Mary of the Forest, ii. 224.
Gelibrande, Sir Laurence, ii. 132.
—— Margaret, his widow, ii. 132, 133.
—— Christiana, her daughter, wife of Duncan Fraser of Tulifour. *Vide* Fraser.
George IV., King, i. 286, 288.
Gerard, William, of Midstrath, i. 213.
Giffard, Andrew, ii. 295.
—— Hugh, i. 24.
—— John, i. 28.
—— Miss, iii. 8.
—— Thomas, of Sheriffhall, ii. 270.
Gight, Laird of. *Vide* Gordon, Laird of Gight.
Gilbert, Earl, ii. 11.
—— Walter, i. 52.
—— son of Walter, i. *inter* 12 and 13.
Gillespie, Mrs., iii. 192.
Gilmour, Mr. Little, iii. 236.
Glamis, Alexander, second Lord, ii. 179.
—— Hon. Agnes Crichton, Lady, his wife, ii. 179.
—— John, third Lord, ii. 179, 305.
—— John, seventh Lord, i. 148; ii. 53.
—— Lady, his mother, i. 148.
—— John, eighth Lord, ii. 62.

Glamis: Hon. Elizabeth Abernethy, Lady, his wife, ii. 62.
—— Lord, ii. 178, 179.
—— Patrick, first Lord, ii. 141, 295.
Glasgow, dean of, ii. 13.
—— Earl of, i. 85.
—— Herbert, bishop of, ii. 10.
—— (John de Cheyam), bishop of, i. 26.
—— John Cameron, bishop of, ii. 206, 305.
—— Joselyne, bishop of, i. 26.
—— Robert, bishop of, ii. 99, 100, 105.
—— Robert, archbishop of, ii. 48.
—— William, bishop of. *Vide* Bondington.
Glen, Duncan de, i. 36, 39.
—— Richard de, his son, i. 36, 39.
—— Richard de, i. 36.
Glencairn, Earl of, i. 208.
Glencharnie, Gilbert de, ii. 132.
Glenelg, Lord, iii. 101.
Glenkindie, Laird of, i. 175.
Gloucester, Earl of, i. 5.
Godfrey, chaplain to bishop of St. Andrews, ii. 14.
Gordon (Gordoun), Sir Adam de (1308), i. 62.
—— Sir Adam de, Lord of Strathbogie, i. 82; ii. 25, 96.
—— Elizabeth de Keith, his wife, i. 82.
—— Adam, of Auchendoun, ii. 61.
—— Adam, of Glenbucket, ii. 66.
—— Adam, i. 174.
—— Alexander, Master of Huntly, Lord, i. 139; ii. 49.
—— Lord Alexander, i. 217.
—— Alexander, ii. 45.

INDEX OF PERSONS.

Gordon, General Benjamin, of Balbithan, i. 214.
—— Catherine, daughter of John of Kinnellar, wife of William Fraser of Park. *Vide* Fraser.
—— Colonel Charles, of Shilogreen, i. 215.
—— Charles, of Wardhouse, i. 214.
—— Charles, of Abergeldie, i. 214.
—— Eleanor, wife of George Fraser, fourteenth Lord Saltoun. *Vide* Fraser.
—— Elizabeth de, heiress of Sir Adam, wife of Sir Alexander de Seton. *Vide* Seton.
—— Sir Ernest, of Cobairdie, i. 214.
—— Sir George, of Haddo, ii. 287.
—— George, of Geicht, i. 144.
—— George, of Schivas, i. 147.
—— George, of Kindrocht and Denend, i. 157.
—— Colonel Harry, of Knockespack, i. 213.
—— Isabel, daughter of Sir Robert of Lochinvar, second wife of Alexander Fraser, ninth of Philorth. *Vide* Fraser.
—— James, of Techmuiry, ii. 147.
—— Jane Fraser, his wife, ii. 147.
—— James, son of Elizabeth, Lady Lochinvar, i. 164.
—— James, of Rothiemay, i. 186; ii. 163.
—— James, younger of Park, i. 198.
—— Hon. Helen Fraser, his wife, i. 198.
—— Sir James, of Lesmoir, i. 198.
—— Jean, Duchess of, i. 219.
—— Sir John, Lord of, i. 124.
—— John, his natural son, i. 124.
—— Sir John, of Lochinvar, i. 161.

Gordon: Dame Elizabeth Maxwell, his wife, i. 161.
—— John, first Viscount Kenmure. *Vide* Kenmure.
—— Sir John, of Park, i. 198; ii. 69, 70.
—— John, of Scourdargue, ii. 42.
—— John, his son, ii. 42.
—— Hon. Elizabeth Abernethy, his wife, ii. 42.
—— John, of Kinellar, i. 198, 205; ii. 155.
—— Hon. Henrietta Fraser, his wife, i. 198, 205; ii. 155.
—— John, of Craig, i. 213.
—— John, of Balmoir, i. 214.
—— John, of Lenturk, i. 214.
—— John Byron, of Gight, i. 215.
—— John, ii. 45.
—— John, i. 150.
—— J. W., of Cairness, i. 115.
—— Lady Mary, daughter of first Earl of Aberdeen, wife of Alexander Fraser, twelfth Lord Saltoun. *Vide* Fraser.
—— Laird of Gight, i. 172, 173; ii. 63, 64, 148, 149.
—— Hon. Jean de Abernethy, his wife, i. 172; ii. 63-65.
—— Peter, younger, of Abergeldie, i. 214.
—— Sir Robert, of Lochinvar, i. 167, 168.
—— Robert, of Hallhead, i. 214.
—— Hon. Robert, brother to the Earl of Huntly, ii. 59.
—— Robert, i. 150.
—— Thomas, of Litillgowill, ii. 277.
—— Thomas, of Premnay, i. 214.

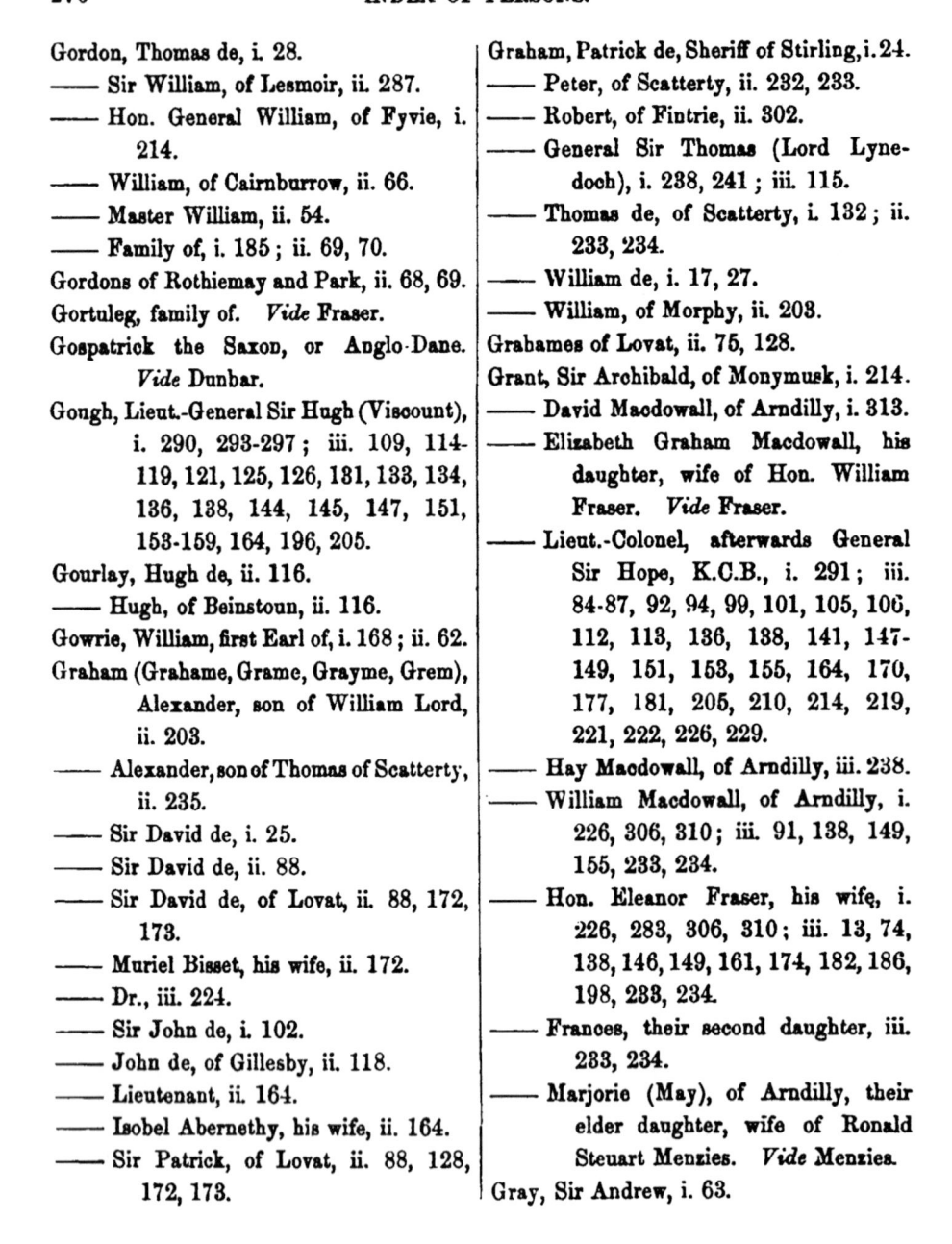

Gordon, Thomas de, i. 28.
—— Sir William, of Lesmoir, ii. 287.
—— Hon. General William, of Fyvie, i. 214.
—— William, of Cairnburrow, ii. 66.
—— Master William, ii. 54.
—— Family of, i. 185; ii. 69, 70.
Gordons of Rothiemay and Park, ii. 68, 69.
Gortuleg, family of. *Vide* Fraser.
Gospatrick the Saxon, or Anglo-Dane. *Vide* Dunbar.
Gough, Lieut.-General Sir Hugh (Viscount), i. 290, 293-297; iii. 109, 114-119, 121, 125, 126, 131, 133, 134, 136, 138, 144, 145, 147, 151, 153-159, 164, 196, 205.
Gourlay, Hugh de, ii. 116.
—— Hugh, of Beinstoun, ii. 116.
Gowrie, William, first Earl of, i. 168; ii. 62.
Graham (Grahame, Grame, Grayme, Grem), Alexander, son of William Lord, ii. 203.
—— Alexander, son of Thomas of Scatterty, ii. 235.
—— Sir David de, i. 25.
—— Sir David de, ii. 88.
—— Sir David de, of Lovat, ii. 88, 172, 173.
—— Muriel Bisset, his wife, ii. 172.
—— Dr., iii. 224.
—— Sir John de, i. 102.
—— John de, of Gillesby, ii. 118.
—— Lieutenant, ii. 164.
—— Isobel Abernethy, his wife, ii. 164.
—— Sir Patrick, of Lovat, ii. 88, 128, 172, 173.

Graham, Patrick de, Sheriff of Stirling, i. 24.
—— Peter, of Scatterty, ii. 232, 233.
—— Robert, of Fintrie, ii. 302.
—— General Sir Thomas (Lord Lynedoch), i. 238, 241; iii. 115.
—— Thomas de, of Scatterty, i. 132; ii. 233, 234.
—— William de, i. 17, 27.
—— William, of Morphy, ii. 203.
Grahames of Lovat, ii. 75, 128.
Grant, Sir Archibald, of Monymusk, i. 214.
—— David Macdowall, of Arndilly, i. 313.
—— Elizabeth Graham Macdowall, his daughter, wife of Hon. William Fraser. *Vide* Fraser.
—— Lieut.-Colonel, afterwards General Sir Hope, K.C.B., i. 291; iii. 84-87, 92, 94, 99, 101, 105, 106, 112, 113, 136, 138, 141, 147-149, 151, 153, 155, 164, 170, 177, 181, 205, 210, 214, 219, 221, 222, 226, 229.
—— Hay Macdowall, of Arndilly, iii. 238.
—— William Macdowall, of Arndilly, i. 226, 306, 310; iii. 91, 138, 149, 155, 233, 234.
—— Hon. Eleanor Fraser, his wife, i. 226, 283, 306, 310; iii. 13, 74, 138, 146, 149, 161, 174, 182, 186, 198, 233, 234.
—— Frances, their second daughter, iii. 233, 234.
—— Marjorie (May), of Arndilly, their elder daughter, wife of Ronald Steuart Menzies. *Vide* Menzies.
Gray, Sir Andrew, i. 63.

INDEX OF PERSONS.

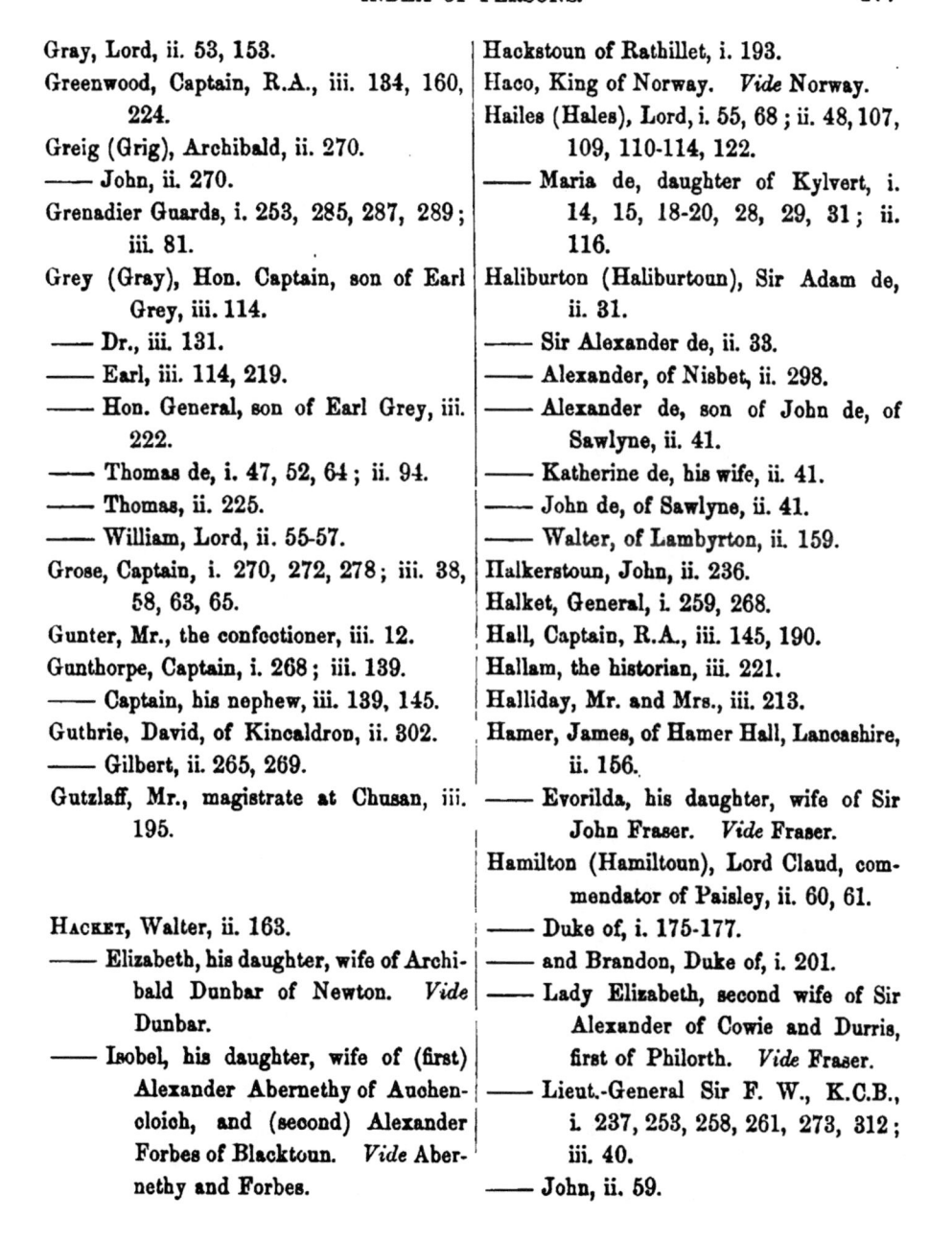

Gray, Lord, ii. 53, 153.
Greenwood, Captain, R.A., iii. 134, 160, 224.
Greig (Grig), Archibald, ii. 270.
—— John, ii. 270.
Grenadier Guards, i. 253, 285, 287, 289; iii. 81.
Grey (Gray), Hon. Captain, son of Earl Grey, iii. 114.
—— Dr., iii. 131.
—— Earl, iii. 114, 219.
—— Hon. General, son of Earl Grey, iii. 222.
—— Thomas de, i. 47, 52, 64; ii. 94.
—— Thomas, ii. 225.
—— William, Lord, ii. 55-57.
Grose, Captain, i. 270, 272, 278; iii. 38, 58, 63, 65.
Gunter, Mr., the confectioner, iii. 12.
Gunthorpe, Captain, i. 268; iii. 139.
—— Captain, his nephew, iii. 139, 145.
Guthrie, David, of Kincaldron, ii. 302.
—— Gilbert, ii. 265, 269.
Gutzlaff, Mr., magistrate at Chusan, iii. 195.

HACKET, Walter, ii. 163.
—— Elizabeth, his daughter, wife of Archibald Dunbar of Newton. *Vide* Dunbar.
—— Isobel, his daughter, wife of (first) Alexander Abernethy of Auchencloich, and (second) Alexander Forbes of Blacktoun. *Vide* Abernethy and Forbes.
Hackstoun of Rathillet, i. 193.
Haco, King of Norway. *Vide* Norway.
Hailes (Hales), Lord, i. 55, 68; ii. 48, 107, 109, 110-114, 122.
—— Maria de, daughter of Kylvert, i. 14, 15, 18-20, 28, 29, 31; ii. 116.
Haliburton (Haliburtoun), Sir Adam de, ii. 31.
—— Sir Alexander de, ii. 33.
—— Alexander, of Nisbet, ii. 298.
—— Alexander de, son of John de, of Sawlyne, ii. 41.
—— Katherine de, his wife, ii. 41.
—— John de, of Sawlyne, ii. 41.
—— Walter, of Lambyrton, ii. 159.
Halkerstoun, John, ii. 236.
Halket, General, i. 259, 268.
Hall, Captain, R.A., iii. 145, 190.
Hallam, the historian, iii. 221.
Halliday, Mr. and Mrs., iii. 213.
Hamer, James, of Hamer Hall, Lancashire, ii. 156.
—— Evorilda, his daughter, wife of Sir John Fraser. *Vide* Fraser.
Hamilton (Hamiltoun), Lord Claud, commendator of Paisley, ii. 60, 61.
—— Duke of, i. 175-177.
—— and Brandon, Duke of, i. 201.
—— Lady Elizabeth, second wife of Sir Alexander of Cowie and Durris, first of Philorth. *Vide* Fraser.
—— Lieut.-General Sir F. W., K.C.B., i. 237, 253, 258, 261, 273, 312; iii. 40.
—— John, ii. 59.

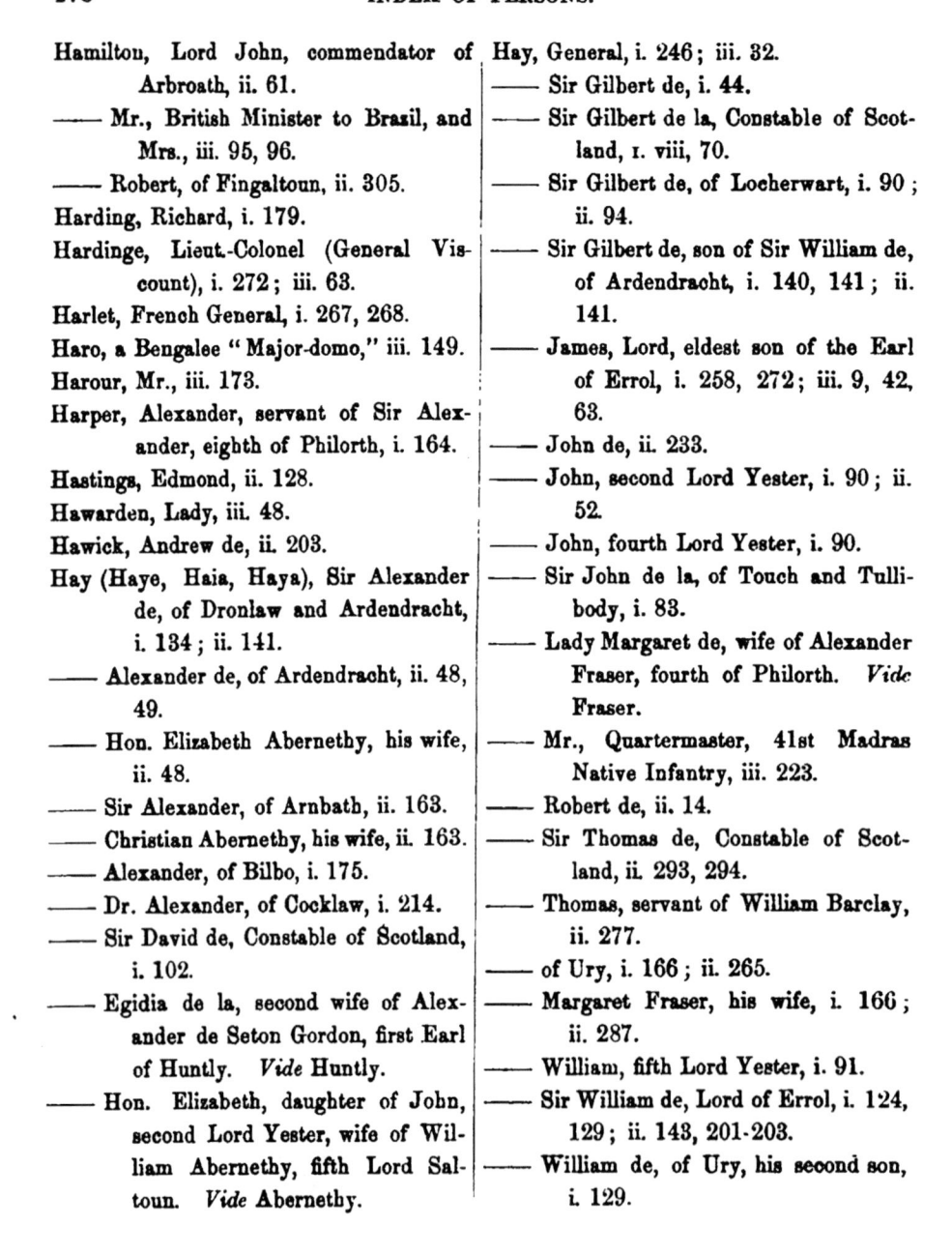

Hamilton, Lord John, commendator of Arbroath, ii. 61.
―― Mr., British Minister to Brazil, and Mrs., iii. 95, 96.
―― Robert, of Fingaltoun, ii. 305.
Harding, Richard, i. 179.
Hardinge, Lieut.-Colonel (General Viscount), i. 272; iii. 63.
Harlet, French General, i. 267, 268.
Haro, a Bengalee "Major-domo," iii. 149.
Harour, Mr., iii. 173.
Harper, Alexander, servant of Sir Alexander, eighth of Philorth, i. 164.
Hastings, Edmond, ii. 128.
Hawarden, Lady, iii. 48.
Hawick, Andrew de, ii. 203.
Hay (Haye, Haia, Haya), Sir Alexander de, of Dronlaw and Ardendracht, i. 134; ii. 141.
―― Alexander de, of Ardendracht, ii. 48, 49.
―― Hon. Elizabeth Abernethy, his wife, ii. 48.
―― Sir Alexander, of Arnbath, ii. 163.
―― Christian Abernethy, his wife, ii. 163.
―― Alexander, of Bilbo, i. 175.
―― Dr. Alexander, of Cocklaw, i. 214.
―― Sir David de, Constable of Scotland, i. 102.
―― Egidia de la, second wife of Alexander de Seton Gordon, first Earl of Huntly. *Vide* Huntly.
―― Hon. Elizabeth, daughter of John, second Lord Yester, wife of William Abernethy, fifth Lord Saltoun. *Vide* Abernethy.
Hay, General, i. 246; iii. 32.
―― Sir Gilbert de, i. 44.
―― Sir Gilbert de la, Constable of Scotland, i. viii, 70.
―― Sir Gilbert de, of Locherwart, i. 90; ii. 94.
―― Sir Gilbert de, son of Sir William de, of Ardendracht, i. 140, 141; ii. 141.
―― James, Lord, eldest son of the Earl of Errol, i. 258, 272; iii. 9, 42, 63.
―― John de, ii. 233.
―― John, second Lord Yester, i. 90; ii. 52.
―― John, fourth Lord Yester, i. 90.
―― Sir John de la, of Touch and Tullibody, i. 83.
―― Lady Margaret de, wife of Alexander Fraser, fourth of Philorth. *Vide* Fraser.
―― Mr., Quartermaster, 41st Madras Native Infantry, iii. 223.
―― Robert de, ii. 14.
―― Sir Thomas de, Constable of Scotland, ii. 293, 294.
―― Thomas, servant of William Barclay, ii. 277.
―― of Ury, i. 166; ii. 265.
―― Margaret Fraser, his wife, i. 166; ii. 287.
―― William, fifth Lord Yester, i. 91.
―― Sir William de, Lord of Errol, i. 124, 129; ii. 143, 201-203.
―― William de, of Ury, his second son, i. 129.

INDEX OF PERSONS.

Hay, William de, of Ardendracht, son of Sir Alexander de, of Dronlaw, i. 134, 140.
—— William, of Ury and Crimond (1560), i. 150 ; ii. 147.
—— Sir William de, Laird of Louchqworwart, ii. 224.
—— W. de, ii. 11.
—— Family of, i. x, 141 ; ii. 124.
Hays of Ardendracht, i. 128.
—— of Dronlaw, ii. 141.
—— of Locherwart, ii. 94.
—— of Tallo, i. 91.
Hayling (Heyling), Chinese Commissioner, i. 301 ; iii. 202.
Haythorne, Sir Edmund, Lieut.-General, K.C.B., iii. 147, 160, 172, 198.
Henderson, Patrick, ii. 270.
Henry I., King, i. 10.
—— II., King, i. 2, 3, 7, 8.
—— III., King, i. 4, 5, 22, 23 ; ii. 17, 18.
—— IV., King, i. 279 ; ii. 35 ; iii. 67.
—— Prince of Scotland, i. 8, 159.
Hepburn, A., i. 176.
—— Adam, ii. 116.
—— Adam, of the Craigs, ii. 47, 48.
—— Elizabeth Ogstoune, his wife, ii. 47, 48.
—— Colonel, i. 264 ; iii. 53.
—— David, of Wauchtoun, ii. 305.
—— Sir Patrick de, ii. 219.
Herbert, Captain Sir Thomas, R.N., iii. 110, 145, 186.
Herries (Heris), Agnes Lady, wife of Sir John Maxwell, Lord. *Vide* Maxwell.
—— N. de, i. 25.

Herwy, Henry, ii. 197.
Hill, General Sir Rowland (Viscount), i. 238-240, 243-245, 248, 277, 290 ; iii. 18, 24, 42, 64, 67, 103, 162.
Hoga, Adam de, ii. 95.
—— Henry de, his father, ii. 95.
Holinshed, the historian, i. 8.
Holland, King of, iii. 52, 53.
Holyrood, Elyas, abbot of, i. 22.
Home, Sir Everard, iii. 141.
—— George, Depute Clerk-Register, i. 208.
—— John, of Carrelsyid, ii. 253, 254.
—— Patrick, of Fastcastle, ii. 48.
—— William de, son of Patrick, brother of Waldeve, Earl of Dunbar, i. 15.
—— Ada de, daughter of Patrick, Earl of Dunbar, his wife, i. 15.
Hope, Captain, R.N., iii. 142.
—— Sir John, General, i. 236, 246 ; iii. 32.
Hoppringill, Thomas de, ii. 33.
Hospitalfield, family of. *Vide* Fraser.
Houston, Mr., iii. 5.
Hoveden, ancient chronicler, i. 3.
Howard, General, iii. 15.
—— Lady Charlotte, his wife, iii. 15.
Howqua, a Chinese merchant, iii. 199.
Hughes, James, groom to the sixteenth Lord Saltoun, i. 273, 276, 280, 281, 283 ; iii. 26, 35, 36-38, 43, 45, 46, 48, 55, 60, 66, 68, 69, 71.
Hume, Dr., iii. 145.
Hunter, John, i. 25.
—— Joseph, the antiquary, i. 8.
Huntercombe, Sir Walter de, i. 36 ; ii. 81, 83.

280   INDEX OF PERSONS.

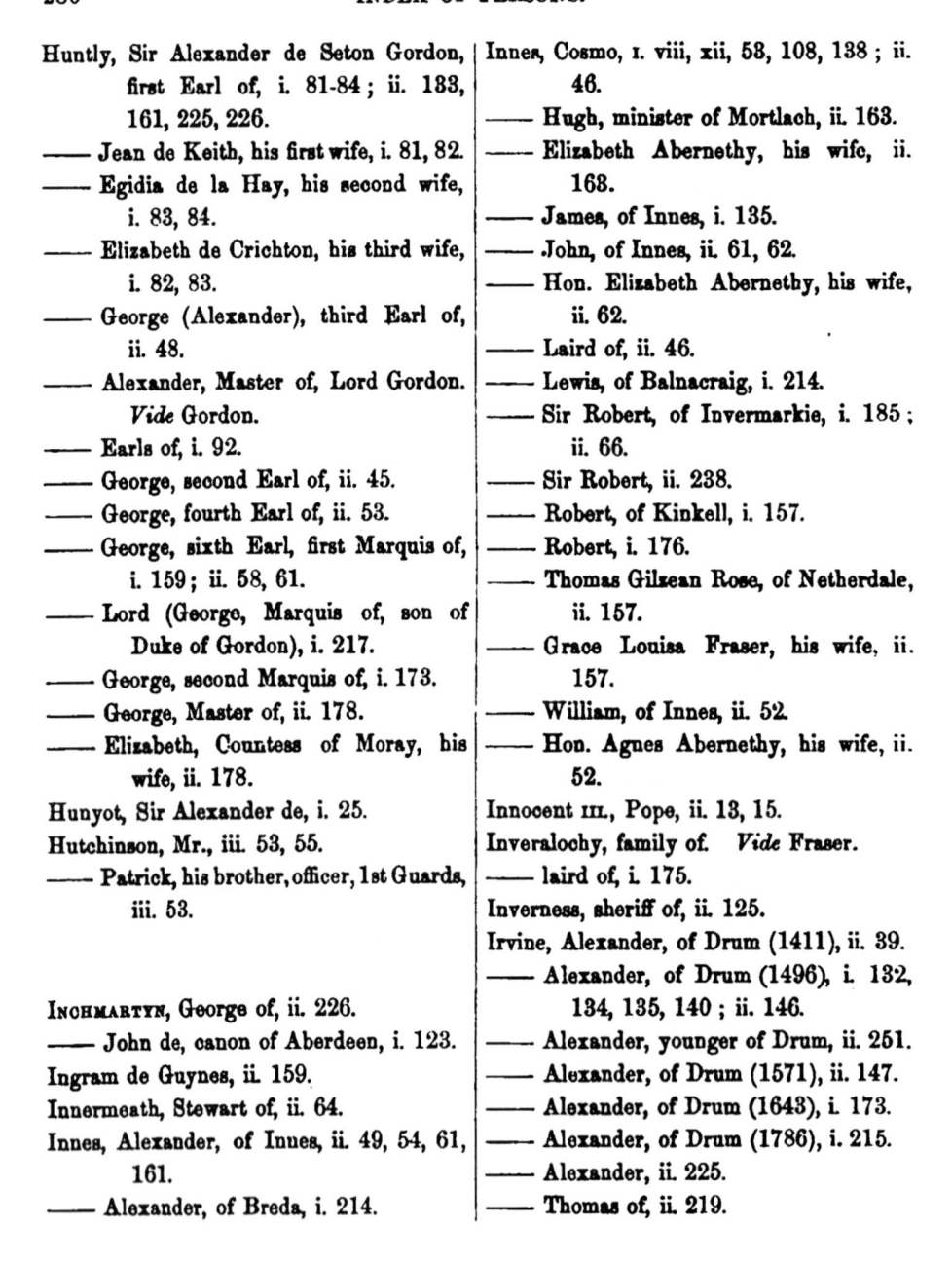

Huntly, Sir Alexander de Seton Gordon, first Earl of, i. 81-84; ii. 183, 161, 225, 226.
—— Jean de Keith, his first wife, i. 81, 82.
—— Egidia de la Hay, his second wife, i. 83, 84.
—— Elizabeth de Crichton, his third wife, i. 82, 83.
—— George (Alexander), third Earl of, ii. 48.
—— Alexander, Master of, Lord Gordon. *Vide* Gordon.
—— Earls of, i. 92.
—— George, second Earl of, ii. 45.
—— George, fourth Earl of, ii. 53.
—— George, sixth Earl, first Marquis of, i. 159; ii. 58, 61.
—— Lord (George, Marquis of, son of Duke of Gordon), i. 217.
—— George, second Marquis of, i. 173.
—— George, Master of, ii. 178.
—— Elizabeth, Countess of Moray, his wife, ii. 178.
Hunyot, Sir Alexander de, i. 25.
Hutchinson, Mr., iii. 53, 55.
—— Patrick, his brother, officer, 1st Guards, iii. 53.

INCHMARTYN, George of, ii. 226.
—— John de, canon of Aberdeen, i. 123.
Ingram de Guynes, ii. 159.
Innermeath, Stewart of, ii. 64.
Innes, Alexander, of Innes, ii. 49, 54, 61, 161.
—— Alexander, of Breda, i. 214.

Innes, Cosmo, i. viii, xii, 58, 108, 138; ii. 46.
—— Hugh, minister of Mortlach, ii. 163.
—— Elizabeth Abernethy, his wife, ii. 163.
—— James, of Innes, i. 135.
—— John, of Innes, ii. 61, 62.
—— Hon. Elizabeth Abernethy, his wife, ii. 62.
—— Laird of, ii. 46.
—— Lewis, of Balnacraig, i. 214.
—— Sir Robert, of Invermarkie, i. 185; ii. 66.
—— Sir Robert, ii. 238.
—— Robert, of Kinkell, i. 157.
—— Robert, i. 176.
—— Thomas Gilzean Rose, of Netherdale, ii. 157.
—— Grace Louisa Fraser, his wife, ii. 157.
—— William, of Innes, ii. 52.
—— Hon. Agnes Abernethy, his wife, ii. 52.
Innocent III., Pope, ii. 13, 15.
Inveralochy, family of. *Vide* Fraser.
—— laird of, i. 175.
Inverness, sheriff of, ii. 125.
Irvine, Alexander, of Drum (1411), ii. 39.
—— Alexander, of Drum (1496), i. 132, 134, 135, 140; ii. 146.
—— Alexander, younger of Drum, ii. 251.
—— Alexander, of Drum (1571), ii. 147.
—— Alexander, of Drum (1643), i. 173.
—— Alexander, of Drum (1786), i. 215.
—— Alexander, ii. 225.
—— Thomas of, ii. 219.

Isles, Donald, Lord of the, i. 123, 124, 132 ; ii. 36-38, 167.
—— Margaret de Leslie, Countess of Ross, his wife, i. 123, 125, 132, 133 ; ii. 36.
—— Alexander, Earl of Ross, Lord of the, i. 125, 133 ; ii. 171, 177.
—— John, Earl of Ross, Lord of the, i. 125, 132-134, 140, 141, 206 ; ii. 47.
—— Lord of the, i. 133, 134, 139, 141, 166 ; ii. 35-37.
—— Ranald, Lord of the, i. 101, 111.

JAMES I., King, i. 126, 127, 129 ; ii. 38-40, 142, 176, 204, 218.
—— II., King, i. 82, 128, 129 ; ii. 40, 44, 178, 226.
—— III., King, i. 132, 134, 136, 139, 141 ; ii. 42, 43, 46, 50, 51, 178, 297-303.
—— IV., King, i. 141, 147 ; ii. 46, 49, 123, 236.
—— V., King, i. 148, 149 ; ii. 49, 148, 240, 243.
—— VI., King, i. 151, 153, 154, 158, 159-161, 171, 222 ; ii. 40, 58, 60, 62, 64, 65, 149, 150, 254, 262, 265, 278, 283, 284, 287.
—— Anne of Denmark, his queen, i. 158.
—— the novelist, iii. 186.
Janitor (porter), Robert, of Kincardine, i. 74 ; ii. 126, 128, 196, 197.
Jardine and Matheson, iii. 150, 157, 168, 218.

Jeffray (Jaffray), John, at Craigellie, ii. 155.
Jejeebhoy, Sir Jamsetjee, iii. 226.
Jerome (Bonaparte), Prince, i. 261.
Jeshair, a black servant, iii. 183.
John, King of England, ii. 109.
—— Pope, XXII., i. viii, 70, 87 ; ii. 80, 134.
—— chaplain, i. *inter* 12 and 13.
Johnstone, Mr., iii. 122.
—— Elizabeth, wife of Alexander Chalmers. *Vide* Chalmers.
—— William, in Doveransyd, i. 146.
Joliffe, Mr., iii. 19.
Jopp, James, of Cotton, i. 215.
Justice, Captain, iii. 142.

KARNYS, William, vicar of Glammis, ii. 212, 213.
Kearney, Captain (Commodore), iii. 150, 170.
Keith, Lady Alison de, daughter of fourth Earl Marischal, wife of Alexander Abernethy, sixth Lord Saltoun. *Vide* Abernethy.
—— Lady Beatrice de, daughter of Robert, Master of Marischal, wife of Alexander Fraser, eldest son of Alexander Fraser, seventh of Philorth. *Vide* Fraser.
—— Christian or Christiana de, third daughter of William the Marischal, and Margaret Fraser, wife of Sir William de Lindesay of the Byres. *Vide* Lindesay.

INDEX OF PERSONS.

Keith, Sir Edward de. *Vide* Marischal.
—— Elizabeth de, daughter of Sir William the Marischal and Margaret Fraser, and wife of Sir Adam de Gordon. *Vide* Gordon.
—— Elizabeth de, daughter of Sir Gilbert Keith of Inverugie, wife of Sir William Fraser, sixth of Philorth. *Vide* Fraser.
—— family of de, i. 13.
—— Colonel George, of Aden, ii. 287.
—— Sir Gilbert de, of Inverugie, i. 137, 139, 140.
—— Janet de, daughter of Sir William the Marischal and Margaret Fraser, and first wife of Philip de Arbuthnot. *Vide* Arbuthnot.
—— Jean de, daughter and heiress of Sir Robert de Keith, first wife of Alexander de Seton Gordon, first Earl of Huntly. *Vide* Huntly.
—— John de. *Vide* Marischal.
—— John of, Lord of Inverugy, ii. 293, 294.
—— John de, eldest son of Sir William the Marischal and Margaret Fraser, i. 81.
—— —— daughter of King Robert II., and wife of John de, i. 81.
—— John, of Balmuir, i. 146.
—— Murielle de, daughter of Sir William the Marischal and Margaret Fraser, second wife of Robert Stewart, Duke of Albany. *Vide* Albany.
—— Sir R., of Athergill, i. 166.
—— Elizabeth Fraser, his wife, i. 166.

Keith, Robert, commendator of Deir, ii. 162.
—— Sir Robert de. *Vide* Marischal.
—— Sir Robert de, son of John de Keith, and grandson of Sir William the Marischal and Margaret Fraser, i. 81, 84.
—— William de, son of Robert de Keith, the Marischal, ii. 145.
—— Sir William de. *Vide* Marischal.
Kellett, Captain, iii. 213.
Kellie, second Earl of, i. 187.
—— third Earl of, i. 187.
—— Earl of, i. 208, 224.
Kelso, monks of, i. 12, 23; ii. 96.
Kemble, Miss A., iii. 164, 165.
Kench, John de, ii. 32, 33.
Kenmure, John, first Viscount, i. 168.
Kennedy, Captain Clarke, iii. 128.
—— Gilbert, Lord, ii. 300, 302.
—— author of "Annals of Aberdeen," i. 78.
—— Rev. Hugh, ii. 153.
—— John, ii. 253, 254.
—— Rachel, daughter of the Rev. Hugh, wife of William Fraser of Fraserfield. *Vide* Fraser.
Kent, private, 1st Guards, i. 269.
Keppel, Captain Hon. Henry, now Admiral of the Fleet, Hon. Sir Henry, G.C.B., i. 303; iii. 229.
—— Hon. Mrs. William, daughter of seventeenth Lord Saltoun, iii. 234.
Kerr, Lady Ann, daughter of William Earl of Lothian, and first wife of Alexander, Master of Saltoun, son of Alexander, tenth Lord Saltoun. *Vide* Fraser.

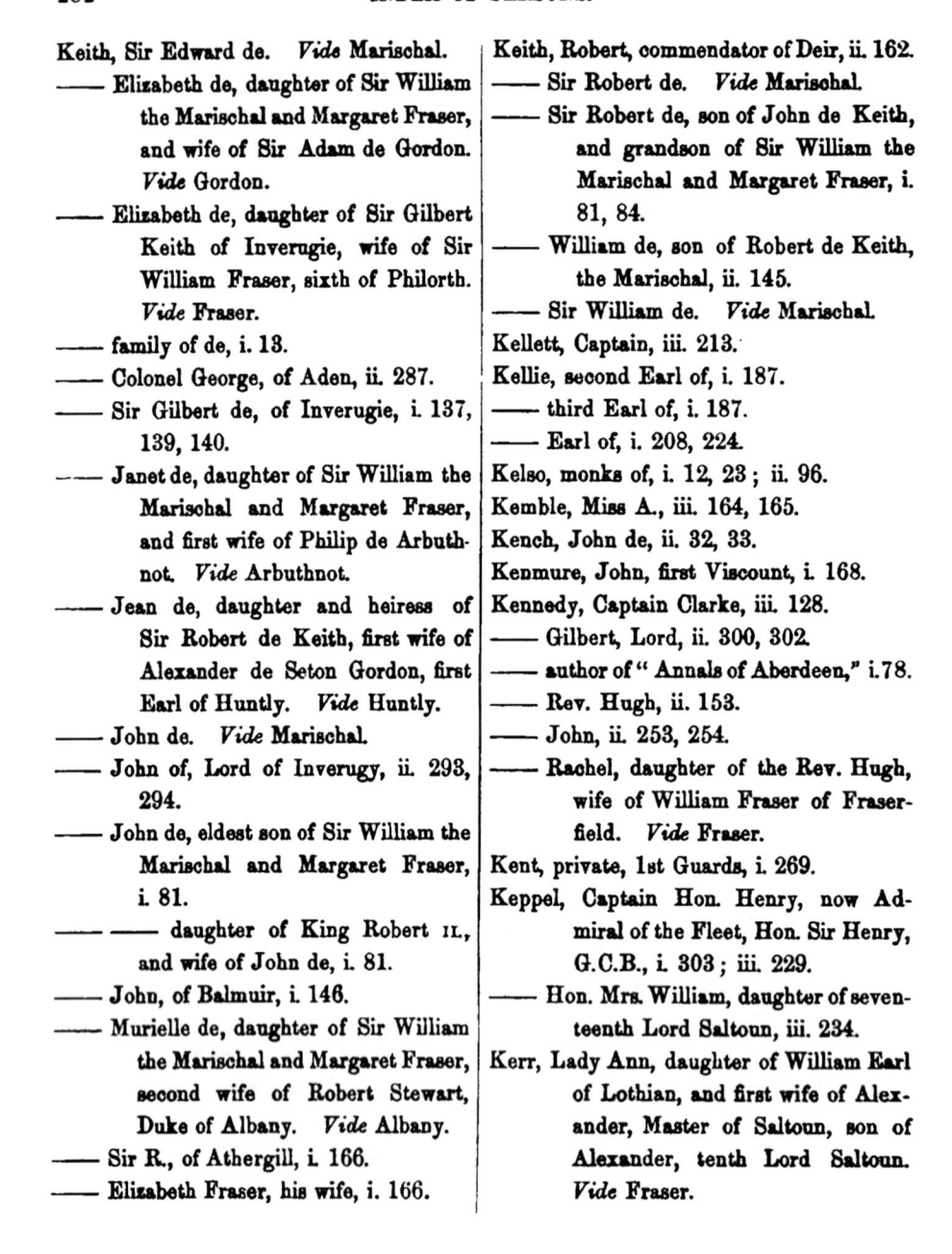

Kerr, George, of Samuelston, ii. 298.
—— Mr., iii. 197, 198.
—— Mrs., iii. 198.
—— Sir William, of Hadden, ii. 288.
Key Ing, Chinese Chief Commissioner, i. 301; iii. 184, 188, 194, 195, 201, 202.
Kilgour, William, ii. 276.
Killigrew, Mr. H., ii. 61.
Kincardine in the Mearns, Robert, Janitor of, ii. 196, 197.
Kingcombe, Captain, of H.M.S. "Belle-Isle," i. 291; iii. 84, 92, 150.
—— Frederick, his son, iii. 92, 150.
Kingedward (Kinedwart), John, Baron of. *Vide* Isles, John, Lord of the.
Kinghorn, William de, ii. 109.
Kingston, Duke of, i. 208.
—— John de, Constable of Edinburgh Castle, ii. 82-84.
Kinnaird (Kinnarde), Lord, i. 208.
—— Lady, i. 282; iii. 71.
—— Thomas de, i. 72.
Kinninmond (Kininmunth), Alexander, bishop of Aberdeen, i. 109.
—— Alexander (second), bishop of Aberdeen, i. 109.
—— Elye de, i. 42, 44.
Kirkcaldy, Laird of Grange, ii. 60.
Kirkland, John of, ii. 95.
—— William, grandson of John of, ii. 95.
Knight, an artist, iii. 145.
—— Colonel Henry, of Pittodrie, i. 214.
Knowles, Lieut.-Colonel, iii. 224.
Kylvert (Culvut, Kylward), i. 13-16, 18, 19, 20, 26, 27, 29-31; ii. 116.

Kymbdy, Duncan, ii. 196, 197.
—— John, ii. 197, 198.
Kynbuk, Joachim de, i. 99.

LACY, Spanish General, i. 238.
Ladizabel, Spanish General, i. 238.
Laing, Henry, author of "Ancient Scottish Seals," i. 90, 138; ii. 16, 137, 144.
Lambert, General, i. 180.
Lamberton (Lambyrton), John de, sheriff of Stirling, i. 24, 96; ii. 117.
—— William de, bishop of St. Andrews, ii. 82, 110, 114.
Lanark, Earl of, i. 176.
—— English sheriff of, ii. 93.
Lancaster, barons of, ii. 103.
Landels, John de, Chamberlain of Scotland for Edward I., i. 40; ii. 74.
Lang, William, rector of the church of Turriff, ii. 221, 223, 224.
Langtoft, Pierre de, metrical chronicler, i. 27; ii. 87, 90.
Langton, Walter de, bishop of Chester, ii. 82.
Lansdowne, Lady, iii. 8, 9.
Lask, Thomas of, ii. 293, 294.
La Peña, Spanish General, i. 238.
Lascelles, Ensign, i. 272; iii. 63.
Latham, Dr., i. 225.
Latimer, Sir William de, ii. 84, 88.
Latour, Ensign, i. 244; iii. 23.
Lauder (Laweder, Lowedir), Alexander, provost of Edinburgh, ii. 286.
—— George of, ii. 224.

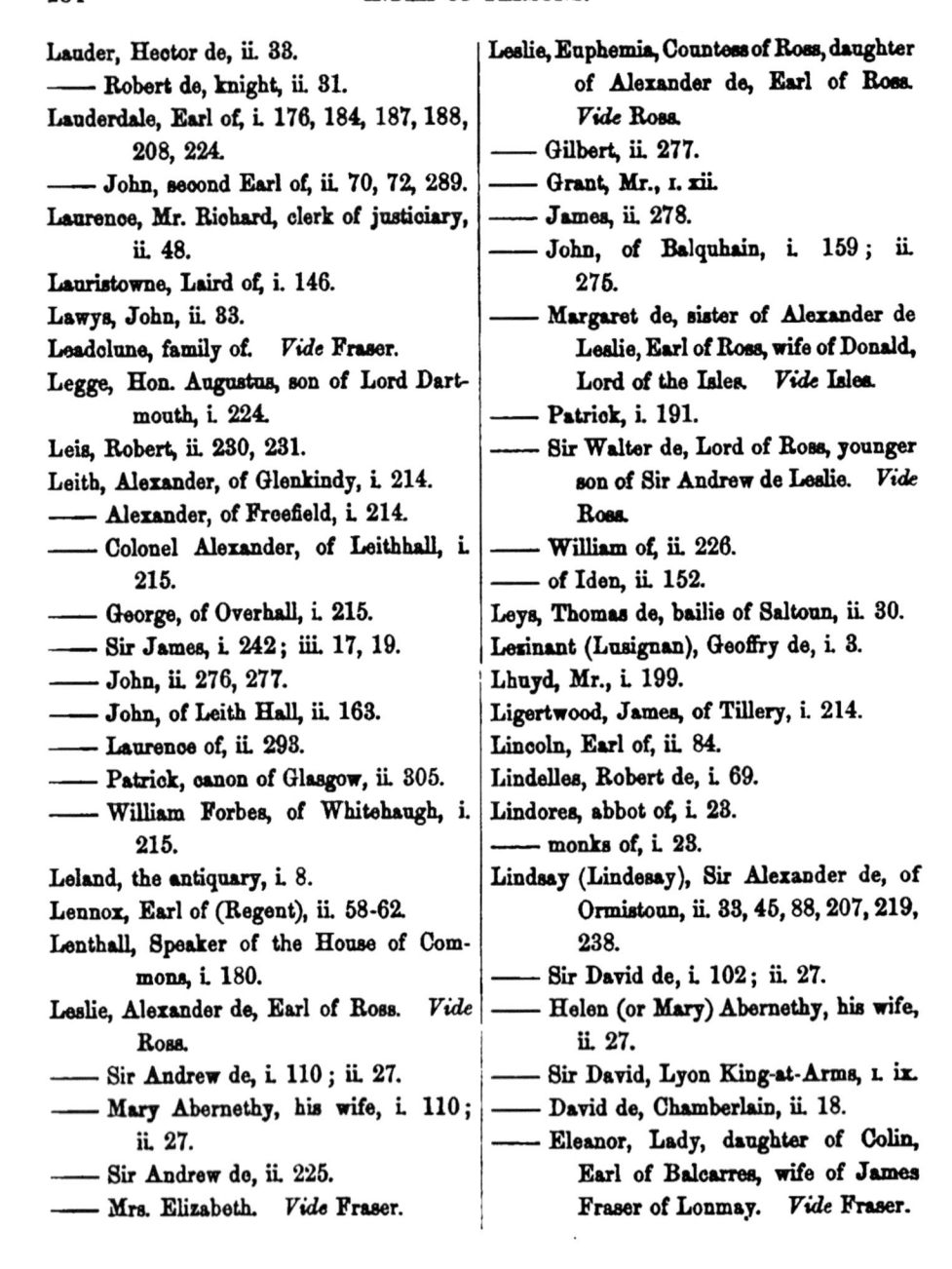

Lauder, Hector de, ii. 33.
—— Robert de, knight, ii. 31.
Lauderdale, Earl of, i. 176, 184, 187, 188, 208, 224.
—— John, second Earl of, ii. 70, 72, 289.
Laurence, Mr. Richard, clerk of justiciary, ii. 48.
Lauristowne, Laird of, i. 146.
Lawys, John, ii. 33.
Leadclune, family of. *Vide* Fraser.
Legge, Hon. Augustus, son of Lord Dartmouth, i. 224.
Leis, Robert, ii. 230, 231.
Leith, Alexander, of Glenkindy, i. 214.
—— Alexander, of Freefield, i. 214.
—— Colonel Alexander, of Leithhall, i. 215.
—— George, of Overhall, i. 215.
—— Sir James, i. 242; iii. 17, 19.
—— John, ii. 276, 277.
—— John, of Leith Hall, ii. 163.
—— Laurence of, ii. 293.
—— Patrick, canon of Glasgow, ii. 305.
—— William Forbes, of Whitehaugh, i. 215.
Leland, the antiquary, i. 8.
Lennox, Earl of (Regent), ii. 58-62.
Lenthall, Speaker of the House of Commons, i. 180.
Leslie, Alexander de, Earl of Ross. *Vide* Ross.
—— Sir Andrew de, i. 110; ii. 27.
—— Mary Abernethy, his wife, i. 110; ii. 27.
—— Sir Andrew de, ii. 225.
—— Mrs. Elizabeth. *Vide* Fraser.
Leslie, Euphemia, Countess of Ross, daughter of Alexander de, Earl of Ross. *Vide* Ross.
—— Gilbert, ii. 277.
—— Grant, Mr., i. xii.
—— James, ii. 278.
—— John, of Balquhain, i. 159; ii. 275.
—— Margaret de, sister of Alexander de Leslie, Earl of Ross, wife of Donald, Lord of the Isles. *Vide* Isles.
—— Patrick, i. 191.
—— Sir Walter de, Lord of Ross, younger son of Sir Andrew de Leslie. *Vide* Ross.
—— William of, ii. 226.
—— of Iden, ii. 152.
Leys, Thomas de, bailie of Saltoun, ii. 30.
Lezinant (Lusignan), Geoffry de, i. 3.
Lhuyd, Mr., i. 199.
Ligertwood, James, of Tillery, i. 214.
Lincoln, Earl of, ii. 84.
Lindelles, Robert de, i. 69.
Lindores, abbot of, i. 28.
—— monks of, i. 28.
Lindsay (Lindesay), Sir Alexander de, of Ormistoun, ii. 33, 45, 88, 207, 219, 238.
—— Sir David de, i. 102; ii. 27.
—— Helen (or Mary) Abernethy, his wife, ii. 27.
—— Sir David, Lyon King-at-Arms, i. ix.
—— David de, Chamberlain, ii. 18.
—— Eleanor, Lady, daughter of Colin, Earl of Balcarres, wife of James Fraser of Lonmay. *Vide* Fraser.

INDEX OF PERSONS.

Lindsay, Sir Henry, of Carraldstoun, twelfth Earl of Crawford. *Vide* Crawford.
—— Sir James of, ii. 219.
—— Sir James de, of Crawford, i. 84.
—— Christiana de Keith, mentioned as his wife, i. 84.
—— James, Provost of Lincluden, ii. 300.
—— Jane, daughter of Sir John of Kinfauns, ii. 63.
—— Sir John de, i. 85; ii. 78.
—— Sir John of, Lord of the Byres, ii. 216.
—— Sir John, of Kinfauns, ii. 63.
—— Hon. Jean de Abernethy, his wife, ii. 63, 65.
—— Johneta de, daughter of Alexander de, of Ormystoun, ii. 33.
—— Lords of the Byres, i. 85.
—— Margaret, daughter of Sir John of Kinfauns, ii. 63.
—— Margaret de, ii. 140.
—— Simon de, i. 28.
—— Sir William de, Lord Chamberlain of Scotland, i. 69; ii. 238.
—— Sir William de, of the Byres, i. 84, 85, 88, 89.
—— Christian de Keith, his wife, i. 84, 85, 88, 89.
—— William de, of Borthwickshiells, ii. 159.
—— . . . i. 146.
Linqua, a Chinese gentleman, iii. 199-201.
Lisle, John de, i. 52.
Little, Captain, Madras Artillery, iii. 90, 108.

Liverpool, Lord, iii. 74-77.
Livingstone, Sir James, Chamberlain of Scotland, ii. 228.
—— Patrick, ii. 253, 254.
—— Sir William de, ii. 31.
Lloyd, Miss, wife of Hugh Fraser of Fraserfield. *Vide* Fraser.
Lochleven, Culdees of, ii. 8.
Lochore, David de, ii. 18.
Lockhart, Mrs., iii. 192.
Logan, James, ii. 236.
Logy, John of, ii. 209.
Londres (London, Lundin), John de, i. 19-21.
—— Nesius de, i. 18-21; ii. 122.
—— Robert de, i. 21.
—— William de, i. 21.
—— Family of, i. 31.
Long, Colonel Samuel, i. 306.
Lonmay, family of. *Vide* Fraser.
Lorens, Hugh, i. 12.
—— Eda Fraser, his wife, i. 12, 13, 86.
—— Eda, their daughter, wife of Philip the Marischal. *Vide* Marischal.
Lorn, John of. *Vide* Macdougal.
Lorymer, Robert, ii. 212.
Lothian, Earls of, i. 14.
—— Frasers in. *Vide* Fraser.
—— Mr. John, Dean of, ii. 14.
—— Marquis of, i. 201.
—— William, Earl of, i. 181, 187.
Louis XVIII. of France, i. 270, 273, 278, 279, 282; iii. 33, 60, 65, 67, 74.
Lovat, Alexander Fraser, fourth Lord, i. 197; ii. 149, 181.

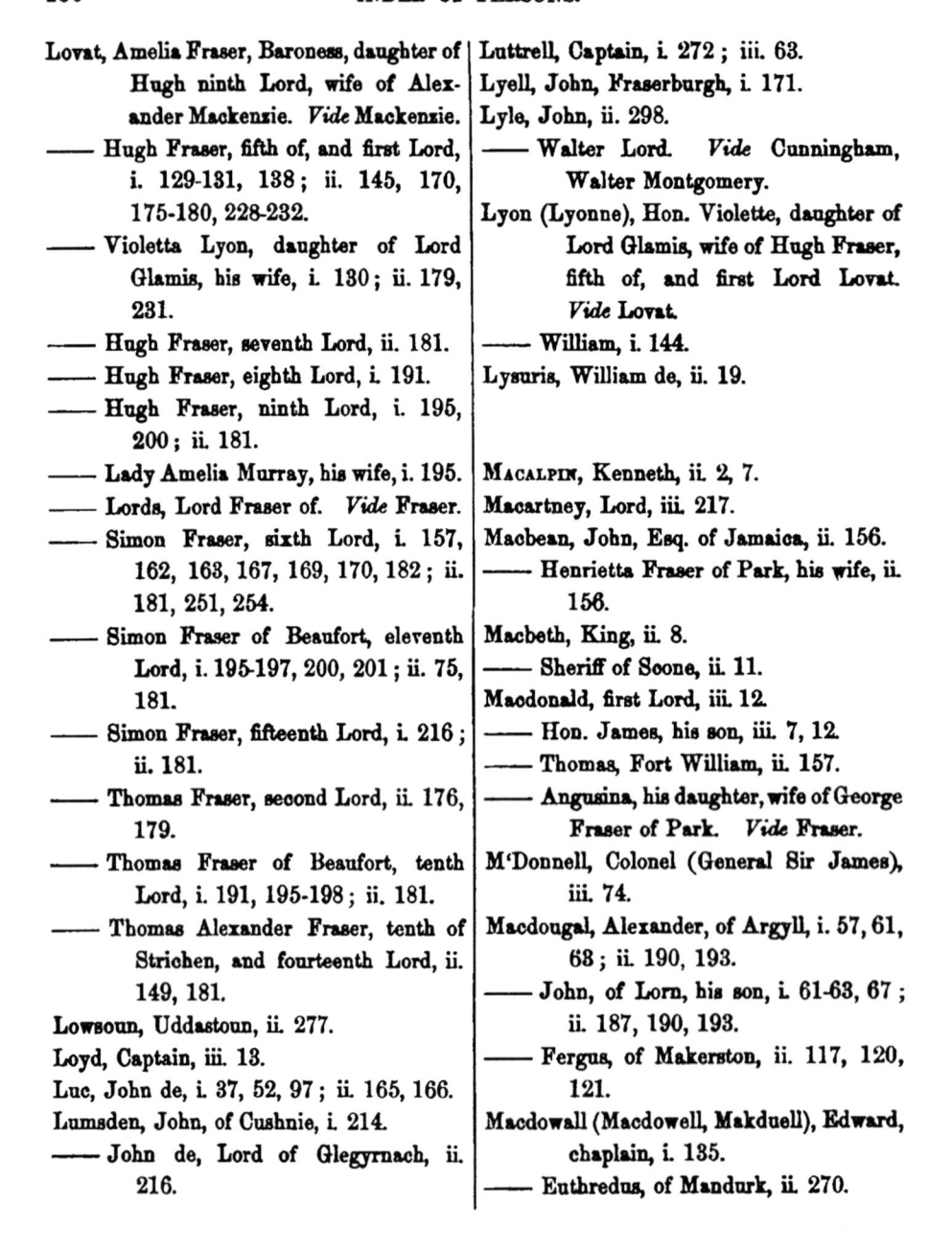

Lovat, Amelia Fraser, Baroness, daughter of Hugh ninth Lord, wife of Alexander Mackenzie. *Vide* Mackenzie.
—— Hugh Fraser, fifth of, and first Lord, i. 129-131, 138; ii. 145, 170, 175-180, 228-232.
—— Violetta Lyon, daughter of Lord Glamis, his wife, i. 130; ii. 179, 231.
—— Hugh Fraser, seventh Lord, ii. 181.
—— Hugh Fraser, eighth Lord, i. 191.
—— Hugh Fraser, ninth Lord, i. 195, 200; ii. 181.
—— Lady Amelia Murray, his wife, i. 195.
—— Lords, Lord Fraser of. *Vide* Fraser.
—— Simon Fraser, sixth Lord, i. 157, 162, 163, 167, 169, 170, 182; ii. 181, 251, 254.
—— Simon Fraser of Beaufort, eleventh Lord, i. 195-197, 200, 201; ii. 75, 181.
—— Simon Fraser, fifteenth Lord, i. 216; ii. 181.
—— Thomas Fraser, second Lord, ii. 176, 179.
—— Thomas Fraser of Beaufort, tenth Lord, i. 191, 195-198; ii. 181.
—— Thomas Alexander Fraser, tenth of Strichen, and fourteenth Lord, ii. 149, 181.
Lowsoun, Uddastoun, ii. 277.
Loyd, Captain, iii. 13.
Luc, John de, i. 37, 52, 97; ii. 165, 166.
Lumsden, John, of Cushnie, i. 214.
—— John de, Lord of Glegyrnach, ii. 216.

Luttrell, Captain, i. 272; iii. 63.
Lyell, John, Fraserburgh, i. 171.
Lyle, John, ii. 298.
—— Walter Lord. *Vide* Cunningham, Walter Montgomery.
Lyon (Lyonne), Hon. Violette, daughter of Lord Glamis, wife of Hugh Fraser, fifth of, and first Lord Lovat. *Vide* Lovat.
—— William, i. 144.
Lysuris, William de, ii. 19.

MACALPIN, Kenneth, ii. 2, 7.
Macartney, Lord, iii. 217.
Macbean, John, Esq. of Jamaica, ii. 156.
—— Henrietta Fraser of Park, his wife, ii. 156.
Macbeth, King, ii. 8.
—— Sheriff of Scone, ii. 11.
Macdonald, first Lord, iii. 12.
—— Hon. James, his son, iii. 7, 12.
—— Thomas, Fort William, ii. 157.
—— Angusina, his daughter, wife of George Fraser of Park. *Vide* Fraser.
M'Donnell, Colonel (General Sir James), iii. 74.
Macdougal, Alexander, of Argyll, i. 57, 61, 68; ii. 190, 193.
—— John, of Lorn, his son, i. 61-63, 67; ii. 187, 190, 193.
—— Fergus, of Makerston, ii. 117, 120, 121.
Macdowall (Macdowell, Makduell), Edward, chaplain, i. 135.
—— Euthredus, of Mandurk, ii. 270.

INDEX OF PERSONS.

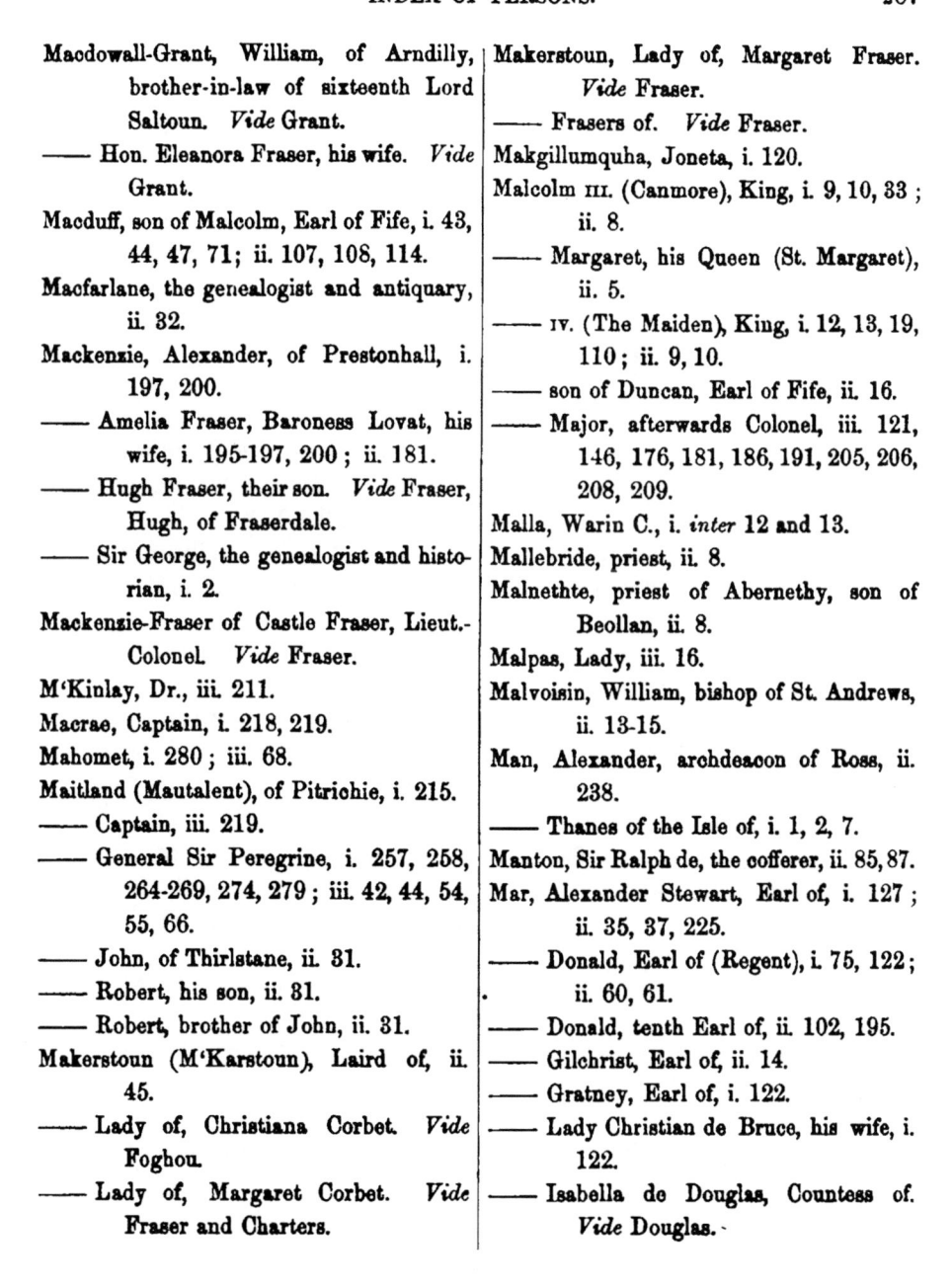

Macdowall-Grant, William, of Arndilly, brother-in-law of sixteenth Lord Saltoun. *Vide* Grant.
—— Hon. Eleanora Fraser, his wife. *Vide* Grant.
Macduff, son of Malcolm, Earl of Fife, i. 43, 44, 47, 71; ii. 107, 108, 114.
Macfarlane, the genealogist and antiquary, ii. 32.
Mackenzie, Alexander, of Prestonhall, i. 197, 200.
—— Amelia Fraser, Baroness Lovat, his wife, i. 195-197, 200; ii. 181.
—— Hugh Fraser, their son. *Vide* Fraser, Hugh, of Fraserdale.
—— Sir George, the genealogist and historian, i. 2.
Mackenzie-Fraser of Castle Fraser, Lieut.-Colonel. *Vide* Fraser.
M'Kinlay, Dr., iii. 211.
Macrae, Captain, i. 218, 219.
Mahomet, i. 280; iii. 68.
Maitland (Mautalent), of Pitrichie, i. 215.
—— Captain, iii. 219.
—— General Sir Peregrine, i. 257, 258, 264-269, 274, 279; iii. 42, 44, 54, 55, 66.
—— John, of Thirlstane, ii. 31.
—— Robert, his son, ii. 31.
—— Robert, brother of John, ii. 31.
Makerstoun (M'Karstoun), Laird of, ii. 45.
—— Lady of, Christiana Corbet. *Vide* Foghou.
—— Lady of, Margaret Corbet. *Vide* Fraser and Charters.

Makerstoun, Lady of, Margaret Fraser. *Vide* Fraser.
—— Frasers of. *Vide* Fraser.
Makgillumquha, Joneta, i. 120.
Malcolm III. (Canmore), King, i. 9, 10, 33; ii. 8.
—— Margaret, his Queen (St. Margaret), ii. 5.
—— IV. (The Maiden), King, i. 12, 13, 19, 110; ii. 9, 10.
—— son of Duncan, Earl of Fife, ii. 16.
—— Major, afterwards Colonel, iii. 121, 146, 176, 181, 186, 191, 205, 206, 208, 209.
Malla, Warin C., i. *inter* 12 and 13.
Mallebride, priest, ii. 8.
Malnethte, priest of Abernethy, son of Beollan, ii. 8.
Malpas, Lady, iii. 16.
Malvoisin, William, bishop of St. Andrews, ii. 13-15.
Man, Alexander, archdeacon of Ross, ii. 238.
—— Thanes of the Isle of, i. 1, 2, 7.
Manton, Sir Ralph de, the cofferer, ii. 85, 87.
Mar, Alexander Stewart, Earl of, i. 127; ii. 35, 37, 225.
—— Donald, Earl of (Regent), i. 75, 122; ii. 60, 61.
—— Donald, tenth Earl of, ii. 102, 195.
—— Gilchrist, Earl of, ii. 14.
—— Gratney, Earl of, i. 122.
—— Lady Christian de Bruce, his wife, i. 122.
—— Isabella de Douglas, Countess of. *Vide* Douglas.

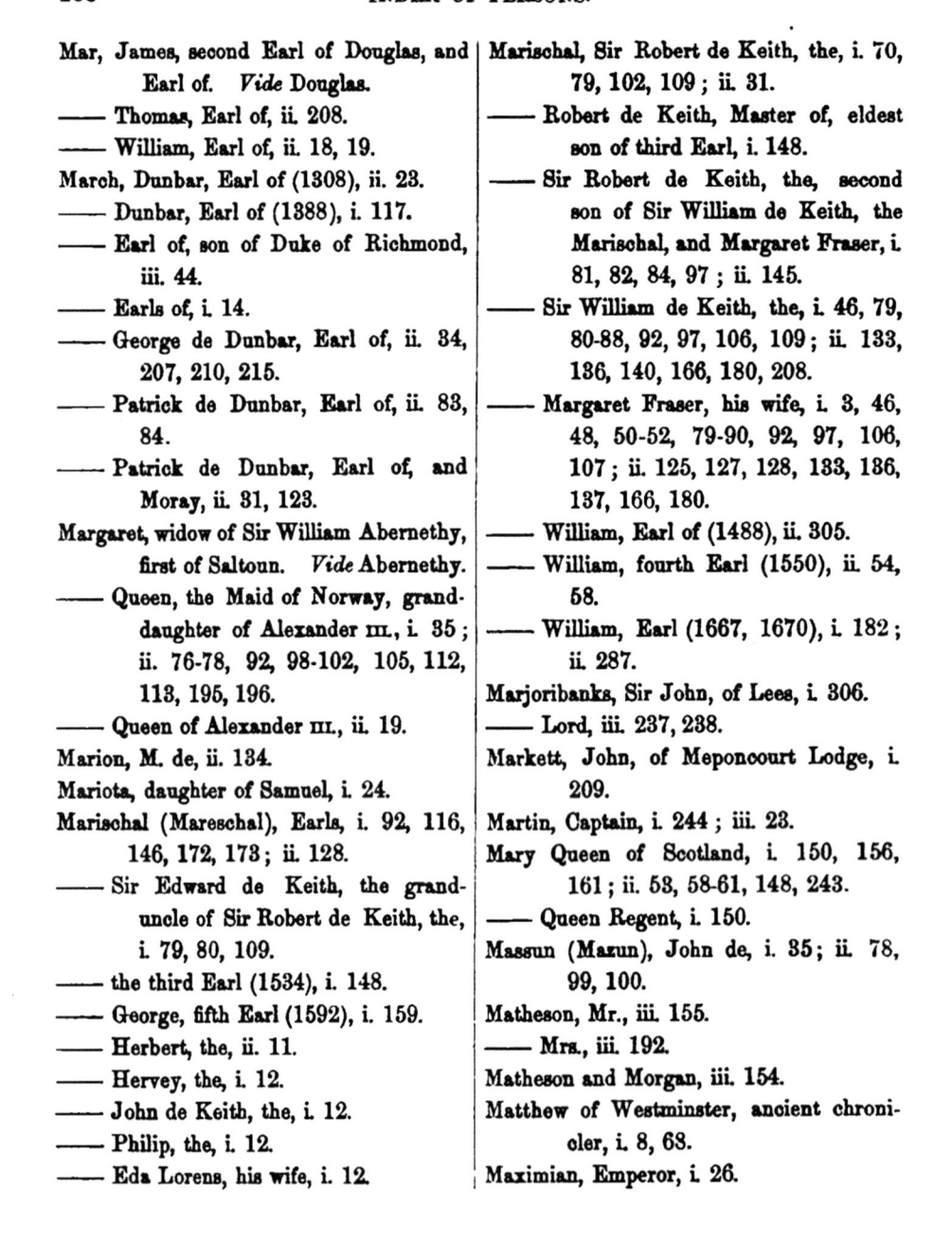

Mar, James, second Earl of Douglas, and Earl of. *Vide* Douglas.
—— Thomas, Earl of, ii. 208.
—— William, Earl of, ii. 18, 19.
March, Dunbar, Earl of (1308), ii. 23.
—— Dunbar, Earl of (1388), i. 117.
—— Earl of, son of Duke of Richmond, iii. 44.
—— Earls of, i. 14.
—— George de Dunbar, Earl of, ii. 34, 207, 210, 215.
—— Patrick de Dunbar, Earl of, ii. 83, 84.
—— Patrick de Dunbar, Earl of, and Moray, ii. 31, 123.
Margaret, widow of Sir William Abernethy, first of Saltoun. *Vide* Abernethy.
—— Queen, the Maid of Norway, granddaughter of Alexander III., i. 35; ii. 76-78, 92, 98-102, 105, 112, 113, 195, 196.
—— Queen of Alexander III., ii. 19.
Marion, M. de, ii. 134.
Mariota, daughter of Samuel, i. 24.
Marischal (Mareschal), Earls, i. 92, 116, 146, 172, 173; ii. 128.
—— Sir Edward de Keith, the granduncle of Sir Robert de Keith, the, i. 79, 80, 109.
—— the third Earl (1534), i. 148.
—— George, fifth Earl (1592), i. 159.
—— Herbert, the, ii. 11.
—— Hervey, the, i. 12.
—— John de Keith, the, i. 12.
—— Philip, the, i. 12.
—— Eda Lorens, his wife, i. 12.

Marischal, Sir Robert de Keith, the, i. 70, 79, 102, 109; ii. 31.
—— Robert de Keith, Master of, eldest son of third Earl, i. 148.
—— Sir Robert de Keith, the, second son of Sir William de Keith, the Marischal, and Margaret Fraser, i. 81, 82, 84, 97; ii. 145.
—— Sir William de Keith, the, i. 46, 79, 80-88, 92, 97, 106, 109; ii. 133, 136, 140, 166, 180, 208.
—— Margaret Fraser, his wife, i. 3, 46, 48, 50-52, 79-90, 92, 97, 106, 107; ii. 125, 127, 128, 133, 136, 137, 166, 180.
—— William, Earl of (1488), ii. 305.
—— William, fourth Earl (1550), ii. 54, 58.
—— William, Earl (1667, 1670), i. 182; ii. 287.
Marjoribanks, Sir John, of Lees, i. 306.
—— Lord, iii. 237, 238.
Markett, John, of Meponcourt Lodge, i. 209.
Martin, Captain, i. 244; iii. 23.
Mary Queen of Scotland, i. 150, 156, 161; ii. 53, 58-61, 148, 243.
—— Queen Regent, i. 150.
Massun (Mazun), John de, i. 35; ii. 78, 99, 100.
Matheson, Mr., iii. 155.
—— Mrs., iii. 192.
Matheson and Morgan, iii. 154.
Matthew of Westminster, ancient chronicler, i. 8, 68.
Maximian, Emperor, i. 26.

INDEX OF PERSONS.

Maxwell, Elizabeth, Lady Lochinvar, daughter of Lord John Herries, wife of Sir John Gordon of Lochinvar, and second wife of Sir Alexander Fraser, eighth of Philorth. *Vide* Gordon and Fraser.
—— Sir Emery de, ii. 117.
—— Eustace of, ii. 219.
—— Herbert, son of Sir Emery de Maxwell, ii. 117.
—— Sir Herbert, Laird of Carlaverock, ii. 40.
—— Sir Herbert de, i. 35; ii. 75.
—— Sir John, Lord Herries, i. 152, 161.
—— Lady Agnes, his wife, i. 161.
—— Sir John de, ii. 31.
—— William, ii. 154.
—— Rachel Fraser, his wife, ii. 154.
—— William, Lord Herries, i. 161.
—— Sir William, i. 218, 219.
May, Isle of, monks of, i. 22.
—— prior of, i. 22.
Maydenstane, Mr. Walter of, ii. 25.
Meldrum, Andrew, official of St. Andrews, ii. 277.
—— David, canon of Dunkeld, ii. 211-213, 216.
—— Patrick (sometime of Iden), i. 174.
—— Patrick, ii. 198.
—— Sir Philip de, ii. 297.
—— William, of Fyvie, i. 132.
—— William de, i. 109; ii. 208.
Melrose, abbot of, ii. 13.
—— Ernauld, abbot of, i. 26.
—— monks of, i. *inter* 12 and 13, 13, 16; ii. 77.

Melville (Malvil, Malvill, Malvyin, Mulevill, Melvin, Melwein), Andrew, ii. 291.
—— Lord, i. 307; iii. 235.
—— Sir Robert, ii. 39.
—— Walter, in Craig, i. 146.
—— William de, i. 25.
—— Memsie, family of. *Vide* Fraser.
Menilevre, Michael de, i. 69.
Menteith (Menethet), Alexander de, ii. 21.
—— Allan, Earl of, i, 81.
—— Sir John de, i. 66.
—— John de, I. viii, ix.
—— Lady Margaret de, daughter of Allan, Earl of. *Vide* Albany.
—— Murdoch, Earl of, i. 75, 76.
—— Walter Comyn, Earl of. *Vide* Comyn.
Menzies, Alexander de, laird of Forthyrgill, ii. 237, 238.
—— Andrew, i. 144; ii. 211, 230, 231.
—— Gilbert, of Pitfodels, Provost of Aberdeen, i. 142, 144, 146, 150.
—— Katherine, his daughter, wife of Alexander Fraser, seventh of Philorth. *Vide* Fraser.
—— Gilbert, of Findon, i. 128.
—— Gilbert, younger of, i. 125, 128; ii. 226.
—— Isabella Fraser, his wife, i. 125, 126, 128; ii. 226.
—— James, i. 146; ii. 280.
—— John, of Pitfoddels, ii. 226.
—— Joneta de, daughter of Alexander, laird of Forthyrgill, ii. 237, 238.

290 INDEX OF PERSONS.

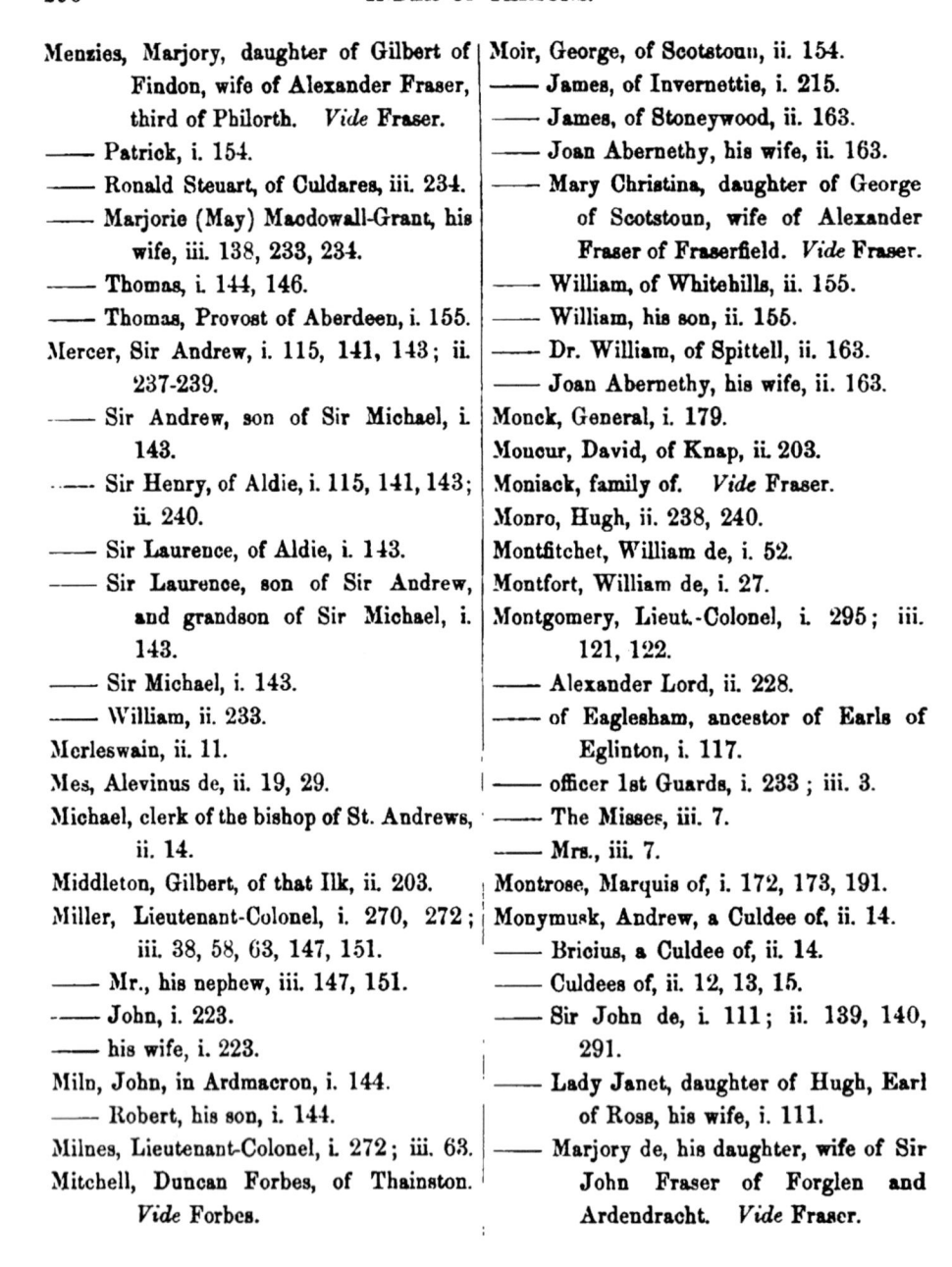

Menzies, Marjory, daughter of Gilbert of Findon, wife of Alexander Fraser, third of Philorth. *Vide* Fraser.
—— Patrick, i. 154.
—— Ronald Steuart, of Culdares, iii. 234.
—— Marjorie (May) Macdowall-Grant, his wife, iii. 138, 233, 234.
—— Thomas, i. 144, 146.
—— Thomas, Provost of Aberdeen, i. 155.
Mercer, Sir Andrew, i. 115, 141, 143; ii. 237-239.
—— Sir Andrew, son of Sir Michael, i. 143.
—— Sir Henry, of Aldie, i. 115, 141, 143; ii. 240.
—— Sir Laurence, of Aldie, i. 143.
—— Sir Laurence, son of Sir Andrew, and grandson of Sir Michael, i. 143.
—— Sir Michael, i. 143.
—— William, ii. 233.
Merleswain, ii. 11.
Mes, Alevinus de, ii. 19, 29.
Michael, clerk of the bishop of St. Andrews, ii. 14.
Middleton, Gilbert, of that Ilk, ii. 203.
Miller, Lieutenant-Colonel, i. 270, 272; iii. 38, 58, 63, 147, 151.
—— Mr., his nephew, iii. 147, 151.
—— John, i. 223.
—— his wife, i. 223.
Miln, John, in Ardmacron, i. 144.
—— Robert, his son, i. 144.
Milnes, Lieutenant-Colonel, i. 272; iii. 63.
Mitchell, Duncan Forbes, of Thainston. *Vide* Forbes.

Moir, George, of Scotstoun, ii. 154.
—— James, of Invernettie, i. 215.
—— James, of Stoneywood, ii. 163.
—— Joan Abernethy, his wife, ii. 163.
—— Mary Christina, daughter of George of Scotstoun, wife of Alexander Fraser of Fraserfield. *Vide* Fraser.
—— William, of Whitehills, ii. 155.
—— William, his son, ii. 155.
—— Dr. William, of Spittell, ii. 163.
—— Joan Abernethy, his wife, ii. 163.
Monck, General, i. 179.
Moncur, David, of Knap, ii. 203.
Moniack, family of. *Vide* Fraser.
Monro, Hugh, ii. 238, 240.
Montfitchet, William de, i. 52.
Montfort, William de, i. 27.
Montgomery, Lieut.-Colonel, i. 295; iii. 121, 122.
—— Alexander Lord, ii. 228.
—— of Eaglesham, ancestor of Earls of Eglinton, i. 117.
—— officer 1st Guards, i. 233; iii. 3.
—— The Misses, iii. 7.
—— Mrs., iii. 7.
Montrose, Marquis of, i. 172, 173, 191.
Monymusk, Andrew, a Culdee of, ii. 14.
—— Bricius, a Culdee of, ii. 14.
—— Culdees of, ii. 12, 13, 15.
—— Sir John de, i. 111; ii. 139, 140, 291.
—— Lady Janet, daughter of Hugh, Earl of Ross, his wife, i. 111.
—— Marjory de, his daughter, wife of Sir John Fraser of Forglen and Ardendracht. *Vide* Fraser.

Monymusk, Prior of, ii. 15.
Moore, Sir John, General, i. 232-235.
—— Major, iii. 172.
Moray (Moravia, Murreff, Murray), Sir Alexander, of Abercairnie, i. 111.
—— Lady Janet, daughter of Hugh, Earl of Ross, his wife, i. 111.
—— Alexander, bishop of, ii. 170-173, 238.
—— Lady Amelia, wife of Hugh Fraser, ninth Lord Lovat. *Vide* Fraser.
—— Sir Andrew, of Bothwell, ii. 20, 22, 29.
—— Sir Andrew, of Bothwell, i. 77-79, 92, 98-100, 119, 120, 122; ii. 131, 169, 174.
—— Lady Christian de Bruce, his wife, i. 122.
—— . . . his daughter, wife of Alexander Fraser, probably younger son of Sir Simon Fraser. *Vide* Fraser.
—— Andrew, bishop of, ii. 48, 305.
—— Angus, ii. 270.
—— Archibald, bishop of, ii. 173.
—— bishop of, ii. 53, 54, 62; ii. 136, 172.
—— Bricius, bishop of, i. 16.
—— Christian, daughter of Freskin de, wife of William de Fedreth. *Vide* Fedreth.
—— David, bishop of, ii. 302.
—— Dunbar, Earl of. *Vide* Dunbar.
—— Earl of, ii. 129, 176.
—— Freskin de, Dominus de Duffus, i. 45.
—— Johanna, Lady of Strathnaver, his wife, i. 45.

Moray, James, "the bonny," Earl of, i. 159; ii. 64.
—— James Earl of, Regent, ii. 58, 62.
—— Janet Dunbar, Countess of, i. 86; ii. 138.
—— Johanna or Jean, of Bothwell, wife of Sir Archibald, third Earl of Douglas. *Vide* Douglas.
—— John Dunbar, Earl of, ii. 138, 174, 182.
—— John, of Bothwell, eldest son of Sir Andrew, i. 100, 101, 120.
—— John Randolph, Earl of, i. 102, 111; ii. 123, 129-131, 134, 297.
—— Euphemia, daughter of Hugh, Earl of Ross, his wife, i. 111; ii. 208.
—— Sir John, of Tullibardine, ii. 24.
—— John de, son of John de Londres, i. 19, 21.
—— John, bishop of, ii. 297.
—— Margaret, daughter of Sir Andrew of Bothwell, wife of Sir William Fraser of Cowie and Durris. *Vide* Fraser.
—— Mary, Lady of Duffus, daughter of Freskin de, widow of Sir Reginald le Chen (junior). *Vide* Chen.
—— Lord Mungo, i. 196.
—— Sir Patrick Keith, of Ochtertyre, i. 88.
—— Patrick de Dunbar, Earl of March and, ii. 31, 123.
—— Patrick de, Laird of Culbardy, ii. 295.
—— Thomas Dunbar, Earl of, ii. 138, 171, 178.

Moray, Sir Thomas Randolph, Earl of (Regent), i. 52, 62, 66, 67, 69, 75.
—— Thomas Randolph, Earl of (son of the Regent), i. 75.
—— Sir Thomas, ii. 39.
—— Sir Thomas, of Bothwell, second son of Sir Andrew, i. 119, 131; ii. 132, 169.
—— William, of Tulibardine, ii. 228.
—— William de, ii. 233.
—— Family of, i. 104; ii. 169.
Mordingtoun, Lord, i. 183.
Moreri, historian, i. 6, 7.
Morgan, Mr. and Mrs., iii. 150, 151, 157, 164, 192.
Morham, John de, i. 28.
Morrison, Alexander, of Bognie, i. 214.
—— Mr., a missionary, iii. 217.
—— Mr., his son, interpreter, iii. 181, 217.
Mortier, iii. 40.
Mortimer, Robert, of Balandro, ii. 203.
—— Roger de, ii. 11.
Morton, Earl of (Regent), i. 154, 156, 157; ii. 58-62.
Morville, family of, ii. 28.
Mountain, Colonel, iii. 110.
Mowat, Alexander, of Loscragy, ii. 305.
—— Mr. James, i. 155.
—— William, canon of Moray, ii. 217.
Mowbray (Mobray, Mobra, Moubre, Mubray), Sir John de, i. 56, 57, 59, 60.
—— John de la, i. 69.
—— Sir Philip de, i. 59; ii. 187, 190.
—— Roger de, ii. 26.
—— Roger de, ii. 122.

Muchalls, Laird of. *Vide* Fraser.
Murat, Marshal, iii. 38, 46, 52.
Mure, Ensign, i. 272; iii. 63.
Muryn, i. 27.

Napier, Sir Charles, G.C.B., iii. 219.
—— Sir George, Governor of the Cape Colony, iii. 99-101.
—— Lady, iii. 100.
—— . . ., author of "History of the Peninsular War," i. 235.
Napoleon I., i. 235, 236, 247, 251, 253, 261, 264-266, 270, 271, 277, 279-282; iii. 7, 24, 25, 30, 32, 33, 38, 41-46, 49, 51-54, 56, 58, 59, 61, 62, 64, 66, 67, 69, 70, 71, 103.
Nassau troops, the, i. 260, 261.
Nectan, King, ii. 2, 5.
Nelson, Lord, iii. 85.
Nesius, son of Nesius, i. 19, 20, 24, 27, 30.
—— son of William, i. 19.
Ness, ii. 8.
Netherlands, King of, iii. 56.
Neukeen, Chinese Commissioner, relative of the Emperor of China, iii. 133, 134.
Newbottle, monks of, i. 18, 20, 21, 24, 26-29; ii. 31, 116.
—— Richard, abbot of, i. 28.
Ney, Marshal, i. 266; iii. 40, 41, 46, 103.
Nicholas, John, son of, ii. 291.
—— III., Pope, ii. 97.
—— V., Pope, ii. 197.
Nisbet, Alexander, author of works on Heraldry, i. 39, 48, 85, 86; ii. 50, 157, 169.

INDEX OF PERSONS.

Nixon, an officer 1st Guards, iii. 64.
Noble, or Nobilis, James, i. 304.
—— Randulphus, i. 19.
—— William, i. 19, 27, 28.
Normandy, William of, i. 7.
Normans, The, i. 2; ii. 1, 111.
Normanville, Thomas de, i. 85; ii. 99.
Northumberland, Gospatrick, Earl of. *Vide* Dunbar.
—— barons of, ii. 108.
Norway, Eric, King of, ii. 99, 100.
—— Ambassadors of, ii. 101.
—— Haco, King of, i. 110.
—— Maid of. *Vide* Margaret, Queen.
Norwegians, The, ii. 7.
Nory, Thomas, ii. 298.

Ochiltree, James Stewart, Lord, i. 185; ii. 66-68.
Ochterlony, Mr., ii. 157.
Ogilvie, Alexander, of Auchirries, i. 213.
—— Alexander, of Deskford, ii. 48.
—— Hon. Janet Abernethy, his wife, ii. 48.
—— Sir Alexander, sheriff of Angus, ii. 37.
—— Alexander of, ii. 226.
—— George, of Carnousie, i. 162; ii. 251, 254.
—— Sir George, his son, i. 162.
—— Sir George, of Dunlugus, ii. 246, 251, 252.
—— James, i. 146; ii. 69.
—— James, of Finlater, ii. 305.
—— James, of Cardell, ii. 54.
—— Sir John, of Mylnetown, i. 142.
Ogilvie, Sir John, of Scattertie, his son, i. 142; ii. 49.
—— John, parson of Cruden, ii. 253.
—— Magdalene, daughter of Sir Walter of Dunlugas, first wife of Sir Alexander, eighth of Philorth. *Vide* Fraser.
—— Mary, mentioned as wife of Sir Bernard Fraser, i. 23.
—— Michael, of Cults, ii. 245.
—— Sir Patrick, of Boynd, ii. 287.
—— Hon. Patrick, ii. 155.
—— Sir Walter, of Findlater, ii. 246.
—— Sir Walter, treasurer of Scotland, ii. 206.
—— Sir Walter, of Boyne, i. 137, 139, 142.
—— Sir Walter, nephew of Sir Walter of Boyne, i. 142.
—— Sir Walter, of Dunlugus, i. 152.
—— Walter, ii. 225.
—— Sir William, of Strathearn, i. 142.
Ogstoune (Ogistoun), Elizabeth, wife of Adam Hepburn. *Vide* Hepburn.
—— Robert, ii. 276.
—— Thomas, ii. 235.
—— Walter, Laird of the Crag, ii. 48, 305.
Oliphant, Lord of, ii. 45.
—— John, of the Dron, ii. 45.
—— Mrs., iii. 115.
—— Thomas, ii. 45.
Oliver, the son of Kylvert, i. 15, 16, 18, 19, 26-31; ii. 116.
Oliver-Castle, family of. *Vide* Fraser.
Onslow, Jane, iii. 179.

Onslow, Mr., iii. 179, 180.
Orange, Prince of, i. 223, 252, 255, 256, 279; iii. 42, 50, 51, 56, 66.
Orkney, Earls of. *Vide* Caithness.
Orlando, paladin of Charlemagne, iii. 20.
Orleans, Duke of, iii. 147.
Orme, Alexander, Depute Clerk-Register, i. 208.
Ormistoun, George, ii. 45.
—— Laird of, ii. 55, 57.
Oswald, General, iii. 15.
Othadin (O'Thady), Signor, iii. 227.
Otterburne, Thomas, of Reidhall, ii. 246, 252, 253.
—— Thomas, his son, ii. 252.
Overtoun, family of. *Vide* Fraser.
Ovide, Adam, ii. 14.
Oyly, D', Lieut.-Colonel Francis, i. 257, 264, 265, 272.
—— Lieut.-Colonel H., i. 272; iii. 63.
Oysel, Nicholas, ii. 88.

Paip, Richard, ii. 278.
Paisley, George, abbot of, ii. 123.
Papedi, Stephan, i. *inter* 12 and 13.
Pardoe, Ensign, i. 272; iii. 63.
Park, family of. *Vide* Fraser.
Parker, Sir Charles C., Vice-Admiral, I. x.
—— Lady, I. x.
—— Admiral Sir William, i. 294; iii. 117, 118, 121, 122, 124, 125, 129, 133, 144, 151, 160, 165, 171, 179, 181, 188, 191, 192, 196, 198, 207, 208, 210, 214, 222, 225-227.
Paton, John, of Grandhome, i. 214.

Paton, Roger, ii. 286.
Paul, Dr., iii. 236.
Pearson (Personi), iii. 13.
Peche, Egidius, i. 5.
—— William, i. 5.
Peebles, Robert de, Chamberlain, i. 72, 73.
—— Sheriff of, i. 38.
Peel, Sir Robert, iii. 203.
Pembroke, Aymer de Valence, Earl of, i. 51, 53, 55; ii. 89, 187, 188, 190, 191, 194.
Pencaitland, John de, i. 35; ii. 75.
Penycook, W. de, i. 25.
Penyngtone, Allan, i. 36.
Percy, Sir Henry, i. 117, 118; ii. 34, 186, 189.
—— Sir Henry de, ii. 22, 84.
—— Lord, i. 102.
—— Sir Ralph, brother of Sir Henry, i. 117, 118.
—— Sir Walter de, ii. 20, 22, 98.
Perel, William, Sheriff of Traquair, ii. 77, 79.
Peresby, Hugh de, ii. 76.
Perry, James, i. 219, 220.
Peter, chaplain to bishop of St. Andrews, ii. 14.
—— Mr., of Dryburgh. *Vide* Dryburgh.
Peterborough, Benedict of, i. 3.
—— Earl of, ii. 144.
Pethcox, Gamel of, i. *inter* 12 and 13.
Philip, King of France. *Vide* France.
Phillips, Thomas, valet to sixteenth Lord Saltoun, i. 291; iii. 101, 127, 132, 204.
—— Mrs., his wife, iii. 235-237.
Philorth, family of. *Vide* Fraser.

INDEX OF PERSONS.

Philp, Margaret, ii. 286.
Phopachy, family of. *Vide* Fraser.
Pickmore, Admiral, iii. 26.
Pictish Royal Family, ii. 2.
—— Kings, ii. 6.
Picts, The, ii. 3, 5, 6.
Picton, General Sir Thomas, i. 255, 265; iii. 79.
Pinkerton, the historian, i. 222.
Pinto, Silviara de, Portuguese Governor at Macao, iii. 197.
Pirie, Professor, M.D., iii. 236.
Pitsligo, Alexander, Lord, ii. 287.
—— Lord, ii. 59, 60.
—— Tutor of, i. 172.
Pius II., Pope, ii. 297.
Platt, Captain, iii. 155.
Poer (Power), Sir Robert, i. 4.
Poitou, Richard, Count of. *Vide* Richard I.
Pope, The, ii. 12, 20, 25, 93.
Poret, French General, i. 267.
Portduvine, William of, ii. 203.
Porteous, Robert, Snowdoun Herald, i. 89.
Portland, Duke of, i. 224.
—— first Earl of, i. 223.
—— great-grandson of Earl of, i. 223.
Portugal, King of, i. 233.
—— Prince Regent of, iii. 11.
Portuguese troops, The, i. 253.
Pottinger, Sir Henry, i. 292-294, 296-299, 301, 302; iii. 107, 109, 118, 119, 121, 129, 131, 133, 134, 136, 137, 149, 151, 154-159, 162-166, 171, 177-179, 184, 191, 192, 201-203, 205, 207, 208, 213, 217, 224, 226-228.

Pottinger, Major, his nephew, iii. 213.
Pratt, Christian, ii. 45.
Predicant Friars in Paris, ii. 110.
Prendergast, Henry de, ii. 89.
Preston, Symon de, Sheriff of Lothian, ii. 33.
—— Henry de, Lord of Formartine. *Vide* Formartine.
Primrose, Sir Archibald, Clerk-Register, i. 184.
Prince, Mr., iii. 72.
Princess Royal, The, iii. 226.
Pringle, Miss Emily, iii. 156, 172.
Pritchard, The Misses, iii. 12.
Prot, George, i. 165.
Prowdy, David, ii. 198.
Prussian Guards, i. 282.
—— troops, The, i. 265, 270, 271, 277, 279, 280, 282.

Quarrelbuss, family of. *Vide* Fraser.
Queensberry, Duke of, i. 208.

Radulph, chaplain to William the Lion, ii. 11.
—— chaplain to Earl Waldeve, i. *inter* 12 and 13.
Raglan, Lord. *Vide* Lord Fitzroy Somerset.
Rainforth, Miss, iii. 164.
Ramsay, Alexander, of Hawthornden, ii. 159.
—— Constantine, ii. 270.
—— Sir George, of Banff, i. 206, 218, 219.

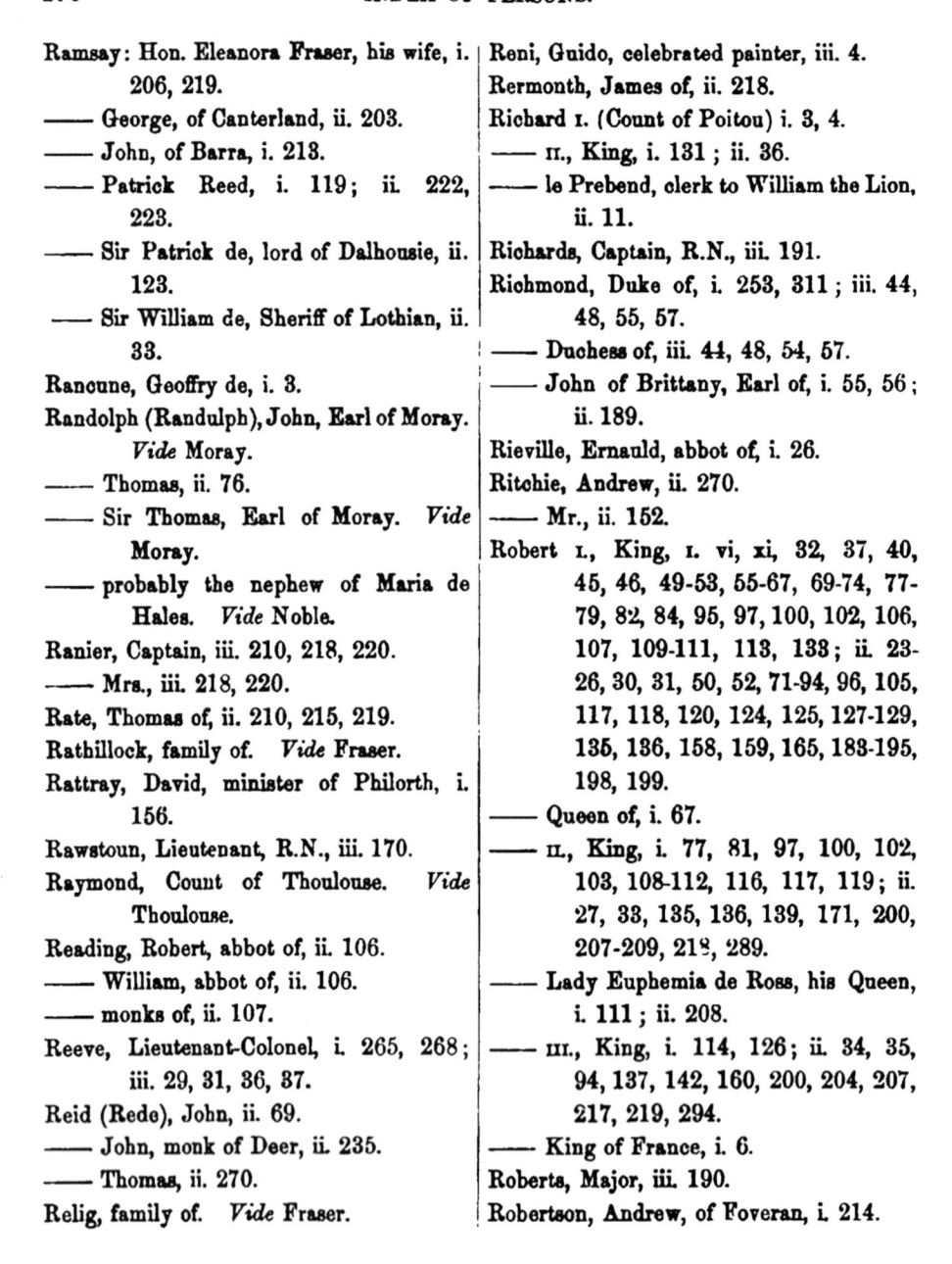

Ramsay: Hon. Eleanora Fraser, his wife, i. 206, 219.
—— George, of Canterland, ii. 203.
—— John, of Barra, i. 213.
—— Patrick Reed, i. 119; ii. 222, 223.
—— Sir Patrick de, lord of Dalhousie, ii. 123.
—— Sir William de, Sheriff of Lothian, ii. 33.
Rancune, Geoffry de, i. 3.
Randolph (Randulph), John, Earl of Moray. *Vide* Moray.
—— Thomas, ii. 76.
—— Sir Thomas, Earl of Moray. *Vide* Moray.
—— probably the nephew of Maria de Hales. *Vide* Noble.
Ranier, Captain, iii. 210, 218, 220.
—— Mrs., iii. 218, 220.
Rate, Thomas of, ii. 210, 215, 219.
Rathillock, family of. *Vide* Fraser.
Rattray, David, minister of Philorth, i. 156.
Rawstoun, Lieutenant, R.N., iii. 170.
Raymond, Count of Thoulouse. *Vide* Thoulouse.
Reading, Robert, abbot of, ii. 106.
—— William, abbot of, ii. 106.
—— monks of, ii. 107.
Reeve, Lieutenant-Colonel, i. 265, 268; iii. 29, 31, 36, 37.
Reid (Rede), John, ii. 69.
—— John, monk of Deer, ii. 235.
—— Thomas, ii. 270.
Relig, family of. *Vide* Fraser.

Reni, Guido, celebrated painter, iii. 4.
Rermonth, James of, ii. 218.
Richard I. (Count of Poitou) i. 3, 4.
—— II., King, i. 131; ii. 36.
—— le Prebend, clerk to William the Lion, ii. 11.
Richards, Captain, R.N., iii. 191.
Richmond, Duke of, i. 253, 311; iii. 44, 48, 55, 57.
—— Duchess of, iii. 44, 48, 54, 57.
—— John of Brittany, Earl of, i. 55, 56; ii. 189.
Rieville, Ernauld, abbot of, i. 26.
Ritchie, Andrew, ii. 270.
—— Mr., ii. 152.
Robert I., King, I. vi, xi, 32, 37, 40, 45, 46, 49-53, 55-67, 69-74, 77-79, 82, 84, 95, 97, 100, 102, 106, 107, 109-111, 113, 133; ii. 23-26, 30, 31, 50, 52, 71-94, 96, 105, 117, 118, 120, 124, 125, 127-129, 135, 136, 158, 159, 165, 183-195, 198, 199.
—— Queen of, i. 67.
—— II., King, i. 77, 81, 97, 100, 102, 103, 108-112, 116, 117, 119; ii. 27, 33, 135, 136, 139, 171, 200, 207-209, 212, 289.
—— Lady Euphemia de Ross, his Queen, i. 111; ii. 208.
—— III., King, i. 114, 126; ii. 34, 35, 94, 137, 142, 160, 200, 204, 207, 217, 219, 294.
—— King of France, i. 6.
Roberts, Major, iii. 190.
Robertson, Andrew, of Foveran, i. 214.

Robertson, David, of Ladykirk. *Vide* Lord Marjoribanks.
—— Dr., i. 78.
Robinson, George, of Gask, i. 215.
—— George, ii. 47.
Rodney, Sir George (Lord) Admiral, ii. 156.
Roger, the son of Finlay, of Twydyn. *Vide* Tweedie.
Rokeby, Thomas de, ii. 32.
Rome, King of, iii. 59.
Ronald (Ranald), Lord of the Isles. *Vide* Isles.
Ros, John de, English Admiral, ii. 131.
Rose, Hugh de, of Kilravock, ii. 172, 177.
—— Maria, daughter of Sir Andrew de Bosco, his wife, ii. 172.
Ross, Alexander de Leslie, Earl of, i. 123, 132, 133; ii. 36.
—— Isabel de, daughter of Robert, Duke of Albany, his wife, i. 123; ii. 36.
—— Alexander, bishop of, ii. 225, 238, 240.
—— Alexander, Lord of the Isles, Earl of. *Vide* Isles.
—— an officer of Coldstream Guards, iii. 6.
—— Earls of, i. 141, 166; ii. 169, 174, 191, 192, 194.
—— Lady Euphemia de, daughter of Hugh, Earl of, wife (first) of John Randolph, Earl of Moray; (secondly), of King Robert II. *Vide* Moray and Robert II.
—— Euphemia, Countess of, daughter of Alexander de Leslie, Earl of, i. 123-125, 132, 133, 141, 143, 166; ii. 36, 207, 210-215, 238, 239.

Ross, Ferquhard, Earl of, i. 110.
—— Hugh, Earl of, son of William, i. 110, 111, 113; ii. 191, 232.
—— Jean, daughter of Walter, Steward of Scotland, his first wife, i. 111.
—— Lady Matilda de Bruce, his second wife, i. 111.
—— Hugh, of Rarichies, second son of Hugh, Earl of, i. 111-115, 121, 166, 205, 206; ii. 208, 209, 232, 233.
—— Isabella, daughter of William, Earl of, wife of Sir Edward de Bruce. *Vide* Bruce.
—— Janet, daughter of Hugh, Earl of, wife of (first) Sir John de Monymusk; and (second), Sir Alexander Moray of Abercairny. *Vide* Monymusk and Moray.
—— Lady Johanna de, daughter of William, Earl of, wife of Sir Alexander Fraser of Cowie and Durris. *Vide* Fraser.
—— John de, second son of William, Earl of, i. 110, 111, 113.
—— Margaret Comyn, daughter of Earl of Buchan, his wife, i. 110, 113.
—— John, Earl of. *Vide* Isles, John, Lord of the.
—— John, deacon of the church of, ii. 225.
—— John, of Arnage, i. 214.
—— Sir John, of Hawkhead, ii. 218.
—— Malcolm, Earl of, i. 110.

Ross, Margaret Leslie, Countess of, wife of Donald, Lord of the Isles. *Vide* Isles.
—— Munro, of Pitcalnie, i. 205.
—— Robert de, ii. 18.
—— Roger, bishop of, ii. 297.
—— Sir Walter de Leslie, Lord of, i. 110-113, 115, 116, 119, 125, 126, 128, 132, 141, 143; ii. 27, 36, 170, 174, 207-217, 237-239.
—— Euphemia, Countess of, and daughter of William, Earl of, his wife, i. 111-113, 115, 121, 125, 126, 132, 134, 141, 143, 206; ii. 27, 36.
—— William, Earl of, son of Ferquhard, i. 110.
—— William, Earl of, his son, i. 44, 57, 67, 110.
—— William, Earl of, son of Hugh, i. 101, 103, 111-115, 125, 134, 205, 206; ii. 27, 36, 206-209, 233, 238, 297.
—— William, his son, i. 111.
Rothes, Earl of, ii. 56.
—— Earls of, ii. 27.
—— Leslie, Earl of, ii. 27.
Rothesay, David, Duke of, ii. 205, 295.
Roxburgh, Alderman and Bailies of, i. 73.
—— Constable of, ii. 83.
—— Earl of, ii. 72.
—— Sheriff of, i. 38; ii. 83.
Rufus, Radulph, ii. 11.
Rule, Henry, of Balmerino, ii. 10.
Russell, Alexander, of Old Deer, i. 214.
—— Lord John, afterwards Earl, i. 307-309; iii. 235.
Russia, Emperor of, i. 281; iii. 69.
Russian troops, The, i. 277-279.
Rutherford, Nicholas de, ii. 19.
Ruthven, Lady Isabell, daughter of William, first Earl of Gowrie, i. 168.
Rydel, Richard, i. 27.
Ryklyntoun, Alexander de, ii. 123.
Rynde, Henry, ii. 198.

St. (Santa) Agatha, i. 229.
St. Andrews, Ernulphus or Arnold, bishop of, ii. 10, 13.
—— Bishop of, ii. 14.
—— Canons of, ii. 12, 16.
—— Culdees of, ii. 10, 12-14.
—— Deans of, ii. 13.
—— Gilbert I., prior of, i. 17, 18.
—— Gilbert II., prior of, i. 17.
—— Henry, bishop of, ii. 213.
—— James, bishop of, ii. 300, 302.
—— John, prior of, ii. 48.
—— Robert, bishop of, ii. 13.
—— Simon (Gilbert), prior of, i. 17.
—— Thomas, prior of, ii. 14.
—— Walter, bishop of, ii. 200, 206, 295.
—— William Fraser, bishop of. *Vide* Fraser.
—— William de Lambyrton, bishop of. *Vide* Lambyrton.
—— William Landale, bishop of, ii. 219.
—— William, prior of, ii. 32.
St. Augustine, ii. 15.
St. Bride (Bridget), ii. 5, 16.
St. Carthach, ii. 3.
St. Columba, ii. 1-5.

St. Cuthbert, i. 33 ; ii. 16.
St. Faith, ii. 102, 196.
St. Francis, iii. 2.
St. James the Apostle, i. 4 ; ii. 38.
St. John, John de, ii. 189.
St. Margaret, Queen of Scotland. *Vide* Malcolm III.
St. Martin, Alexander de, Viccoomes, i. 24.
St. Michael, John of, ii. 225.
—— Roger, ii. 16.
St. Nicholas, bishop, i. 26.
St. Palladius, ii. 2.
St. Patrick, ii. 5.
Salomons, Mr. Philip, iii. 183.
Saltoun, Abernethies and Frasers, Lords. *Vide* Abernethy and Fraser.
Saltoun and Glencorse, Fletchers of, ii. 70.
Salviaco, Bertram de, Count of Campania, ii. 25.
Samuel, i. 24.
Sanderson, Andrew, ii. 270.
Sawers, John, herald painter, i. 89.
Saxons, i. 2 ; ii. 1.
Say, Mr. Tradescant, iii. 208.
Sayis, Spanish General, i. 238.
Schewas (Scheues), John, ii. 198.
—— John, canon of Glasgow, ii. 216.
Schoedde, General, i. 295, 296, 299, 300, 302 ; iii. 122, 125, 126, 139, 144.
Schorswald, George. *Vide* Brechin, bishop of.
Scotland, Alexander the Steward of, ii. 77.
—— Barons of, ii. 90, 92, 93, 98, 100, 103, 109.
—— Chamberlain of, for Edward I., ii. 89.
—— Estates of, ii. 58.

Scotland, Kings of, ii. 99.
—— James, Prince of. *Vide* James IV.
—— James, Senescallus or Steward of, i. 66 ; ii. 98, 105.
—— Lieutenant of, for Edward I., ii. 89.
—— Lord Paramount of. *Vide* Edward I.
—— Lord Register for, i. 208.
—— Nicol, Chancellor of, ii. 10.
—— Prelates of, ii. 98, 100, 103.
—— Regents or Guardians of, ii. 98, 103-105, 113.
—— Sir Simon Fraser, guardian of. *Vide* Fraser, Sir Simon (filius).
—— Walter, the Steward of, i. 67, 238 ; ii. 32.
Scots, The, ii. 2, 3.
Scott, David, i. 145.
—— Thomas, ii. 277.
—— Sir Walter, of Abbotsford, iii. 20.
—— Sir Walter, of Buccleuch, ii. 60, 61.
—— William, ii. 298.
Scottish Church, ii. 4.
Scovell, Sir George, iii. 197.
Scriven, the antiquary, i. 8.
Scrymgeour, Alexander, of Aberbrothoc, ii. 136, 291.
—— Sir James, Constable of Dundee, ii. 38, 53.
—— James, of Dudup, ii. 305.
Segrave, Sir John de, ii. 85, 86, 88, 89.
Seillun, Peter, i. 3.
Selkirk, Earl of, i. 208, 209, 224.
—— Forest, guardian of. *Vide* Fraser, Sir Simon (filius).
Seton (Seytoun), Sir Alexander de, of Touchfraser, i. 83, 84.

INDEX OF PERSONS.

Seton, Sir Alexander de, Lord of Gordon, i. 82; ii. 161, 225, 226.
—— Elizabeth de Gordon, his wife, i. 82.
—— Alexander, of Meldrum, i. 169, 170.
—— Alexander de, ii. 31.
—— Elizabeth, daughter of Alexander of Meldrum, second wife of Alexander Fraser, tenth of Philorth, tenth Lord Saltoun. *Vide* Fraser.
—— John, ii. 291.
—— Sir George de, of Seton, first Lord, i. 83.
—— Jean or Margaret Stewart, his wife, i. 83.
—— of Meldrum, ii. 62, 251.
—— . . . daughter of Alexander Abernethy, sixth Lord Saltoun, his wife, ii. 62.
—— Lord, ii. 59.
—— William of, ii. 225, 226.
—— of Touchfraser, family of, i. 83, 92.
Seton-Gordon, Sir Alexander de, first Earl of Huntly, eldest son of Sir Alexander Seton, Lord Gordon, and Elizabeth de Gordon. *Vide* Huntly.
Seton-Gordons of Huntly, ii. 180.
Sextus Fourth, Pope, ii. 217.
Seymour, Captain, iii. 141.
Shadwell, an officer 98th Regiment, son of Vice-Chancellor Shadwell, iii. 143, 144.
Shand, Alexander, minister of Inch, ii. 163.
—— Elizabeth Abernethy, his wife, ii. 163.

Sharpe, James, Archbishop of St. Andrews, i. 193.
—— Margaret, his daughter, wife of William Fraser, eleventh Lord Saltoun. *Vide* Fraser.
—— Mr., iii. 169.
—— Robert, ii. 288.
Shaw, historian, ii. 133.
Shean, groom to sixteenth Lord Saltoun, i. 291; iii. 103, 127, 188.
Shifner, Captain, i. 246; iii. 32.
Shuttleworth, Mary Elizabeth, wife of William Fraser of Woodhill. *Vide* Fraser.
Sibbald, Sir Robert, i. 199.
—— Thomas, ii. 203.
Siborn, Captain W., iii. 78-83.
Silkyfurth, William de, i. 44.
Simeon, Sir Richard, Bart., i. 227.
Simpson (Symsone), Captain, i. 272; iii. 63.
—— Alexander, vicar of Aberkerdor, ii. 161.
—— General Sir James, i. 287.
—— John, ii. 253.
—— Thomas, ii. 270.
Sinclair (St. Clair, Sancto Claro), Alexander de, son of Thomas de, i. 115.
—— Euphame de, ii. 170.
—— Sir James, ii. 34.
—— John the, Lord of Herdmanston, ii. 40.
—— John, ii. 253.
—— John de, i. 107.
—— Thomas, ii. 298.

INDEX OF PERSONS.

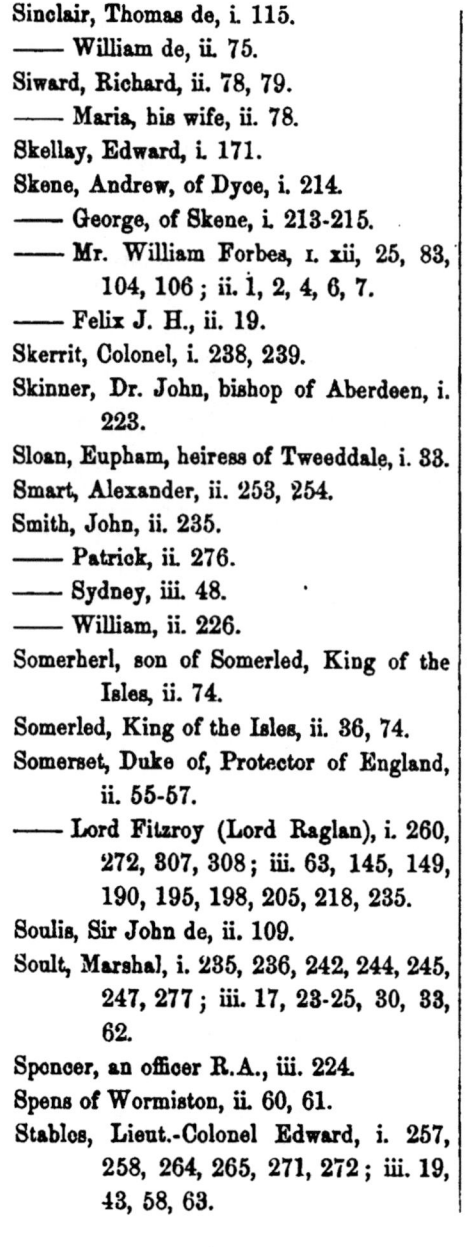

Sinclair, Thomas de, i. 115.
—— William de, ii. 75.
Siward, Richard, ii. 78, 79.
—— Maria, his wife, ii. 78.
Skellay, Edward, i. 171.
Skene, Andrew, of Dyce, i. 214.
—— George, of Skene, i. 213-215.
—— Mr. William Forbes, I. xii, 25, 83, 104, 106; ii. 1, 2, 4, 6, 7.
—— Felix J. H., ii. 19.
Skerrit, Colonel, i. 238, 239.
Skinner, Dr. John, bishop of Aberdeen, i. 223.
Sloan, Eupham, heiress of Tweeddale, i. 33.
Smart, Alexander, ii. 253, 254.
Smith, John, ii. 235.
—— Patrick, ii. 276.
—— Sydney, iii. 48.
—— William, ii. 226.
Somerherl, son of Somerled, King of the Isles, ii. 74.
Somerled, King of the Isles, ii. 36, 74.
Somerset, Duke of, Protector of England, ii. 55-57.
—— Lord Fitzroy (Lord Raglan), i. 260, 272, 307, 308; iii. 63, 145, 149, 190, 195, 198, 205, 218, 235.
Soulis, Sir John de, ii. 109.
Soult, Marshal, i. 235, 236, 242, 244, 245, 247, 277; iii. 17, 23-25, 30, 33, 62.
Sponcer, an officer R.A., iii. 224.
Spens of Wormiston, ii. 60, 61.
Stables, Lieut.-Colonel Edward, i. 257, 258, 264, 265, 271, 272; iii. 19, 43, 58, 63.

Stacey, Joseph, Ross Herald, i. 89.
Stanhope, Lieutenant-Colonel, i. 274.
Stanley, Lord (late Earl of Derby), i. 301.
Stevens, Robert, of Broadland, i. 214.
Stewart (Senescallus, Steward, Stuart), Sir Alexander, of Bonkill, i. 62.
—— Alexander, Earl of Mar. *Vide* Mar.
—— Andrew, brother of John, Earl of Buchan, i. 81, 84.
—— Andrew, the historian, ii. 134.
—— Hon. Anne, daughter of first Lord Blantyre, second wife of John Abernethy, eighth Lord Saltoun. *Vide* Abernethy.
—— Sir Archibald, of Blackhall, i. 185, 186; ii. 67-69.
—— Sir Charles, British Ambassador, iii. 52.
—— David, bishop of Moray, ii. 177.
—— Harry, of Craigehall, ii. 252, 254.
—— Lady Isabel, daughter of Robert, Duke of Albany, wife of Alexander de Leslie, Earl of Ross. *Vide* Ross.
—— James, Lord Stewart, of Newton, Chancellor of Scotland, ii. 246.
—— Sir James, Steward of Scotland. *Vide* Scotland.
—— James, Earl of Buchan, uterine brother of James III. *Vide* Buchan.
—— James, of Killeith, afterwards Lord Ochiltree. *Vide* Ochiltree.
—— John Glass Gordon, ii. 157.
—— Evorilda Eliza Maria Fraser, his wife, ii. 157.

Stewart, John, Archdeacon of Aberdeen, ii. 245.
—— John, Earl of Buchan, son of Regent Albany. *Vide* Buchan.
—— Sir John, of Bonkill, ii. 136.
—— Sir John, of Frendraught, his son, i. 87; ii. 134-136.
—— John, of Cragyhall, ii. 305.
—— John, of Murene, ii. 246.
—— John, natural brother of King Robert III., ii. 218.
—— Major-General, M.P., i. 221.
—— Margaret, daughter of Sir John of Frendraught, wife of Sir James Fraser, brother of the Chamberlain. *Vide* Fraser.
—— Lady Margaret, daughter of James, Earl of Buchan, and wife of Alexander Abernethy, fourth Lord Saltoun. *Vide* Abernethy.
—— Lady Margaret, daughter of Earl of Athole, wife of George Abernethy, seventh Lord Saltoun. *Vide* Abernethy.
—— Lady Maria, daughter of Robert, Duke of Albany, and wife of Sir William Abernethy, sixth of Saltoun. *Vide* Abernethy.
—— Lady Mary, daughter of Earl of Moray, first wife of John Abernethy, eighth Lord Saltoun. *Vide* Abernethy.
—— Mrs., iii. 198.
—— Murdoch, son of Robert, Duke of Albany, ii. 34.
—— Patrick, i. 144.

Stewart, Robert (Steward of Scotland). *Vide* Robert II.
—— Robert, Duke of Albany. *Vide* Albany.
—— Robert, his son, i. 81, 84, 124.
—— Robert, of Clawak, i. 139.
—— Sir Robert, of Innermeth, ii. 219.
—— Sir Thomas, of Garnetulie, ii. 246.
—— Sir Walter, Steward of Scotland. *Vide* Scotland.
—— Sir Walter, ii. 240.
—— Walter, of Morfy, ii. 45.
—— Sir William, of Jedworth, ii. 34.
—— Colonel Hon. William, i. 256, 257, 272; iii. 63.
—— William, notary in Fraserburgh, i. 174.
—— of Innermeath, family of, ii. 64.
Stirling (Stryveline), John, of Craigbernard, ii. 48.
—— Hon. Margaret Abernethy, his wife, ii. 48.
—— Peter de, ii. 171.
—— John, his son, ii. 171.
—— Sheriff of, i. 38.
Stoneywood (Stenewod), Laird of (1531), i. 146.
Stopford, General, i. 246; iii. 32.
Stormont, Viscount, i. 208, 224.
Stowe, the antiquary, i. 8.
Strachan, Patrick, of Kinaldie, i. 175.
—— Sir Richard, Admiral, i. 236, 237.
Straiton (Straton, Stratoune), Alexander, ii. 39.
—— Alexander, of Lowrenstoun, ii. 305.
—— Alexander, of that Ilk, ii. 203.
—— Andrew, of Cragy, ii. 203.

Straiton, John, i. 146.
Strathallan, Lord, iii. 196.
Strathard, Thainus de, ii. 11.
Strathbogie, David de, Earl of Athol. *Vide* Athol.
—— Presbytery of, i. 173-175.
Stratheach, Wallevus de, ii. 116.
Strathearn (Strathern), Constantin, judge of, ii. 11.
—— Malise (sixth), Earl of, i. 111; ii. 21, 23, 129.
—— Isabella, daughter of Magnus, Earl of Caithness, his wife, ii. 129.
—— his daughter, mentioned as wife of William, Earl of Ross, i. 111.
—— Maria, wife of Sir Hugh de Abernethy, afterwards Countess of. *Vide* Abernethy.
—— Robert, Steward of Scotland, Earl of. *Vide* Robert II.
—— Earls of, ii. 22.
Stratheth, John de, ii. 203.
—— Alexander, of Monbodow, ii. 203.
Strathnaver, Johanna, Lady of. *Vide* Moray.
Streatfield, Captain, i. 244, 272; iii. 28, 63.
Strichen, family of. *Vide* Fraser.
—— Lord. *Vide* Fraser.
—— Laird of, ii. 286.
Strivelyn del Cars, Johan de, i. 36.
Struy, family of. *Vide* Fraser.
Stutewill, William de, dean of Dunkeld, ii. 18.
Stylle, Henry, of Saltoun, ii. 30.
Suchet, Marshal, iii. 30.
Sullivan, Sir Henry, i. 246; iii. 32.
—— Mrs., iii. 218.

Surrey, John de Warrenne, Earl of, Governor of Scotland, i. 44; ii. 102, 196, 308.
Sussex, Duke of, iii. 192.
Sutherland, of Kinminity, i. 185.
—— James, of Duffus, ii. 149.
—— Violet Fraser, his wife, ii. 149.
Swinbourne, author, iii. 3.
Swinburn, officer 1st Guards, i. 266.
Swinton, John, i. 207.
Sydserfe, Archibald, i. 176.

Taylor (Tailzour), George, i. 135.
—— John, of Portertoun, i. 215.
Techmuiry, family of. *Vide* Fraser.
Thom, Mr., interpreter, iii. 181.
Thomas, Lieut.-Colonel, i. 272; iii. 31, 39, 63.
Thompson, Alexander, ii. 270, 287.
—— Captain, i. 244; iii. 23.
—— Surgeon-General, iii. 185, 187, 188.
Thorntons, of that Ilk, i. 128.
—— William, ii. 217.
Thorold, William, i. 36.
Thoulouse, Raymond, Count of, i. 3, 4.
Thuadel, a Culdee, ii. 8.
Thurlow, Lord Chancellor, i. 226, 241.
—— Catharine, his daughter, wife of Alexander George Fraser, sixteenth Lord Saltoun. *Vide* Fraser.
—— Caroline, his daughter, wife of General Samuel Brown. *Vide* Brown.
—— Maria, his daughter, wife of Colonel (Sir David, Bart.) Cunynghame. *Vide* Cunynghame.
Tighernac, Irish annalist, ii. 2, 6.

Tilliol, Robert de, keeper of Lochmaben Castle, ii. 85.
Timousky, author, iii. 89.
Tolloch, Alexander, ii. 305.
Tolquhon, Laird of, ii. 286.
Tomlinson, Lieutenant-Colonel, i. 293; iii. 109, 110.
Torrens, General Sir Henry, iii. 36, 77.
Torry, abbot, John de, ii. 137.
Touchfraser, family of. *Vide* Fraser.
Townshend, Colonel, i. 247, 272; iii. 38, 63, 141.
Traquair, Earl of, i. 176.
Trevor, Lieut.-Colonel, iii. 126, 127.
Troubridge, Admiral Sir Thomas, iii. 85.
Turner, John, of Turnerhall, i. 214.
—— Robert, of Menie, i. 214.
Turyne, Andrew de, Laird of Fovern, ii. 293, 294.
Tweeddale, Earl of, i. 188.
—— Marchioness of, iii. 205.
—— Marquis of, i. 90, 303; iii. 205.
Tweedie, James, of Drumelzier, ii. 118.
—— Roger, son of Finlay, ii. 117-119.
—— William of (Skirling), ii. 118.
—— of Drumelzier, ii. 117, 118.
Twydyn, Finlay of, ii. 117, 118.
Tyrell, the antiquary, i. 55.
Tytler, the historian, ii. 114.
Tzing, Governor of Provinces, China, iii. 133, 134, 155.

Udny, Alexander, of Udny, i. 213.
—— laird of, ii. 284.
Ulton, Earl of, ii. 88.

Umphraville, Gilbert de, Earl of Angus. *Vide* Angus.
—— Sir Ingrahame de, i. 61; ii. 109.
Uniack, Major, iii. 126.
Urie (Ury, Urry), Lady, daughter of Alexander Fraser, eighth of Philorth. *Vide* Hay.
—— Gilbert, ii. 291.
—— Johanna, his wife, ii. 291.
Urquhart (Wrchard), Adam of, Sheriff of Cromartie, ii. 233, 238, 240.
—— Adam, of Meldrum, ii. 287.
—— James, of Old Craig, i. 173, 174.
—— Keith, of Meldrum, i. 214.
—— Walter, of Crombie, i. 173.
—— William, of Craigston, i. 214; ii. 154.
—— Mary Fraser, his wife, ii. 154.
Uxbridge, Lord, iii. 46, 47.

Valence, Sir Aymer de. *Vide* Pembroke, Earl of.
Vallibus, J. de, Vicecomes de Edinburgh, i. 25.
—— William de, i. 27, 28.
Valoines, Adam de, i. 42, 44.
Valois, daughter of Charles, Count of, ii. 109.
Vandame, iii. 64.
Venator. *Vide* Hunter.
Versey, Sir Robert, ii. 128.
Victor, French General, i. 239.
Victoria, Queen, i. 306-309; iii. 116, 134, 135, 141, 178, 184, 188, 191, 192, 201, 226, 235.

INDEX OF PERSONS.

Ville, Sir Ralph de la, i. 191.
Villiers, Mrs., i. 232.
Vivian, General, i. 281; iii. 70, 103.
Vocat, John, ii. 211.

Wake, John, ii. 84.
Waldeve, Earl, son of Gospatrick, Earl of Dunbar. *Vide* Dunbar.
Wales, Edward Prince of. *Vide* Edward II.
—— Prince of, iii. 226.
—— Princess of, iii. 12.
Wallace (Waleys), Sir William, i. 37; ii. 23, 88-91, 93.
Walsingham, Mr. Secretary, ii. 61.
Walter, son of Allan, "dapifer" to William the Lion, i. 16, 18.
—— chaplain to William the Lion, ii. 11.
—— chaplain to Earl Waldeve, i. *inter* 12 and 13.
—— Steward of Scotland. *Vide* Scotland.
—— Jean, his daughter, first wife of Hugh, Earl of Ross. *Vide* Ross.
Ward, General, iii. 5.
Wardlaw, Robert, ii. 236.
Warrender, Lady, iii. 48.
Warrenne, Earl of. *Vide* Surrey.
Watertoun, Laird of, ii. 286.
Wauchop, Archibald, of Little Niddry, ii. 305.
Waus, John, ii. 226.
Weddale, the black priest of, ii. 9.
Wellesley, Captain, R.N., nephew of the Duke of Wellington, iii. 144.
—— Marquis of, iii. 166.

Wellington, Duke of, i. 235, 238, 240-242, 244-246, 252, 253, 260, 261, 263-269, 271, 273, 274, 276, 278, 279, 281-284, 289, 297, 301, 302, 304, 308; iii. 7, 11, 18, 23, 25, 28-30, 35, 38, 41, 42, 44-46, 48-50, 52, 53, 56, 59, 61, 64, 66, 69, 70-72, 78, 80, 83, 116, 144, 145, 191, 195, 197, 205.
Wemyss, Earl of, i. 306.
—— Sir John de, ii. 24.
—— Sir John, of Strathardill, ii. 42, 47.
—— Hon. Christiana Abernethy, his wife, ii. 42, 48.
—— William, of Craighall, i. 214.
Westmoreland, barons of, ii. 103.
Weston, John de, i. 52; ii. 173.
—— Thomas de, ii. 173.
Whang, Chinese Commissioner, i. 301; iii. 202.
Whately, Rev. Edward, ii. 157.
—— Leslie Anne Fraser, his wife, ii. 157.
White, Captain, i. 246; iii. 32.
Whitelaw, Archibald, ii. 300, 302, 305.
Whittle, Miss, iii. 214.
Wigton (Wigtown), Earls of, ii. 94.
—— John, Earl of. *Vide* Fleming.
—— Malcolm Fleming, Earl of. *Vide* Fleming.
Wilbraham, Mr., brother of first Lord Skelmersdale, i. 224.
William the Conqueror, i. 2, 9, 10; ii. 8.
—— Rufus, King, i. 10.
—— the Lion, King, i. 12, 13, 16, 18-21; ii. 10-12, 16, 17.
—— Ermengarde, his Queen, i. 20; ii. 17.

William IV., King, i. 289.
—— called Wolf, ii. 30.
Williamson, John, ii. 236.
Willingham, Colonel, iii. 75.
Wilson, Colonel, iii. 214.
—— Mrs., his wife, iii. 192, 214.
—— Dr., iii. 236-238.
—— Miss, wife of Simon Fraser of Ness Castle. *Vide* Fraser.
—— Mr., iii. 169, 211.
Winton (Wyntoun), Henry de, Governor of Forfar Castle, ii. 23.
—— the historian, i. 76, 84, 98, 101 ; ii. 8, 9, 20, 29, 86, 124, 134.
—— Thomas, ii. 278.
Wishart (Wischard, Wisheart), Adam, of Logie, ii. 50.
—— of Pittarrow, ii. 50.
—— Robert, bishop of Glasgow, ii. 98.
—— Thomas, ii. 298.
—— William, of Plenderleith, ii. 50, 52.
—— William, Chancellor, bishop of St. Andrews, ii. 19, 97.
—— Family of, ii. 50, 51.
Wisman, Sir William, i. 63.
Woburn, Captain, i. 246 ; iii. 32.

Wolstropp, Sir Oswalde, ii. 57.
Wood, Walter, of Bobigno, ii. 253, 254.
—— Mr., editor of Douglas Peerage, i. 122, 143, 148; ii. 32, 63, 129, 130, 158, 167, 175, 179.
Woodford, Colonel (afterwards Field-Marshal Sir) Alexander, i. 264.
Wynyard, Montagu, an officer Coldstream Guards, iii. 6.
—— General, iii. 163.
—— Miss, his daughter, iii. 163.

Yester, Hay, Lord, i. ix.
—— Lords of, i. 90, 192.
York, Archbishop of, i. 102; ii. 57, 84.
—— Duke of, i. 178, 193, 279 ; iii. 1, 66, 75-78.
—— barons of, ii. 103.
Young (Zonge), Dr., iii. 164.
—— John, vicar of Drone, ii. 217.
—— officer R A., iii. 224.

Zhalolok (Yhalulok), Duncan, notary, ii. 212, 217.

Index of Places.

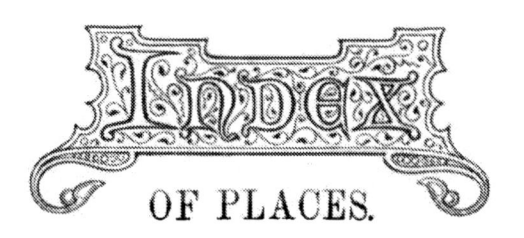

Abbeville House, near Exeter, iii. 237.
Aberbrothok. *Vide* Arbroath.
Aberbuthnot. *Vide* Arbuthnot.
Abercorn, barony of, ii. 221, 225.
Aberdeen, burgh, city, and county of, i. 57, 58, 66, 70-73, 78-81, 83, 109, 112, 113, 116, 119, 123, 125, 129, 134-137, 139, 140, 143-145, 148, 149, 153-155, 159, 172, 173, 175, 176, 178, 191, 195, 196, 198, 202, 205, 211, 213, 219, 311; ii. 17, 37, 48, 53, 59, 60, 128, 145, 153, 154, 163, 166, 180, 181, 183, 186, 187, 190, 205, 206, 209-211, 214, 215, 218-222, 225-228, 230-244, 247, 248, 254, 255, 261, 262, 269, 274, 277-280, 289-291, 293-295; iii. 7, 236.
—— Cathedral Church of, ii. 197.
—— chapter of, i. 73.
—— church of St. Nicholas, i. 109.
—— diocese of, ii. 15, 133, 185.
—— district of, i. 88.
—— King's College, i. 157, 169, 187, 189, 193.
Aberdour (Abredover), barony of, i. 122, 128, 129; ii. 220-222, 255.
Aberdour, fourscore merk land in, i. 102, 103.
—— lands of, i. 119, 167, 170; ii. 151, 226, 227, 254, 256, 259, 261, 262, 278, 279, 286.
—— lordship of, i. 119, 120; ii. 218, 219.
—— parish of, i. 114.
Abergardine, in Aboyne, ii. 45.
Aberkerdor (Aberkirder), barony of, ii. 49, 54, 63.
Aberlour, land of, ii. 64.
Abernethy, barony or lordship of, in Fife, ii. 27, 41.
—— church of, ii. 5, 6, 11, 12.
—— college of, ii. 16.
—— Culdee establishments of, ii. 5, 7, 11.
—— monastery of, ii. 1, 6.
—— round tower of, ii. 7.
—— territory of, ii. 11.
—— grange of Henry Lord, ii. 41.
—— barony of, in Rothiemay, ii. 43, 62-64, 66, 67, 70, 303-307.
—— lands and estates, i. 184, 194; ii. 70.
Abertarf, lands of, ii. 175-177.
Aboyne (Obyne), barony of, i. 81, 82; ii. 45.

INDEX OF PLACES.

Aboyne, lands of, i. 65, 82-84.
Achichdonachy, lands of, ii. 196, 197.
Achlochery (Auchleuchries), lands of, ii. 140, 294-296.
Achlun, lands of, i. 127; ii. 220.
Aden, in Arabia, i. 303; iii. 166, 212.
—— estate of, Aberdeenshire, i. 115.
Admore, ii. 8.
Adour, river, i. 244-246; iii. 24-26, 28, 29.
Adur, river, iii. 28.
Affghanistan, iii. 166, 213.
Africa, ii. 156.
Agrigentum. *Vide* Girgenti.
Aigas, island of, i. 196.
Ajen, i. 247; iii. 33.
Albania (Scotland), ii. 3.
Alduides, valley of the, iii. 19-21.
Alesick (Alesek, Elsick), lands of, i. 117; ii. 200.
Alexandria, i. 304; iii. 206, 209, 230-233.
Ali-Wann, iii. 180.
Alicata, iii. 3.
Alost, iii. 40.
Altre, lands of, ii. 173.
America, i. 277, 279; iii. 8, 34, 62, 66, 84, 166.
Amherst Rocks, i. 293; iii. 116.
Amiens (Amess), i. 145, 147.
Amoy, i. 294, 302; iii. 110, 119, 134, 144, 151, 167, 171, 209.
Anauch (Annauch, Annack, Aynachil), lands of, i. 100, 101.
—— water, i. 100.
Anestan, i. 4.
Angers, i. 203.

Anglet, i. 246; iii. 28.
Angus, district of, ii. 27.
Anjou, province of, i. 6-8, 10.
Annandale, district of, ii. 129.
—— lands in, ii. 120.
Añover, i. 240.
Antwerp, i. 236, 237, 252; iii. 6, 88-40, 43, 54.
—— cathedral of Nôtre Dame, iii. 39.
—— church of St. Jaques, iii. 39, 40.
Aran river, iii. 28.
Aranjuez, i. 239, 248.
Arauntz, iii. 26.
Aravaca, i. 240.
Arbroath (Aberbrothok), abbey of, i. 69; ii. 11, 12, 16, 26, 136, 219, 292.
—— lands of, i. 65.
—— town of, i. 70.
Arbuthnot (Aberbuthnot), thanage of, i. 78, 81, 84.
Arcangues, iii. 26, 28.
Ard (Airde), the lands and barony of, ii. 170, 172, 174-177, 230, 231.
Ardelach, lands of, ii. 220.
Ardendracht, i. 103, 131; ii. 140, 141, 180, 295, 296.
—— two towns of, ii. 293, 294.
Ardglassey, lands of, i. 113; ii. 210, 278.
—— mill of, ii. 278.
Ardlaw, lands of, i. 124, 150.
Ardlogie, i. 69, 73.
Ardmakren (Ardmuchorne), lands of, i. 113, 144; ii. 146, 210, 278.
Ardmale, lands of, ii. 49.
Argyle, district of, i. 57, 62-64, 67, 219; ii. 2, 74, 193.

Ariadne Rocks, iii. 141.
Arkelton, i. 34, 38.
Armabedy, lands of, ii. 280.
Arola, mountain of, iii. 21.
Arosa, iii. 22.
Arran, island of, i. 52.
Arringrosk, lands of, ii. 123.
Arteville, ii. 110.
Arun, river, iii. 28.
Astorga, in Leon, i. 235.
Ath, i. 253; iii. 35, 42, 43, 54.
Athelstaneford, i. 81.
Athole, ii. 191.
Auchanayouche, lands of, ii. 41.
Aucheries, estate of, i. 115.
Auchincarnie (Auchincairnie), tenement of, i. 50, 72, 95, 96; ii. 198.
Auchincloich, ii. 163.
Auchincross, lands of, i. 65.
Auchindaveris, lands of, ii. 49, 63.
Auchinmare, lands of, ii. 133.
Auchinroth shooting lodge, i. 305, 308-310; iii. 235-237.
Auchinshogill, lands of, i. 113, 116, 121, 128, 134, 140; ii. 137, 140, 141, 210, 211, 214, 215, 289, 290.
Auchintuin, lands of, i. 113; ii. 210.
Auchmacludy, lands of, i. 113; ii. 210, 220, 221.
Augusta, town of, i. 228, 229.
Auldearn, ii. 192.
Australia, iii. 157.
Awe, loch, i. 62, 63.
—— river, i. 63.
Ayr, county of, i. 101.

BADAJOS, iii. 126.
Badechale. *Vide* Bodychell.
Baden, iii. 24.
Badenoch, district of, i. 57.
Bagshot, iii. 8.
Balbrennin, lands of, ii. 10.
Balchern (Balcharn, Balcharne), lands of, i. 113; ii. 142, 204, 210.
Balchirewell, ii. 11.
Baldredestan, i. *inter* 12 and 13.
Baldwins, Kent, i. 225.
Balecolly, ii. 11.
Balfuthachy, lands of, ii. 142, 204, 205.
Balgounie, bridge of (Aberdeen), i. 134, 140; ii. 146.
—— estate of, ii. 153.
—— (Fife), ii. 160.
Ballebrochy, lands of, i. 65.
Ballinbreich (Balnebreig) (Fife), lands of, ii. 16, 27.
Ballintraille, lands of, ii. 133.
Ballintrey, lands of, ii. 21.
Balmadethyn, lands of, ii. 10.
Balmariot, lands of, ii. 138.
Balmerino (Balmurenach), lands of, ii. 17.
—— monastery of, ii. 17.
Balnedan, lands of, ii. 17.
Balnedard, lands of, ii. 17.
Baltrody, lands of, ii. 21.
Balvenie, barony, estate, or lands of, i. 185-187, 189; ii. 64, 66.
Balvraid, ii. 230.
Bamborough Castle (Brembre), i. 37.
Banca, straits of, iii. 104.

Banff, county of, i. 57, 109, 116, 122, 128, 143, 148, 149, 159, 175, 185, 198, 211, 219, 226, 313; ii. 30, 31, 37, 41, 43, 49, 50, 53, 63, 133, 157, 180, 224-226, 239, 241, 247, 248, 254, 262, 279, 287, 288, 296, 299, 301, 303, 304, 306.
—— kirk of, ii. 251, 252.
—— town of, i. 148; ii. 166, 245, 251, 287.
Bankwall, lands of, ii. 278, 286.
Bannockburn, battle of, I. xi, 67, 102; ii. 128, 158.
Barrie (Barre), lands of, ii. 41, 162.
Barriere de Roule, i. 279, 280; iii. 66, 67.
Barrosa, battle of, i. 237, 238.
Bastan, valley of, iii. 21.
Bath, iii. 102, 105, 128, 138, 146, 159, 164, 175, 236, 237.
Battersea, iii. 88.
Battle Abbey, monastery of, i. 8.
Batz, Fort, i. 236; iii. 6.
Bautzen, iii. 103.
Bavay, i. 271; iii. 58.
Bayonne, i. 244-247; iii. 23, 24, 28-30, 33, 41, 42.
—— Citadel of, i. 246.
Beaucotte, iii. 29.
Beauly, priory of, i. 132, 171.
—— river, i. 196; ii. 170, 172.
—— town of, i. 196.
Belcors, lands of, i. 123.
Belgium, i. 252; iii. 51.
Belhelvie (Balhelvy), i. 198.
—— Berclay, ii. 294, 295.
—— -Boneville, lands of, ii. 140, 293, 294.
Beltun, i. *inter* 12 and 13.

Beluch, lands of, ii. 11.
Ben Cruachan, i. 62.
Bengal, iii. 125, 126, 130, 131, 137, 149, 155, 157, 164, 210.
Benzietown (Bounzeltoun), i. 170, 171; ii. 278.
Bergen-op-Zoom, i. 252; iii. 6, 12, 38, 40.
Bernera, island of, ii. 74.
Berwick, Castle of, i. 37, 68; ii. 82.
—— shire, i. 57, 71, 306; ii. 28, 30, 43, 53, 63, 95, 123, 173, 299, 301, 303, 304, 306; iii. 114.
—— town of, i. 37, 38, 44, 68, 70; ii. 56, 81-83, 85, 86, 114, 117, 118, 122, 158, 165.
Beveland, South, island of, i. 236; iii. 6.
Biarritz, iii. 28.
Bickleigh Down, i. 228.
Bidart, i. 244; iii. 23, 26.
Bidassoa river, i. 243; iii. 15, 17, 18, 20.
Bidouse river, iii. 28.
Biggar, ii. 86.
Bilboa, iii. 5, 16.
Binche, i. 271; iii. 58.
Bintang, island of, iii. 104.
Blackheath, i. 234.
Blackwall passage, iii. 116.
Blair Mormond, lands of, i. 150.
Blaktoun, lands of, i. 113, 123; ii. 210, 286.
Blaretoune, lands and tenandry of, ii. 140, 294.
Bledelaw (Bledlow), i. 5.
Bodychell (Badechale), lands of, ii. 278.
—— mill of, i. 124, 150, 220, 221.
Bogheid, lands of, ii. 278, 286.

Bois de Bossu, i. 254, 255, 270; iii. 58.
Bois de Boulogne, i. 278, 280; iii. 65, 67.
Bolden, lands of, ii. 96.
Bombay, iii. 108, 121, 134, 148, 149, 151, 154, 155, 157, 160, 165, 166, 168, 169, 173, 174, 176, 178, 179, 181, 182, 185, 186, 189, 195, 196, 204-206, 208, 209, 212, 214, 215, 217, 218, 220, 222, 224-227, 229-232.
Bonavista, island of, iii. 89.
Bonn, iii. 210.
Bordeaux, i. 203, 246, 247; iii. 23, 32, 33.
Bordlands, lands of, ii. 41.
Borlum, lands of, i. 210.
Borneo, island of, iii. 212, 214, 217.
Borthwick, barony of, i. 150.
Borthwickshiels, ii. 159.
Bothkyl, i. *inter* 12 and 13.
Bothwell, i. 57; ii. 187.
Botriphnie, lands of, ii. 64.
Boulogne, ii. 25; iii. 67.
Bounzeltoun. *Vide* Benzietown.
Bourget (Bourjet), le, i. 277, 278; iii. 63, 65, 70.
Bourtry, i. 84.
Boussiers, i. 273; iii. 59.
Braine-le-Comte, i. 253, 254, 270; iii. 54, 58.
Braklawmoir, lands of, i. 113; ii. 210.
Brakours, the two, i. 113; ii. 210.
Bramby Moor Inn, i. 288.
Branbridge, ii. 156.
Brancepeth, i. 117.
Brazil, i. 233, 234; iii. 94.

Brechin, castle of, ii. 24, 59.
—— Culdee establishment at, ii. 5.
—— round tower at, ii. 7.
—— town of, ii. 59.
Breky, Easter, lands of, ii. 171.
Brembre. *Vide* Bamborough.
Bremlaw, lands of, ii. 279.
Briggham, i. 32, 35, 110; ii. 76, 100, 112, 113.
Brighton, i. 251; iii. 27, 29.
Britain, Great, i. 2, 7, 10, 26, 208, 220, 222-224; ii. 2, 93; iii. 22, 202.
—— North, i. 200.
Broadland, ii. 157.
Broadsea (Braidsea), lands of, i. 170, 304.
—— seatown of, i. 304.
—— tower of, ii. 276, 277.
Brokeiston. *Vide* Utlaw, New.
Bromley, iii. 234.
Brompton, iii. 13.
Brotherton, lands of, ii. 128, 131.
Brounmoldy, lands of, ii. 133.
Brucklay, estate of, i. 115.
Bruges, i. 252; iii. 35.
Brunswick, iii. 45, 53.
Brussels, i. 253, 257, 258, 269; iii. 35, 36, 38, 40, 42, 43, 45, 48, 52-54, 56.
Bruxie, lands of, ii. 278.
Bruyere, Le Grand, iii. 51.
Buchan, district of, i. 61, 79, 114-116, 221; ii. 192, 193, 208, 209, 222, 232, 289, 291.
—— earldom of, i. 110, 111, 113, 115; ii. 145, 214, 217, 234, 235, 293.
Buckingham, county of, i. 5.
—— Palace, i. 307.

Bulgeny (Bulgny), Middle, lands of, i. 127; ii. 220, 221.
—— mill of, ii. 220, 221.
—— Nether, lands of, i. 127; ii. 220, 221.
—— Over, lands of, i. 127; ii. 220, 221.
Bunchrew, wood of, i. 196.
Burgh-on-Sands, i. 55.
Burgos, i. 235, 240.
Burgundy, iii. 186.
Byrnes (Birnes), lands of, ii. 162.
Byth (Beth), lands of, i. 132, 136, 139, 141; ii. 232-234.

CABUL, iii. 158, 164.
Cadiz, i. 237-239, 248; iii. 7, 84, 86, 88, 103, 118.
Cadzow (Hamilton), ii. 97.
Cairnbulg, castle of, i. 114, 151, 163, 183.
—— lands of, i. 113, 145, 146, 149, 162, 163, 170, 181-183, 205; ii. 144, 210, 278, 286.
—— Point, i. 153.
Cairness, lands of, i. 205.
—— mansion of, i. 115.
Cairney, lands of, ii. 27.
Cairo, i. 303, 304; iii. 230.
Caithness (Catania), district of, i. 175; ii. 125-127, 129, 164.
—— estates in, i. 50.
—— lands in, i. 44-47, 50, 66.
Calabria, Upper, i. 230.
Calais, i. 101; iii. 68.
Calata Girone, iii. 2.

Calcutta, i. 303; iii. 105, 121, 122, 146, 154, 161, 165-167, 177, 182, 188, 194, 196, 203, 206, 221, 225, 229-232.
Callao, iii. 91.
Calvary, Mount, iii. 40.
Cambestone, lands of, ii. 137.
Cambov, Moor of, ii. 198.
Cambray, i. 283.
Cambridgeshire, i. 5.
Canada, iii. 78, 80.
Canton, i. 302; iii. 150, 155-160, 162, 164, 166, 169, 171, 177, 180, 181, 183, 184, 188, 189, 194, 196-199, 202, 203, 207-209, 214-218, 222, 226.
Can-si-Ming, iii. 130.
Cantonment Hill, Hong-Kong, i. 298; iii. 167.
Cape of Good Hope, i. 292; iii. 90, 95-97, 99, 102, 104, 105, 107, 124, 136, 138, 144.
Cape de Verd Islands, iii. 87, 89, 93.
Cardenye, lands of, i. 72, 82.
Cardno, lands of, i. 210.
Carham-on-Tweed, i. 35; ii. 78.
Carlaverock Castle, ii. 84, 95.
Carlisle, i. 7, 55, 117, 179; ii. 82, 187-190.
Carneglas, lands of, ii. 280.
Carnemure, lands of, ii. 278.
Carnoustie, lands of, ii. 137.
Carrick, district of, i. 52; ii. 183, 185-187, 189, 194.
Carrickfergus, battle at, i. 69.
Carrion, valley of the, i. 235.
Cartmyris, lands of, ii. 279, 281, 282.

INDEX OF PLACES.

Caskiben, estate of, ii. 286.
Castellega, i. 239.
Castille, province of, iii. 7.
Castor, temple of, at Girgenti, iii. 4.
Catalonia, province of, iii. 30.
Catania, in Sicily, i. 228, 229; iii. 1, 2, 4.
Cateau (le Cateau Cambresis), i. 273; iii. 59, 60.
Caulaincourt (Coulaincourt), i. 275; iii. 60.
Caza Gardens, Macao, iii. 201.
Ceuta, i. 233.
Ceylon, i. 303; iii. 181, 182, 229.
Chamberlain Newton, feu of, ii. 19, 27.
Changhai. *Vide* Shanghai.
Chapelle, la, i. 277; iii. 63.
Chapoo, i. 293, 294; iii. 110, 115, 119.
Charleroi, i. 257, 269; iii. 54.
Chatham, i. 236.
Chester Castle, ii. 156.
Chiclana, i. 238.
China, i. 290-292, 294, 296, 300, 304, 305; iii. 83, 89, 94, 99-101, 104, 108, 119, 121, 123, 126, 143, 148, 150, 153, 156, 175, 177, 185, 191, 195, 199, 203, 232.
Chinghai, i. 294; iii. 119, 134, 142.
Chin-kiang-foo, i. 295, 296, 300; iii. 124-127, 129, 130, 133, 137, 139, 140, 206.
Choissi (Choisi), i. 277; iii. 61, 63.
Chuck-Choo, i. 298; iii. 149, 163, 167, 169, 180, 183, 188-190, 192, 202, 206, 212, 215, 216, 221, 222.
Chuk-Pi-Wann, iii. 172, 178-180.
Chuk-Wann, iii. 179, 180.

Chusan (Thusan), i. 294, 299, 300; iii. 113, 114, 116, 119, 133, 134, 141-143, 146, 148, 149, 151, 153, 159, 167, 171, 186, 192, 195, 198, 207, 221, 223, 225.
Cien Pozuelos, i. 240.
Cintra, i. 241; iii. 10.
Ciudad Rodrigo, i. 240.
Clackmannan, county of, ii. 124.
——— manor of, ii. 24.
Clevedon, iii. 234.
Clogstone, barony of, i. 120.
Closerath, lands of, i. 120.
Cluny, barony of (Aberdeen), i. 72, 82; ii. 133.
——— lands of, i. 82.
Clydesdale (Strathclyde), i. 80; ii. 20.
Coburty, lands of, i. 149, 150; ii. 278.
Cocherel, i. 117.
Coignafearn, i. 284, 305; iii. 207.
Colansoo, near Amoy, iii. 134, 144, 207.
Colbanston, tenement of, i. 44; ii. 20.
Coldinghame, i. 13, 18, 23.
Coldstream, i. 306.
Collie. *Vide* Cowie.
Cologne, iii. 210.
Colynstoun, lands of, ii. 140, 294.
Compeigne, abbey of, ii. 150.
——— town of, i. 277; iii. 62.
Concord, temple of, at Girgenti, iii. 4.
Connaught Place. *Vide* London.
Constantia, Cape of Good Hope, iii. 101.
Constantinople, iii. 96.
Contessa, i. 229, 230.
Conveth, i. 66.
Copenhagen, i. 224.

Cork, i. 213.
Corncairn, barony of, ii. 42, 43, 52, 62, 66, 69, 164, 301, 303, 304, 306, 307.
Cornetoun, lands and estate of, i. 52, 97; ii. 165, 166.
Corskie (Quorsque), lands of, ii. 49, 53, 62.
Corteby, lands of, ii. 17.
Cortes, mansion of, i. 115.
Corunna, i. 235, 236; iii. 5, 47, 103.
Couchy, iii. 62.
Coulaincourt. *Vide* Caulaincourt.
Countryhills (Fife), ii. 27.
Cowie, barony of, i. 108, 117, 121, 122, 124; ii. 142, 143, 180, 196, 200-205, 289, 290.
—— estate of, i. 93-96, 124, 129.
—— forest of, i. 51, 73, 74, 77, 81, 95-97, 106, 107; ii. 199.
—— thanage of, i. 51, 73, 77, 92, 93, 95-97, 100, 101, 103, 104, 106-108; ii. 196, 199.
Cowlie, lands of, i. 150.
Craigellie, ii. 155.
Craighouse, Lothianburn, i. viii.
Craigie, forest of. *Vide* Cowie.
Craiginning Glasculloche, i. 73, 97.
Craigs or Cragy, lands of, ii. 48.
Crawford Priory, i. 85.
Crechie, lands of, i. 167; ii. 151.
Crechyrosy, lands of, ii. 133.
Crekiltoun. *Vide* Kregiltoun.
Cressy, iii. 61.
Crey, estate of, i. 43; ii. 107.
Crichie, Meikle, estate of, i. 150.

Crimond, church of, i. 153, 154; ii. 255, 259, 260, 263, 265, 279, 280, 282.
—— park of, i. 150.
Crimonmogate, mansion of, i. 115.
Cristoun, lands of, ii. 121.
Cromby, lands of, ii. 53, 286.
Culbreny, lands of, ii. 239.
Culburty, lands of, i. 122, 127; ii. 220, 221, 225, 278.
Culcoak, lands of, i. 127; ii. 220, 221.
Culmesty, lands of, ii. 137.
Culpressache, lands of, i. 65.
Cultram (Cultran), church of, ii. 11.
—— lands of, ii. 17.
Cumberland, county of, i. 9; ii. 103.
Cumnock, i. 55; ii. 186-190.
Cunningham (Conynghame), barony of, i. 101.
—— district of, i. 100; ii. 187, 190.
Cupar, castle of, i. 64.
—— monastery of, ii. 19.
—— town of, i. 64.
Cupermaculty, lands of, ii. 137.

Dalcross, lands of, ii. 230.
Dalders, lands of, ii. 43, 52, 299, 301, 303, 304, 306, 307.
Dalgarnock, ii. 189.
Dalkeith, castle of, i. 117.
—— town of, ii. 55.
Dalriada, kingdom of, ii. 2-4.
Daltilichs, the two, ii. 230.
Dalton, ii. 173.
Dartmouth House, Blackheath, i. 234.

Deer, bridge of, ii. 147.
Delgady (Dalgedy, Dalgetty, Dalgathy, Delgattie), lands of, i. 113, 116, 121, 128, 134, 140; ii. 43, 63, 139, 141, 210, 289-291, 299, 301, 303, 304, 306.
Dendermonde, iii. 40.
Denend, half of, i. 151, 152, 157, 162; ii. 146, 255, 257, 259, 261, 280.
Denmark, i. 158.
Derby, county of, i. 4; iii. 28.
Desolation, island of, iii. 102.
Deveron (Doverne), valley of the, i. 116; ii. 139.
―― water of, ii. 248, 255, 256, 259, 279.
Devonshire, iii. 236.
Dingwall, ii. 235.
―― castle of, ii. 240.
Dives, church of, Normandy, i. 8.
Dolbethok, lands of, ii. 14, 15.
Don, river, i. 134.
Donaldston, ii. 173.
Doncaster, ii. 99.
Donibristle (Dynnibirsell), house of, i. 159.
Douglas Castle, ii. 20, 29, 186, 187, 189, 190.
Douglasdale, ii. 186.
Doune, in Menteith, ii. 237.
Douro, river, i. 242.
Doveransyd (Dovernsyid), i. 146; ii. 249.
Downie, Castle, i. 196.
―― lands of, in Angus, ii. 27.
Downs, the, i. 228.
Drem, chapel and lands at, i. 17.
―― estate of, i. 17, 22.

Dremes-sheles, i. 22.
Dripp, or Dripps, in Stirlingshire, lands of, i. 42, 50, 52, 82-84; ii. 23, 25.
Dron, chapel of, ii. 11.
Drumalban, ii. 2.
Drumblait, parish of, ii, 187.
Drumdowle, lands of, i. 120.
Drumelzier, i. 28, 30-32; ii. 79, 117, 118, 123.
Drumquhendill, lands of, i. 113; ii. 220.
―― Little, i. 119; ii. 210, 222, 223, 279, 286.
―― Meikle, ii. 210.
Dryburgh, abbey of, i. 73, 220, 221, 223; ii. 29-32.
Dublin, iii. 78, 128.
Duffus, lands of, i. 45, 66.
Dulmernak, lands of, ii. 137.
Dumbarton, i. 67.
Dumfries, county of, i. 34, 37, 38, 71, 112, 113; ii. 206.
―― town of, i. 57; ii. 189.
Dunbar, i. 177, 180; ii. 56, 57, 80, 109.
Dunboig, lands of, ii. 27.
Dunbulc̄, chapel of, ii. 11.
Dundarg, castle of, i. 78.
Dundee, i. 99; ii. 24, 286.
Dundonald, ii. 218.
Dunfermline, abbey of, i. 110.
Dunkeld, church of, ii. 3, 6.
Dunkirk, iii. 53.
Dunmanin, church of, ii. 122.
Dunnottar, castle of, i. 85, 88.
―― estate of, i. 88.
―― lands of, i. 84, 85, 88.
Dunse, i. 306.

Dunse, Nesbit House at, i. 290.
Dunstaffnage, castle of, i. 63; ii. 193.
Dupplin, i. 75-77, 98, 100, 107; ii. 26, 129.
Durada, i. 242; iii. 13.
Durham, i. 15, 33, 34, 79, 101, 102, 104, 107, 109, 111, 117; ii. 16, 17, 31, 32, 85, 39, 123, 130, 131.
—— county of, i. 9.
Durris, forest of, i. 73, 95.
—— lands and barony of, i. 93, 94, 103, 106-109, 116, 120, 124; ii. 139, 141-144, 180, 196, 200, 201, 204, 205.
—— thanage of, i. 97, 98, 100, 101, 103, 104, 106, 107, 116; ii. 200.
—— castle of Mount, i. 106; ii. 139, 289.
Dyle, river, iii. 104.

Ebro, river, iii. 5.
Echallar, pass of, iii. 20.
Edane, town of, i. 123.
Eddirstone, lands of, Northumberland, i. 38.
Edinburgh, Advocates' Library, i. xii.
—— castle of, i. 98, 99; ii. 61, 81-83, 130, 164.
—— county of, i. 52, 71; ii. 30, 236, 250, 299, 301, 303, 304, 306.
—— General Register House, i. xii, 70.
—— garrison of, i. 57.
—— town of, i. viii, 7, 146, 148, 152, 155, 164, 171, 173, 176, 177, 179, 183, 191, 201, 208, 215, 216, 218, 221, 288; ii. 19, 40, 43, 57, 60, 61, 63, 65, 71, 159, 200, 209, 221-223, 236, 237, 246, 256, 262, 269, 287, 299-301, 305; iii. 236.
Edrigford, ii. 187, 190.
Egham, iii. 8.
Eglinton, iii. 102.
Eglismenythok, lands of, ii. 13, 15.
Egypt, iii. 137.
Elba, i. 251.
Elgin, i. 66; ii. 170, 238, 297; iii. 236.
Elihok (Elcho), i. 111.
Ellon, ii. 162.
Enghien, i. 252, 253; iii. 35, 44, 46, 48, 54, 55.
Ennerurie. *Vide* Inverurie.
Erne (Earne), river, i. 75.
Erolyn (Erroll), chapel of, ii. 11.
Esculapius, temple of, iii. 4.
Escurial, The, i. 240.
Eskidels, Wester, ii. 230.
Eskyltuh. *Vide* Essintuly.
Eslingoloh, i. *inter* 12 and 13.
Espinar, i. 240.
Esse, lands of, ii. 170-172.
Essick, i. 195.
Essintuly (Essuly, Eskyltuh), lands of, i. 65, 97, 100.
—— Wester, lands of, i. 103, 106, 116; ii. 139, 289.
Estspot, lands of, ii. 123.
Etna, Mount, i. 228, 229.
Eton, i. 227.
Europe, i. 9, 203, 223, 251; iii. 14, 15, 32, 46, 47, 95, 177, 221.

Ewnysedale, i. 79.
Exeter, iii. 237.

FAITHLIE, burgh of (*vide* also Fraserburgh), i. 149, 152-154; ii. 263, 265, 266, 269, 281, 282.
—— lands of, i. 141, 143, 149, 170; ii. 237-243, 255-257, 259, 261-263, 279, 280.
—— port or harbour of, i. 149, 154; ii. 255, 256, 259, 262, 279-282.
—— village of, i. 115, 149.
Falkirk, battle of, ii. 90, 136.
Falkland, ii. 203.
Falmouth, i. 241; iii. 8, 9, 11, 15, 26, 196.
Faryndonalde (Ferdonald), lands of, i. 113; ii. 210, 214, 215.
Fatteheid (Fetyhede, Forttieheid), lands of, i. 142; ii. 241-243, 247, 279.
Faudon, ii. 96.
Fayrelehope, lands of, ii. 171.
Fern (Fearn), abbey of, i. 110.
Fernell (Fernel), i. 93, 94; ii. 117.
Fetteresso, i. 88.
Fife, county of, i. 42, 47, 52, 64, 65, 71, 75, 88, 179, 193, 211; ii. 30, 41, 43, 98, 101, 126, 236, 299, 301, 303, 304, 306.
—— earldom of, i. 43; ii. 99, 107, 108.
—— House, iii. 74, 77.
Finellan House, i. 196.
Fingask (Feingyeask), ii. 178, 272.
Fintrie, Meikle, lands of, i. 113, 123; ii. 210, 214, 215.
Flanders, i. 37, 41, 47; iii. 186.

Fleurus, i. 270; iii. 58.
Flisk, church of, ii. 11.
Flodden, battle of, i. 142, 148; ii. 49.
Flushing, i. 236.
Fochabers, i. 308, 309.
Foghou (Fogo), church of, i. 22.
—— estate of, i. 15; ii. 120.
Fonte-viros, i. 240.
Fordoue, lands of, ii. 137.
Forfaldis, lands of, ii. 241-243, 248, 279.
Forfar, castle of, ii. 23.
—— county of, i. 57, 61, 65, 71, 79, 93, 94, 211; ii. 21, 35, 37, 43, 52, 63, 157, 160, 171, 172, 174, 193, 230, 232, 299, 301, 303, 306.
—— Platan of, The, ii. 209.
—— town of, ii. 19.
Forgie, i. 173.
Forglen, lands of, i. 103, 116, 131; ii. 140, 180, 291-294.
Formosa, island of, iii. 113, 178.
Forn, water of, ii. 170, 172.
Fornathy, lands of, ii. 14.
Forres, ii. 164.
Forteviot, ii. 6, 7.
Forth, Firth of, i. 22, 99, 105, 177, 211; ii. 106.
—— river, i. 133, 179; ii. 22-25, 98.
Forton, East, lands of, i. 19.
—— lands of, East Lothian, i. 19, 20, 31.
—— West, lands of, i. 21.
Fortrie of Innerrowrie, lands of, ii. 147, 255, 256, 259, 261, 279.
Fort William, ii. 157.
Foudland Hills, i. 59.
Fourgy, lands of, ii. 123.

France, i. 1, 7, 37, 77, 142, 145, 147, 198, 213, 220, 246, 265, 269, 280, 285; ii. 20, 94, 109, 110, 130, 173; iii. 18, 19, 21, 22, 24, 25, 27, 30, 38, 45, 47, 49, 51, 56, 68, 70, 88, 156.
Frankfort, iii. 24.
Fraserburgh (*vide* also Faithlie), bay of, i. 114.
—— castle and lighthouse of, i. 152, 155, 162, 164, 165, 190.
—— kirk of, i. 165, 190, 198.
—— parish of, i. 114.
—— port or harbour of, i. 154, 155; ii. 259, 261, 263, 266, 267, 270-273, 279-282.
—— regality of, i. 154, 155, 171.
—— Saltoun Arms Hotel, i. 305.
—— town of, i. vii, 115, 141, 149, 154-156, 161, 166, 170, 171, 174, 183, 189, 190, 198, 202, 203, 215, 217, 226, 234, 289, 304, 305, 311; ii. 6, 155, 257, 259-261, 263, 265-277, 279, 281, 282, 286; iii. 34.
—— University and Colleges of, i. 154, 155; ii. 263, 265, 268, 279-283.
Fraserfield, estate of, ii. 153-155.
Frendraught, barony of, ii. 137.
—— place, and lands of, ii. 54, 135, 136.
Frézelière, Seigneurie of, i. 6, 7, 10.
Frio, Cape, iii. 94.
Frosterseit, lands of, ii. 63.
Fruid, lands of, ii. 118, 119.
Fuentes d'Honore, i. 240.
Fynletor, lands of, ii. 239.
Fyvie, castle of, i. 84; ii. 140, 183.
—— King's park at, i. 69.
—— lands of, i. 73.

GAIRNTULLY, i. 143.
Gallegos, i. 240.
Galloway, i. 55, 56, 61, 64, 127; ii. 180, 186, 187, 189-191, 194.
—— lordship of, ii. 214, 217.
—— tenandries in, i. 118.
Galston (Gawlistone), ii. 187.
Garonne, river, i. 247; iii. 33.
Garvocks (Garuocis), lands of, i. 65.
Gascony, i. 35; ii. 78, 99; iii. 28.
Germany, i. 178.
Ghent, i. 252; ii. 81; iii. 35, 36, 43.
Gibraltar, i. 209; ii. 156; iii. 47.
Gight, castle of, i. 172.
Gillecameston, lands of, ii. 16.
Girgenti, i. 233; iii. 3, 4.
Glasgow, i. 172, 221; ii. 82; iii. 150.
—— kirk of, i. 88.
Glaslach, lands of, i. 127; ii. 220, 221.
Glencorse, 20 merk land of, ii. 19.
—— barony of, ii. 43, 49, 63, 67, 70, 299, 301, 303, 304, 306, 307.
—— estate of, ii. 28.
Glen-Dochart, i. 62.
Glendroggyn, lands of, ii. 10.
Glenelg, lands of, ii. 175-177, 230.
Glenmuick, lands of, i. 82.
Glenrustok, lands of, ii. 94.
Glensauche, Little, lands of, ii. 137.
Glentanner, lands of, i. 82.
Glentruell, ii. 187, 188, 190.
Gloucestershire, i. 4.
Golden Island, iii. 124, 128, 140.
Gomez, Villa Nueva de, i. 240.
Gonesse, i. 277; iii. 63.

INDEX OF PLACES.

Gordon Castle, i. 219.
—— district of, ii. 95.
—— lordship of, i. 82.
Gough's Island, iii. 114.
Gourmignies, i. 270, 273; iii. 57, 59.
Grammont, iii. 42, 46, 48, 54.
Grampian Mountains, The, i. 57, 64; ii. 184, 185, 187, 191.
Grand-Bruyere, le, ii. 51.
Gravesend, iii. 165.
Great Cumberland Street. *Vide* London.
Great George Street. *Vide* London.
Greenlaw, lands of, ii. 241-243, 247.
Greenwich, meridian of, iii. 96, 98.
Green Street. *Vide* London.
Grosvenor Street. *Vide* London.
Gunstatt Rock, iii. 116.
Gushachan, ii. 230.

HADDINGTON, Constabulary of, ii. 164, 250, 297-299, 301, 303, 304, 306.
—— shire, ii. 43.
—— town of, ii. 56.
Hague, The, iii. 52.
Hainan Island, iii. 113.
Hal, iii. 35, 54.
Haldeyhardsted, lands of, ii. 79.
Hales (Hale), lands of (East Lothian), i. 15, 26-30; ii. 116.
—— North, i. 19, 21, 24, 29-31; ii. 116.
—— South, i. 29; ii. 116.
Halidon Hill, i. 49, 77, 98, 100, 111; ii. 31, 118, 124, 129, 130, 134, 136, 168-170, 181.
Hamer Hall, ii. 156.

Hampshire, iii. 25.
Hanover, ii. 156.
Harlaw, battle of, i. 123, 124, 133; ii. 37-40, 51.
Harrow, i. 312.
Hasparen, iii. 28.
Hautain Caroll, i. 254.
Havre, i. 277; iii. 62.
Hawthornden, castle of, ii. 159.
Hebrides (Western Isles), i. 67; ii. 36, 47.
Hercules, temple of, at Girgenti, iii. 4.
Hesilyard, lands of, ii. 79.
Highlands, The, i. 195; ii. 155, 167, 194; iii. 172.
—— Western, i. 57; ii. 193.
Hill, The, iii. 102, 161, 221.
Holland, i. 236; iii. 27, 31, 54.
Holy Land, The, ii. 160.
Holyroodhouse (Halyruidhous), i. 21, 157, 158, 208; ii. 72, 263, 269.
—— chapel, i. 288.
Home, lands of, i. 15.
Homildon, battle of, ii. 34.
Honan Island, iii. 199.
Honemener, lands of, ii. 94.
Hong-Kong, i. 292, 293, 296, 297, 299, 301, 303; iii. 105-109, 111-114, 118, 134, 136, 137, 139, 144-146, 148, 151, 154, 155, 159, 161, 164, 166, 168, 175, 176, 179, 180, 182, 183, 185, 189, 191, 193, 196, 197, 202-204, 207, 209, 215, 216, 218, 219, 222, 224, 226, 229-231, 233.
—— Little, iii. 171, 172.
Hopcartane, lands of, ii. 79.

Hopkelchock, lands of, i. 25; ii. 121.
Hopprew (Hoprewe), lands of, i. 27; ii. 79, 88, 94.
Hougomont, château and orchard of, i. 253, 258-261, 263-266, 268, 269; iii. 78, 79, 81.
Hove, i. 252, 254, 270; iii. 36-39, 41, 44-46, 48, 50, 51, 53, 55, 57, 58.
Huelva, i. 239, 240.
Humber, river, i. 9.
Humbie, parish of, i. 12.
Huntly, barony of, i. 82-84.
—— earldom of, i. 82-84.

Inchetomoch, place of, ii. 46.
Inchkeith, island of, i. 99.
India, i. 290, 296, 297; ii. 157; iii. 100, 104, 106, 122, 128, 145, 147, 150-152, 154-157, 160, 163, 166, 174, 177, 179, 196, 205, 206, 208, 214, 221, 222, 226.
Indies, West, i. 206, 210; iii. 205.
Ingolfhiston, i. 25.
—— Chapel of St. Mary of, i. 25.
Innernethy, ii. 11.
Innerwic, i. *inter* 12 and 13.
Inverallochy, ii. 246.
—— lands and barony of, i. 113, 148, 154, 162, 182; ii. 147, 181, 210, 255-257, 259, 261, 279.
Inverbervie, i. 100; ii. 128.
Inverleith, lands of, ii. 75.
Inverlethan, town of, i. 25.
Invernairn, lands in, ii. 177.
Inverness, castle of, ii. 183, 191.
Inverness, county of, i. 113, 175, 209, 211, 284; ii. 119, 125, 132, 172, 174, 176, 210, 214, 230, 232; iii. 207.
—— district of, i. 60, 127; ii. 180, 191, 192.
—— town of, i. vii, 57, 61, 64, 139, 195, 196, 210; ii. 2, 36, 42, 58, 127, 170, 171, 177, 184, 186, 189-192, 194, 209, 301, 302.
Invernorth, lands of, i. 162, 170, 182, 205; ii. 278.
Inverury (Ennerurie), i. 58-62, 78; ii. 147, 187, 188, 191, 193, 194.
—— battle of, i. 60, 61; ii. 183-185, 192, 193.
Iona, island of, ii. 2.
Ipswich, i. 275.
Ireland, i. 67, 69, 157, 178, 212, 222; ii. 2, 3, 7; iii. 80, 220, 227.
Irun, i. 242; iii. 13, 15, 16, 18, 20.
Irvine river, i. 100.
Italy, iii. 5, 38, 52.

Jamaica, ii. 156.
Jarama, river, i. 240.
Java, iii. 105.
—— Head, iii. 98, 104, 105.
Jedburgh, St. Mary's Church of, ii. 122.
Jersey (Jarsey), i. 178.
Juno Lucina, temple of, at Girgenti, iii. 4.
Jupiter Olympius, temple of, at Girgenti, i. 233; iii. 3.
Just-in-the-Way Island, iii. 114.

INDEX OF PLACES.

KAERMERDIN, castle of, i. 4.
Keith, church of (Aberdeenshire), ii. 53, 54, 62, 64.
—— church of (East Lothian), i. 12.
Keith-Hervey, district of, i. 12.
Keith-Hundeby, district of, i. 12.
Keith-Marshall, district of, i. 12.
Keith-Simon, district of, i. 12.
Kellie, castle of (Aberdeenshire), i. 172.
Kelso, i. 12, 13.
—— abbey of, ii. 11, 95, 96.
Kenmure, i. 161.
Kensington, iii. 74, 78.
Kent, county of, i. 209, 225.
Kerpul, ii. 11.
Kian-Kong, iii. 125.
Kian-Shan. *Vide* Golden Island.
Kildrummy (Kildrumie, Kildromie, Kyndromie), castle of, i. 67, 110; ii. 185, 224.
Kilravock, estate of, ii. 172.
Kiltarlity (Kyntallergy), ii. 170-172.
Kinbog, lands of, i. 113; ii. 210, 278.
Kincardine, i. 129; ii. 203.
—— county of, i. 57, 61, 65, 71, 73, 79, 97, 100, 108, 129, 159, 211; ii. 37, 126, 128, 137, 142, 193, 200, 202, 204, 205, 289, 290.
—— O'Neil, ii. 59.
—— royal manor of, i. 72; ii. 196-198.
—— thanage of, i. 72; ii. 199.
Kinchyle, lands of, i. 210.
Kindrocht, half of, i. 151, 152, 157, 162; ii. 146, 255, 257, 259, 261, 280.
Kinfauns, iii. 95.

Kingedward (Kynedwart, Kynnedor), barony of, i. 123, 125, 132, 139, 141; ii. 233, 234, 237-240, 255, 262.
—— Miltoun of, i. 123.
—— tenement of, ii. 232.
Kinghorn, i. 202; ii. 22, 98.
—— royal manor of, ii. 160.
Kingildore, lands of, ii. 79.
Kinglasser (Kinglassie), lands of, i. 113, 150; ii. 210, 278.
Kinmundy, lands of, ii. 166.
Kinnaird Head, i. 115, 153, 155, 170, 205.
—— castle of. *Vide* Fraserburgh, castle of.
Kinnaltie (Kynyaultie, Kynaltie), lands of, ii. 35, 160.
Kinnarde, barony of, i. 72.
Kinnell, barony and estate of, i. 130; ii. 171, 172, 174, 176, 230-232.
Kinrara, i. 234, 285.
Kinross, county of, i. 211.
—— town of, i. 72, 211; ii. 18, 199.
Kintore, burgh of, ii. 153.
Kintyre, lordship of, i. 133.
Kirkcudbright, stewartry of, i. 161.
Kirkham, ii. 80.
Kirkintilloch, ii. 85.
Kirkomyr, ii. 230.
Kirkton, lands of. *Vide* Philorth, kirktoun of.
Kirkton Tyrie. *Vide* Tyrie.
Kirpool, lands of, ii. 21.
Knockorthie, lands of, ii. 49, 62.
Kregiltoun, castle of, i. 113; ii. 210.
—— lands and barony of, i. 113; ii. 210, 214, 215.

VOL. III.

Kyle, district of, ii. 187, 190.
Kynclonyes, lands of the two, ii. 142, 204.

LA BELLE ALLIANCE, i. 266, 268, 269.
La Haye Sainte, i. 266.
Ladrone Islands, iii. 107, 108.
Ladykirk, mansion of, i. 306.
Lambyrton, manor of, ii. 158.
Lammermoor, i. *inter* 12 and 13.
Lanark, county of, i. 71; ii. 30, 118.
Lancashire, i. 179; ii. 103, 156.
Langholm, parish of, i. 34.
—— town of, ii. 117.
Langside, ii. 58.
Laon, iii. 59.
Lauderdale, bailiary of, ii. 303, 304, 306.
—— lordship of, ii. 29, 31, 299, 301.
Lavajos, i. 240.
Lees, house of, i. 306; iii. 233.
Leicester Fields, iii. 8.
—— shire, i. 288.
Leinach, lands of, ii. 230.
Leipsic, iii. 43.
Leis, the three, ii. 230.
Leith Hall (Aberdeenshire), ii. 163.
Leith, town of, ii. 81.
Lenton, ii. 189.
Leon, province of, i. 235.
—— Isla de, i. 237.
Lessindrum, lands of, ii. 162.
Lessines, iii. 54.
Lethanhope, pastures of, i. 25.
Leuchars (Looris), ii. 101, 102, 196.
Liddel, castle of, i. 101.
Lillo, iii. 6.

Linlithgow, garrison of, i. 57.
—— town of, ii. 58, 295.
Lintin Island, iii. 203.
Linton, East Lothian, i. 19, 21, 31.
—— barony of, ii. 171.
Lisbon, i. 235, 241; iii. 7, 9-11, 96, 97, 103, 197.
—— Black Horse Square, in, iii. 96.
Lisle, iii. 53.
Littlehampton, iii. 28.
Liverpool, iii. 91.
Lochdoune, castle of, i. 66.
Lochirmagus (Longformacus), lands of, ii. 34.
Lochleven, castle of, i. 67; ii. 58.
—— Culdee establishment of, ii. 5, 8.
Lochmaben, castle of, ii. 22, 85, 120.
Logie (Morayshire), ii. 157.
Loire, river, i. 278; iii. 65.
Loncardy, lands of, i. 113, 116, 121; ii. 139, 141, 210.
London, i. 191, 202, 204, 209, 211, 225, 245, 279, 283, 284, 288, 290, 305, 310, 312, 313; ii. 65, 67, 89, 90, 156; iii. 10, 16, 27, 31, 41, 47, 49-51, 61, 66, 80, 117, 128, 144, 162, 169, 195, 221, 227, 282, 234, 236.
—— Beefsteak Club, i. 285.
—— Bird-cage Walk, i. 286.
—— Bridge, ii. 90.
—— British Museum, i. xii.
—— Caledonian Asylum, i. 285.
—— Catch Club, i. 285.
—— Connaught Place, i. 279; iii. 66.
—— Great Cumberland Street, i. 284, 285; iii. 65.

London, Great George Street, i. 286.
—— Green Street, iii. 12.
—— Grosvenor Street, iii. 8, 9, 33, 34.
—— Madrigal Society, i. 285; iii. 115.
—— Portman Square, iii. 10.
—— Record Office, I. xii, 48; ii. 27.
—— St. James Square, iii. 9.
—— Somerset House, iii. 7.
—— Staples Inn, i. 212.
—— Storey's Gate, i. 286.
—— Strand, iii. 49.
—— Tower of, ii. 32.
—— Tyburn, i. 279; iii. 66.
—— Vauxhall, iii. 16.
—— Whitehall, i. 184; ii. 289.
Lonmay, house and estate of, ii. 155.
—— parish of, ii. 155.
Lorn, i. 63, 64.
Lossidwyn, barony of, ii. 137.
Lothian, i. 9; ii. 17.
—— East, i. 11, 15, 19, 24, 29-31, 35; ii. 10, 27, 28, 45, 75.
—— West, i. 221.
Lothians, the, i. 57.
Lothianburn, I. viii.
Loudoun Hill, battle of, i. 52, 55, 57; ii. 187, 188, 190, 194.
—— town of, ii. 187.
Louvre, the, iii. 67.
Lovat, lordship, barony, and estate of, i. 130, 195; ii. 75, 167, 168, 172-174, 176, 177, 179-182, 230-232.
Lyelstoune, lands of, ii. 43, 66, 299, 301, 303, 304, 306, 307.
Lytilkethic, lands of, ii. 137.

MACAO, i. 301-303; iii. 108, 110, 148, 155, 157, 158, 160, 162, 164-166, 168-171, 176-181, 183-185, 188, 189, 192, 194, 196-199, 201, 203, 209, 211, 213, 214, 216, 217, 221, 222, 224-226.
Macclesfield Banks, the, iii. 107.
Mackyspoffil, ii. 158.
Madeira, i. 292; iii. 84, 87, 88.
Madras, i. 303; iii. 90, 108, 110, 121, 125-127, 130, 134, 137, 163, 165, 167, 180, 189, 190, 205, 212, 220, 223, 225, 229, 230.
Madrid, i. 238, 240.
Madrigal Society. *Vide* London.
Mafra, i. 241; iii. 10.
Magus Moor, i. 193.
Mai, Champ de (Paris), iii. 45, 48, 52.
Maida, battle of, i. 230.
Makarston, estate of, i. 15; ii. 117, 120, 121, 123.
Malazzo, iii. 1.
Malines (Mechlin), iii. 39.
Malmaison, i. 277; iii. 64.
Malta, iii. 196, 231, 232.
Maman, Mont, iii. 80.
Man, Isle of, i. 12.
Manilla, i. 302; iii. 157, 163, 214, 225, 226, 229.
Many, tenandry of, ii. 294.
—— lands of, ii. 140.
Manzanilla, i. 239.
Mar, earldom of, i. 129.
March, the, ii. 196.
Markinch, Wester, lands of, i. 85, 87, 88.

INDEX OF PLACES.

Marlowe, i. 5.
Marne, river, iii. 59.
Marq, i. 252.
Marseilles, iii. 196.
Marstino, island of, i. 229.
Mathers, West, lands of, i. 81.
Maubeuge, iii. 53, 54, 56.
Mauls, lands of, ii. 230.
May, Isle of, i. 22; ii. 106.
Maya, pass of, iii. 20-22.
Mayen, estate of, ii. 163.
—— house of, ii. 69.
Mayorga, i. 235.
Mearns, coast of the, i. 88.
—— sheriffdom of the, i. 74; ii. 128, 197, 201.
Mediterranean islands, iii. 47.
—— Sea, iii. 100, 229.
Melrose, ii. 99.
—— abbey and monastery of, i. *inter* 12 and 13, 13, 16; ii. 77, 79, 96, 116, 158.
Memsie (Mamesy, Mamissy, Mamsy), lands of, i. 127, 135, 136, 194; ii. 146, 220, 225, 235, 278.
Meneicht, lands of, ii. 133.
Meponcourt Lodge, Kent, i. 209.
Mere Hall, ii. 156.
Merton, ii. 173.
Messina, i. 228-231; iii. 1.
—— citadel of, i. 230.
—— Straits of, i. 229-231.
Methven, battle of, i. 51, 53, 64, 97; ii. 89-92, 166, 186.
Metz, iii. 54.
Milazo, i. 232.
Milia, i. 230.

Milnehalech of North Hales, i. 18, 20, 29-31; ii. 116.
Minto, church of, ii. 34, 51.
—— territory of, ii. 34.
Moguere, Petite, iii. 26.
Monadhliadh Mountains, i. 284, 305; iii. 207.
Mondarin, iii. 22.
Mondeo, i. 240.
Mons, iii. 54.
Mont St. Jean, i. 258.
Mont Martre, i. 277, 278; iii. 64, 65.
Montauban, i. 247; iii. 38.
Month, The, the Grampian Mountains, i. 53, 56, 58; ii. 184, 187, 188, 194.
Montrose, iii. 237.
Monymusk, ii. 14.
—— Culdee establishment at, ii. 5.
—— parish church of, ii. 13, 14.
Moray, county or district of, i. 57, 60, 61, 66, 128, 175, 211; ii. 37, 133, 157, 180, 190, 192.
—— earldom of, ii. 132, 137, 176, 179.
—— Firth, i. 105.
—— regality of, ii. 230.
—— see of, ii. 173.
Mordwheit (Morthwayt), lands of, i. 12.
Mormond Hill, i. 114, 115.
Morpeth, i. 44.
Moscow, iii. 23.
Mother-bank, the, i. 304; iii. 232, 233.
Muchalls, ii. 166.
Muckavie, ii. 230.
Muiralehouse, lands of, ii. 49, 54.
Muir Hall, ii. 159.
Mukedrum, ii. 11.

Mulbyne, lands of, ii. 133.
Musselburgh, town of, i. 218.

NAIRN, county of, i. 133, 211; ii. 180.
Namur, i. 254; iii. 54.
Nanka Island, iii. 104.
Nankin, i. 296; iii. 124, 126, 128, 130, 132, 134, 138, 146, 155.
Nel Spraida, iii. 7.
Nesbit House, Dunse, i. 290.
Neale, i. 276; iii. 61.
Ness Castle, estate of, i. 210.
Netherdale (Nathyrdole), ii. 157, 164, 239.
Nevis (West Indies), i. 206.
New Forest (Aberdeenshire), estate of, i. 115; ii. 145.
New Muircroft, barony of, i. 150.
Newbottle, abbey of, i. 12, 24, 181.
Newcastle-on-Tyne, i. 36, 43, 117; ii. 80, 104; iii. 117.
Nigg, lands of, ii. 16.
—— parish of, i. 66.
Nine Maiden Hill, near Fraserburgh, ii. 6.
Ningpo, i. 294; iii. 100, 119, 153, 209, 216.
—— river, iii. 119, 134, 142.
Ninove, iii. 45, 46, 54.
Nithsdale, ii. 159.
Nive, river, i. 244, 245; iii. 22, 24, 26, 28.
Nivelles, river, i. 244; iii. 22, 81.
—— town of, i. 254, 258, 259, 270, 271; iii. 54, 58.
Norfolk, county of, i. 5, 287.

Norham, i. 36, 43; ii. 78, 103, 104.
—— garrison of, ii. 84.
Normandy, i. 8, 283; iii. 72.
North Berwick, monastery of, ii. 16.
Northumberland, county of, i. 9, 10, 37, 38, 44, 117; ii. 103.
Norway, ii. 98, 101, 195.
Nottingham, county of, i. 4.
Noyers, abbey of, i. 6, 7.
Noyon, abbey of, ii. 150.
Nuebla, i. 239.

OBYNE. *Vide* Aboyne.
Ochtirothirstruthir. *Vide* Struthers.
Old Deer, ii. 148, 149.
Old Meldrum, i. 60; ii. 184.
Oleron, i. 244; iii. 24.
—— Gave d', iii. 29.
Oliver Castle, Tweeddale, i. 16, 27, 30-33, 38, 39; ii. 75, 94, 165, 168.
—— barony of, i. 91.
Oporto, i. 241, 242; iii. 9, 10, 12-14.
Orba (Inheritance land), the, i. 105, 106.
Orchirenchd, lands of, ii. 133.
Orde, lands of, i. 27.
Ordichoys, lands of, ii. 133.
Orkney, county of, i. 175.
—— earldom of, ii. 44.
—— Isles, ii. 101, 102, 195, 196.
Orleans, i. 203.
—— New, iii. 86.
Ormiston, estate of (Lothian), ii. 10, 27, 29.
—— (Roxburgh), ii. 29, 45.

Ostend, i. 252; iii. 35, 46.
Otterbourne, battle of, i. 117, 118, 122; ii. 34.
Ourcq, Canal de l', i. 277; iii. 64.
Oxford, shire of, i. 4.
—— University of, i. 104, 199.
Oyarzun, iii. 14, 18, 19.

PALAGONIA, iii. 2.
Palencia, i. 242.
Palermo, iii. 1, 2, 4.
Palma, i. 239; iii. 3.
Pampeluna (Pamplona), iii. 5, 14, 16, 21, 22.
Panbryde, barony of, i. 82.
—— lands of, i. 65.
Paracels Banks, the, iii. 107.
Paris, i. 6, 142, 203, 247, 253, 276-283; ii. 109, 151; iii. 34, 37, 42, 45, 46, 48, 56, 59-62, 64-69, 71, 72, 96, 123, 129.
—— church of Carmelites in, ii. 147.
—— church of Franciscans in, ii. 150.
—— church of Predicant Friars in, ii. 110.
—— Scots College in, ii. 147.
—— University of, ii. 150, 151.
Park, estate of (Aberdeenshire), ii. 155-157, 164.
—— estate of (Banffshire), ii. 52, 69, 70.
—— house of (Banffshire), ii. 50, 53.
Passero, Cape, iii. 1.
Pau, i. 244; iii. 24.
—— Gave de, iii. 28, 29.
Peebles, county or district of, i. 36, 71; ii. 75, 116.

Peebles, sheriffdom of, i. 80; ii. 94, 171.
—— town of, i. 25.
Peffer, lands in, i. 19.
Pei-Ho river, iii. 120.
Pekin, i. 294; iii. 89, 119, 120, 131, 134, 138, 157, 175, 184, 188, 217.
Pembroke Lodge, in Richmond Park, i. 307, 309.
Penang, iii. 212.
Pencaitland, lands of, i. 85; ii. 40, 75.
Pendreche, i. 72.
Peronne, town and fortress of, i. 273-276; iii. 60, 70.
Perth, garrison of, i. 57.
—— shire or district of, i. 58, 61, 211; ii. 21, 133, 137, 180, 193.
—— town of, i. 100, 101, 111, 112, 144, 160, 161, 177, 178; ii. 11, 100-102, 129, 134, 195, 196, 202, 206, 207, 218, 225, 226, 240; iii. 226.
Peterhead, i. 114; iii. 106.
Petinlouer, lands of, ii. 11.
Petpollok (Pitteloch), ii. 19, 98.
Philorth, barony or lordship or manor of, i. 114-116, 119, 126, 128, 140, 142, 152, 163, 167, 169, 170; ii. 170, 180, 226-229, 240-243, 247, 254-263, 277-283, 290.
—— bay of, i. 114, 153.
—— castle and tower of, ii. 241, 242, 259, 262, 281.
—— church of, i. 111, 153, 154, 170; ii. 255, 259, 260, 262, 279, 280, 282.
—— estate or lands of, i. 113, 121, 128, 143, 170, 182, 192, 210; ii. 152, 206, 209, 210, 226-229.

INDEX OF PLACES.

Philorth, kirktoun of, i. 113; ii. 210, 274, 278.
—— mill of, i. 150; ii. 278.
—— old manor place of, i. 114-116, 151, 162, 163, 169, 181, 183; ii. 236, 281.
—— parish of, ii. 274.
—— present house of, I. xii, 115, 188, 190, 202, 206, 207, 210, 211, 216, 226, 234, 251, 284, 285, 304, 305, 311; iii. 34, 51, 73, 75, 76, 176, 238.
—— water of, i. 114; ii. 272.
Pictavia, ii. 3, 4, 7.
Piedmont, iii. 186.
Pinkie, battle of, ii. 55, 144, 147.
Pitblae, estate and lands of, i. 115, 170.
Pitcarlie, lands of, i. 149.
Pitfour, estate of, i. 115.
Pitsligo (Pitsligach, Petsligach), lands of, i. 122, 127; ii. 220, 221.
—— parish of, i. 114; ii. 286.
Pittalochy, lands of, i. 150, 152; ii. 243-246, 278.
Pittendreich (Petyndreiche), i. 85, 88; ii. 166, 239.
Pittendrum, lands of, i. 170, 189, 194; ii. 244.
Pittenweem (Petenueme), i. 187.
Pittullie (Pittouly), lands and house of, i. 145, 146, 152, 159, 167, 170, 189, 190, 194; ii. 71, 244, 284.
—— Nether, lands of, i. 122, 127; ii. 220, 221, 225, 247, 249, 278.
—— Over, lands of, i. 122, 127; ii. 220, 221, 225, 247, 249, 278.
—— mill of, ii. 247, 249.

Plady, lands of, i. 113, 116, 121, 128, 134, 140; ii. 139, 141, 210, 289-291.
Planchenoit, i. 265.
Platane of Forfar. *Vide* Forfar.
Plenderlaith (Prenderlaith), lands and barony of (Roxburgh), ii. 43, 50, 51, 63, 299, 301, 303, 304, 306, 307.
Plymouth, i. 228, 291, 293; iii. 25, 84, 89, 92, 93, 106, 107, 116, 117, 132, 147.
Poitou, i. 3.
Polgony, bridge of. *Vide* Balgounie.
Pompey's Pillar, at Alexandria, iii. 231.
Pootoo, island of, iii. 142, 143.
Portarstoun, ii. 197.
Portland, iii. 232.
Portman Square. *Vide* London.
Portsmouth, i. 236; iii. 61, 234.
Portugal, i. 235, 248; ii. 153; iii. 11, 198.
Pouerhov, East Lothian, i. 24.
Poyang Lake, iii. 132.
Prussia, i. 223; iii. 43.
Puente Larga, i. 240.
Puerto de Viscayret, iii. 20.
Pulo-Penang, i. 303.
Punjab, iii. 166.
Put-Foo-Lun, iii. 172.
Pyrenees, The, i. 242, 243; iii. 14, 15, 20, 21.

Quarrelbuss, lands of, i. 151; ii. 151.
Quatre-Bras, i. 253, 254, 258, 270, 271, 306; iii. 58, 78, 80.
Queensferry, i. 211.
Querell, the, i. 113; ii. 210, 220, 289-291.

Quorsque. *Vide* Corskie.
Quytingeham. *Vide* Whittinghame.
Quytsom, ii. 123.

RACHRIN, island of, i. 52; ii. 93.
Ramoir (Romore), lands of, ii. 49, 63.
Ramsgate, i. 228, 252; iii. 35.
Rareys, estate of, i. 43; ii. 107, 108.
—— house of, i. 44, 47; ii. 108.
Rathen, church of, i. 73, 154, 170, 182; ii. 259, 260, 263, 279, 280, 282.
—— lands of, i. 127, 194; ii. 220, 221, 225, 278.
—— parish of, i. 114, 151; ii. 146, 286.
Rathhilloch (Rathilloch), lands of, i. 150; ii. 151.
Raza Island, near Rio Janeiro, iii. 94, 97.
Reading, monastery of, ii. 106, 107.
Record Office. *Vide* London.
Regio, i. 230.
Renfrew, ii. 206.
Rethie (Rethy, Redy), barony of, ii. 35, 43, 51, 52, 63, 160, 299, 301, 303, 304, 306, 307.
Rhine, river, iii. 40.
Rieville, abbey of, i. 26.
Rig, lands of, i. 34.
Rigfoot, i. 34.
Rio Janeiro, i. 292; ii. 153; iii. 87-90, 93-99, 105, 107, 138.
Roberton, lordship of, i. 101.
Rome, i. 128; ii. 12, 97.
Roncesvalles, pass of, i. 243; iii. 18-22.
Roskelyn, lands of, ii. 75.
Roslin, battle of, ii. 85-87.

Ross, district of, i. 111, 113, 127, 133; ii. 180, 208-211, 214.
—— earldom of, i. 110, 112-114, 123-125, 133, 134, 166, 206; ii. 36, 206, 217.
—— shire, ii. 172, 180.
Rothes, i. 305, 308.
Rothiebrisbane, lands of, i. 135.
Rothiemay, house of, ii. 58, 60.
—— kirk of, ii. 49, 62-64.
—— lands and barony of, i. 185; ii. 31, 41-44, 69, 70, 296, 299-301, 304.
Rotnachie, lands of, ii. 286.
Roundabout Island, iii. 114.
Round-tree Point, iii. 141.
Roxburgh, castle of, i. 67.
—— county of, i. 71; ii. 27, 30, 43, 51, 117, 120, 137, 159, 299, 301, 303, 304, 306.
—— town of, i. 68, 73; ii. 51.
Roye, iii. 61, 70.
Rugged Islands, the, iii. 142.
Russia, iii. 7, 89.
Rutherglen, garrison of, i. 57.

SADLER'S WELLS THEATRE, iii. 20.
St. Andrews, Culdee establishment at, ii. 5, 9.
—— kirk of, i. 88; ii. 14, 101, 110, 212.
—— priory or convent of, i. 17, 65; ii. 8.
—— town of, ii. 4, 7, 47, 114, 193.
—— church of St. Leonard at, ii. 211, 216, 217.
St. Bernard, Convent of, i. 246; iii. 29, 30, 32.

INDEX OF PLACES.

St. Cloud, i. 277; iii. 64.
St. Cruz, in Teneriffe, iii. 86, 88.
St. Cuthbert, chapel of, at Kingildore, ii. 79.
—— shrine of, at Durham, i. 15, 33; ii. 16.
St. Denis, i. 277; iii. 63.
St. Etienne, i. 246.
St. Germain, bridge of, i. 277; iii. 64.
St. Helena, island of, iii. 103.
St. James of Compostella, shrine of, i. 4.
St. James Square. *Vide* London.
St. Jaques, church of. *Vide* Antwerp.
St. Jean Pied de Port, iii. 20, 22, 26.
St. Jean de Luz, i. 245; iii. 22, 24, 26-28, 41.
St. Jose, church of, Macao, iii. 201.
St. Martin, iii. 62, 70.
St. Maxence, Pont, iii. 62.
St. Nicholas, church of, Aberdeen. *Vide* Aberdeen.
St. Paul, island of, iii. 102.
St. Pe, iii. 22.
St. Pierre, iii. 26.
St. Sebastian, castle of, iii. 17.
—— town and fortress of, i. 242, 243; iii. 14, 15, 17-19, 33, 94, 126.
Saithlie, lands of, i. 157, 162.
Sal, island of, Cape de Verd Islands, iii. 89.
Salamanca, i. 240.
Saline (Sawlyne), barony of, ii. 41.
Salisbury, ii. 99.
Saltoun (Salton), lands and barony of, ii. 42, 43, 49, 58, 63, 69, 70, 250, 297-299, 301, 303, 304, 306, 307.
—— brewhouse in the town of, ii. 30.

Saltoun, churchlands of, ii. 67.
—— estate of, i. 185; ii. 10, 17, 28, 29.
—— house of, ii. 55.
—— mill of, ii. 32.
—— Nether, tenement in, ii. 32.
Sambre, river, iii. 54.
San Carlos, valley of, iii. 21.
San Lucar le Major, i. 239.
San Munos, i. 241.
Santa Catherina, Monte de, Lisbon, iii. 10.
Santander, port of, iii. 15.
Sarawak river, Borneo, iii. 214.
Sauchieburn, ii. 46.
Saxony, iii. 43.
Scatterty, lands of, i. 132, 136, 139, 141, 167; ii. 232-234, 241-243, 248, 255, 256, 259, 261-263, 279.
Scheldt, river, i. 286.
Scilla, castle of, i. 230.
Scone, i. 82, 107, 177; ii. 7, 76, 77, 98, 106, 201.
Scotia, ii. 3, 6, 7.
Scotland, thanages of, i. 104.
Scotscraig, i. 193.
Seatoun, Fraserburgh, i. 190; ii. 247, 249.
Seine, river, i. 277; iii. 63, 64, 123.
Selkirk, county of, i. 71.
—— Royal Forest of, ii. 78, 80, 84, 94.
Sempring, ii. 173.
Senlis, i. 277; iii. 63, 70.
Serain, i. 273, 275; iii. 59, 60.
Seres, Fort, iii. 22.
Severn, river, i. 179, 180.
Seville, i. 239; iii. 115.
Seywaan, iii. 169.

VOL. III. 2 T

Shanghai, i. 293; iii. 117, 118, 141, 209, 216.
Shannon estate, the, i. 213.
Shetland, lordship of, ii. 44.
Shoreham, iii. 28.
Shropshire, i. 179.
Siam, gulf of, iii. 106.
Sicily, island of, i. xi, 228-231, 233; iii. 1-32.
Silver Island, iii. 129.
Simons Bay, i. 292; iii. 99, 101.
Sinclair Hills, i. 115.
Singapore, i. 292; iii. 91, 101, 104, 106, 107, 109, 118, 121, 122, 127, 141, 145, 147, 149, 155, 156, 158, 161, 166, 169, 173, 186, 193, 205, 210, 212, 214, 219, 224, 228.
Skene, loch of, i. 72.
Skirling (Scraveline), barony of, ii. 118.
Skye, lordship of, i. 112; ii. 206.
Slaines, i. 59; ii. 296.
—— lands of, ii. 49.
Slethmanan (Slamannan), lands of, ii. 117.
Slevach, burn of the, i. 59; ii. 183-188, 190, 191.
Smithill, Kingedward, i. 123.
Snottingham, burgh of, i. 9.
Soignies, iii. 54.
Soissons, iii. 59.
Solway, i. 144.
Somerset House. *Vide* London.
Somme, river, i. 274.
Souchu, iii. 209.
Southampton, i. 304; iii. 231-233.
Southrig (Suythrig), in South Hale, i. 28.
Southton, i. 5.
Southwark bridge, iii. 49.
Spa, iii. 54.

Spain, i. 75, 159, 223, 231, 235, 238, 241, 252, 285; ii. 153; iii. 5, 6, 8-10, 12, 14, 42, 44, 47, 56, 88, 202, 228.
Spey, river, i. 305; ii. 177; iii. 236.
Spraida, i. 240.
Spynie, i. 128; ii. 228.
Stanhouses, ii. 22, 85.
Stapilgorton, ii. 117.
—— old manor of, i. 34.
Staples Inn. *Vide* London.
Steinkirk, i. 254.
Stewarton, i. 100.
Stirling (Stryvelin), district or shire of, i. 22-24, 31, 32, 37, 42, 52, 58, 71, 72, 82, 83; ii. 43, 52, 63, 126, 165, 166 193, 299, 301, 303, 304, 306.
—— castle or garrison of, i. 57; ii. 88.
—— estates in, i. 30, 31, 34, 37, 39, 42.
—— sheriffship of, i. 30, 31, 50.
—— town of, i. 31, 44, 57, 67, 136; ii. 18, 47, 60, 83, 85, 88, 128, 199.
Stobhou (Stobo), lands of, i. 24, 27.
Stockbridge, iii. 117.
Stocket, forest of the, i. 70.
Stonehaven, i. 211.
Stonywood (Stanywood), ii. 166.
Storey's Gate. *Vide* London.
Strachan (Strathean, Strathechin), lands of, i. 65, 79.
Strand. *Vide* London.
Strathaveth (Strathalbeth), barony of, i. 122; ii. 224-226.
Strathbogie, i. 59, 60, 173; ii. 59, 184, 192.
Strathbogie, lordship of, i. 82.
Strathclyde, i. 80.
Strathdee, ii. 6.

Strathearn, earldom of, ii. 1.
Stratherrick (Strathardok), i. 195, 201, 209; ii. 177, 230.
Strathglas (Straglas), ii. 177, 230.
Strathisla, ii. 41, 162.
—— lands of, ii. 62.
Strathnaver, i. 46, 66.
Strichen, lands, barony, and estate of, i. 115; ii. 147-150.
—— parish of, i. 114, 216.
Struthers (Ochtirothirstruthir, Uchtrethrestrother), estate of, i. 47, 48, 50, 52, 64, 71, 85, 87, 88, 97; ii. 126.
Subhill, ii. 63.
Suez, i. 303; iii. 182, 206, 209, 225, 229, 231.
Sunda Straits, iii. 102, 104.
Surat-Galley passage, iii. 148.
Sussex, iii. 28.
Sutherland, lands in, i. 44.
Sydney, iii. 91, 157.
Syracuse, i. 228, 229.
Sy-Wann, iii. 179, 180, 210.

Tagus, river, i. 240.
Tain, i. 67.
Taixalium, promontory of (Kinaird's Head), i. 115, 152.
Talavera, i. 239.
Tarbert, isthmus of, i. 67.
Tartary, iii. 120.
Tarwathie, i. 145, 146.
Tay, river, i. 62; ii. 87.
Techmuiry, ii. 146.
Teme, river, i. 180.

Teneriffe, island of, i. 292; iii. 84-86, 88-90, 93.
Terra Nova, iii. 2, 3.
Terregles, i. 161.
Thames river, i. 227.
Tibarty (Tibberty), lands of, i. 122, 127-129, 135, 148, 167; ii. 224-227, 241-243, 248, 254, 256, 259, 261-263, 279.
Tinghay, iii. 119.
Titam, iii. 169, 180, 183.
Toledo, i. 239.
Torax (Torres), lands of, ii. 49, 54, 63.
Tordesillas, iii. 13.
Toro, i. 242; iii. 18.
Torrietuthill, lands of, ii. 278.
Torry (Turry), lands of, i. 50, 66; ii. 165.
Touch (Tulche, Tullich), church of, ii. 6, 59.
—— lands of, i. 82.
Touchfraser (Tulch-fraser), estate of, i. 22, 26, 31, 32, 37, 40-43, 48-51, 71, 81-84; ii. 125-127, 165.
Toulouse (Thoulouse), i. 4, 203, 247; iii. 33, 41.
Touraine, i. 6, 7.
Tournay, iii. 43, 45.
Tours, i. 247; iii. 84.
Tower, the. *Vide* London.
Traquair, ii. 77.
—— Royal Forest of, ii. 78, 80, 94.
—— sheriffship of, i. 80; ii. 80, 94.
Trent river, i. 5, 41, 42, 44, 47, 51, 102.
Trigeras, i. 239.

Tristan D'Acunha, island of, iii. 98.
Truxillo, i. 239.
Tuath (tribal district), the, i. 105.
Tuilleries, The, i. 276; iii. 61.
Tulicultry, lands of, ii. 19, 29, 69.
Tullibody, i. 83, 84; ii. 124.
Tullidoch (Tullidoven, Tullidoun), lands of, ii. 63.
Tulyfour, lands of, ii. 45, 183.
Tulykeraw, lands of, i. 150; ii. 45.
Tulymald, half lands of, i. 123.
Tulynamolt, lands of, i. 127; ii. 221.
Tulyoich, lands of, ii. 138.
Turnberry, castle of, ii. 186, 189.
Turriff, i. 73.
Tuti-Wann, iii. 180.
Tweed, river, i. 177, 221; ii. 104.
Tweeddale, i. 15, 16, 30, 31, 33; ii. 79, 88, 117, 118.
Tyburn. *Vide* London.
Tyndrum, i. 62.
Tyne, river, i. 117.
Tynewald, ii. 189.
Ty-Py-Wann, iii. 171.
Tyrie, church of, i. 153, 154, 170; ii. 255, 259, 260, 263, 279, 280, 282.
—— Easter, lands of, i. 115, 162.
—— house of, ii. 152.
—— lands of, i. 115, 141, 143, 210; ii. 152, 238-243, 255, 256, 259, 261-263, 279, 281, 282, 285.
—— lands of Kirkton, ii. 255, 256, 259, 261, 262, 281, 282.
—— Muircroft of Kirkton, i. 150.
—— parish of, i. 114, 157.

Ugie, river, i. 114; ii. 149.
Ugistone (Ulkestone), lands of, ii. 28, 43, 299, 301, 303, 304, 306, 307.
—— mill of, ii. 29-31.
Ugtrethrestrother. *Vide* Struthers.
Ulm, iii. 103.
Unthank, lands of, i. 101.
Upsetlington, ii. 104.
Urdax, iii. 21.
Urogne, i. 244, 249; iii. 19-21.
—— Hill of, iii. 20.
Urquhart, barony of, ii. 130.
—— castle of, ii. 130.
Urt, iii. 26.
Ushant, iii. 84.
Ustaritz, i. 244; iii. 24.
Utlaw, lands of, i. 122, 127-129, 135, 149, 167; ii. 224-227, 241-243, 254, 256, 259, 261, 262.
—— New, lands of, ii. 247, 279.
—— Old, lands of, ii. 247.

VALLADOLID, iii. 12.
Vauxhall. *Vide* London.
Vendee, La, iii. 49, 56.
Vera, Pass of, i. 244; iii. 20.
Vermand, i. 273-275; iii. 60.
Verneuil, battle of, i. 141.
Versailles, i. 277; iii. 64.
Vethi, burn of, ii. 198.
Victoria (Hong-Kong), i. 301; iii. 212.
Vienna, i. 223.
Vigo, iii. 84.
Villa Abba, i. 239.
Ville Franche, iii. 26.

Villette, i. 278; iii. 65, 67.
Viscayret, Puerto de, iii. 20.
Viseu, i. 240, 248.
Vittoria (Victoria), town and battle of, i. 242; iii. 13.
Vrmothe, lands of, ii. 278.

WALCHEREN, island of, i. 236, 237, 310; iii. 6.
Wales, New South, iii. 192.
Wark, i. 144; ii. 76.
Warkeworth, castle of, ii. 57.
Waterloo (Waterlude), i. xi, 253, 269-271, 278, 295, 306; iii. 57, 58, 61, 66, 74, 78, 79, 103, 145, 234.
Wavre, iii. 103.
Wemyss, ii. 23.
West Point, Hong-Kong, i. 298; iii. 167, 209.
Western Isles. *Vide* Hebrides.
Westminster, i. 286; ii. 23.
Westmoreland, county of, i. 9; ii. 103.
Whampoa, iii. 171, 208, 216, 229.
Whang-Ho river, iii. 124.
Whelplaw, lands of, ii. 53, 66.
Whitehall. *Vide* London.
Whittinghame (Quytingeham), ii. 123.

Wigtoun, county at, i. 112, 113, 121; ii. 206, 214.
Windsor, barracks at, i. 288.
—— bridge, i. 227.
—— Park, i. 288.
Wodley, lands of, ii. 278.
Woodhill, ii. 154.
Woolwich, ii. 154.
Woosung Harbour, iii. 120.
—— town of, i. 293; iii. 116-118, 123, 140, 143.
Worcester, battlefield of, i. 190.
—— city of, i. 179, 190.
Worshipping Island. *Vide* Pootoo Island.
Worthing, iii. 42.
—— house, i. 251.
Wylughton (Wyleighton), manor and castle of, ii. 26.

YANG-TSE-KIANG (Yang-tze-Kan) river, i. 293-296; iii. 110, 113, 114, 116, 117, 119, 139, 144.
Yellow Sea, iii. 120.
Yetholm, lands of, ii. 121.
York, i. 22; ii. 84, 189.
—— county of, ii. 103.

ZAGARAMURDI, iii. 21.

ERRATA.

Vol. I.

Page
ii, line 24, *for* " G.C.B." *read* " K.C.B."
35, 38, note 1, *for* " 305 " *read* " 309."
47, note 4, *for* " 303, 314 " *read* " 304, 313."
52, note 2, *for* " 303, 305 " *read* " 314."
52, note 3, *delete* " 314."
130, note 3, *for* " V." *read* " IV."
134, line 2, *for* " fugitive " *read* " monk in the Abbey of Paisley."
240, line 25, *for* " elected " *read* " re-elected."
244, line 5, *for* " Wora " *read* " Vera."
Portrait of sixteenth Lord Saltoun, *for* "G.C.B.," *read* " K.C.B."

Vol. I.

Page
289, line 4, *for* " 1812 " *read* " 1807.'
291, line 25, *for* " 29th " *read* " 20th."
301, line 17, *for* " Macao " *read* " Hong-Kong."

Vol. II.

75, line 18, *after* " name" *add* " Earl of Dunbar."
84, note 5, *for* " No." *read* " Introduction, p."
180, line 15, *for* " and Nairn " *read* " Nairn and Forfar."